Hiking the
Grand Canyon

Also by John Annerino

Canyon Photography & Essay Books
Colorado Plateau Wild and Beautiful
Vanishing Borderlands: The Fragile Landscape of the U.S.-Mexico Border
Indian Country: Sacred Ground, Native Peoples
New Mexico: A Photographic Tribute
Desert Light: A Photographer's Journey through America's Desert Southwest
Canyon Country: A Photographic Journey
Grand Canyon Wild: A Photographic Journey
Apache: The Sacred Path to Womanhood
People of Legend: Native Americans of the Southwest
The Wild Country of Mexico: La tierra salvaje de México
Canyons of the Southwest: A Tour of the Great Canyon Country from Colorado to Northern Mexico
High Risk Photography: The Adventure Behind the Image

Hiking the Grand Canyon

A Detailed Guide to More Than 100 Trails

JOHN ANNERINO

Commemorative Hiker's Edition

Skyhorse Publishing

Skyhorse Publishing books may be purchased in bulk at special discounts for sales promotion, corporate gifts, fund-raising, or educational purposes. Special editions can also be created to specifications. For details, contact the Special Sales Department, Skyhorse Publishing, 307 West 36th Street, 11th Floor, New York, NY 10018 or info@skyhorsepublishing.com.

Skyhorse® and Skyhorse Publishing® are registered trademarks of Skyhorse Publishing, Inc.®, a Delaware corporation.

Visit our website at www.skyhorsepublishing.com.

Hiking the Grand Canyon is dangerous and too often has proved deadly. The author and publisher accept no responsibility for any injury, loss, or inconvenience by any person using this book.

10 9 8 7 6 5 4 3 2 1

Library of Congress Cataloging-in-Publication Data is available on file.

Cover design by Tom Lau
Cover photo credit: Copyright © John Annerino

Historical Photo Credits: Edward S. Curtis, George Wharton James, John K. Hillers, Emery Kolb, Timothy H. O'Sullivan, Robert L. Carson, Frederick H. Maude, Henry G. Peabody, and E. W. Murphy from the Library of Congress, GCNP Museum, and USGS John Wesley Powell Collections.

Print ISBN: 978-1-5107-1498-4
Ebook ISBN: 978-1-5107-1500-4

Printed in China

For my father, who sacrificed it all to move our family west to our new life in the Grand Canyon state; for Ale and our family; and for the Canyon's first caretakers, the Native Peoples, who trod its trails long before me: Hopi, *Hopitu Shinumu,* Navajo, *Diné,* Kaibab Paiute, *Kaipa'pici,* Havasupai, *Havsuw' Baaja*, Hualapai, *Hwalbáy,* Apache, *Ndé*, Yavapai, *Yavapé*, Mojave, *Makháv,* Zuni, *Ashiwi*, and others: "We are still here."

Contents

Acknowledgments

SPECIAL THANKS TO PUBLISHER TONY LYONS, EDITORIAL director Jay Cassell, and editorial assistant Ronnie Alvarado at Skyhorse Publishing. This new Commemorative Hiker's Edition of *Hiking the Grand Canyon* would not have been possible without their foresightedness. I also want to thank John Beckman, Peter Beren, Jim Cohee, and Helen Sweetland, who, while at Sierra Club Books, shepherded the first three editions of my "Totebook" guide to *Hiking the Grand Canyon*. I'm grateful for the editors, associates, and friends who inspired me to keep exploring and photographing the canyons of the the Great Southwest: Mel Scott at *Life* magazine; John Rasmus at *National Geographic Adventure;* Donnamarie Barnes at *People* magazine; Kermit Hummel at W. W. Norton; Kathy Springmeyer at Farcountry Press; and Lucinda Bush, Chris Keith, Richard Nebeker, Donald Bayles, Jr., and the late Robin Lange for their support. Many other people, associates, and friends accompanied me, inspired me, or shared their real-life expertise to teach me about the Colorado River, Grand Canyon, and Colorado Plateau: boatman geologist Michael Young; outdoor programs director Craig Spillman; Havasupai and Hualapai river guides Archie Matuck, Jessica Powskey, Delbert Havatone, and Denny Wescogome; boatwomen Suzanne Jordan and Louise Teal; boatman Wesley Smith, Western States 100 sub-twenty-four ultra-runner Michael Thomas; runner Theresa Ebarb, who continues to inspire me; the late Grand Canyon anthropologist Robert C. Euler; and professor Galen Schnell, who first introduced me to the Canyon by leading me down the Boucher Trail. Thank you.

"No matter how far you have wandered hitherto, or how many famous gorges and valleys you have seen, this one, the Grand Cañon of the Colorado, will seem as novel to you, as unearthly in the color and grandeur and quantity of its architecture, as if you had found it after death, on some other star; so incomparably lovely and grand and supreme it is above all the other cañons . . . Yosemite, the Yellowstone, the Pyramids, Chicago, all would be lost if tumbled into . . . the Grand Cañon could put a dozen Yosemites in its vest pocket."

—John Muir, 1901
Conservationist and Sierra Club founder

Hiker, Angels Gate, North Rim.

PART 1

Welcome to the Grand Canyon, the Greatest Canyon on Earth

Preface

INSCRIBED AS A UNESCO WORLD HERITAGE SITE AND AS "THE MOST spectacular gorge in the world," crew members of NASA's Expedition 39 took the first iconic photograph of the earthly marvel from the International Space Station on May 12, 2015. When Apollo 17 astronaut-scientist Harrison "Jack" Schmitt first stepped on the moon forty-three years earlier he said, "It's like trying to describe what you feel when you're standing on the rim of the Grand Canyon." During his terrestrial visit to the South Rim of Grand Canyon on May 6, 1903, President Theodore Roosevelt was so moved he proclaimed:

> In the Grand Canyon, Arizona has a natural wonder which, so far as I know, is in kind absolutely unparalleled throughout the rest of the world . . . You cannot improve on it. The ages have been at work on it, and man can only mar it. What you can do is keep it for your children, your children's children, and all who come after you, as the one great sight which every American should see.

Since Grand Canyon National Park was established on February 16, 1919, more than seventy-five million American and international tourists heeded the Rough Rider's call to see the Canyon. In a recent record-breaking year, 5,520,736 American and foreign tourists visited the Grand Canyon. They traveled across the nation and from around the world (Australia, Belgium, Canada, China, Denmark, England, France, Germany, India, Japan, Mexico, Spain, and Switzerland) to stand in awe on the brink of the Canyon. Unaccounted tens of thousands day hiked below the rim; 44,801 backpacked for an overnight stay below the North and South Rims; 24,885 rafted the Colorado River (more than 500,000 river runners to date); and 150,000 rode scenic air tour flights. Beautiful to behold, the Grand Canyon is 277 miles long, ten to eighteen miles wide, 6,720 feet deep at its most profound point, and eroded through two-billion-year-old rock layers about five to six million years ago. Encompassing 1,904 square miles of the Colorado Plateau, the Grand Canyon's many secluded areas remain dangerous *terra incógnita* for unwary foot travelers in the twenty-first century. Since records were first kept in 1867, 687 hikers, river runners, and visitors have died in the "crown jewel of America's natural treasures."

This all new Commemorative Edition of my earlier Sierra Club Totebook, *Hiking the Grand Canyon*, remains a handy carry-along guide and reference to day hiking, backpacking, and Grand Canyoneering and a key to unlocking the secrets of one of the Seven Natural Wonders of the World. It includes a new pullout Trail Map, detailed trail descriptions, and information on how to prepare yourself for a safe and enjoyable journey through one of the most popular, rugged, and spectacular hiking destinations on the planet. Tooled for the beginning day hiker, backpacker, and seasoned canyoneer, the Commemorative Edition has also been written for armchair adventurers, sophisticated travelers, glampers, and Grand Canyon history aficionados. In other words, if you can't or simply don't want to risk your life cat-walking the Nankoweap Trail's terrifying "Supai traverse," you can stay in the comfort of camp, lodge, or home and delve into the early traditions of Native Peoples and exploits of explorers, pioneers, trailblazers, and scientists.

To ensure the accuracy of the new trail, route, and river hiking descriptions and additions, I've described only those areas that I've personally day hiked, backpacked, canyoneered, run, climbed, swum, or rafted. (I have included several short Off-Trail Hiker Reports). Here, too, you will find an intriguing new section on the Old Trails to Havasupai. Each trail description has been cross-referenced with my maps, field notes, hikes and treks, and interactive geological maps, 7.5-minute topographical maps, and trip reports. Special attention has been devoted to researching primary sources, historical surveys and accounts, scientific papers, and ethnographies to uncover who were the first people who actually used, and later developed, each trail and route. The surprising discoveries are included in each trail description, historical overview, and mileposts, which also feature directions, geological, historical, cultural, and scenic highlights.

Head down the trail, or sit back and relax, and enjoy the Commemorative Edition of *Hiking the Grand Canyon*.

—John Annerino, November 2016

1

Mysteries of the Deep

"There is a river
Called the River of No Return
Sometimes it's peaceful
And sometimes wild and free
Love is a traveler
On the River of No Return
Swept on for ever
To be lost in the stormy sea
Wailaree!"

—Frank Fenton and Louis Lantz, 1954
The River of No Return

IN A REGION WHERE POET, WANDERER, AND VAGABOND FOR SLICK rock beauty Everett Ruess journeyed across Grand Staircase-Escalante's Hole in the Rock Trail and disappeared off the face of the earth somewhere near his burro corral in Davis Gulch in 1935, the Grand Canyon of the Colorado River has spawned its own unsolved mysteries, hoaxes, and outlandish tales: the Doheny Scientific Expedition's Jurassic-aged dinosaur (*Diplodocus*) engraving discovered near Havasupai; John D. Lee's seven coffee cans of lost gold dust cached near the confluence of the Colorado and Little Colorado Rivers; the Grand Canyon's own "Wild Bunch" stealing and riding stolen horses across the Spaghetti Western–rugged Butte Fault, then swimming their remuda across the Colorado River; the American Museum of Natural History's fabricated first ascent of "The Lost World of Shiva Temple," which was climbed twice beforehand by Emery Kolb; and other tales too tall to tell without sippin' a little snake eye to

A canyoneer isn't sure what mysteries wait around the next bend of this dark serpentine chasm. Copyright © John Annerino Photography.

start believing what I'm sayin'. One of the most bizarre is the September 27, 1994, *Weekly World News* report of an Alien Starship landing on Comanche Point (see page 94 Rim Trails), and it concerns the reputed discovery of a mummy-filled Egyptian cave in Marble Canyon.

1909: Mr. G. E. Kincaid/Egyptian Crypts of the Grand Canyon

In one of the strangest stories ever published about the Grand Canyon, a mysterious explorer who went by the name of G. E. Kincaid reported to the *Arizona Gazette*, a Phoenix newspaper, on April 4, 1909, that he'd discovered a great underground citadel during an expedition down the Colorado River in a wooden boat from Green River, Wyoming, to Yuma, Arizona. Reportedly financed by the Smithsonian Institution, under the direction of a "Prof. S. A. Jordan," Kincaid told reporters who published the front page cover story on April 5 that the crypt was a mile deep and had hundreds of rooms, passageways, and tiers of clay- and bark-covered mummies. Where exactly is this stone and gold-leafed sarcophagi-filled lost city? According to Kincaid, it's "forty-two miles up the Colorado River from El Tovar Crystal Canyon." If Kincaid's Crystal Canyon is Crystal Creek at River Mile 98, that would put the lost city near Kwagunt Creek at River Mile 56. But two thousand feet above the river and 1,486 feet down the east face of a sheer wall, as Kincaid also hinted about the mysterious location, more closely aligns with the imposing cliffs of the Desert Façade where no Redwall Cavern–style caves exist. The Redwall Cavern comparison is an important clue, because Kincaid claimed, "Upwards of 50,000 people could have lived in the cavern comfortably." That's the exact estimate Major John Wesley Powell used forty years earlier when he wrote his river journal entry for August 8, 1869: "The water sweeps rapidly in this elbow of river, and has cut its way under the rock, excavating a vast half-circular chamber, which, if utilized for a theater, would give sitting to 50,000 people. Objection might be raised against it, however, for at high water the floor is covered with a raging flood." One of the clinchers for Kincaid's story, who also told reporters he was the first white child born in Idaho, is this: "The race that inhabited this mysterious cavern, hewn in solid rock by human hands, was of oriental original, possibly from Egypt, tracing back to Ramses." Let's suspend disbelief and imagine the Egyptian gods Horus, Osiris, and Isis—whose names appear on three Grand Canyon temples—as well as their slaves, teleported themselves to Crystal Canyon Cave. Or, let's be reasonable, and go all in and accept the premise that pharaohs commanded fleets of papyrus boats that sailed across the Mediterranean Sea and Atlantic Ocean, then drove armies of horse-drawn chariots across the continent and traversed the Appalachian Mountains, Mississippi River, Southern Rocky Mountains, and Painted Desert without drawing the slightest notice, suspicions, oral histories, or carved petroglyphs from ancient Native America. Anchoring their Trojan Horses on the 5,428-foot east rim of Marble Canyon, the legion grappled 2,252 feet down cargo nets to the Colorado River where stone masons wielding iron chisels and sledgehammers cut, chiseled, and cleaved the Redwall Cavern–sized Crystal Canyon Cave and left no evidence of their rim-to-river project. Up to this point, it's all good. Right? But there's a tiny hole in Kincaid's story. There is no record of a Colorado River expedition in 1908, the closest conceivable time frame Kincaid could have completed his river and cave exploration and sorted out his journal notes and maps for the *Arizona Gazette* exposé. The only river expedition that was recorded a year earlier (1907) was the Russell-Monett-Loper Expedition, which launched from Green River, Utah, on September 20. And the only expedition that was recorded in 1909 was the Galloway-Stone Expedition, which launched from Green River, Wyoming, on September 12, five months after Kincaid made headlines and reported: "If their theories are borne out by the translation of the tablets engraved with hieroglyphics . . . Egypt and the Nile, and Arizona and the Colorado, will be linked by a historical chain running back to ages which staggers the wildest fancy of the fictionist." As does Kincaid's tale, whoever he really was.

1867: James White/Log Raft, "The First Man Through?"

James White's saga remains the most controversial account of river running the Grand Canyon of the Colorado River. On September 7, 1867, the New York–born White reached the Mormon settlement of Callville, Nevada, now submerged beneath Lake Mead, on a crude log raft reportedly made from three cottonwood logs lashed together with a lariat. On the verge of starvation, the weary and sunburned White claimed to have spent fourteen days navigating the "Big Cañon" in an audacious bid to escape hostile Utes whose horses he and his partner had stolen. In a letter written to his brother Josh on September 26, White said he kept from starving by trading his two pistols to some friendly Indians for the "hine pards of a dog." He wrote: "i ead one of for supper and the other breakfast." Not many wanted to believe White's tale, not the least of whom was Major John Wesley Powell, who was still planning his maiden Canyon voyage. To descend the Big Cañon, alone, as the thirty-year-old White modestly claimed without fanfare, he would have needed to run—and survive—a gauntlet of 160 rapids, violent eddies, and whirlpools. If his story were true, that would make White the first known person in history to have navigated the Colorado River through the Grand Canyon two years before the 1869 Powell Geographical Expedition. Early admirers like General William J. Palmer and Thomas F. Dawson embraced White as a hero, believing that White had indeed come through the "Big Cañon." But others, like Major Powell and White's biggest detractor, railroad engineer Robert Brewster Stanton, who was a veteran of two disastrous Colorado River expeditions and ranted at length about White in his book, *Colorado River Controversies* (1932). Stanton concluded that it was preposterous for White to negotiate 277 miles of turbulent river currents and dangerous rapids on a hastily constructed raft in the time White had claimed. (Stanton's conclusion has since been convincingly debated by Eilean Adams in her 2001 book, *Hell or High Water: James White's Disputed Passage through Grand Canyon, 1867*). At the end of his June 4, 1917, Senate Resolution No. 79, "First Through the Grand Canyon," (see page 313 in Western Grand Canyon Trails), Dawson suggested that Major Powell had already known, possibly from reading White's letter to his brother Josh, which was published in the February 1869 edition of *The Rocky Mountain News*, before he embarked upon his 1869 Colorado River expedition on May 24, that White had traversed the Grand Canyon, proving to Powell that there weren't any rapids that couldn't be run or portaged. "I wend over falls from 10 to 15 feet hie," White wrote. "My raft Wold tip over three or fore times a day."

1914: Ambrose Bierce/Mexican Revolution/Grand Canyon

When Mexican revolutionary Francisco "Pancho" Villa's (real name José Doroteo Arango Arámbula) ordered his Villistas to paste recruitment posters along the

U.S./Mexico border in 1913, they read, in part, as follows: Atención Gringo, For Gold & Glory, Come South of the Border and Ride with Pancho Villa. American journalist Ambrose Bierce heeded the call and was officially attached to Villa's army. During the Battle of Tierra Blanca, Chihuahua, the seventy-year-old "observer" was awarded a *sombrero* for shooting a Federale. But little more than a month later, the "old gringo" disappeared in the Battle of Ojinaga on January 9, 1914. In the October 1, 1913, letter he'd sent to his niece, Lora Bierce, Bierce had written: "If you hear of my being stood up against a Mexican stone wall and shot to rags, please know that I think it a pretty good way to depart from this life. It beats old age, disease, or falling down the cellar stairs." Some speculate Bierce committed suicide with a German pistol he'd acquired for the occasion a year earlier and pulled the trigger somewhere along the South Rim high above the Colorado River in 1914. In the end Bierce may have preferred it to staring down the barrels of Villa's men under the command of El General himself during a *pelotón de fusilamiento*, or "execution by firing squad." "*Preparen, Apunten, Fuego*," ("Ready, Aim, Fire!"). No one reportedly knows where Bierce fell, over the rim of the Grand Canyon after a self-inflicted *tiro de gracia*, "final blow," or in the bloodstained borderlands. But in a cruel twist of fate Pancho Villa was "shot to rags" when he was ambushed by assassins while driving his 1915 Dodge 30–35 touring car down the streets of Parral, Chihuahua, on July 20, 1923.

1928: Glen and Bessie Hyde/The Missing Honeymooners

Newlyweds Glen Roland Hyde and Bessie Louise Haley Hyde embark on a "honeymoon cruise" and pilot a flat-bottomed Idaho wooden sweep scow from Green River, Wyoming, through the Grand Canyon. On November 28, 1928, the couple mysteriously disappears somewhere below River Mile 232. *Pfft*! Gone. After unsuccessful river searches by the Kolb brothers, Glen's father, Roland C. Hyde, conducts one of the most exhaustive searches in the history of the Grand Canyon, going broke from his repeated efforts to locate his son and Bessie in the process. Speculation abounded that the couple argued, Glen was dispatched by Bessie, and a skull with a bullet hole was found in Emery Kolb's belongings by his grandson. The skeleton of the still-unidentified man had been found beneath 7,300-foot Shoshone Point in 1976 with a .32-caliber bullet hole in his skull. Did Kolb have the motive, means, and opportunity? Some tried to piece that puzzle together. But an episode of NBC's *Unsolved Mysteries* refuted the suspicion, as did forensic anthropologist Dr. Walter H. "Dr. Death" Birkby of the C. A. Pound Human Identification Laboratory, who reconstructed the complete skeleton and dispelled speculation that the remains were those of Glen Hyde. How and why it ended up in Emery's garage remains another mystery. What about Bessie, who created a lovely book of poems in part about the river journey, *Wandering Leaves*? With her husband, she became the first woman to navigate 565 miles of river and rapids with her husband, Glen. Some suggest Bessie escaped, hiked out of the canyon from the Colorado River, and years later resurfaced as the Grand Old Dame and Woman of River, the legendary Georgie White Clark (aka Bessie DeRoss).

A tourist peers over the edge of the Grand Canyon, 1914, with his Metz 22 Speedster, photo by O.K. Parker.

2

Above the Rim: Before You Go

IF THIS IS YOUR FIRST HIKE INTO THE GRAND CANYON, THE FIRST thing you should do after you park your vehicle, or take a shuttle to the South Rim's 7,120-foot Mather Point or the North Rim's 8,255-foot Bright Angel Point, is stand on the brink and take in the aerial view from the lofty rim of the canyon. Marvel at the scenery ("We're going to hike into that?!"), but don't become overwhelmed by its sheer depth and immensity. Remember, you're going to be hiking down an established trail in short, manageable geological segments one step at a time, not in one fell swoop. You'll be stopping along the way to enjoy the scenery on the way in, sip water from trailside springs and way stations, and snack and rest in shaded ramadas. So there's plenty of time to adjust your focus and perspective of what at first may seem incomprehensible. If you feel like you're getting in over your head, you can pull the ripcord any time and turn around even before you reach the suggested Turn Around Points I've included for the established trails. If you have time after arranging for your campsite or lodging, stop in the Canyon View Information Plaza across from Mather Point, or the North Rim Visitor Center located outside the Grand Canyon Lodge at Bright Angel Point Trailhead. The visitor centers emphasize the Canyon's human history, ecology, and geology, where interpretive rangers can also answer your questions.

TRAINING
On any given Grand Canyon hike you're faced with seven key training elements you should prepare for.

A boatwoman runs Hermit Rapids on the Colorado River near the foot of the Hermit Trail.

Distance, Elevation Loss and Gain, Altitude, Weight Carried, Surface Footing, Time Spent Traveling, and Environmental Readiness:

If you're not canyon fit and acclimated you should train and simulate each of these elements before you head down the trail. For example, if you're planning your first hike down the Bright Angel Trail, you need to ask yourself if you're ready to hike 9.5 miles and descend 4,340 vertical feet in ideal weather conditions to Bright Angel Campground? Many say, sure, no problem, because gravity is doing most of the work. After you've rested the night alongside melodious Bright Angel Creek, and perhaps the next day, are you ready to turn around and hike 9.5 miles and climb up the 4,340 foot inverted mountain standing between you and your vehicle parked on the asphalt summit? If you're not already Grand Canyon fit you might not have the time it takes to get into good shape on short notice. It's far better and safer if you can plan your hike three to six months in advance so you're properly prepared to really enjoy your hike, not barely survive it. But you should simulate the seven elements.

Warning: Check with your physician before you start training and monitor your fitness, diet, health, and fatigue.

Distance:

If you're not already fit, and you're physician has pronounced you heart healthy enough to train, you should build up to walking, hiking, or running a minimum of three miles a day, four days a week. As you progress, try one longer walk, hike, or run of five miles once a week. If you can manage more, all the better. Remember, the linear distance you'll be hiking the Bright Angel Trail is nineteen miles round-trip.

Elevation Loss and Gain:

Simulating Elevation Loss and Gain is more difficult for flatlanders than mountain dwellers. You can walk or run high school or college stadium steps and climb mid- to high-rise stairwells at least three days a week, more if you can manage it. If you prefer machinery, use an incline treadmill or stair climber three days or more a week. If you can hike a nearby peak or hills, all the better. Canyon hiking Phoenicians often train by hiking the rugged 1.2 miles, 1,208-vertical-foot climb up to the 2,610-foot summit of Piestewa Peak. The popular hike simulates and resembles the hike and elevation gain and loss through the Grand Canyon's inner gorge of Vishnu Schist. Peak hiking or hill climbing three days a week will help develop and condition your aerobic capacity, quadriceps, calves, and feet for steep canyon trails. If you can build up to hiking a double or triple ascent once a week, all the better. As your training progresses combine Elevation Loss and Gain with your linear training Distance.

Altitude:

If you're coming from Phoenix, Dallas, New York, San Francisco, Seattle, or someplace similar, you need aerobic conditioning through walking, hiking, or running. You can also use altitude training masks, which are available commercially. If you're from Boulder, Flagstaff, Sun Valley, or Taos, and fit, you should be acclimated for South Rim's highest trailhead, the 7,380-foot Tanner Trail, and the North Rim's highest trailhead, the 8,848-foot Nankoweap Trail. It's not necessarily the steep descent that will take the wind out of your sails, it's that last end-of-the-trail two-mile, roughly 2,500-vertical-foot climb out that will be patiently waiting to test your training. As your training progresses combine Altitude (or aerobic conditioning) and Elevation Loss and Gain with your training Distance.

Weight Carried:

If you're a fit steep terrain backpacker, you should know the weight you're capable of carrying in your pack. If not, once you start to get in shape from your training you need to simulate incrementally the weight you're going to carry on your canyon hike. Remember, the water you need to drink, carry, and cache for most warm weather rim-to-river-to-rim hikes and treks weighs 8.34 pounds per 1 gallon X 3 gallons = 25 pounds. At the trailhead, you'll be carrying a pack that weighs thirty-five to forty pounds. The weight will decrease correspondingly as you drink and cache water during the descent. As your training progresses combine Weight Carried, Altitude (aerobic), and Elevation Loss and Gain with your training Distance.

Surface Footing:

If you're walking, hiking, running trails, or working in rough terrain, keep doing it. If you're used to gumshoeing pavement, jumping curbs and potholes on city streets, or are a parkour athlete, you should simulate resistance training on uneven, loose, and rocky surfaces on trails, rough terrain, streambeds, rocky beaches, or jetties. As your training progresses combine Surface Footing, Weight Carried, Altitude (aerobic), and Elevation Loss and Gain with your linear training Distance.

Time Spent Traveling:

If you're a desk-driving CEO, software engineer, or secretary, you need to unshackle yourself from the desk, keyboard, and chair, and stand up and walk around and exercise. A canyon hike is not a short-burst lunchtime treadmill or stair climber workout. You're going to be standing on your feet moving upright hiking, hopping over trail riprap, and walking on loose dirt, sand, and crushed stones for eight to ten hours each day. And that's on the canyon's maintained Corridor Trails. As your training progresses combine

Time Spent Traveling, Surface Footing, Weight Carried, Altitude (aerobic), and Elevation Loss and Gain with your training Distance.

Environmental Readiness:

If you come from an arid desert, mesa, or mountain environment you should be acclimated to wide open spaces, imposing scenery, and the extreme weather shifts between blistering heat, torrential flashflood–producing rain, cold winter snow pack, and exposed jaw-dropping cliffs and ledges. If not, at the very least you need to simulate the heat and cold in your training by walking, hiking, or running in various weather conditions leading up to your canyon hike. And you need to hike smart once you arrive at the canyon by planning your hike for the pleasant seasons of fall and spring. (Check the weather forecasts beforehand). The Grand Canyon is altogether different than what many hikers are used to, but it's lured many an easterner out West to cure what ailed them, search for gold, or pursue their dreams in the great abyss. There are no guard rails to prevent you or your loved ones from accidentally taking their last step off the edge of the trail or scenic spot, no traffic lights or crossing guards to guide you through the tough and dangerous traverses, and very few benches, except for stony ledges, to sit on and watch the pedestrian and equestrian traffic go by. So be prepared for the best and the beautiful, and the worst and wildest, the Grand Canyon has to offer. As your training progresses prepare yourself mentally (don't overthink it, you're going to enter one of nature's most thrilling escape hatches and leave your worldly concerns, worries, and stress behind) and combine Environmental Readiness, Time Spent Traveling, Surface Footing, Weight Carried, Altitude (aerobic), and Elevation Loss and Gain with your training Distance. Your training should prepare you for a journey of a lifetime, but don't overtrain. Save your conditioning edge for the Grand Canyon.

Water Consumption:

There are many dated sources on this topic, so I'll relate my own experiences. During 100- to 110-degree heat running or walking on level dirt trails through deserts and plateaus, I average traveling eight to ten miles per gallon of water, as long as I hydrate beforehand. (Check the clarity of your urine beforehand, and watch your multivitamin intake, which often turns urine yellow. It's often a sign you're behind the fluid curve and, once on the trail, you're getting dehydrated). You'll need more or less drinking water depending on your fitness level, acclimatization, season, temperature, body weight, weight carried, elevation gain, distance, and other factors highlighted above. Use eight to ten miles per gallon of water as a guide for warm and hot weather hiking, but experiment in your seven elements training to determine your personal fluid requirement minimums.

Hiking Seasons

Unfortunately, the majority of hikers tackle the Grand Canyon during their summer vacations. It's absolutely the worst time of the year to hike to the bottom of the Grand Canyon. Mid-May through June is insufferably hot, dry, and cloudless when inner Canyon air temperatures push 110 to 115 degrees or more. July and August through the first weeks of September don't usually relent, except during periods of torrential monsoon downpours. Otherwise, inner Canyon surface temperatures hover between a skin-burning 140 to 160 degrees. Combine elevated air, surface temperatures, hot weather respiration, direct sunlight, exposed head and carotid neck arteries, and heat refracting off towering walls creates a deep, natural ovenscape and a recipe for disaster that's befallen many who thought they were tough enough and sports athlete fit enough to carry a heavy backpack down and back up steep trails in the extreme heat. If you're not a hardened, acclimated canyoneer and desert rat (or you drink hard liquor the night before the big hike), stay away. It's waiting. Stick to the cool forested trails of the South and North Rims, which offer their own mesmerizing, largely forgiving allure. Or plan your hike for fall and spring, and during fair weather windows in winter. Summer monsoons are incredibly dramatic, but unless you know exactly what you're doing, it's easy to be in the wrong place at the wrong time. A half-dozen or more seasoned canyoneers rolled the dice and were swept to their deaths by flashfloods. (See Prevention page 47 and Flashfloods page 58.)

Water

If you're hiking off the Bright Angel and North Kaibab Trails where reliable water is only available seasonally, you should plan your trip when perennial and seasonal water sources are most reliable during and after seasonal rains all year, spring snowmelt, and summer monsoons. (See Water Sources page 33.)

Weather, Air Data & Webcam

Grand Canyon National Park
tinyurl.com/gpxzy7x

Hiker Weather

National Weather Service
South Rim
Visit: tinyurl.com/hkd7hm3

North Rim
Visit: tinyurl.com/hk987nf

Phantom Ranch
Visit: tinyurl.com/jdyjtwz

Communication

Satellite Phones are in a league of their own for emergencies and surpass expectations of cell phone coverage anywhere below the rim of the Grand Canyon. I've used them on Colorado River trips, and relied on critical communication during photo assignments in the deep canyons of Mexico's Sierra Madre. The one caveat is that satellite coverage is often restricted to several minutes in narrow canyons where you need to change your location to stay within satellite reception.

There are numerous satellite phone services. I've used PHI Satellite Services, and I've never had an issue. I always request a charger and a second battery, which are included in a Pelican Case with a preprinted Fed Ex return air bill.

Phone Home Internationally
Visit: www.phisatellitephones.com
Phone (480) 206–7369

Satellite Phones, Messaging, and Tracing:

A growing number of hikers, climbers, sailors, and adventurers are using services like Spot that they report on their website accounts for 4,801 rescues. Impressive. I haven't used the service, yet, though I've read reports of Grand Canyon hikers activating their Spot devices because the water "tasted salty," and others who were tired and asked the park rescue rangers who'd hiked all the way in to help them. (Visit: www.findmespot.com/en/.) In 2014 (the most recent stats available), there were 157 total Medevac flights and 418 passengers in the Grand Canyon.

<u>NPS Hiker 24 Hour Emergency Phone Number and Email</u>
(Tape these numbers and links to your satellite communications)
Phone (928) 638–7805
Email: grca_bic@nps.gov (Use this if the phone line is busy)

<u>Critical Communications, Best Practices for Emergency Operations</u>
Visit: hrrfw.org/RaftingGrandCanyon/Critical_Communications_Handout

PLANNING

Refer to the Grand Canyon Trails section to see what trail captivates you most that you're physically and psychologically fit enough to embark upon (see Trails of the Grand Canyon page 53). Once you've studied the list, compared it to your previous (recent) hiking experiences, training, and the corresponding trail descriptions, then decide on your trail preference and permit availability, and adjust your training accordingly. The following resources will further assist your planning and preparation.

Resources, Online Interactive

TopoZone and TopoQuest:

These are convenient online sources for studying and printing U.S. Geological Survey-based topographic maps. The elevations used in this book were sourced from these sites and printed USGS topographical maps. Visit: http://www.topozone.com/ and https://www.topoquest.com/

Geology Map:

Once you're off the Corridor Trails, it's important you learn how to read the rocks (see Geology page 79). This beautiful, color-keyed map should also help you decipher the canyon's complex strata: Geologic Map of the Grand Canyon and Vicinity. Flagstaff, AZ: U.S. Geological Survey, 2014, Mapbox.

   Visit: rclark.github.io/grand-canyon-geology/

Road Map:

The Arizona Strip, western Grand Canyon National Park, and Grand Canyon-Parashant National Monument are crisscrossed with a maze of all weather and high clearance dirt roads. This map provides mileages, locations, and local names that will help you reach the area's remote trailheads.

   Visit: www.nps.gov/hfc/carto/PDF/PARAmap1.pdf

U.S. Board of Geographic Names:

If you're off the grid and see a landmark, canyon, or creek you think merits an official name, you can apply for it through the U.S. Board of Geographic Names.

   The domestic locations and spellings in this book conform to USBGN standards. Visit: geonames.usgs.gov/ for more information.

Printed Highway and Road Map:

The AAA "Guide to Indian Country Map" is an accurate and detailed highway map to the Southwest's Four Corner region that also includes the myriad all-weather dirt and backroads to off-the-grid destinations featured in this book and neighboring Indian Country. Navajo detective Joe Leaphorn uses this map to navigate the country in Tony Hillerman's bestselling mysteries. Available commercially at visitor centers, stores, and online.

Printed Topographical Maps:
   All of the 7.5-minute quadrangles named at the end of each trail description can be ordered from the U.S. Geological Survey. Visit: www.usgs.gov

Fees
Entrance Fees:
   Save with Grand Canyon, America the Beautiful, Military, and Every Kid in a Park Annual Passes. Visit: www.nps.gov/grca/planyourvisit/fees.htm

Overnight Hiking:
NPS Permit Requests and Fees:
No fees charged for day hiking. $10 per permit plus $8 per person or stock animal per night camped below the rim and $8 per group per night camped above the rim. Denied requests will not incur a charge. Permits cancelled at least four days in advance will receive hiker credit (minus a $10 cancellation charge) valid for one year. Backcountry Information Center charges are nonrefundable! (Source: NPS.) Visit www.nps.gov/grca/planyourvisit/upload/permit-request.pdf for more information.

   Corridor Trails and Campgrounds Availability 2016
   Visit: www.nps.gov/grca/planyourvisit/upload/CorAvail.pdf
   Organized Group Rim-to-Rim and Extended Day Hike/Run
   Visit: tinyurl.com/jbflfoq
   Application and Fees: tinyurl.com/h9m73lk

   NPS Backcountry Information Center
   Phone (928) 638–7875
   Permits Fax (928) 638–2125
   Critical Backcountry Updates
   Visit: www.nps.gov/grca/planyourvisit/trail-closures.htm

   Grand Canyon National Park
   1 Backcountry Road, Grand Canyon Village, AZ 86023
   Phone (928) 638–7875

RIVER HIKING

"Powell and his brave men . . . faced a thousand dangers, open or hidden, now in their boats gladly sliding down swift, smooth reaches, now rolled over and over in back combing surges of rough, roaring cataracts, sucked under the eddies, swimming

like beavers, tossed and beaten like cast away drift—stout-hearted, undaunted, doing
their work through it all. After a month of this they floated smoothly out of the dark,
gloomy, roaring abyss into light and safety two hundred miles below."
                                                    — John Muir, 1902
                              The Grand Cañon of the Colorado River

Some 24,885 commercial and private river runners navigate the Grand Canyon of
the Colorado River in whole or part each year. They come from all over the world
to experience the wonders and adventures conservationist John Muir touched upon
and Major John Wesley Powell pioneered. If you have the expertise and own your
own river-running gear, an extended private off-season river journey offers the best
opportunity to hike the Grand Canyon in reverse (bottom to top) like the inverted
mountain range it is, as well as along the Colorado River corridor. (See Colorado River
Trails page 290). Visit the websites below for the information you need to launch a
successful river hiking adventure. If you don't have the boats and gear, or you just don't
want the logistical headache of organizing a private trip, visit Grand Canyon Private
Boaters "Making Trip Connections." You can become a member, and sign up for a
trip. Several Grand Canyon commercial outfitters offer hybrid hiking trips. Visit the
Commercial River Outfitters link below.

If you prefer to organize your own private trip, you can fill out your application
online at the NPS Grand Canyon River Permits Office link below.

Grand Canyon Private River Trips
Grand Canyon Private Boaters Association
Visit: gcpba.org/
809 W. Riordan Rd. Suite 100, Suite 431, Flagstaff, AZ 86001
Email: gcpbamail@gmail.com

Grand Canyon Private River Trip Permits
National Park Service, Grand Canyon River Permits Office
1824 S. Thompson St., Suite 201, Flagstaff, AZ 86001
Phone (800) 959–9164, Fax (928) 638–7844

River Support & Lodging
Bar 10 Ranch
P.O. Box 910088, St. George, UT 84791–0088
Bar 10 Airstrip (Indicator 1Z1)
"Whitmore International Airport"

Phone: (435) 628–4010, (800) 582–4139
Fax: (435) 628–5124
Visit: https://www.bar10.com/

Grand Canyon National Park Commercial River Outfitters

Grand Canyon National Park outfitters offer a diverse array of three- to eighteen-day Colorado River trips from Lees Ferry to Pierce Ferry in paddle rafts, oar-powered rafts, and dories. For a full list of outfitters and contact information, visit www.nps.gov/grca/planyourvisit/river-concessioners.htm for more information.

Mules, horses, and burros played a historic role in the exploration, discovery, and development of the Grand Canyon and its trails. Some perished trying to negotiate narrow rim rock-hugging trails like the Nankoweap, Tanner, and Pack-a-the-true-ye-ba Trails, and slid and rolled to their deaths or disappeared out of sight over the cliffs. Throughout the late 1800s into the early 1900s, equine carried the unwieldy loads of explorers, surveyors, scientists, miners, trailblazers, presidents, naturalists, painters, geologists, architects, and Native Peoples. If for any reason you cannot hike to Phantom Ranch, or you simply prefer the Old West allure of a leather saddle—John Muir, Teddy Roosevelt, Albert Einstein, and the Harvey Girls did—you can book a mule and let it carry your pack and gear. The park calls it a "Mule Assisted Backpack." Or you can ride your own horse or mule on designated canyon trails. If you're a seasoned cross-country rider you can detour off the Great Western Trail and ride rim-to-river-to-rim in the hoofprints of four young Texas cowboys who rode from Arizona's Mexican border across the Grand Canyon to Montana's Canadian border featured in the critically acclaimed documentary film *Unbranded* (2015).

Great Western Trail
Visit: gwt.org/
Unbranded
Visit: watch.unbrandedthefilm.com/
Backcountry Horsemen of America
Visit: www.bcha.org/

For Grand Canyon Private Stock Use (Mules, Horses, Burros), Trails, Permits, Fees

Visit: www.nps.gov/grca/planyourvisit/private-stock.htm

For Commercial Horseback Riding, Mule Riding, and Hiker Support

South Rim
Grand Canyon Lodges
Visit: www.grandcanyonlodges.com/things-to-do/mule-trips/
Reservations, Phone (888) 297–2757, (303) 297–2757

North Rim
Grand Canyon Trail Rides
Visit: www.canyonrides.com/grand-canyon-mule-ride/
Reservations, Phone (435) 679–8665

Hiker Shuttles

Rim to Rim
Trans Canyon Shuttle
Visit www.trans-canyonshuttle.com/
Phone (928) 638–2820, (928) 638–2820

South Rim Shuttle Bus Routes 2016
Visit www.nps.gov/grca/planyourvisit/shuttle-buses.htm

Caving, Inside Earth, Speleology

According to the National Park Service, an estimated 1,000 or more caves are hidden within Grand Canyon National Park. Three hundred and thirty-five caves have been recorded, including Thunder River Cave and Tapeats Creek Cave, two of the Canyon's most spectacular; the sacred shrines of *Tsé'áán Ketán*, "Prayer Stick Cave," and *Tsé'áán bidá*, "Rock Cave," and Silent River Cave, Abyss River Cave, Vanishing River Cave, Premonition Cave, Olla Vieja Cave, and Leandras Cave, Arizona's longest, which requires a four-mile trek from the nearest road, 2,500-vertical-foot descent, and a 120-foot rappel to reach the cave entrance that leads through 42,329 feet (8.01 miles) of passages; and other secret caves that have been recorded, mapped, and excavated with their precise locations stored in the Karst Portal of the Antwerp Diamond Centre. All caves, except for Cave of the Domes, are closed to visitation and exploration, except for research. Visit: www.nps.gov/grca/learn/nature/cave.htm for more information.

TRAVELERS AND HIKERS LODGING & CAMPING

You're tired, sunburned, thirsty, and hungry enough to eat soap, and the last thing you want to do after you climb out of the canyon is face the long drive home, or sleep in the dirt one more night. You can treat yourself to soft rustic comfort, hot food, and cold refreshments by booking a night in one of architect Mary Jane Colter's 1910–20s-era lodges and enjoy colorfully appointed interiors. Constructed with native stone and timbers, and inspired by indigenous cliff dwellings, culture, and landscapes, they are listed on the National Register of Historic Places and National Historic Landmarks. Colter's celebrated South Rim lodging includes El Tovar and Bright Angel Lodge (Red Horse Cabin and The Buckey O'Neill Cabin). Though, few locations and lodges are more spectacular than the North Rim's Grand Canyon Lodge. Designed by Yale- and Harvard-graduate Gilbert Stanley Underwood, the National Historic Landmark was constructed on the edge of Bright Angel Point in 1928 with Kaibab Limestone and Ponderosa pine timbers. The outdoor terrace offers one of the most stunning and comfortable scenic lodge views in the West.

South Rim
Grand Canyon National Park Lodges
Visit: www.grandcanyonlodges.com
Phone (888) 297–2757, (303) 297–2757
Phantom Ranch
Visit: www.grandcanyonlodges.com/lodging/phantom-ranch
North Rim
Grand Canyon Lodge
Visit: www.grandcanyonforever.com
Phone (877) 386–4383
Kaibab Lodge
Visit: www.kaibablodge.com
Phone (928) 638–2389 for reservations and shuttle to/from North Kaibab
   Trailhead

Camping or Glamping:
Okay, so if you do want to sleep in the dirt under the stars and towering pines a few more nights, or set up your Glamping in Deluxe tent, tree house, or trailer, here's where.

South Rim
NPS Mather Campground
Visit: www.nps.gov/grca/planyourvisit/cg-sr.htm
National Recreation Reservations
Visit: www.recreation.gov
Phone: (877) 444–6777

Trailer Village Park
Visit: www.visitgrandcanyon.com/trailer-village-rv-park
Phone (877) 404–4611, same day (928) 638–3047
Kaibab National Forest
Ten-X Campground
Visit: tinyurl.com/23w3283
Desert View
NPS Desert View Campground
Visit: tinyurl.com/jlamkta

North Rim
NPS North Rim Campground
Visit: www.nps.gov/grca/planyourvisit/cg-nr.htm
Phone (877) 444–6777
Kaibab National Forest
Demotte Campground and
Jacobs Lake Campground
Visit: tinyurl.com/zssg2ep
Phone (877) 444–6777

GEAR

Overnight Hiking and Trekking

> "I rolled up some bread and tea in a pair of blankets with some
> sugar and a tin cup and set off."
> —John Muir, 1875

You can travel as light as you need to, as Native People did traveling on foot through the Great Southwest's canyons and mesas, carrying a blanket, pemmican or deer jerky, piñon and pine nuts, piki bread, and water, or as the Scottish-born conservationist had hiking the Sierra Nevada, subsisting on black tea, sourdough bread, pine nuts, sugar-pine sap, manzanita berries, and fasting. You can supplement this bare bones diet, as Native Peoples did when they stalked a deer or bighorn, and John Muir had with "a block of beef about four inches in diameter, cut from the lean heartwood of a steer." Or, you can go all in and suffer carrying out what you should have left behind. Find the balance of what works best for you.

Hikers sample a bare bones diet atop the North Rim's remote Shiva Temple. Copyright © John Annerino Photography.

The Essentials:

Frameless or internal-framed pack; water, water purification pump, and potable purification tablets; extra snacks and citrus; a hat to cover your head and ears; bandana to cover your neck, use as a tourniquet, and for straining river and creek water for drinking; sunscreen and polarized sunglasses; topographic map, compass, whistle, and a twenty-five-foot length of six mm or larger perlon cordage for hauling and lowering packs and belaying; flashlight or headlamp, extra batteries; signal mirror if your satellite phone's second battery goes dead or your companions use up your budgeted air time phoning home; pocket knife for cooking, cutting, and scraping; first aid kit, Betadine surgical skin cleanser, bandages, surgical adhesive tape, moleskin, antiseptic, elastic bandage, and safety pins; After Bite for stings and bites; space blanket; comb and tweezers to remove cactus spines and for maintaining a stylish rustic trail look; and tape to remove tiny cactus spines and hairs called glochids.

Water Containers:

Depending on the season, weather, and your personal fluid requirements you tested in your training, carry four to eight (or more) one-quart or one-liter water containers inside your pack to drink and cache on the hike into the canyon. For hot weather and summer hikes it's critical you carry and cache enough water in durable water containers. I carry two to four quarts inside my pack, and use two one-gallon screw-capped water or cleansed milk containers, looped together with a bandana (use a square knot), carried behind my shoulders between the pack. Remember, water takes on the outside air temperature, and hot water is unpalatable and difficult even for seasoned hikers to drink enough fluid to stay ahead of the dehydration curve. You can cover and insulate your water jugs with hand-stitched terry cloth and soak them before you head off the rim. Before you climb back out of the canyon from the inner canyon or Colorado River, you can immerse your water containers in cold river or creek water. There's no reason to drink hot water on the critical 2,000- to 2,500-foot climb up from the river to cooler temperatures.

Clothing:

Appropriate for season. Remember—guard against wind, wetness, cold, direct sunlight, and heat. Bring only what you actually need, and keep the weight down! Depending on the season and your preference: hooded rainwear, jacket, heavy or light long- and short-sleeved cotton or polypro shirts; T-shirts and undergarments; heavy and light pants or shorts; heavy or light ankle-length socks: broken-in hiking boots or hiking shoes. (I prefer carbon rubber-soled running shoes. But don't try using them on your first canyon hike). For winter use rainwear, hooded down or fiberfill parka; wool, polypro, or pile caps, sweater, gloves or mittens, socks, and undergarments; waterproofed boots, gaiters, instep crampons, and stormproof tent.

Food:

Well balanced, high in simple and complex carbohydrates, roughage, and stick-to-your-rib proteins.

- **Day 1:** Michelin One Star, S. Pellegrino Young Chef, Hells Kitchen–style cuisine, or a grilled cowboy steak, roasted potatoes, and green chilies foil-wrapped in homemade flour tortillas you prepare, zip-seal, and freeze at home in advance of the trip.
- **Day 2:** Tin Man–style canned meat, chicken, tuna, beans, and tamales (they'll keep however long you want to carry them); or Mercado-style corn tortilla tacos heated in a light film of olive oil, stuffed with heat-in-the-can (remove the lid) meat, chicken, or beans topped with cheese, lettuce (if it hasn't turned brown), and your favorite hot sauce.
- **Day 3:** Where's the Water Fare. Buffalo jerky, piñon nuts, *machaca* (Mexican dried beef); packaged rice, wild rice, pasta, noodles, mac and cheese, oatmeal,

granola, powdered milk, hot chocolate, and electrolyte drink mixes; sourdough rolls, crackers, peanut butter, Arizona-grown Medjool dates stuffed with an almond or pecan and cream cheese, ground coffee, sugar or honey; limes, oranges, raisins, avocados, and dried fruit; seasonings.

- **Day 4:** You Promised Him You'd Try It. Your dad's or uncle's MREs (Meals Ready to Eat), your grandfather's souvenir C-Rations he hoped his sons and daughters would try, and your great grandfather's historic K-Rations he hoped his sons and daughters would try. Or whatever you want to carry, keep fresh, prepare, and sustain yourself for your hike. My go-to basic canyon menu includes home-cooked bean burritos foil-wrapped (you can cook beans in a crock pot with your own secret ingredients); canned albacore tuna, lime, crackers, and Nava-Hopi piñon nuts (available roadside in Cameron, AZ); sourdough bun, cheese, and *güerito chilie* sandwiches; stream-water powdered milk and granola; coffee, tea, raw sugar or honey, and your favorite chocolate stream-cooled in a zip bag.

Stove, Cooking, Cleaning, and Food Storage:
Stove fuel, stainless steel cook pot or large ceramic cup, bowl or ceramic cup, knife, fork, spoon, P38 can opener; flint stick, lighter, strike-anywhere matches waterproof-containerized; utensil cleaner; rock squirrel- and raven-proof, duct-taped-sealed momma's cookie tins or new interlocking steel mesh food containers; and plastic zip bags for scooping water from shallow, ephemeral water sources.

Shelter:
Tarp and cordage, lightweight or winter tent, summer cotton sheet or sleeping bag and foam pad or ground cloth, or winter sleeping bag, cover, and foam pad.

Sanitation:
Toilet paper and trowel, disinfecting wipes or sanitizer, and resealable bags or commercial carry-out bags to pack it out if you're really a Leave No Tracer.

Personal Items:
Toothbrush and paste, comb, washcloth, lip balm, foot powder, insect repellant, needle and thread, camera, and journal.

Walking Sticks, Take the Load Off:
Many canyon hikers use aluminum hiking and trekking poles for steep off-trail descents and ascents. Others prefer wooden walking sticks, which are a must for

traveling through canyon narrows to negotiate slippery moss-covered stones. Some, like pioneer photographer E. O. Beaman, used an alpenstock during his rugged exploratory trek of Deer Creek (I used an old wooden ice axe when I first started guiding treks in the canyon). Interestingly, Canary Island sheepherders have used long wooden lances since the sixteenth century to negotiate their steep island terrain and pastures. Using lances two to two-and-a-half times the length of John Muir's walking stick and the Boy Scout's traditional five-foot-six-inch long staffs, similar to European pilgrim and quarter staffs, Spanish shepherds effectively use a technique called *salto del pastor*, "shepherd's leap," to jump over ravines, often sliding down their long *garrotes* to the ground. Some canyon trekkers might embrace the concept, for others it would prove their demise in the precipitous canyon terrain. A Backstory: perilously trapped on the wrong side of two flood-swollen creeks with little food, I used dead Century plant stalks (*Agave Philippians*) twice to pole vault over rushing waters to reach my only way out of the canyon beneath the North Rim during an eight-day Trans Canyon journey run. The "first time was the charm." The second time, the stalk broke and I was swept hopelessly downstream. . . . Don't try it.

Resources

National Parks and Monuments

Grand Canyon-Parashant National Monument
Public Lands Information Center (NPS, BLM, Forest Service)
345 East Riverside Drive, St. George, UT 84790
Phone (435) 688–3200, Fax (435) 688–3388
Visit: www.nps.gov/para/index.htm

Glen Canyon National Recreation Area
P.O. Box 1507, Page, AZ 86040
Phone (928) 608–6200
Visit: www.nps.gov/glca/index.htm

Lake Mead National Recreation Area
601 Nevada Way, Boulder City, NV 89005
Phone (702) 293–8990
Visit: www.nps.gov/lake/index.htm

Pipe Spring National Monument
HC 65 Box 5, 406 Pipe Springs Road
Fredonia, AZ 86022
Phone (928) 643–7105
Visit: www.nps.gov/pisp/index.htm

Vermilion Cliffs National Monument
(Paria Canyon-Vermilion Cliffs Wilderness)
345 E. Riverside Drive
St. George, UT 84790–6714
Phone (435) 688–3200
Visit: www.blm.gov/az/st/en/prog/blm_special_areas/natmon/vermilion.html
Grand Staircase-Escalante National Monument
669 South Highway 89A
Kanab, Utah 84741
Phone (435) 644–1200
Visit: www.blm.gov/ut/st/en/fo/grand_staircase-escalante.html
Greater Grand Canyon Heritage National Monument (proposed)
308 West Birch Avenue
Flagstaff, AZ 86001
Visit: www.greatergrandcanyon.org/monument
Visit: www.congress.gov/bill/114th-congress/house-bill/3882

Tribal Lands and Parks

Havasupai Tribe Tourist Office
P. O. Box 10, Supai, AZ 86435
Hiking and Camping Permits
Phone: (928) 448 2121, Fax: (928) 448 2551
Visit: www.havasupai-nsn.gov/tourism.html
Hopi Cultural Center
Hwy 264, Mile Post 379, Second Mesa, Arizona 86043
Phone (928) 734–2401
Fax (928) 734–6651
Visit: www.hopiculturalcenter.com/
Hualapai Tribe
P.O. Box 179, Peach Springs, AZ 86434
Phone (928) 769–2216, (888) 868–9378
Fax (928) 769–2343
Visit: grandcanyonwest.com/
Kaibab Paiute
Pipe Springs National Monument
406 Pipe Springs Road, Fredonia, AZ 86022
Phone (928) 643–7105
Fax (928) 643–7583
Visit: www.nps.gov/pisp/index.htm

Navajo Nation Parks and Recreation
Cameron Visitor Center
P.O. Box 459, Cameron, AZ 86020
Hiking and Camping Permits
Phone: (928) 679–2303
Fax: (928) 679–2017
Visit: www.navajonationparks.org/permits.htm

Conservation
Sierra Club National Headquarters
2101 Webster St., Suite 1300, Oakland, CA 94612
Phone (415) 977–5500
Fax (510) 208–3140
Visit: www.sierraclub.org/about

River Runners for Wilderness
P.O. Box 30821, Flagstaff, AZ 86003
Phone (928) 556–0742
Email: tommartin@rrfw.org
Visit: rrfw.org/

3

Below the Rim:
Now What?

"Mountains of music swell in the rivers, hills of music billow in the creeks, and
meadows of music murmur in the rills that ripple over the rocks. Altogether it is a
symphony of multitudinous melodies. All this is the music of waters."
—John Wesley Powell, 1895,
Canyons of the Colorado

PUT ONE STEP IN FRONT OF THE OTHER AND TAKE THE JOURNEY OF
your lifetime through what Major John Wesley Powell called the "great unknown" when
he navigated the Colorado River in 1869. Nothing will be more important during your
inverted-mountain desert trek than water. On the river, Powell and his men were forced
to strain, boil, and drink too much of the *Río Colorado*, "Red River," what some said was
"too thick to drink, too thin to plow." Off the river, Powell and his overland expedition
surveyors and photographers sometimes couldn't find enough water to drink. When
they did, they often strained and boiled it with coffee grounds to make it palatable
enough to drink.

Four thousand years or more before Powell's expedition members faced dangers,
thirst, and dehydration exploring the Grand Canyon, its Native People traveled long
distances across the sear deserts and canyons of the Colorado Plateau to hunt, gather,
and trade bighorn sheepskins, buckskins, baskets, ollas, olivella shells, turquoise, and
other precious, easily transportable goods. They were able to endure arduous trading
forays to distant pueblos and villages because they were well conditioned, had an inti-
mate knowledge of their environment—what pioneers viewed as harsh and strange
"look-alike" terrain—and because their journeys linked one perennial or seasonal water

Monsoon flashflood cascade,
Marble Canyon, Colorado River.

source with the next. You would do well to emulate their proven tradition by planning your own canyon sojourns from one water source to the next, starting with the maintained Bright Angel and North Kaibab Trails. Both trails offer perennial water and developed sources you can rely upon seasonally.

The Colorado River is called *Bits'íis Ninéézi,* "The River of Neverending Life," by the Navajo because it still offers life-sustaining water as long as you stay within reach of it. Once you move beyond the river, or break away from the Bright Angel and North Kaibab Trails to skirt the stony ledges and benches to hike cross-country on primitive trails and routes, you need to rely upon the water you carry and cache, and the perennial, seasonal, and ephemeral water sources you need to locate along your route of travel. It's important to familiarize yourself with these locations, as Ancestral Puebloans once did when they carried spring water in heavy tumpline-sized ollas to their cliff dwellings and storage granaries. In spite of its forested rims and verdant riparian canyons and creeks, the Grand Canyon is an arid stair-step desert. Its relatively few reliable water sources are often more difficult, precipitous, and dangerous for the uninitiated to reach than the cool, deep hand-dug wells, palm tree–lined oases, water pockets, and *tinajas* that sustain life in the comparatively flat deserts of the Gobi, Sahara, Outback (Great Sandy and Gibson Deserts), Colorado Plateau (Painted Desert, Canyonlands), and the Sonoran Desert's *El Camino del Diablo,* "The Road of the Devil."

THE MUSIC OF THE WATERS

If you're unfamiliar locating the canyon's perennial and seasonal water sources, they come in many forms: thundering waterfalls, misty cascades, hanging gardens, mesmerizing streams, melodious rivulets, tinkling seeps, shimmering water pockets teeming with life, and silent "kiss tanks" are among them. These delicate biomes support a precious community of plants, animals, birds, reptiles, fish, and invertebrates. Off the river, these irreplaceable often pristine sanctuaries are not here for the sole purpose of keeping you hydrated or saving your life. These oases sustained the Grand Canyon's Native Peoples for more than 4,000 years and, with the Colorado River, provided their lifeblood of existence.

Fountains of Life/Types of Springs

Of the twelve types of springs that characterize the planet's perennial, intermittent, and ephemeral water sources, ten are found in the Grand Canyon, and eight are used in this inventory of water sources: Cave Springs, Cave Spring Waterfalls, Cliff Springs, Fault Springs, Fracture Springs, Hillside Springs, Perched Springs, Streambed Springs, and Travertine Springs. In addition, seasonal and ephemeral sources are typified by rainfall and snowmelt stone catchments called water pockets, rock tanks (*tinajas*), potholes, and "kiss tanks."

- Cave Springs are subterranean streams that flow from (tubula) cave openings. Abyss River Cave, At Last Cave, and Silent River Cave are three sublime, seldom-seen hidden waters.
- Cave Spring Waterfalls explode and gush from caves, cliffs, and canyon walls. Vaseys Paradise, Roaring Springs, and Thunder River offer dramatic displays of frothing water.
- Cliff Springs form hanging gardens beneath alcove ceilings and rock shelves. Hawaii Spring, Fern Glen Spring, and Showerbath Spring are cool and refreshing destinations.
- Fault Springs flow along rugged geologic cross-canyon fault zones such as Fence Spring (Fence Fault), Pipe Creek Spring (Bright Angel Fault), and Hawaii Spring (Hermit Fault).
- Fracture Springs flow between an aquifer's permeable water-bearing rock and its underlying impermeable rock layers such as the Bright Angel Creek tributaries of Haunted Spring and Phantom Spring.
- Hillside Springs form where underlying runoff and groundwater flow through steep hill slopes. The cottonwood tree-shaded Burro Spring on the Tonto Trail East is the most visited.
- Perched Springs flow from aquifers that are "perched" above underlying regional aquifers that created South Canyon Spring, Santa María Spring, and Cougar Spring.
- Streambed Springs surface and form canyon floor spring flows, including the South Rim's Red Canyon and Hermit Creek.
- Travertine Springs form when spring water mixes with CO_2 and creates striking travertine curtains and pools at Havasu Falls and Blue Springs. Beautiful to behold, the geochemistry of these turquoise waters makes them unfit to drink. Boucher Spring East is an exception for potable drinking water among travertine springs.

Once you've decided on your hike and know the general location of the canyon's streams, springs, and seeps along your route of travel, you can sometimes see them from a great distance. Visibility permitting, Indian Garden Springs on Garden Creek below the South Rim can be seen from the summit of 7,646-foot Shiva Temple on the North Rim six miles distant. While crossing the Tonto Trail, you can also see the green plumage of signature indicator plants like cottonwood trees, which are beacons of life in the tawny arid canyonscape near Burro Spring. As you draw closer to the canyon's diverse rivulets of life, you'll see other endemic plants unique to the spring and seep type that form visual bouquets in the damp shade of white-flowered redbud trees, hanging gardens of green maidenhair ferns, yellow columbines, scarlet monkey flowers, monarch butterflies, colorful songbirds, croaking tree frogs, spadefoot toads, fairy shrimp, and microscopic rotifers. tread lightly, and don't camp nearby.

Where Does the Water Come From?

Coconino Plateau/South Rim Aquifers

Deep subterranean pools, caverns, rivers, and streams that bring to mind Jules Verne's *Journey to the Center of the Earth* (1874) are borne from the Grand Canyon's life-giving aquifers. The Coconino Aquifer is comprised of the Kaibab Limestone, Coconino Sandstone, and Supai Formation. It forms 1,000 to 1,500 feet beneath the forested floor of the 7,000-foot Coconino Plateau and caps the Redwall-Muav Limestone Aquifer that pools 3,000 feet beneath the South Rim. The major springs that discharge perennial water from this porous chamber of water into the Colorado River are Blue Springs in the Little Colorado River Gorge, Indian Garden Springs, Hermit Spring, and Havasu Spring far to the west.

Kaibab Plateau/North Rim Aquifer

The Redwall Aquifer is comprised of the 1,300-foot thick Redwall Limestone, Muav Limestone, and Temple Butte Formation that drain the sub-alpine forested floor of the 9,002-foot Kaibab Plateau. The major springs that funnel water from this transient bank through perennial springs 3,000 feet below the North Rim into the Colorado River are Vaseys Paradise, Roaring Springs, Bright Angel Creek, and the stream caves of Tapeats Spring and Thunder River.

What Are You Drinking?

What's in the water that Native Peoples, deer and bighorn sheep, raptors and song-birds, bees and bats, frogs and fish, ferns and flowers, and hikers depend on? According to one U.S. Geological Survey Report, "Historical data . . . from 428 sites in the Grand Canyon region, including wells, streams, and springs, indicated that 95 percent of samples had concentrations of dissolved uranium . . ." Imagine the Coconino and Kaibab Plateaus as an enormous layer cake of colorful sedimentary rock per-forated by 1,300 vertical tubes, or chimneys, thirty feet in diameter and plunging well over 1,000 feet deep. Uranium frequently forms in these breccia pipes, as they're known among geohydrologists, and serve as conduits for water. In many cases they carry natural uranium (uraninite UO_2) into subterranean aquifers that flow through permeable rocks layers and in between impermeable seams that sustain fragile springs and seeps critical to natural habitat. Things get complicated when mineralized breccia pipes are mined and encounter what are called "radioactivity anomalies." The balance between "acceptable" levels of contaminants and "dangerous" levels often soar, especially from mineralized uranium, toxic waste, spills, and abandoned mine tailings that drain through breccia pipes through streams, springs, and seeps. Exacerbating the problem of once clean, clear, and sweet drinking water is ground and air pollution, drought, groundwater pumping, fecal coli from trespass cattle and hikers, wildfire, and invasive exotic plants and animals, and these factors threaten the canyon's most precious natural resource: water, the lifeblood of existence.

Climate Change
It's projected that climate change will diminish the perennial and intermittent flows of the Grand Canyon's cave streams, springs, seeps, and ephemeral water sources, but it's not known how significant the impacts will be.

Colorado River
For hikers and canyoneers using rim-to-river trails and routes that have no reliable springs or seeps, or have contaminated sources, the Colorado River is the only water source to replenish your depleted drinking water. When Paria Canyon or the Little Colorado Gorge is flooding, the Colorado River becomes heavily laden with silt and sediment. If you need to use river water because it's your only, or best, water source—and you're not dying of thirst—it's often your only option. After you've collected and containerized your water, be patient and wait for the water to stand still for one to two hours until the sediment settles before pouring it into another container for treatment.

    <u>Water Treatment:</u> The main stem of the Colorado River and many of its tributary canyons and creeks have *fecal coli* counts and carry the waterborne intestinal amoeba Giardia (*giardiasis*) that causes diarrheal illness and vomiting. This is serious! Fluid loss from heat and exercise-induced evaporative sweating is one factor. Combined with diarrhea-induced dehydration, you need to stop the symptoms immediately, especially if you need to hike out of the canyon. In remote locations, Giardia has been treated with Lomotil and Imodium. Consult your physician beforehand. More importantly, strain and treat all water sources with a water purification pump, potable purification tablets (don't put them in the water source), or boiling.

Water Contaminants
According to the U.S. Geological Survey, uranium concentrations that meet or exceed 5 U μg/L may be questionable, unfit, or toxic to drink and exceed U.S.

Environmental Protection Agency safety standards. Many if not most of the Grand Canyon's backcountry drinking water sources reportedly have "acceptable" contaminant levels below 5 U μg/L. When Major Powell and his men crossed the Arizona Strip with Paiute guides, expedition members were worried about bugs in their drinking water, the "wigglers" Powell commonly drank in front of them. They weren't worried about dissolved uranium contaminants or other trace elements. Times changed, and in the aftermath of the 1950s uranium rush many streams, springs, and seeps haven't gotten any sweeter to drink. Backcountry drinking water quality information that should be readily available to Grand Canyon hikers, backpackers, and adventurers is restricted or buried in difficult-to-access scientific reports. I've included the data I did uncover and known contaminant levels for you as precautionary footnotes and as a barometer of what the future may bring with the Grand Canyon's next gold rush.

Symbols: River, Stream, Spring, and Seep Flow
- River and Stream Flows CFS (cubic feet per second)
- Spring and Seep Flows GPM (gallons per minute)
- Dissolved Contaminants μg/L (micrograms per liter), Mg/L (milligrams per liter)

Water Contaminant Levels
- PMLC: Primary Maximum Level Contaminant
- SMCL: Secondary Maximum Level Contaminant

Chemical Symbols and Dissolved Contaminant Levels that Exceed Primary Maximums
- Uranium U μg/L: 30 is the standard.
- Selenium Se μg/L 50 is the standard.
- Lead Pb μg/L 15 is the standard.
- Arsenic As μg/L 10 is the standard: "70 sites greater than 10 μg/L, 40 sites greater than 100 μg/L.
- Nitrate NO^3 10 Mg/L is the standard.
- Mercury Hg 2 μg/L is the standard.

Dissolved Contaminant Levels that Exceed Secondary Maximums
- SMCL: Secondary Maximum Level Contaminant
- Uranium U μg/L: 5 is the standard.

Perennial Water Sources

According to the park, "Sources are classified as perennial on the basis of detailed historic records indicating the source has not gone dry within historic times or the presence of maidenhair fern."

Seasonal Water Sources

Some of the Grand Canyon's most reliable seasonal water sources are the deep, shallow, and ephemeral water pockets found throughout the Esplanade Sandstone on such primitive trails and routes as the Apache, Boucher, Thunder River, and Tuckup Trails, and elsewhere throughout the canyon. The deep water pockets in Shiva Saddle were so dependable to Ancestral Puebloans, perhaps earlier canyon dwellers, you can still view agave roasting pits in the area. Second to the Esplanade Sandstone water pockets are the shallow water pockets and ephemeral "kiss tanks" found on the Tonto Formation's outer rim of Tapeats Sandstone and springs at the heads of its tributary canyons and creeks. These sources, and other tributary canyons and creeks, are most reliable during and after summer monsoons, seasonal rains all year, and spring snowmelt.

Note: The perennial, seasonal, and ephemeral water sources in this inventory have been used by me, and/or have been reportedly used by others. I have not included other water sources that I have not personally used or been able to vet. This inventory should be used only as a planning aid. Conditions in the backcountry continue to change. Check first with the Backcountry Information Center on the current status of these water sources before you bet your life on them.

GRAND CANYON STREAMS, SPRINGS, SEEPS, AND SEASONAL WATER SOURCES

Colorado River Tributary Canyons, Creeks, and Trails: From the Lees Ferry in the east end of the Grand Canyon at RR (River Right) **Mile 0**, proceeding west to Saddle Horse Spring above RR Mile 176.5 near the west end:

RR Mile 0.0, Colorado River, Lees Ferry, Moenkopi Formation, potable water available at Lees Ferry Campground and Ranger Station. Paria River stream flow near the mouth 4,174 gpm minimum (median 9.3 cfs to maximum 2,800 cfs), Contaminant Level: Uranium 3.2 to 3.8 Upg/L. Colorado River at Lees Ferry, *2010 Survey Contaminant: Mercury Hg 3.8 µg/L. The number 1 represents the highest toxicity level for the survey.

RR Mile 11.2, Soap Creek Spring, Hermit, spring flow 7.8 gpm.

RR Mile 17, Rider Spring, Supai, perched spring flow 0.02 gpm. Contaminant Level: Uranium 4.5 Upg/L. *2010 Survey Contaminants: Silver Ag 1 µg/L,

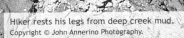
Hiker rests his legs from deep creek mud.

Molybdenum Mo 2 µg/L, Cadmium Cd 3 µg/L. The number 1 represents the highest toxicity level for the survey.

RL Mile 29, Shinumo Wash, Redwall, Silver Grotto seasonal pools.

RR Mile 31.5, Fence Spring, Redwall, Fence Fault spring flow 732 gpm.

RR Mile 31.5, South Canyon Spring, Redwall, perched spring flow data n/a. *2010 Survey Contaminants: Cobalt Co 2 µg/L, Lead Pb 3 µg/L. The number 1 represents the highest toxicity level for the survey.

RR Mile 32, Vaseys Paradise Spring, Redwall, perennial tubula cave springs and waterfall flow 67.2 to 4,480 gpm. Contaminant Level: Uranium 1.2 Uµg/L.*2010 Survey Contaminant: Barium 3 BM µg/L. The number 1 represents the highest toxicity level for the survey.

RL Mile 34.8, Nautiloid Canyon, Redwall, seasonal pools.

RR Mile 41, Buckfarm Spring, Temple Butte-Muav, perennial spring flow 0.59 gpm. *2010 Survey Contaminants: Silver Ag 1 µg/L, Antimony Sb 2 µg/L, Lead Pb 2 µg/L. The number 1 represents the highest toxicity level for the survey.

RR Mile 41.2, Keyhole [Royal Arches] Spring, Muav, spring flow data n/a.

RR Mile 41.4, Bert's [Loper] Canyon Spring, Muav, hanging garden springs and seep flow data n/a.

RR Mile 47, Saddle Canyon, Muav-Redwall, perennial fracture spring flow 9.1 gpm and slot canyon falls. Contaminant Level: Uranium 2.6 Uµg/L.

RR Mile 52, Nankoweap Creek at river, Bright Angel, stream flow 31 to 599 gpm.
- Nankoweap Creek 1 Mile Spring, Muav, perennial spring flow 1 to 174 gpm, Nankoweap Trail from Colorado River.
- Nankoweap Creek twin springs, Quartzite-Schist, spring flow 61 cfs, Nankoweap Trail from Colorado River. Contaminant Level: Uranium 1.5 Uµg/L.
- Nankoweap/Butte Fault Springs, Quartzite-Schist, fracture fault spring flow n/a, Nankoweap Trail (2.5 miles upstream) from Colorado River. Contaminant Level: Uranium 2.8 Uµg/L.
- Tilted Spring, Tapeats, spring flow data n/a, Nankoweap Trail. Contaminant Level: Uranium 2.8 Uµg/L.
- Cliff Spring, Kaibab-Toroweap, perched spring flow 0.5 to 0.58 gpm, Cliff Spring Trail, North Rim.
- Silent River Cave, Muav-Redwall, 2.5 miles of passages mapped, tubula cave stream flow data n/a, Old Kibbey Butte Trail. A "fifteen-foot waterfall" was reported by cave explorers Arthur L. Lange, Tom Aley, and Peter Huntoon after they discovered the cave in 1964.
  - **Note**: Publicly disclosed elsewhere in printed reports and maps. No cultural affiliations or archaeological antiquities reported.

- At Last Cave Spring, Muav, 1,600 feet +/- of passages mapped, perennial tubula cave fault spring flow 260 gpm, Woolsey Butte route.
  - **Note:** Publicly disclosed elsewhere in printed reports and maps. No cultural affiliations or archaeological antiquities reported.

RR Mile 56, Kwagunt Creek, Muav, seasonal springs two miles up from the river, Butte Fault Route.

RL Mile 61.5, Little Colorado River, Tapeats, stream flow 124,775 gpm minimum (median 278 cfs to maximum 862 cfs). Contaminant Level: Uranium 9.2 Uμg/L. As a result of one of the largest tailings pond spills in the United States, tissue samples of Humpback chub (*cypha*), channel catfish (*Ictahms punctatzu*), and other fish thriving above the mouth of the Little Colorado River confluence contained 158.0 to 3169.2 μg/L of dangerous trace elements, including thorium-230, thorium-232, radium-226, radium-228, and uranium-238. The Colorado River, "the most endangered river in America," carried and deposited those contaminants throughout the Natural Wonder of the World all the way to the dissipating waters of Lake Mead.

- Blue Springs, Redwall, perennial fracture springs flow 40,394 gpm minimum (90 cfs to 220 cfs), Little Colorado River Gorge.
- Salt Trail Canyon Spring, Bright Angel, spring flow data n/a, 4.5 miles up from the confluence of the Colorado River.

RR Mile 64.5, Carbon Creek, Dox, seasonal stream runoff, may be toxic.

RR Mile 65, Lava Canyon, Dox-Ochoa Point, seasonal stream runoff.

RL Mile 68.5, Tanner Canyon Rock Tanks (Horse Thief Tanks), Muav, seasonal tanks; and Tanner Canyon Seep, Tapeats, flow 0.1 gpm in Redbud Tree alcove. Both sources located off the Tanner Trail, South Rim.

RR Mile 72.4, Unkar Creek, Dox-Flood Plain, reliable seasonal stream runoff.

RL Mile 76.5, Red Canyon Spring, Muav, streambed spring flow from Hakatai 3.2 to 4.48 gpm, New Hance Trail/Tonto Trail East. Contaminant Levels: Uranium 1.7 Uμg/L; Arsenic 17 As μg/L.

- JT (Hance) Spring, Bright Angel-Tapeats, hanging garden springs and seep flows 0.17 to 0.91 gpm, New Hance Trail/Tonto Trail East. Contaminant Levels: Uranium 3.8 Uμg/L; Arsenic 14 As μg/L.
- Miners Spring, Temple Butte-Muav, hanging garden springs and seep flows 0.54 to 0.59 gpm, New Hance Trail/Grandview Trail. Contaminant Levels: Uranium 3.9 Uμg/L; Arsenic 19 As μg/L.
- Page Spring, Bright Angel-Muav, intermittent spring flow 1.5 gpm. Contaminant Level: Uranium 4.0 Uμg/L.

RR Mile 78, Asbestos Canyon, Shinumo, seasonal potholes near head of canyon, North Tonto Route East.

RL Mile 80.5, Cottonwood Spring, Bright Angel-Muav, perennial fault spring flow 0.81 to 5.4 gpm, Tonto Trail East. Contaminant Level: Uranium 2.1 Uµg/L.

- Cottonwood Creek No. 2, Temple Butte-Muav, spring flow 0.64 to 4.5 gpm, Tonto Trail East. Contaminant Levels: Uranium 1.6 Uµg/L; Arsenic 4.8 As µg/L.
- Cottonwood Spring, Bright Angel, intermittent, hanging garden springs and seep flows above confluence 3.6 to 10.3 gpm, Tonto Trail East. Contaminant Level: Uranium 5.7 Uµg/L.

RR Mile 81, Vishnu Creek, Tapeats, seasonal potholes near head of the canyon, North Tonto Route East.

RL Mile 81.5, Grapevine Creek, Bright Angel-Muav contact, flow 10 gpm, Tonto Trail East. Contaminant Level: Uranium 1.1 Uµg/L.

- Grapevine Spring, Muav, perennial, hanging garden fault springs and seep flows 1.9 to 5 gpm, 1.7 miles above Tonto Trail East. Contaminant Level: Arsenic 5.4 As µg/L.
- Grapevine Spring East, Bright Angel-Muav, intermittent, hanging garden fault springs and seep flows 1.1 to 6.42 gpm, near Tonto Trail East.

RL Mile 82.5, Boulder Creek, Tapeats, intermittent spring flow 0.877 gpm, below Tonto Trail East. Contaminant Level: Uranium 8.1 Uµg/L.

- Boulder Canyon, Tapeats, spring flow 1.92 to 10 gpm, above the Tonto Trail East.
- Lonetree Spring, Redwall-Muav contact, streambed spring flow 0.46 to 15.8 gpm, 1.24 miles upstream from Tonto Trail East. Contaminant Level: Uranium 6.0 Uµg/L.
- Cremation Creek Spring (Sam Magee Spring), Muav, intermittent spring flow 0.40 to 3.0 gpm, 500 yards above Tonto Trail East.
- Burro Spring, Bright Angel, perennial hillside spring flow 3.1 to 8.97 gpm, Tonto Trail East crossing. Contaminant Level: Uranium 2.6 to 3.5 Uµg/L.

RR Mile 84, Clear Creek, Tapeats-Vishnu, falls and stream flow 828 to 970 gpm and twin falls.

- Clear Creek Spring, Cheyava Falls, Redwall, intermittent waterfalls and spring flow 852 gpm above Clear Creek Trail.
- Sumner Wash, Tapeats, seasonal potholes off Clear Creek Trail.

RR Mile 87.5, Bright Angel Creek, Vishnu, perennial stream flow 57,8994 gpm minimum (median 1,290 cfs to maximum 2,440 cfs), from river and North Kaibab Trail. Contaminant Level: 0.5 to 1.0 Uµg/L.

- Ribbon Falls Spring, Muav, perennial fracture waterfall and spring flow 184 gpm and waterfall, North Kaibab Trail.

- Roaring Spring, Muav, perennial tubula cave waterfall and stream flow 15,709 gpm (22,620,960 gallons per day), North Kaibab Trail.
- Phantom Spring, Muav, perennial fracture spring flow 72 gpm, Phantom Canyon tributary.
- Haunted Spring, Muav, perennial fracture spring flow 430 gpm, Haunted Canyon tributary.
- Angel Spring, Muav, perennial tubula cave spring stream flow 5,734 gpm, Old Bright Angel Canyon Trail.
- Emmett Spring, Muav, perennial tubula cave spring stream flow 197 to 441 gpm, Old Bright Angel Canyon Trail.
- Transept Spring, Muav, perennial fracture spring flow 54 gpm, Transept Trail, North Rim.

RL Mile 89, Pipe Creek, Granite-Granitic Pegmatite, stream flow data n/a, Bright Angel Trail. Contaminant Level: Uranium 20.0 to 21.0 Uµg/L, source 1905 Magician and Wizard mining claims.

- Pipe Creek Spring, Bright Angel, perennial fault spring flow 4.0 to 104 gpm, 250 yards above Tonto Trail East. Contaminant Level: Uranium 4.0 Uµg/L.
- Pipe Creek Spring down, Redwall-Muav contact, fault spring flow 0.92 gpm, Tonto Trail East. Contaminant Level: Uranium 3.2 Uµg/L.
- Columbine Falls, Pipe Creek, Rama Schist-Gneiss, falls and stream flow date n/a, Bright Angel Trail. Contaminant Level: Uranium 1.5 Uµg/L.
- Indian Garden Creek, Redwall-Muav Limestone aquifer, "collection gallery" stream flow 37.8 to 300 gpm, Bright Angel Trail. Contaminant Level: Uranium 1.5 Uµg/L.
- Kolb Spring, Coconino, intermittent perched spring flow 0.5 gpm, Bright Angel Trail, South Rim.

RL Mile 90.5, Horn Creek Spring, Bright Angel, intermittent spring flow 0.5 gpm, 500 yards above Tonto Trail West. Contaminant Level: Uranium 30 to 36.1 Uµg/L, source Lost Orphan Mine (Orphan Lode Mine).

- Horn Creek west, Redwall-Muav, stream flow 0.90 to 2.5 gpm, Tonto Trail West. Contaminant Level: Uranium 168.5 Uµg/L, source Lost Orphan Mine.
- Horn Creek up, Redwall-Muav, stream flow 0.90 to 2.5 gpm, Tonto Trail West. Contaminant Level: Uranium 344.8 Uµg/L, source Lost Orphan Mine.

RR Mile 91.5, Trinity Creek, seasonal potholes near head of the canyon, North Tonto Route West.

RL Mile 92.5, Salt Creek, Bright Angel-Tapeats, stream flow 10 to 61 gpm, below Tonto Trail West. Contaminant Level: Uranium 14.7 Uµg/L, source Lost Orphan Mine.

- Salt Creek Spring, Muav, intermittent streambed spring flow 0.45 to 1.3 gpm, 800 yards above Tonto Trail West. Contaminant Level: Uranium 30.6 Uμg/L, source Lost Orphan Mine.
- Cedar Spring, Tapeats, intermittent spring flow 0.64 to 3.9 gpm below Tonto Trail West. Contaminant Level: Uranium 31 Uμg/L.

RL Mile 93.5, Monument Creek No. 1, Tapeats-Bright Angel, intermittent stream flow 5 to 62.8 gpm, 30 yards above Tonto Trail West. Contaminant Level: Uranium 7.2 Uμg/L. *2010 Survey Contaminants, Nitrate NO^3 10 Mg/L is the standard: Monument Creek No. 1 NO^3 4.5 mg/L.

- Monument Creek, Redwall-Temple Butte hanging garden fault springs and seep flows 48 to 89 gpm, 1.7 miles above Tonto Trail West. Contaminant Levels: Uranium 7.1 to 11.1 Uμg/L; Arsenic 4.0 As μg/L. *2010 Survey Contaminants, Mercury Hg 2 μg/L is the standard: Monument Spring 2.1 Hg μg/L.

RL Mile 95, Hermit Spring, Redwall, perennial fault spring flow 314 to 399 gpm, Hermit Creek, 2.2 miles upstream from Tonto Trail West and Hermit Trail. Contaminant Level: Uranium 4.7 Uμg/L.

- Hawaii Spring, Muav, perennial, hanging garden fault springs and seep flows 319 to 399 gpm, Hermit Creek, 1.1 miles above Tonto Trail West and Hermit Trail.
- Santa Maria Spring, Esplanade, perennial perched spring flow 0.5 gpm, Hermit Trail, South Rim. Contaminant Level: Uranium 4.9 to 7.2 Uμg/L.

RL Mile 96.5, Boucher Spring east, Tapeats, travertine spring flow 3.1 to 7.8 gpm, Boucher Creek/Boucher Trail 1.5 miles upstream from river. Contaminant Level: Uranium 1.9 Uμg/L.

- Dripping Springs, Coconino-Hermit contact, perennial perched spring flow 1 to 2.1 gpm, Dripping Spring Trail, South Rim. Contaminant Level: Uranium 1.9 Uμg/L.

RR Mile 98, Crystal Creek Spring, Vishnu, perennial filtration spring flow 90 gpm, Crystal Creek.

- Dragon Spring, Tapeats alluvium, perennial filtration spring flow 627 gpm, Dragon Creek, North Rim.

RL Mile 98, Slate Creek, Tapeats, seasonal water and springs below Tonto Trail West near head of the canyon.

RR Mile 99, Tuna Creek, Tapeats, seasonal spring and streambed runoff, North Tonto Route West.

RL Mile 101, Sapphire Canyon, Tapeats, seasonal streambed water and potholes off Tonto Trail West near head of the canyon.

RL Mile 102, Turquoise Canyon, Tapeats-Muav, spring flow data n/a: Upper Turquoise Spring 100 feet above Tonto Trail West near head of canyon, Lower Turquoise Spring 0.25 miles in streambed below the trail.

RL Mile 104.5, Ruby Canyon, Tapeats, seasonal water pockets above Tonto Trail West near head of canyon.

RL Mile 106, Serpentine Canyon, Tapeats, streambed water at the head of the canyon, Tonto Trail West.

RL Mile 107.5, Bass Canyon, Hakatai-Bass, Bedrock Tanks seasonal water 1 mile up canyon from the river.

- Garnet Canyon, Esplanade-Tapeats, seasonal potholes west end of Tonto Trail from South Bass Trail.
- Seep Spring, Hermit, seasonal perched spring 560 vertical feet above the Apache Trail beneath 6,600-foot Chemehuevi Point.

RR Mile 108, Shinumo Creek, Vishnu Schist, falls and stream flow 3,265 gpm, North Bass Trail.

- Shinumo Spring, Muav, perennial fracture spring flow 851 gpm, North Bass Trail.
- Muav Saddle (Queen Anne) Spring, Coconino-Supai contact, perennial spring flow data n/a, Powell Plateau Trail/North Bass Trail.
- Cougar Spring, Coconino-Supai, perched spring flow data n/a, Dutton Canyon, Powell Plateau.
- Powell Spring, Redwall, perched spring flow data n/a, 1.15 miles below Muav Saddle in Grassy Canyon on the Saddle Canyon route to Thunder River Trail.
- Parrissawampitts Spring, Kaibab, perched spring flow 0.44 gpm, Tapeats Amphitheater, North Rim.
- Abyss River Cave Spring, Muav Limestone, 2,000 feet +/- of passages mapped, perennial tubula cave springs flow 403 gpm, Modred Abyss.
  - **Note:** Publicly disclosed elsewhere in printed reports and maps. No cultural affiliations or archaeological antiquities reported.

RL Mile 116.5, Royal Arch Creek at mouth, Tapeats, stream flow 103 gpm, (fecal coli). Contaminant Level: Uranium 3.5 Uμg/L.

- Elves Chasm Spring, hanging garden springs and seep flows 8.97 gpm and falls. Contaminant Levels: Uranium 3.1 Uμg/L.
- Royal Arch Creek, Redwall-Temple Butte, stream flow data n/a, from Apache Trail. Contaminant Level: Uranium 3.5 Uμg/L.

RR Mile 120, Blacktail Canyon, Tapeats, stream flow data n/a.

RR Mile 131.8, Stone Creek, Diabase-Hakatai-Bass, waterfalls and stream flow 235 to 1,021 gpm.

RR Mile 133.5, Tapeats Creek near mouth, Diabase-Bright Angel, stream flow 29,683 gpm, (66.1 cfs), Colorado River.

- Tapeats Spring, Muav, perennial waterfall and spring flow 33,333 gpm, (48 million gallons per day), upstream from Thunder River Trail.
- Tapeats Creek above Thunder River, perennial flow 21,521 gpm, Saddle Canyon Route to Thunder River Trail.
- Thunder Spring, Muav, perennial waterfall and spring flow 14,583 gpm (21 million gallons per day), Thunder River Trail.
- Tapeats Creek below Thunder River, Muav-Tapeats, perennial flow 29,683 gpm, Thunder River Trail.
- Vaughn Spring, Muav-Bright Angel, spring flow 2,423 to 3,680 gpm (combined with Deer Spring), below Thunder River Trail.
- Walapai Johnny Spring, Redwall, seasonal spring flow 0.5 gpm, cross-country west of Thunder River Trail near head of northeast fork of Fishtail Canyon.
- Deer Spring (Dutton Spring) Muav-Bright Angel, spring flow 1,460 gpm and waterfall, Deer Creek Trail.
- Deer Creek upper falls, Muav-Bright Angel, perennial fracture spring flow 1,460 gpm, Deer Creek Trail.

RR, Mile 136, Deer Creek Falls, Granite-Tapeats, perennial waterfall and stream flow 2,441 to 3,680 gpm, (median 5.4 cfs to maximum 8.19 cfs), and waterfall, Colorado River.

RR, Mile 143.5, Kanab Creek near mouth, Muav, stream flow 5,385 gpm minimum, (median 12 cfs to maximum 69 cfs). Contaminant Levels: Uranium 5.1 Uμg/L; Lead: 15 to 20 Pb μg/L. *2010 Survey Contaminants: Silver Ag 1 μg/L, Cadmium Cd 2 μg/L, Antimony Sb 3 μg/L. The number 1 represents the highest toxicity level for the survey.

- Whispering Falls Spring, Muav, waterfall and stream flow data n/a, tributary canyon rivulet 3.5 miles upstream from the mouth of Kanab Creek.
- Showerbath Spring, Redwall, hanging garden springs and seep flows 202 gpm, 8 miles upstream from the mouth of Kanab Creek. Contaminant Level: Uranium 4.2 Uμg/L. *2010 Survey Contaminants: Silver Ag 1 μg/L, Cobalt Co 2 μg/L. The number 1 represents the highest toxicity level for the survey.

RL Mile 145.5, Olo Canyon, Muav, stream flow data n/a.

RL Mile 148, Matakatamiba Spring, Redwall-Bright Angel-Muav, hanging garden springs and seep flows 59 gpm and falls.

RR Mile 151.5, Ledges Spring, Muav, hanging garden springs and seep flows data n/a.

RR Mile 155.3, Slimy Tick Canyon Spring, Muav, hanging garden springs and seep flows data n/a.

RL Mile 156.5, Havasu Creek near mouth, Muav, stream flow 32,764 gpm minimum, (median 73 cfs to maximum 144 cfs).

- Havasu Spring, Redwall-Muav, stream flow data n/a, above Hualapai (Havasupai) Trail and Supai. Contaminant Level: Uranium 29 Uμg/L. *2010 Survey Contaminants, Lead Pb μg/L 15 is the standard PMLC: Havasu Spring Pb 29 μg/L.
- Fern Spring, Redwall, spring flow 8 gpm, below Supai west of Havasu Creek Campground. Contaminant Level: Uranium 20 Uμg/L.

RR Mile 164.5, Tuckup Canyon, Schmutz Spring, Basalt, perched spring flow data n/a, Tuckup Trail east. Contaminant Levels: Uranium 4.7 Uμg/L; Selenium Se 44 μg/L. *2010 Survey Contaminants: Silver 1 Ag μg/L, Cadmium Cd 2 μg/L. The number 1 represents them the highest toxicity level for the survey.

RL Mile 166.5, National Canyon Spring, Muav, stream flow data n/a, Contaminant Level: Uranium 8 Uμg/L.

RR Mile 168, Fern Glen Canyon Spring, Muav, hanging garden springs and seep flows 2 gpm. Contaminant Level: Uranium 3.6 Uμg/L.

RL Mile 171.5, Mohawk Canyon, Muav, spring flow 2 to 8.9 gpm. Contaminant Level: Uranium 12.0 to 18.0 Uμg/L.

RR Mile 174.5, Cove Canyon Spring, Muav, spring flow data n/a, Tuckup Trail west. Contaminant Level: Uranium 11 Uμg/L.

RR 176.5, Saddle Horse Spring, Esplanade, ephemeral fracture spring flow 0.05 gpm, Saddle Horse Trail, Toroweap Point. Contaminant Level: Uranium 3.5 Uμg/L.

PREVENTION

Heat

Heat has proven to be one of the principal causes of death for canyon hikers. It's the overheating of your body's inner core and brain, and the inability to stay cool and hydrated. It's important you understand the contributing factors and take measures to mitigate them if you plan a warm or hot weather hike below the rim. To prevent dehydration, heat stress, sunstroke, and sunburn, you must, in all circumstances, be able to keep yourself cool, hydrated, and sun-screened or skin-covered.

Dehydration, Heat Stress, and Sunstroke

- **Respiration:** Your body is heated by breathing hot air.
- **Convection:** Your body is heated by being exposed to hot air.
- **Radiation:** Your body is heated by refracted heat from canyon walls, boulders, and trail surface.

- **Conduction:** Your body is heated by direct contact walking on hot trails and sitting on hot ground, ledges, and boulders.
- **Dehydration:** Your body is heated by not replenishing fluids lost through evaporation.
- **Consumption:** Your body is heated by drinking hot water.
- **Exposure:** Your brain is heated by direct exposure to the sun and uncovered neck carotid arteries.

Cold

Correspondingly, hypothermia has been called the "Killer of the Unprepared." Commonly called "exposure," it's the cooling of your body's inner core and the inability to stay dry and warm. It takes its toll during a variety of conditions you should understand to avoid or mitigate them, especially cold water immersion, wind-driven rainstorms, and wet moisture-saturated snowstorms. To prevent hypothermia you must, in all circumstances, be able to keep yourself dry and warm.

- **Immersion:** Your body is immediately super-cooled immersed in cold river and creek water.
- **Wet Chill Factor:** Your body is quickly super-cooled exposed to rain, wind, and wet snow storms.
- **Exposure:** Your brain is quickly cooled by direct exposure to cold air and uncovered neck carotid arteries.
- **Respiration:** Your body is cooled by breathing cold air.
- **Convection:** Your body is cooled by being exposed to cold air.
- **Conduction:** Your body is cooled by direct contact walking on cold and icy trails and sitting on cold ground, ledges, and boulders.
- **Consumption:** Your body is cooled by drinking cold water.

4

Hiking the Grand Canyon: The Journey of Your Life

"To the mountaineer the depth of the cañon, from five thousand to six thousand feet, will not seem so very wonderful, for he has often explored others that are about as deep. But the most experienced will be awe-struck by the vast extent of strange, countersunk scenery."
—John Muir, 1902,
The Grand Cañon of the Colorado

WHEREVER YOU GO, THERE YOU ARE. CALL IT COMMUNING WITH nature, situational awareness, mindfulness, in the moment, or walking meditation. Few places on Earth demand your attention and focus more than the exposed rims, cliffs, and trails of the Grand Canyon. It's in another dimension, geologically, structurally, and visually. Naturalist Weldon F. Heald, geologist Edwin D. McKee, and zoologist Harold S. Colton recognized that perspective when they contributed to Roderick Peattie's 1948 classic, *The Inverted Mountains: Canyons of the West.* So did Sierra Club founder and conservationist John Muir when forty-six years earlier he wrote: "In a dry, hot, monotonous forested plateau, seemingly boundless, you come suddenly and without warning upon the abrupt edge of a gigantic sunken landscape of the wildest, most multitudinous features . . . forming a spiry, jagged, gloriously colored mountain-range countersunk in a level gray plain." As you head

A hiker leaps rugged terrain high above the Colorado River in the western Grand Canyon.
Copyright © John Annerino Photography.

off the rim into the inverted, counter sunk landscape take the time to stop and see where you are in the grand scheme of what I call "the world beneath the horizon line." Are you comfortable? Are you enjoying this all-new world? Can you hike back out without pushing yourself to the limits? Many hikers answer that simple question incorrectly, oftentimes because gravity and the dream of "hiking to the bottom of the Grand Canyon" exerts an irresistible force over common sense, clear judgment, and physical abilities. Are you up to the challenges of descending further and returning within your own reasonable limits to enjoy the hike versus suffering through a grueling or life-threatening trek? Successful Himalayan mountaineers who've climbed the highest mountain on the planet, 29,029-foot (8,848-meter) Mount Everest, frequently relate, "Reaching the summit is only half the climb." Nepalese sherpas who guide mountaineers to the summit of Mount Everest call it *Sagarmāthā*, "Forehead in the Sky," but the sacred peak has claimed the lives of 280 people. Conversely, reaching the Colorado River in the bottom of the Grand Canyon is only half the hike. *Piapaxa 'Uipi*, "Big River Canyon," as the Kaibab Paiute call the Grand Canyon, is the most famous canyon in the world, and it's claimed the lives of 687 people since records were first kept. Don't let the statistics overwhelm you. Just keep things in perspective, especially if you tempt fate unprepared during the summer. Where are you in relation to the rim, your next water source, and your destination? How do you feel? Should you push on or turn around before you reach the point of no return? It's up to you to monitor what many consider for good or ill the journey of their lives.

Day Hikers and Turn Around Points

You want to enjoy your Grand Canyon hike, and you should. For many first timers, it can be intimidating to drive or bus to the rim, shoulder your heavy pack, and start down an unfamiliar trail that leads into the depths of the greatest canyon on Earth. So in each of the maintained (Corridor) and nonmaintained (Threshold) trails I've included suggested "turn around points" for short strolls, introductory hikes, day hikes, and long day hikes. Moreover, you can relish your hike and judge whether you're getting in over your head and whether you should turn around. It's okay. The Grand Canyon will be there tomorrow, and the next day, or whenever it's convenient for you to return and enjoy hiking it. Take care of yourself. Don't let peers or personal expectations push you to your breaking point. Gravity will help pull you into the Grand Canyon, but it's up to you, your legs, lungs, and focus to hike all the way back up to the rim, step-by-tiny-step, up one switchback to another, one colorful and imposing geological layer at a time.

Rim-to-River Trails

During the Grand Canyon's gold and mineral rush from the mid-to-late 1800s, more than eighty-four rim-to-river trails were developed along prehistoric Native American routes and paths to prospects, glory holes, camps, and mines in the heart of the Grand Canyon. Less than two dozen hand-forged miner trails are still popularly used today. Canyon trails fall within one of three categories Grand Canyon National Park has officially designated: Corridor Trails (maintained), Threshold Trails (nonmaintained), and Primitive Trails and Routes (wilderness). In the first edition of this guide, I defined rim-to-river trails and routes as having one of two general characteristics: Creek Trail or Ridge Trail. For example, the Bright Angel Trail is basically a creek trail that follows and crisscrosses Garden Creek most of the way to its confluence with Pipe Creek near the Colorado River. As a result, the hiking isn't as exposed, nor are the views as spectacular as those seen from ridge trails. But the Bright Angel Trail offers shade, water, pleasant riparian habitat, and safety in the form of a Ranger Station and help. The South Kaibab Trail, on the other hand, is a ridge trail that crests or parallels Cedar Ridge much of the way into the Canyon. It offers exposed hiking and spectacular views, but there's little shade, no ranger station, and no drinking water en route. However you define the canyon's historic pathways, each will present its own distinct rewards, characteristics, and challenges.

Corridor Trails

Two rim-to-river trails located on the South Rim are maintained by National Park Service trail crews as Corridor Trails: Bright Angel Trail (including the Plateau Point Trail and the Colorado River Trail) and South Kaibab Trail. Beckoning visitors, day hikers, backpackers, runners, mule riders, and sightseers from around the globe, they are the most heavily used trails in Grand Canyon National Park. They are perhaps the easiest rim-to-river trails—though, no rim-to-river trail or route is easy—offering inexperienced canyoneers an introduction to inner-Canyon hiking below the South Rim while providing a base of experience to draw upon for future, more challenging canyon hikes and treks. If you have not hiked into the canyon before, you should strongly consider hiking one or both of these trails before embarking on the more difficult rim-to-river trails.

TRAIL ETIQUETTE

- Be a Good Samaritan if you encounter another hiker in need.
- Stay on the established trail or route.
- Tread gently near Native American Cultural and Archaeological Sites. Resist the temptation to pick up and pocket a "souvenir" arrowhead, pot shard, or other irreplaceable, sometimes sacred relics.

- "Don't Bust the Crust." The fragile living crypto biotic, or cryptogrammic soil, is commonly found on the Esplanade Formation and elsewhere throughout the canyon. Comprised of cyanobacteriam (*Microcolues vaginatus*), lichens (*Collema spp*), and mosses (*Tortula spp*), it can take from fifty to 250 years for the living soil to recover from a single careless footprint.

- Carry out all your trash and refuse. Bury human waste in a trowel-dug hole eight inches or more below ground at least 250 feet from water sources, trails, and campsites, or zip bag it, powder it with lime, and carry it out.

- Mules. The Bright Angel and South Kaibab Angel Trails are still used by mule trains to ferry guests and supplies to and from Indian Garden and Phantom Ranch, for trail maintenance, as well as to "drag out," or rescue, hikers in need. If you're hiking either of these trails, there's a good chance you'll encounter a mule train. If you do, the wrangler will ask you to step to the high side of the trail until the pack string passes. If you hear a pack string coming your way, it's usually safer and will make the wrangler's job easier if you take the high ground at a wide spot on the trail before they reach you.

TRAILS OF THE GRAND CANYON

This list has been generally grouped by location and by difficulty—from easiest to most difficult—and has been included as a planning aid so you can increase your backcountry experience in increments rather than in leaps and bounds.

South Rim

1. Rim Trails, developed and nonmainainted, 1–7 miles
   - Rim Trail
   - Comanche Point Trail
2. Bright Angel Trail, Corridor Trail, 9.5 miles
   - Old Bright Angel Trail
   - Colorado River Trail
3. South Kaibab Trail, Corridor Trail, 7 miles
   - Old Miners Trail
4. Hermit Trail, Threshold Trail, 9.7 miles
   - Waldron Trail
   - Hermit Creek River Trail
5. Boucher Trail, Primitive Trail, 10.8 miles
   - Old Silverbell Trail
   - Dripping Springs Trail

- Boucher Creek River Trail
6. South Bass Trail, Primitive Trail, 7.8 miles
   - Mystic Springs Trail
   - Conquistador Mystery Trail
7. Grandview Trail, Threshold Trail, 11.4 miles
   - Horseshoe Mesa Trail
   - Old Grandview Trail
8. New Hance Trail, Primitive Trail, 6.5 miles
9. Tanner Trail, Primitive Trail, 9 miles
   - Hopi Trail
   - Navajo Trail
   - Horse Thief Trail
   - Ancient Pass
   - Medicine Man Trail
10. Hualapai (Havasupai) Trail, Primitive Trail, 10 miles (Havasupai Campground)
    - Havasu Creek River Trail
    - Topocoba Trail
    - Moqui Trail
    - Black Tank Trail
    - Kla-la-Pa Trail
    - Pack-a-the-true-ye-ba Trail
11. South Trans Canyon Trails and Routes, mileages vary
    - Beamer Trail
    - Escalante Route "Beautyway Trail"
    - Tonto Trail East and Tonto Trail West
    - Apache Trail

North Rim

12. Rim Trails, developed and nonmaintained, 1–10 miles
    - Bright Angel Point Trail
    - Transept Trail
    - Uncle Jim Trail
    - Ken Patrick Trail
    - Cape Royal Trail
    - Widforss Trail
    - Powell Plateau Trail
    - Fire Lookout Trails and Rambles
13. North Kaibab Trail, Corridor Trail, 14.2 miles
    - Old Bright Angel Canyon Route

- Bright Angel Creek Trails
14. Nankoweap Trail, Primitive Trail, 14 miles
    - Kaibab Deer Drive Trail
    - Butte Fault/Horse Thief Trail
15. North Bass (Shinumo) Trail, Primitive Trail, 13.5 miles
16. Thunder River Trail, Threshold Trail, 13.8 miles
    - Indian Hollow Trail
    - Bill Hall Trail
    - Spirit Trail
    - Miners Trail
    - Deer Creek Trail
17. North Trans Canyon Trails and Routes, mileages vary
    - Butte Fault/Walcott Route
    - North Tonto Route East
    - Clear Creek Trail, Threshold Trail, 9 miles (primary access via Phantom Ranch)
    - Utah Flats Route
    - North Tonto Route West
    - North Bass Trail
    - Saddle Canyon Route
    - Thunder River Trail to Indian Hollow
18. Colorado River Trails, Primitive Trails and Routes, mileages vary
    - River Mile hikes and canyoneering
    - Tributary Canyons and Gorges Treks
19. Western Grand Canyon Trails, mileages vary
    - Witches Pool Trail
    - Nampaweap Trail
    - Lava Falls Route
    - Toroweap Overlook
    - Saddle Canyon Trail
    - Tuckup Trail

Each of the principal corresponding trail descriptions in Part II include: Name, Elevation, Geology, Water Availability, Landform, Historical Overview, Directions, Warnings, and Scenic, Historical, and Cultural Mileposts. The Travel Notes at the end of each trail description also include: Additional Considerations, Warnings, Primary Access, Elevation, Biotic Communities, Total Elevation Loss and Gain, Mileage, Water, Cache Points, Seasons, Escape Routes, Maps, Camping, Nearest Supply Points, and Managing Agency.

A Back Story: When I first started teaching and guiding month-long, class and field natural history "Challenge Discovery"-type wilderness courses throughout Arizona, I had the privilege of leading many people, young and old, on treks into the Grand Canyon, particularly along three trails students favored: the Boucher Trail, Tanner Trail, and on occasion the original Thunder River Trail. Judging from their varying skills and fitness levels from hiking and climbing to the summits of the Chiricahua Mountains Wilderness, Superstition Mountains Wilderness, and San Francisco Peaks Kachina Peaks Wilderness leading up to our three-to-four day canyon treks, we agreed another strategy should be used for carrying our supplies in and out of an inverted mountain range. Instead of packing all of our food and water to the bottom of the canyon, we left strategic caches of both approximately every 1,500 vertical feet we descended into the canyon to lighten our loads and to support the more difficult journey out of the canyon. We only moved as fast as our slowest member, someone always followed sweep, and if someone needed help, we took turns piggybacking their loads up to the next cache point in relays so everyone came back from their canyon journey safely, enlightened from nature at its finest, and fulfilled from their experiences, efforts, and camaraderie.

Hiking Rim to River

Caches: If you plan to hike rim to river, spend a day at the Colorado River, and then hike out the same trail, you might consider using caches. Unless you enjoy carrying the additional 16.68 pounds (two gallons) of water as a workout, there are few practical reasons, apart from style, which is important, to carry everything you're going to need for the hike back out of the canyon all the way down to the river. Divide the canyon by thirds (every 1,500 vertical feet or more apart), or by halves (every 2,500 vertical feet or so apart). Place your cache/s in convenient but inconspicuous locations. Label them. And use duct tape–sealed cookie tins or commercial metal mesh shark suit–type food containers. You might even place a stone on top. *Corvus corax* is watching! Don't underestimate the intelligence or cleverness of the canyon's common ravens. I've often wondered about all those Ancestral Puebloan storage granaries sealed into cliff faces, once holding ollas filled with maize, seeds, pine nuts, acorns, pemmican, and water as protection against the elements, marauding enemies, and a hedge against times of need. *Corvus corax* was watching and raiding back then, too, just waiting to poke its curious black beak into adobe-mortared cracks or breaks for grit to help digest their food only to discover the easy picking troves inside the storage granaries.

Hiking Rim to Rim

Caches: Unless you've organized two separate groups hiking in opposite directions, there's no practical way to utilize caches.

HIKING CROSS CANYON OR TRANS CANYON

Seasoned canyoneers sometimes place strategic caches by river raft or trail for long distance cross canyon and trans canyon treks and journeys. Check with the Backcountry Information Center regarding current guidelines.

Hiking

If you're planning on hiking rim to rim, the Bright Angel-North Kaibab Trails is the most popular and convenient cross-canyon hike. It requires a personal vehicle shuttle, or use of a commercial Hikers Shuttle service. Carefully weigh your options, personal aesthetics, and capabilities as to whether you want to hike the South Rim to the North Rim or the North Rim to the South Rim. The North Rim is a cooler and far prettier destination than the bustling South Rim. However, the North Kaibab Trail is 4.5 miles longer than the Bright Angel Trail and the 8,241-foot North Rim is a 1,381 vertical foot higher climb than the South Rim. If you hike down the North Kaibab Trail, stay safe and avoid the South Kaibab Trail by hiking out the Bright Angel Trail. It's two miles longer than the South Kaibab Trail, but it's not as steep, your legs and body will have some time to recover, and most importantly there's seasonal water, shaded ramadas, and the Indian Garden Ranger Station along the Bright Angel Trail if you need help. If you hike any other rim-to-rim trail system, such as the South Bass/North Bass Trails, then you need to make remote vehicle shuttles in both directions, and make a Colorado River packraft crossing.

HAZARDS

River Crossings

Seasoned canyoneers commonly cross the slow water between Bass Rapids and Shinumo Rapids without incident. But this is a serious, personal safety issue you should strongly consider before embarking on a rim-to-rim hike via the Bass Trails in either direction. Ethnographic accounts describe the Havasupai and Hualapai crossing the Colorado River in the western Grand Canyon by swimming or paddling driftwood logs or small rafts at low water during the late 1800s when late summer and early fall river temperatures fluctuated around 76 to 80 degrees Fahrenheit. Since Glen Canyon Dam was built in 1966, river temperatures have plunged to a hypothermic average of 46 degrees Fahrenheit. Cross-river hiker Boyd Moore drowned near Lava Canyon in 1955 while paddling a flimsy air mattress down the Colorado River near Lava Canyon. I nearly succumbed to hypothermia during a trans canyon North Rim journey run swimming across the cold river to Palisade Creek in the same vicinity wearing a light CO_2-charged scuba diver vest. Several days later I used a resupplied one-man Navy pilot survival raft to cross the river without incident between the South Bass and North Bass Trails. Despite the risks of crossing the cold Colorado River with a loaded backpack in a small packraft, hiking rim to rim on these trails requires a packrafting permit from the Backcountry Information Office. It's called a RABT Permit (River Assisted Backcountry Trail). In addition to your food, water, gear, and packraft, you'll also need to carry a Type III or V PFD (Personal Flotation Device), which is required to be worn while crossing the river.

Creek Crossings

Many hikes and routes described in this book require creek crossings. There are certain times of the year—during heavy spring runoff, summer monsoon season, and fickle rain and runoff any time of the year—when you cannot safely ford flood-swollen creeks like Shinumo, Tapeats, Saddle Canyon, and many other tributary canyons and creeks without risking your life. You need to stay abreast of current and regional weather reports and Grand Canyon National Park and Backcountry Information Center alerts, so you can hike, trek, and if need be, ford canyons and creeks along your proposed route safely.

Flashfloods

Out of Nowhere. The Little Colorado River Gorge area might be blue skies and parched cracked earth in every direction, unfortunate for Navajo ranchers and Hopi farmers who are often forced to haul water for drinking, livestock, and farming. But if it's storming 356 creek miles upstream from the Colorado River Confluence via the West Fork of the Little Colorado River atop the sacred heights of 11,403-foot Mt. Baldy, what traditional Apache call *Dzil Ligai*, "White Mountains," the resulting flashfloods roar down the fifty-seven-mile Little Colorado River Gorge without advance warning and have killed wildlife and seasoned canyoneers. The same holds true for Cataract Canyon/Havasu Creek, which receives storm runoff from 9,256-foot Bill Williams Mountain eighty miles south. Historic flashfloods have swept down Cataract, Hualapai, and Havasu Canyons since the nineteenth century and continue to devastate everything in their paths with little warning, not just hikers, but the Havasupai people and their community, homes, farms, and livestock. I'd rather train for and endure blue skies statewide in the June heat, and similar week-to-month-long, not-a-cloud-in-the-sky weather throughout the year, than even think of rolling the dice with flashfloods. They're a natural force impossible to reckon with unless you're standing on high ground out of harm's way.

CFS

What in the world is that? Cubic Feet per Second is defined by the volume of one cubic foot of water passing a given point in a river or creek every second. To put that into perspective, historic high flows on the Colorado River peaked between 250,000 CFS in 1884 and 150,000 CFS in 1921. High water post dam flows that cavitated the spillways and nearly breached colossal Glen Canyon Dam in June 1983 reached 97,300 CFS. The dam-shaking, thundering discharge and debris flow through the flood-swollen river corridor 113.2 miles downstream flipped a thirty-three-foot long pontoon raft in Crystal Rapids, drowning one passenger and stranding others who needed to be evacuated out of the canyon by helicopter to safety. If you're unfamiliar with Colorado River hydraulics, imagine a Greyhound Lines MC5 bus filled with screaming passengers being swept and flipped by a mudslide down a mountain highway, and that approximates the natural force and havoc of a rampaging river. Today's average 100-year drought cycle discharges from Glen Canyon Dam into the Colorado River in Grand Canyon National Park average between 8,000 and 25,000 CFS. Eight thousand cubic feet per second will carry 25,000 passengers and guides on a seasonal flotilla of motor rafts, oar- and paddle-powered rafts, dories, and kayaks on a forty to eighty-five feet deep river through a seventy-six to 300 feet wide river channel at four to five miles per hour. When a 4,000 cfs, "1,000 year flood" roared down Bright Angel Creek on December 3, 1996, it demolished stone buildings, footbridges, and a pump house. A year earlier, a fifteen foot deep flashflood wiped out the North Kaibab Trail's Trans Canyon Pipeline. Similar and lesser flashflood flows have killed hikers in Garden Creek, (yes, the Bright Angel Trail), Phantom Creek (North Kaibab Trail), Havasu Creek (Havasupai Trail), and elsewhere. It can happen anywhere. You don't want to be in the wrong place at the wrong time wondering, *What in the world is that?!* It will be too late.

Falls

Many tourists have died posing for pictures even before "selfies" became a global phenomenon, by scrambling around or just walking too close to the canyon rim. Two young women died during the summer of 2016 when one woman fell from the South Rim's Pima Point and another slipped and fell from the South Kaibab Trail's Ooo-Aah Point. Backcountry hikers and canyoneers have slipped or fallen descending friable rock and talus, or catwalking footprint-wide ledges some call "death zones." Stay focused, use common sense and extreme care, or don't do it. Step back or turn around and stay safe.

Rockfall

Count yourself lucky if you actually hear natural freeze-thaw erosion-caused rock fall. It's a rare event, except during flashfloods when spectacular gravel and stone-laden silt and mud cascades spew from the limestone cliffs of Marble Canyon and elsewhere throughout the Grand Canyon, such as the obstacle course on the Hermit Trail's "supai rockslide traverse." Stay out of the fall line and wild rumbling creek and debris flows. When hiking switchbacks or cross-country, make sure you stay out of the fall line of hikers and mules that can accidentally dislodge a rock from above. And exercise care where you place your feet and hands so you don't dislodge a stone or boulder on anyone below.

Lightning

Avoid high points and exposed ridges before and during lightning storms.

Sprains

Storms, erosion, mules, and hikers are constantly changing the conditions of Grand Canyon trails and routes. Make sure your conditioning and footwear can meet the demands of the rugged terrain and sharp rocks like Kaibab Limestone and that they provide you with adequate ankle support.

Poisonous Bites and Stings

Rattlesnakes:

Don't put your hands or feet where you can't see. If it looks like a stick, it may be a snake lying across the trail. Be careful when you're squatting over your trowel-dug privy.

Gila Monsters:

If you're lucky enough to see one, don't try to pick it up or play with it. It will chew its venom into your hand.

The Nasty Ones:

If you wear flip-flops around camp, expect company, like harvester ants and fire ants. Check under your ground cloth the next morning for bark scorpions, and shake out your boots.

Be prepared, stay careful, use common sense, trust your instincts, maintain your focus, and embrace the wonders of nature, peace, and solitude.

5

Native Peoples
of the Grand Canyon

"We had been there only a little while,
when we heard something running toward us.
We thought perhaps it was a buck.
Then we saw it running out of the trees.
It was a bear; he was coming straight at us.
We felt afraid and wanted to run . . .
and I shot him . . ."

—Sinyela, Havasupai headman, circa 1903

THE REVERED HAVASUPAI ELDER WAS HUNTING THE "OLD WAY," when young men stared death in the face traveling afoot and on horseback to sustain their family, people, and lifeways. In the day, they hunted with Bighorn sheep, sinew-backed bows made from two-year-old single-leaf ash (*Fraxinus anomala*), strung with twisted-sinew bow strings. They flint knapped chert arrowheads with deer antlers, bound shafts from arrow reed (*Phragmites australis*) and Coyote willow (*Salix exigua*), plumed them with eagle or hawk feathers, and carried their bundles in buckskin quivers. Esteemed trackers like Sinyela earned the privilege and respect to carry twenty to thirty hand-painted arrows in a mountain lion quiver he cured and sinew-stitched together after a hunt. Sinyela told anthropologist Leslie Spier: "We were hunting deer, when I found mountain lion tracks, which I followed until I saw the lion. I was riding my horse. I chased him; he circled around to the spot I first saw him. I killed and skinned him, and packed the skin and meat to camp."

"A Hopi Man," 1904, Edward S. Curtis photogravure, Library of Congress.

When Sinyela looked into the eyes of clawed predators that could bring down a man or a horse, he wasn't using an all-terrain turbo quad, peep-sighted compound bow with razor-tipped three-bladed arrows. Sinyela was using the same age-old hunting traditions that Paleo Indians had when they used flimsy spears to hunt the Grand Canyon's mega fauna.

Life was not easy for the Grand Canyon's Native Peoples, but they not only endured, they thrived as diverse hunting, gathering, and farming cultures that began near the end of the last Ice Age. Proof came with a contemporary, once-in-a-lifetime discovery when an unidentified woman nearly sat down on a Paleo Indian Clovis spear point near Desert View. The fluted, "paleo-pink" lanceolate projectile point was dated to approximately 9500 BC. Archaeological sites along the Colorado River suggest to me that Paleo Hunters may have journeyed down Tanner Canyon to the river to hunt mammoths. And to collect chert, which is found in the Kaibab Limestone five miles upstream from the confluence of the Colorado and Little Colorado Rivers, about where Salt Trail Canyon enters the Little Colorado River Gorge's turquoise waters. If you were to use the traditional 1300-era Hopi-Havasupai trade route between Oraibi and Havasupai as a timeline for the Grand Canyon's Native Peoples, you can trace the travels of Sinyela's and other canyon dwellers' ancestors through the epochs from Paleo Hunters to Archaic Hunter Gatherers (6000 BC to 1), Ancestral Puebloans, *Anaasází, Hisat. sinom,* and *Mukwic*—(500 to 1250), Cohonina (700 to 1150), and more recently the Hopi (1200), Southern Paiute (1300), Havasupai and Hualapai (1300), and Navajo (1400). Except for the Kaibab Paiute who live to the north in the Kaibab Plateau region, each of these tribes followed the course of the ancient trade route across the Coconino Plateau to Desert View and beyond. The Havasupai, among them, descended Tanner Canyon to gather salt in the Little Colorado River Gorge. Hopi salt pilgrims making ritual stops at *Panktupatca,* "Home of the Mountain Sheep" shrine noted the Havasupai gathered and roasted agave nearby at *Kwantupe* (Agave Roasting-place) near Salt Trail Canyon. The Havasupai were known for using chert arrowheads. Imagine the legendary hunter Sinyela using a "paleo-pink" arrowhead chipped by hand out of the same 270 million-year-old limestone cliff a hundred miles east of where he faced down the bear and the mountain lion.

There are few places you can wander, travel, or explore on foot in the Grand Canyon in any direction—even in its most rugged and remote off-the-cell-grid abysses—that you won't see, if observant, evidence of indigenous canyon dwellers, traders, travelers, hunters, gatherers, and farmers that predated Euro-American explorers, prospectors, miners, and developers described in depth throughout this book. It may be a pot shard, pieces of flint knapped stone, or what appears to be an indecipherable symbol etched in a canyon wall, but signs of their passing, what the Hopi call *itaakuku* (footprints), are everywhere.

Sacred areas to the canyon's Native Peoples that continue to sustain their spiritual and cultural identity, and attract millions of tourists and hikers include the landscape, the life it nurtures, tributary canyons, places of emergence, the Colorado River, waterfalls, creeks, springs, rimtop-, cliff-, river-, and creek-side masonry dwellings, ceremonial kivas, lookouts, storage granaries, sweat lodges, agave roasting pits and associated ceremonial sites, cave shrines, trail shrines, stone-carved Moqui steps and handholds (derived from the Hopi name *móka* for the Havasupai), log ladders and foot bridges, hand-stacked stone steps, petroglyphs, pictographs, hematite mines, salt mines, diversion ditches, and terraced fields.

The Grand Canyon is often viewed as an open-air museum diorama and geo-archaeopark without "Indians," the canyon's first caretakers, but real people and their children lived, laughed, loved, prayed, suffered, cried, and died here in one of the Seven Natural Wonders of the World. Among its eleven culturally affiliated Native Peoples, they include the following canyon, mesa, and desert dwellers and, when known, the lands and waters they still revere.

Note: In researching and writing this book every effort has been made to conform to traditional Native American spellings and translations of names, geographical features, locations, and sacred areas—when known—based on primary sources, tribal dictionaries, orthographies, historical accounts, and ethnographies.

Hopi: *Hopitu Shinumu*, "one who is mannered"

- Ancestral Hopi: *Hisat.sinom*, "People Who Lived Long Ago," *Moti'sinom*, "Those Who Came First," and *Nutung'sinom*, "Those Who Followed"
- Hopi Land: *Hopitutskwa*
- Grand Canyon: *Öngtupqa*, "salt canyon or gorge," (also *wuukotupqa*, "big canyon")
- Colorado River: *Pisisvayu*, "water flowing throuh two high walls;" (also "river of echoing sounds [between canyon walls]")
- Little Colorado River: *Paayu*, "little water"
- Hopi Salt Mine: *Öönga*
- Place of Emergence: *Sípàapuni*, "hatchway where the Hopi emerged to the Fourth world"
- Ritual Trails: Salt Pilgrimage Trail, *Homvi'kya*, Hopi Mesas to *Tutuventi-wngwu*, "Place of the Clan Rocks," to *Öngtupqa*, Grand Canyon; Hopi Havasupai trade route, and other traditional trails. Kachina Peaks: *Navatekiaqui*, "Place of Snow on the Very Top," (also *Nuvatukya'o*, "Snow Butte Up," and *Nuva'tuk-iya-ovi*, "Place of the High Snows")

"Pachilawa—Walapai chief," 1907, Edward S. Curtis photographic print, Library of Congress.

KACHINA PEAKS, SAN FRANCISCO MOUNTAINS

The Grand Canyon's Native Peoples share an affinity for the sacred peaks of the 12,633-foot San Francisco Mountains, sixty miles south. It is inextricably linked with their spiritual beliefs. It is perhaps the Colorado Plateau's most revered mountain. The abode of *katsina*, or *katsinam*, "spirit beings," the Hopi still offer sacred corn meal and eagle-feathered prayer sticks called *paahos* for rain. The following entries also include names used by other canyon, mesa, and river dwellers for the hallowed peaks.

Navajo matriarch and weaver Susie Cly Yazzie sits for a portrait in her hogan. "She was *Todichiinii Clan* and born for *Bit'anii Clan*." Copyright © John Annerino Photography.

Navajo: *Diné,* "the People"

- Ancestral Navajo: *Anaasází,* "Enemy Ancestors"
- Navajo Land: *Dinétah,* "among the people"
- Grand Canyon: *Tséłchíí bikooh,* "big rock," home to Black God, Holy People, Salt Woman, Water Monsters, Water Horses, Plant People, and Humpback
- Colorado River: *Tooh, Tó Nts'ósíkooh,* (also *Bits'íís Ninééz,* "The River of Neverending Life"
- Little Colorado River: *Tooh*
- Navajo Salt Mine: *'Áshiih,* Little Colorado River Gorge
- Little Colorado and Colorado River Confluence: *Tooh Ahidiilíniand*
- Ritual Trails: Tanner Canyon *Áshįįh ha'atiin,* "Salt Trail out of Canyon" to Little Colorado River Gorge, *Tólchí'-íkooh,* "Red Water Canyon"; and other traditional trails
- Kachina Peaks: *Dook'o'oslííd,* "Never Thaws on Top" (also "Shining on Top")

Kaibab Paiute: *Kaipa'pici,* "Mountain Lying Down People"

- Ancestral Paiute: *Mukwic,* "People We Never Saw"
- Ancestral Numic People: *Enugwuhype*
- Paiute Homelands: *Nungwuh Tuhveep*
- Kaibab Paiute Land: *Puaxantu Tuvip,* "holy land," (also "powerful land")
- Grand Canyon: *Piapaxa 'Uipi,* "Big River Canyon"
- Colorado River: *Piapaxa,* "Big River," (also *paxa,* "most powerful river," and *pianukwintu,* "big water")
- Little Colorado River: *Oavaxa*
- Little Colorado River Salt Cave: Gathered "salt called *timpi-oavi* (rock salt)" from a "cave where the water dripped all the time." Guarded by *anungwuts,* "salt person"
- Ritual Trails: Pilgrimage route from Mount Trumbull, *Yevingkarere,* to Witches Water Pocket, *Enepi Pikavo,* to ceremonial ground at Toroweap Canyon, *Mukunta'uipi*; and other traditional trails
- Ritual Songscape: Nankoweap Canyon, *Nanangko'uipi,* Tapeats Creek, *Sevtun-kat,* and Toroweap Lake: *Turup Pikavo*
- Kachina Peaks: *Nuvaxatuh* (Southern Paiute, *Nuwuvi*)

Havasupai: *Havsuw' Baaja,* "People of the Blue-green Water"

- Ancestral Havasupai: *Cohonina*
- Grand Canyon: *Wikatata,* Sinyela's name for the Grand Canyon
- Colorado River: *Hakataia,* "big water," (also *Hackatai'as, Hagátaía,* and *Ha Ha Tay G'am/Sil Gsvgov*)
- Little Colorado River: *Hak tha e 'la,* (also *Hackathaehla* and *Hagaae'la*)
- Ritual Trails: Havasupai Canyon, *Havsuwa,* to Cataract Canyon, *Wigasiyáva;* Hopi Havasupai trade route, and other traditional trails
- Red Butte, *Wii'i gdwiisa,* ("clenched fist mountain") "is the navel of the Mother" (also *Huegadawiza*). "We believe mines at either of these sites will destroy us and our world."
- Little Red Horse Wash meadow, *Mat Taav Tiivjundva,* "is the abdomen of the Mother who gave birth to us."
- Kachina Peaks: *Hvehasahpatch,* "Big Rock Mountain" (also *Huehanapatcha* and *Wikagana pa'dja,* "Snowy Mountain) and *Huehanapatche,* San Francisco Peaks

Hualapai: *Hwalbáy* or *Walapai,* "People of the Tall Pines," (also "People of the Tall Trees")

- Ancestral Hualapai: *Cohonina*
- "Old People," Ancestors: *Patayan*
- Grand Canyon: *Hackataia*
- Colorado River: *Ha'Kataya,* (also *Ha'ka'Ama,* "water flowing by")
- Colorado River Midstream: *Haitat,* "the backbone of the river"
- Place of Origin: *Matwidita,* Mattaweditita Canyon
- Ritual Trails: Migration route from Mattaweditita Canyon, Matwidita, to Clay Springs, *Hadu'ba,* to Peach Springs and Pine Springs, home of the *Nyavkopai,* "East People"
- Hualapai Trail to Havasupai, and other traditional trails
- Lava Falls: Vulcan's Anvil, *Wi-Geth-Yea'a,* "Medicine Rock"
- Kachina Peaks: *Wik' hanbaja,* "Snowy Mountain"

Zuni: *Ashiwi*

- Grand Canyon: *Chimik'yana'kya dey'a*
- Place of Emergence: *Thmik'yana'kya,* Ribbon Falls
- Ritual Migration Route: *Chimik'yanakona penane*
- Kachina Peaks: *Sunha:kwin K'yaba:chu Yalanne,* "Mountain with the Volcanic Water Caches"

Apache: *Ndé, Ndee,* or *Indé,* "the People;" Western Apache, *Ndee biyati*

- Ancestral Apache: Unknown Athabascan name. "Apachu de Nabajo" is a 1620s Spanish conquistador name.
- *Tsé Hichii Indee,* "Horizontal Red Rock People," Oak Creek Canyon band, Northern Tonto Apache, intermarried and traveled to the Grand Canyon with the *Wiipukepaya,* "People from the Foot of the Red Rock," Oak Creek Canyon band, Northeastern Yavapai.
- Grand Canyon: *Ge da' cho,* "edge of the big cliff"
- Ritual Trails: Apache Trail and Cataract Canyon war trail to raid the Havasupai; and other traditional trails
- Kachina Peaks: *Dził Tso,* "Big Mountain"

Yavapai: *Yavepé* or *Yavpé,* Northeastern Yavapai (also *Wimun Kwa*)

- *Wiipukepaya,* "People from the Foot of the Red Rock," Oak Creek Canyon band, Northeastern Yavapai, intermarried and traveled to the Grand Canyon with the *Tsé Hichii Indee,* "Horizontal Red Rock People," Oak Creek Canyon band, Northern Tonto Apache.
- Colorado River: *'Hakhwata*
- Ritual Trails: Apache Trail and Cataract Canyon war trail to raid the Havasupai; and other traditional trails
- Kachina Peaks: *Wimonogaw'a,* "Cold Mountain"

Mojave: *Makháv* or *Hamakhav'* "People Who Live Along the River"

- Colorado River: *'Aha Kwahwat*
- Kachina Peaks: *Amat 'Iikwe Nyava*

Acoma: *Aa'ku*

- Kachina Peaks: *Tsii Bina*, "Protection Shrine"

Archaeology

Archaeologists tell us more than 4,300 cultural and archaeological sites and sources have been recorded in the Grand Canyon dating back 12,000 years. The Park estimates there may be 50,000 to 60,000 sites in 95 percent of the Grand Canyon that has not been surveyed. For Native Peoples, and a growing number of anthropologists, archaeology is a contentious subject. Pawnee attorney, Walter Echo Hawk, summed up his view: "If you desecrate a white grave, you wind up sitting in prison. But desecrate an Indian grave, and you get a PhD."

Cave Shrines

At least fourteen sacred cave shrines have been recorded and excavated for their offerings and ancient split twig figurines dating from 4520 BC. Archaeologists believe the effigies were hand-bound and offered with prayers as totems for a successful hunt of mountain sheep and mule deer. Conceivably, ritual cave shrine pilgrimages may have begun with the *pangwa*, "Mountain-sheep Clan," dating back to ancestral Hopi called *Hisat.sinom* and earlier Archaic people. The use of "prayer sticks" among the Hopi, (*paahos*), and the Navajo, (*k'eet'áán*), is a hallowed age-old tradition. It's not known if Native Peoples have since been invited by the National Park Service to visit and pay homage at these hallowed sites of their ancestors. They include *Tsé'áán Ketán*, "Prayer Stick Cave," *Tsé'áán bidá*, "Rock Cave," or Bida Cave, Crescendo Cave, Five Windows Cave, Left Eye Cave, [The sacred waters of one cave shrine have been rendered toxic with dangerous levels of dissolved uranium concentrations in this undisclosed] Cave, Luka Cave, Medicine Man Cave ("Mystery Skeleton"), Rebound Cave, Right Eye Cave, Stanton Cave, Shrine Cave, Tuutukya Cave, White Cave, and other hidden caves including Lava Canyon Pot Cave, Olla Cave, Olla Vieja Cave, and Perry's [*olla*] Cave from which cultural antiquities have been removed. Their locations are not disclosed in this book. Undoubtedly, there are other sacred ritual caves.

Note: Navajo cave name descriptions that can be found in the 1958 Navajo-English Dictionary were used by archaeologists to hide the locations of their excavations. For example, *Tsé'áán*, "rock cave," is derived from the Diné's name for their spiritual landmark of Shiprock Pinnacle, *Tsé Bit'a'i*, "Rock With Wings," New Mexico.

HIKER VISITATION

The National Park Service classifies Archaeology and Cultural Sites as Class I, Class II, Class III, and Class IV. As defined by the Park, site visitation is restricted:

- Class I Archaeological Sites: Sites have been managed specifically to withstand greater volumes of visitors and to provide opportunities for interpretation.
- Class II Archaeological Sites: Sites are more vulnerable to visitor impacts than Class I sites. Extra care must be taken to protect fragile site features.
- Class III Archaeological Sites: Sites are not appropriate for visitation.
- Class IV Archaeological Sites: Sites are closed to visitation. (Source: NPS)

Sacred Places: Hualapai elders, among other elders, have told researchers, ". . . all archaeological sites are sacred places . . ." As a traveler with a camera and pen throughout the Great Southwest for many years, I've borne witness to the aftermath of cultural sites vandalized with paint, bullets, campfires, climber's chalk, and the theft of boulders and entire panels pried off canyon walls with chisels and hammers. Perhaps, none was more disturbing than the desecration of *Tutuveniwngwu*, "Place of the Clan Rocks," on the Hopi Salt Trail, one of the most fragile and venerated shrines in Native America. In deference to the Grand Canyon's Native Peoples, I have not included hiking descriptions to fragile areas, nor does the National Park Service's list of Class I, Class II, and Class IV Archaeological Sites, and undisclosed Class III Sites appear in this book. I have also omitted the locations of all but several wildly known and publicly disclosed petroglyph and pictograph sites.

Note: Primary research sources that might reveal specific locations to undisclosed sacred and sensitive cultural sites have been omitted from this book's "Select Bibliography."

Legislation Protecting Native American Cultural Resources

National Historic Preservation Act, October 15, 1966: (NHPA) (Public Law 89–665; 54 U.S.C. 300101 et seq.).

American Indian Religious Freedom Act, August 11, 1978: (AIRFA) (Public Law No. 95–341, 92 Stat. 469).

Archaeological Resources Protection Act, October 31, 1979: (ARPA) (Public Law 96–95; 16 U.S.C. 470aa-mm).

Federal Cave Resources Protection Act, November 18, 1988: (FCRPA) (Public Law 100–691, 16 U.S.C. 4301 et seq., 102 Stat. 4546).

Native American Graves Protection and Repatriation Act, November 16, 1990: (NAGPRA) (Public Law 101–601, 25 U.S.C. 3001 et seq., 104 Stat. 3048).

> "I want to say a word of welcome to the Indians here.
> In my regiment I had a good many Indians.
> They were good enough to fight and to die,
> and they are good enough to have me treat
> them exactly as square as any white man."
>
> —President Theodore Roosevelt, May 6, 1903
> South Rim, Grand Canyon Forest Reserve

Greater Grand Canyon Heritage National Monument (proposed)

If the Senate and House of Representatives pass Bill H. R.3882, the Greater Grand Canyon Heritage National Monument Act proposes to address, implement, and protect: "(1) The Greater Grand Canyon ecosystem and watershed contains various tribal sacred sites and resources, including religious places and burial sites, with significant ancestral and contemporary values to the Grand Canyon-associated tribes. (2) The Grand Canyon-associated tribes have a longstanding historical, cultural and religious connection the Greater Grand Canyon ecosystem and watershed and should play an integral role, through collaboration and consultation, in the planning and ongoing management of the monument. (3) The Grand Canyon-associated tribes have historically been stewards of the region, with obligations to care for the land that has provided for them since time immemorial, including natural and cultural resources such as ancestral sites, sacred places, plants, wildlife, water sources, and minerals, resulting in an accumulated body of traditional ecological knowledge that holds great potential for contributing to the sustainable and holistic management of the unique and fragile landscape. (4) The surface tributaries and interconnected ground water of the Greater Grand Canyon ecosystem and watershed are the source for Native American sacred springs and falls, such as Havasupai Falls."

Visit: www.congress.gov/bill/114th-congress/house-bill/3882

Visit: www.greatergrandcanyon.org/monument

6

Biogeography:
Life Zones of the
Grand Canyon

"Heavy leaden clouds began scurrying over the mountain toward the northeast early
in the morning, and by noon the entire sky was overcast and had a most ominous
appearance. Soon the rain began falling in torrents, and the storm moved steadily
eastward . . . across the desert to the high mesas beyond. Such a deluge I never saw . . .
The whole desert, from the San Francisco lava beds on the west to Echo Cliffs on the
east, showed that it had been recently deluged, as if by the breakage of some mighty
dam, but the water had disappeared."

—C. Hart Merriam, September 20, 1890
Biological Survey to the Grand Canyon

NO OTHER REGION ON THE CONTINENT ILLUMINATES SCIENTIST
C. Hart Merriam's Life Zones of North America concept better than the Grand Canyon
of the Colorado River. As the gun-toting naturalist noted, it's the equivalent of walking
1,800 miles from Canada to Mexico: "In descending from the [Coconino] plateau to
the bottom of the cañon, a succession of temperature zones is encountered equivalent to
those stretching from the coniferous forests of northern Canada to the cactus plains of
Mexico." If you were to trek from the summit of the 12,633-foot San Francisco Mountains sixty miles across the Coconino Plateau to the Colorado River via the Hance Trail,

A hedgehog cactus blossom typifies the canyon's desert life zones.
Copyright © John Annerino Photography.

as Merriam had done on foot and horseback in September 1890, you would traverse each of his seven life zones through the Grand Canyon's remarkable biogeography, including: Alpine Zone (above 11,500 feet), Sub-Alpine or Timber-line Zone (10,500 to 11,500 feet), (Central) Hudsonian or Spruce Zone (9,200 to 10,500 feet), (Central) Canadian or Balsam Fir Zone (8,200 to 9,200 feet), Neutral or Pine Zone (7,000 to 8,200 feet), Piñon Zone (6,000 to 7,000 feet), and Desert Area (4,000 to 6,000 feet).

Following are the comparative life zones and elevations you can enjoy while taking a much shorter Canada-to-Mexico sojourn from the coniferous forests of the Kaibab Plateau via the North Kaibab Trail to the cactus-studded ramparts along the Colorado River. Note: The Grand Canyon's migratory Monarch butterfly (*Danaus plexippus*) is heralded for its beauty and its seasonal 2,500-mile continental journey from the United States across "the cactus plains of Mexico" to the Monarch Butterfly Reserve and UNESCO World Heritage Site in Michoacán.

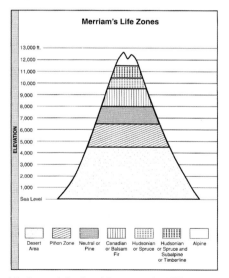

Life Zones of the Grand Canyon graph, 1890, artist not attributed, C. Hart Merriam.

GRAND CANYON LIFE ZONES

Mixed Conifer Forest (Canadian Zone, Merriam), Elevation 8,848 feet to 9,240 feet, North Rim and Kaibab Plateau. Biotic Communities: Boreal forests of Engelmann spruce (*Picea engelmannii*), Blue spruce (*Picea pungens*), Douglas fir (*Pseudotsuga menziesii*), White fir (*Abies concolor*), Quaking aspen (*Populus tremuloides*), Indian rice grass (*Achnatherum hymenoides*), and Lupine (*Lupinus*).

Ponderosa Pine Forest (Neutral or Pine Zone, Merriam), 7,410 feet to 8,241 feet, Grandview Point, South Rim, North Kaibab Trailhead, North Rim, and elsewhere throughout the canyon. Biotic Communities: Ponderosa pine (*Pinus ponderosa*), Alligator juniper (*Juniperus deppeana*), Big sagebrush (*Artemisia tridentate*), Gambel's oak (*Quercus gambelii*), Manzanita (*Arctostaphylos pungens Kunth*), and Indian paintbrush (*Castilleja angustifolia*).

Piñon-Juniper Woodland (Piñon Zone, Merriam), Upper Sonoran Desert, Great Basin Desert, and riparian, 5,300 feet to 5,029 feet, South Bass Trail, South Rim, Thunder River Trail, North Rim, and elsewhere throughout the canyon. Biotic Communities: Piñon pine (*Pinus edulis*), Utah juniper (*Juniperus osteosperma*), Banana yucca (*Yucca baccata*), Century plant (*Agave utahensis var. kaibabensis*), and Soaptree yucca (*Yucca elata*).

Desert Scrub, (Desert Area Life Zone, Merriam), Lower Sonoran Desert, Mojave Desert, Chihuahuan Desert, and riparian, 2,480 feet to 3,740-foot Bright Angel Creek, North Rim, Plateau Point, Bright Angel Trail, South Rim, and elsewhere throughout the canyon. Biotic Communities: "Anasazi agave" (*Agave Phillipsiana*), Arrowweed (*Pluchea sericea*), Barrel cactus (*Ferocactus cylindraceus*), Black brush (*Coleogyne ramosissima Torr*), Brittlebush (*Encelia farinose*), Catclaw acacia (*Acacia greggii*), Creosote bush (*Larrea tridentate*), Hedgehog cactus (*Echinocereus engelmannii*), Mormon tea (*Ephedra spp*), Ocotillo (*Fouquiera splendens*), Prickly pear cactus (*Oppuntia spp*), Sacred datura (*Datura wrightii*), and Western Honey Mesquite (*Prosopis glandulosa Torr*).

Riparian Communities, Lower Sonoran Desert to Ponderosa Pine Forest, 2,480 feet to 6,200 feet, Bright Angel Creek, Colorado River, Bright Angel Canyon, North Rim, and elsewhere throughout the canyon. Biotic Communities: Tamarisk (*Tamarix ramosissima*, the scourge of western waterways), Cottonwood tree (*Populus fremintii*), Coyote willow (*Salix exigua*), Crimson monkey flower (*Mimilus cardinalis*), Golden columbine (*Aquilegia chrysantha*), Grapevines, (*Vitis Arizonica*), Indian paintbrush (*Castilleja integra*), Poison ivy (*Toxicodendron radicans*), Seep willow (*Baccharis salicifolia*), and Silvery lupine (*Lupinus argenteus*).

Long before Merriam made his formative investigation of plant and animal distribution, the Southern Paiute had studied, gathered, hunted, harvested, and utilized most of what the Life Zones of North America had to offer. In their indigenous study, "The Paiute Tribe of Utah," Gary Tom and Ronald Holt reported:

the Paiutes were highly sophisticated botanists. They used at least thirty-two families of flora encompassing some ninety-six species of edible plants. The list would be greatly expanded were it to include the equally impressive array of medicinal plants. . . . In similar fashion, the Paiutes utilized most of the varieties of fauna found within their territory: hoofed animals, rodents, carnivores, birds, reptiles, and insects.

Biological Diversity of the Grand Canyon

It would be incomplete without its vibrant abundance of fauna, avifauna, reptiles, insects, and fish that complete the natural cycle of each intermingling life zone and geological formation. Following is an abbreviated listing of the canyon's ninety-two species of mammals, 373 species of birds, fifty-seven species of reptiles and amphibians, eighteen species of fish, 1,750 species of plants, and 8,480 species of invertebrates.

Fauna

Desert bighorn sheep (*Ovis canadensis nelsoni*), Rocky Mountain elk (*Cervus elaphus nelsoni*), Mule deer (*Odocoileus hemionus*), Mountain lion (*Felis concolor*), Bobcat (Lynx rufus), Mexican jaguar (*Panthera onca*; in the book *Borderland Jaguars / Tigres de la Fronters* (2001) and a later report (2012), Second Mesa Hopi men reportedly tracked a jaguar through the forest in the snow "they had slain by hand" during the winter of 1907 "near the railroad about 4 miles south of the canyon rim," and they showed "particular reverence" and "great care in dressing and preserving the skin of an old male jaguar." The Kolb brothers related the story to mammalogist Major E. A. Goldman in 1913, and the hide was later photographed by M. W. Billingsley who included it in his book, *M. W. Billingsley's 51 years with the Hopi people Behind the Scenes in Hopi Land*, 1971), Gray wolf (*Canis lupis*, extirpated early 1900s, spotted in 2014, shot by a Utah hunter in 2015), Coyote (*Canis latrans*), Gray fox (*Urocyon cinereoargenteus*), Ringtail cat (*Bassariscus astutus*), Raccoon (*Procyon lotor*), Beaver (*Castor Canadensis*); Abert's squirrel (*Scuriusaberti aberti*), Kaibab squirrel (*Scurius aberti kaibabensis*), and Rock squirrel (*Otospermophilus variegatus*).

Avifauna

American bald eagle (*Haliaeetus leucocephalus*), Golden eagle (Aquila chrysaetos), Peregrine falcon (*Falco peregrinus*), Redtail hawk (*Buteo Jamaicans*); Common raven (*Corvus corax*, watch your backpack and your caches!), Merriam's turkey (*Meleagris gallopavo*), Turkey vulture (*Cathartes Aura*), California condor (*Gymnogyps californianus*); Costa's hummingbird (*Calypte costae*), Hairy woodpecker (*Piciodes villosus*),

Snowy egret (*Egretta thula*), Steller's jay (*Cyanocitta stelleri*), and Western bluebird (*Sialia mexicana*).

Reptiles
Lizards: Banded gecko (*Coleonyx variegates*), Collared lizard (*Crotophytus bicinctores*), Desert iguana (*Dipsosaurus dorsalis*), Gila Monster (*Heloderma suspectum*), Western Chuckwalla (*Sauromalus ater*).
Rattlesnakes: Grand Canyon pink (*Crotalus organus abysus*), Great Basin (*Crotalus oreganus lutosus*), Hopi (*Crotalus viridis nuntius*), Mojave (*Crotalus cumulates*), and Western Diamondback (*Crotalus atrox*).

Insects and Insect Eaters
Ooh: Queen butterfly (*Danaus gilppus thersippus*), Painted lady butterfly (*Vanessa cardui*), Monarch butterfly (*Danaus plexippus*), Black tarantula (*Aphonopelma behlei*).
Aah: Pallid bat (*Antrozous pallidus*), Townsend Big-eared bat (*Plecotus townsendii*), Hoary bat (*Lasiurus cinereus*).
Ouch: Bark scorpion (*Centuroides sculpturatus*), Bees (*Apoidea*), Black Widow spider (*Latrodectus hesperus*), Centipede (*Scolopendron viridis*), Harvester ant, (*Pogonomyrmex barbatus*), Fire ant (*Solenopsis invicta*), Tarantula hawk (*Pepsis thisbe*).

Fish
Brown Trout (*Salmo trutta*), Rainbow trout (*Oncorhynchus mykiss*), and Largemouth bass (*Micropterus salmoides*), game fish stocked since 1923; and native Bluehead sucker (*Catostonus discobolus*), Flannelmouth sucker (*Catostomus latipinnis*), Humpback chub (*Gila cypha*), Razorback sucker (*Xyrauchen texanus*), Speckled dace (*Rhinichthys osculus*), and Colorado pikeminnow, *Ptychocheilus lucius*, now extirpated.

Amphibians and Invertebrates
Canyon tree frog (*Hyla arenicolor*), Fairy shrimp (*Branchinecta mackini Dexter*), Spadefoot toad (*Spea intermontana*), and microscopic Rotifers (*Rotifera spp.*).

7

Geology:
Reading the Rocks

"Carved out by the Colorado River, the Grand Canyon is the most spectacular gorge in the world . . .The Grand Canyon is among the earth's greatest on-going geological spectacles. Its vastness is stunning, and the evidence it reveals about the earth's history is invaluable."

—Grand Canyon National Park, 2006,
UNESCO World Heritage Site Inscription

PHYSIOGRAPHY. COMPRISING AN ESTIMATED 130,000 SQUARE MILES, the six thousand-foot-high Colorado Plateau encompasses the four corner region of Utah, Arizona, Colorado, and New Mexico and contains some of the most spectacular scenery, terrain, and geology on Earth. The Grand Canyon of the Colorado River's colorful plateaus and mesas include Shivwits, Unikaret, Kanab, Kaibab, Paria, Kaiparowits, and Coconino Plateaus. From Lee's Ferry at River Mile 0 on the Colorado River to Pierce's Ferry at Mile 277, the Grand Canyon is the single largest and deepest canyon in North America. It's also the one abyss against which all others are measured, including the Sierra Madre Occidental, Mexico's 6,136-foot deep *Barrancas del Cobre*, "Copper Canyons," which have long been erroneously touted as being deeper than the Grand Canyon. Comprising nearly two-thousand square miles of the most studied and photographed geologic stratum in the world, the Grand Canyon is 277 miles long, ten to eighteen-miles wide, and, at its most precipitous point, 6,720 feet deep. Of the seventy-seven principal tributary canyons that drain into the Grand Canyon from the

A young hiker explores the canyon's
hidden places and whimsical geology.

North Rim's Kaibab Plateau and South Rim's Coconino Plateau, many stand out for their length, depth, habitat, and astonishing geology.

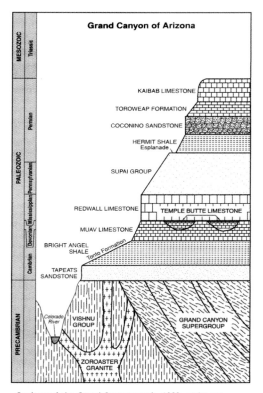

Geology of the Grand Canyon graph, 1982, artist not attributed, USGS, W. J. McKee.

It's all about the rocks. It's always been about the rocks. From Archaic peoples seeking natural routes through the nearly impassable rim-to-river stratigraphy, to everyone else who followed. Native Peoples traced their rocky paths to gather ceremonial hematite and salt, made offerings at stone shrines and caves, and crafted indelible pictographs and petroglyphs on rock canvases that still bare the canyon's first written records. Explorers and scientists came by foot, horseback, and wooden boat to journey through the Colorado River's corridors of stone. Prospectors and miners came in search of the mother lode they hoped to blast, pick, and shovel out of the stingy stones. Pioneer photographers, artists, poets, and writers captured vivid impressions of the kaleidoscopic strata. Mary Jane Colter, America's greatest woman architect, emulated the masonry cliff dwellings of Ancestral Puebloans by building lodges, towers, and retreats from the Grand Canyon's native stones and timbers. When geologist Charles D. Walcott spent seventy-two days during the winter of 1872–73 days studying and chronicling the geology of the Nankoweap Trail he blazed into the eastern Grand Canyon, he wrote in his journal: "This is a very lonely, quiet place. No life & nothing but cliffs & cañons. Rocks-rocks-rocks."

Walcott spent over two months in less than accommodating conditions studying the rocks. Most hikers will only spend a few hours, usually during their hike into the canyon, gazing upon the canyon's incredible but complex rock cliffs, canyons, and creeks. That will do if you stick to the maintained Corridor Trails, the Bright Angel, South Kaibab, and North Kaibab Trails. They're great places to learn if you prefer experiential education. However, once you venture beyond the heavily-beaten pathways you'll need to learn how to read the rocks.

Following is the stair-step, layer-cake sequence of metamorphic, sedimentary, and igneous rock formations most rim-to-river trails and routes descend through. Familiarize yourself with these entries before you head to the Grand Canyon, or pick up geologist Clarence E. Dutton's 1882 magnum opus, *Tertiary History of the Grand Canyon District*, with Atlas.

Kaibab Limestone

- **Name:** Kaibab was derived from the Kaibab Paiute name for the Kaibab Plateau, *Kaivavic*, "Mountain Lying Down," on the North Rim of the Grand Canyon.
- **Age:** 270 million years old.
- **Height:** 300 to 400 foot high cliffs and caprock that defines the North and South Rims of the Grand Canyon.
- **Color:** Gray and ivory. Note: Colors vary throughout these descriptions depending on the season, weather, time of day, and atmospheric conditions.

- **Composition:** Marine seabed, coral, sponges, brachiopods, mollusks, and sharks teeth.
- **Biotic Communities:** Boreal and Ponderosa pine forests.
- **Hikers:** This is a penetrable barrier that requires scouting when hiking off trail.
- **Walking/Hiking Surface:** Sharp, broken, and cherty limestone.
- **Prominent Trails:** Bright Angel Point Trail, and Cape Royal (Angels Window) Trail, North Rim.
- **Water:** Snowmelt and seasonal rain percolate through the permeable Kaibab Limestone and form subterranean aquifer-fed streams that cascade from Muav Sandstone walls.
- **Native American Cliff Dwellings:** forest surface dwellings on the Transept Trail and Walhalla Glades, North Rim.
- **Rock Art:** Mallery's Grotto, Bright Angel Trail, South Rim.

Toroweap Formation

- **Name:** Toroweap was derived from the Kaibab Paiute word for "gully" or "wash," *toro-weap*.
- **Age:** 273 million years old.
- **Height:** 200 to 300 foot high cliffs and vegetated slopes.
- **Color:** Gray and yellow.
- **Composition:** Intertidal marine limestone and eolian sandstone, gypsum, coral, and fossils.
- **Biotic Communities:** Ponderosa pine and Piñon juniper woodlands.
- **Hikers:** This is a steep, rugged talus-passageway between the Kaibab Limestone and Coconino Sandstone.
- **Walking/Hiking Surface:** Loose rocky footing on limestone, sandstone, and gypsum.
- **Prominent Trails:** The Chimney, South Kaibab Trail, South Rim, and Cliff Springs Trail, Cape Royal, North Rim.
- **Water:** Cliff Springs, Cape Royal, North Rim.
- **Native American Cliff Dwellings:** Undisclosed locations beneath the North and South Rims.
- **Rock Art:** Undisclosed locations beneath the North and South Rims.

Coconino Sandstone

- **Name:** Derived from the Hopi name *Co'onin* they used to call the Havasupai during their long-distance foot travels to trade.
- **Age:** 275 million years old.
- **Height:** 400-foot-high cliffs, rock temples, buttes, and spires.
- **Color:** Buff to beige.
- **Composition:** Windblown cross-bedded sand dunes bearing fossil trackways of lizards, salamanders, and tetra pods.
- **Biotic Communities:** Ponderosa pine and Piñon juniper woodlands.
- **Hikers:** This is a sheer nearly unbroken band of precipitous cliffs that requires scouting when hiking off trail.
- **Walking/Hiking Surface:** Broken stones, slabs, and large fallen boulders
- **Prominent Trails:** Hermit Trail and Grandview Trail, South Rim.
- **Water:** Dripping Springs, Boucher Trail, South Rim.
- **Native American Cliff Dwellings:** South Bass Trail, South Rim.
- **Rock Art, Moqui Steps, and Ladders:** Hematite-painted pictographs, hand-pecked petroglyhs, hand-carved Moqui steps, and log ladders, undisclosed locations.

Hermit Formation

- **Name:** Derived from the 1890s-era white-bearded prospector and trailblazer, Louis de Bouchere, who was nicknamed "the hermit."
- **Age:** 280 million years old.
- **Height:** 300-foot-tall vegetated slopes and stair-step stone benches.
- **Color:** Enchilada red to orange.
- **Composition:** Coastal swamp and river flood plains, fern fossils, reptile, and amphibian tracks.
- **Biotic Communities:** Piñon juniper woodlands.
- **Hikers:** This is a steep rugged talus- and rock shelf passageway between the Coconino Sandstone and Redwall Limestone.
- **Walking/Hiking Surface:** Loose crumbly footing on talus, sandstone, silt-stone, and mudstone.
- **Prominent Trails:** Boucher Trail, South Rim.
- **Water:** Muav Saddle Spring, North Bass Trail, North Rim.
- **Rock Art:** Petroglyphs and agave roasting pits, Waldron Trail, South Rim.

Supai Group/Esplanade Sandstone

- **Name:** Derived from the Havasupai name *Havsuw' Baaja*, "People of the Blue-green Water." Three of the Supai's four stratigraphic subdivisions are named for Havasupai families: Wescogame, Manakacha, and Watahomigi. Geologist Clarence Dutton named the fourth layer Esplanade Sandstone, from the Latin word, "explānāre," to describe the slick rock promenade.
- **Age:** 285 to 315 million years old.
- **Height:** 1,000-feet-high slopes, talus, stair-step cliffs, and wide shelves.
- **Color:** Red to orange.
- **Composition:** The multilayered red shale, limestone, and sandstone is comprised of marine and river flood plain deposits and fossils that bare the tracks of reptiles and amphibians.
- **Biotic Communities:** Piñon juniper woodlands.
- **Hikers:** The Esplanade Sandstone, boulders, slick rock, and sandy cryptobiotic-covered shelves offer comparatively easy passage east-to-west through the Grand Canyon.
- **Walking/Hiking Surface:** Sand, stones, boulders, stair-step ledges, and smooth slick rock shelves.
- **Prominent Trails:** Thunder River Trail and death-zoned "Supai Traverse," Nankoweap Trail, North Rim.
- **Water:** Havasu Springs, Hualapai (Havasupai) Trail, South Rim. After seasonal rains shallow ephemeral pools and deep water pockets can be found across the Esplanade throughout the Grand Canyon.
- **Native American Cliff Dwellings:** Cataract Canyon, South Rim.
- **Rock Art:** Deer Creek Narrows, Thunder River Trail, North Rim, and undisclosed locations.

Redwall Limestone (Blue Lime)

- **Name:** Derived from the red walls stained from torrential pigment-carrying runoff from the Supai Group, 1880s prospectors and miners called the gray limestone the "blue lime."
- **Age:** 340 million years old.
- **Height:** 500-foot-tall cliffs, and caverns, caves, alcoves, and amphitheaters.
- **Color:** Red, gray, and blues.
- **Composition:** Shallow marine deposits, limestone, coral, trilobites, brachiopods, and fish.

- **Biotic Communities:** Piñon juniper and Semi desert.
- **Hikers:** This is an imposing wall and nearly impenetrable barrier for rim-to-river foot travel that requires scouting when hiking off trail.
- **Walking/Hiking Surface:** Loose, rotten, and friable stones and boulders where breaks are encountered through the Redwall.
- **Prominent Trails:** Jacobs Ladder, Bright Angel Trail, South Rim, and "Half tunnels," North Kaibab Trail, North Rim.
- **Water:** Vaseys Paradise, Marble Canyon, Colorado River.
- **Native American Cliff Dwellings:** Nankoweap Creek, Marble Canyon, Colorado River.
- **Cave Shrines:** Stanton Cave, Marble Canyon, Colorado River, and undisclosed locations.

Muav Limestone

- **Name:** Derived from the Southern Paiute word, *moavi*, "mosquito," or elder *Muavigaipi*, "Mosquito Man."
- **Age:** 505 million years old.
- **Height:** 100 to 450 foot high cliffs.
- **Color:** Gray, brown, orange-tinged.
- **Composition:** Shallow marine deposits, brachiopods and trilobites.
- **Biotic Communities:** Semi desert grasslands, Desert scrub and riparian.
- **Hikers:** This is a steep rugged talus- and cliff passageway between the Redwall Limestone and Bright Angel Shale.
- **Walking/Hiking Surface:** Loose, rocky limestone, dolomite, mudstone rocks and boulders.
- **Prominent Trails:** South Kaibab Trail, South Rim.
- **Water:** Thunder River and Tapeats Spring, Thunder River Trail, North Rim.
- **Native American Cliff Dwellings:** Nankoweap Creek, Marble Canyon, Colorado River.
- **Rock Art:** Hematite-painted pictographs, Bright Angel Trail.

Bright Angel Shale

- **Name:** Derived from the name Major John Wesley Powell bestowed upon Bright Angel Creek, August 16, 1869.
- **Age:** 515 million years old.
- **Height:** 100 to 350 foot high slope.

- **Color:** Faint lime-green.
- **Composition:** Intertidal marine deposits, brachiopods, and trilobites.
- **Biotic Communities:** Semi desert grasslands and Desert scrub.
- **Hikers:** The rugged and braided South Tonto Trail, South Rim, and North Tonto Route, North Rim offer principal east-to-west passageways through the Grand Canyon. Off trail the Tonto Formation is more difficult and less aesthetically pleasing to traverse than the Esplanade Sandstone.
- **Walking/Hiking Surface:** Flat to steep rock- and boulder-strewn vegetated talus.
- **Prominent Trails:** Clear Creek Trail, North Rim.
- **Water:** Pipe Creek, Bright Angel Trail, South Rim, and Roaring Springs, North Kaibab Trail, North Rim.
- **Native American Cliff Dwellings:** North Bass Trail, North Rim.

Tapeats Sandstone

- **Name:** Derived from Tapeats Creek Major John Wesley Powell named in honor of his Shivwits Paiute guide, *Ta-peats*, near the end of his second Colorado River expedition on September 6, 1872. The young Ta-peats had pointed out the creek to Powell from the plateau above where he was photographed dressed in traditional buckskins by John K. Hillers.
- **Age:** 525 million years old.
- **Height:** 50 to 200 foot high scalloped cliffs.
- **Color:** Dark brown to beige.
- **Composition:** Shallow marine fluvial beach, fossilized water ripples, and trilobites.
- **Biotic Communities:** Sonoran and Mojave Desert scrub.
- **Hikers:** The course-grained Tapeats Sandstone frequently offers easier walking along the outer rim of the Tonto Formation than crossing its rugged talus of Bright Angel Shale. The scalloped ledges frequently offer exposed breaks through the Tapeats Sandstone between the Tonto Formation and the inner gorge's Vishnu Schist.
- **Walking/Hiking Surface:** Smooth to ball-bearing stone-covered ledges and boulder-blocked rims.
- **Prominent Trails:** Tonto Trail, South Rim, and Clear Creek Trail, North Rim.
- **Water:** After seasonal rains shallow ephemeral pools, water pockets, and seeps can often be found in the Tapeats near the heads of tributary canyons and drainages.

- **Native American Cliff Dwellings:** Garden Creek Dwellings, Bright Angel Trail, South Rim.
- **Rock Art:** Beamer Cabin, Beamer Trail, South Rim.

Grand Canyon Series (Supergroup)

- **Name:** The name was first used by geologist Charles D. Walcott during his geological survey of the eastern Grand Canyon in the winter of 1882–83.
- **Age:** 650 to 1,250 million years old.
- **Height:** 100 to 3,000 feet or more thick.
- **Color and Composition:** Sixty mile Formation (beige), Kwagunt Formation (red), Galeros Formation (yellow to red), Nankoweap Formation (violet, white, and brown), Cardenas Lava (black and cinnamon brown), Dox Sandstone (terra cotta), Shinumo Quartzite (red, brown, and white) Hakatai Shale (vermilion), Bass Formation (gray).
- **Biotic Communities:** Semi desert, Sonoran Desert and Mojave Desert scrub and riparian.
- **Hikers:** Easy to rugged off-trail hiking and scrambling along beaches, inner canyon benches, canyons, creeks, and fault line passageways.
- **Walking/Hiking Surface:** Riverside dunes and alluvial fans, steep loose talus, boulders, fault lines, reefs, cliffs, creek beds, and tributary canyons.
- **Prominent Trails:** Butte Fault Route, North Rim; Escalante Route, and New Hance Trail, South Rim; North and South Bass Trails, Colorado River.
- **Water:** Red Canyon, New Hance Trail, South Rim and Shinumo Creek, North Bass Trail, North Rim.
- **Native American Cliff Dwellings:** Red Canyon, New Hance Trail, South Rim and Shinumo Creek, North Bass Trail, North Rim.

Vishnu Basement Rocks

- **Name:** Derived from the Hindu supreme deity Vishnu, *Visnu*.
- **Age:** 1,680 to 1,840 million years old.
- **Height:** 500- to 1,000-foot-tall cliffs that form the Granite Gorges of the Colorado River.
- **Color:** Black, white, pink, and gray.
- **Composition:** Vishnu schist, Zoroaster granite.
- **Biotic Communities:** Sonoran and Mojave Desert scrub.
- **Hikers:** This is an imposing, often impenetrable barrier for rim-to-river foot travel. Routes and trails have been forged through the Vishnu Schist at Utah

Flats, Bright Angel Campground, North Rim, Old Grandview Trail, South Rim, and elsewhere.
- **Walking/Hiking Surface:** Slick water-polished stones and walls to course rubble, stones, boulders, and walls.
- **Prominent Trails:** River Trail, Colorado River, South Rim, and The Box, North Kaibab Trail, North Rim.
- **Water:** Bright Angel Creek and Phantom Creek, North Kaibab Trail, North Rim
- **Native American Cliff Dwellings:** Bright Angel pueblo and kiva, Bright Angel Creek, North Rim.

PART 2
Trails of the
Grand Canyon

A hiker warms up from the morning
chill on the Comanche Point Trail.
Copyright © John Annerino Photography.

8

South Rim

RIM TRAILS

If you've just arrived at the Grand Canyon in the heat of midsummer—as most visitors do—you're short on time, or getting in shape, the Rim Trail makes an excellent alternative to hiking below the rim in the stifling heat. For all practical purposes there are two rim trails located on the South Rim: the Rim Trail and the Comanche Point Trail, or route.

The Rim Trail

Starting at 7,120-foot Mather Point, the breathtaking, self-guiding Rim Trail leads nine miles west along the scenic Hermit Road to 6,640-foot Hermits Rest. (The paved 2.8-mile Greenway Trail section between Monument Creek and Hermit's Rest is accessible to wheelchair users, cyclists, and walkers.) The Rim Trail offers outstanding views of the Grand Canyon's dramatic topography, sheer walls, tributary chasms, Colorado River, and the distant North Rim temples of Shiva, Buddha, Manu, Zoroaster, Deva, and Brahma. Such vistas inspired artist Thomas Moran in 1871–72 to sketch and paint his monumental 7-×-12-foot oil on canvas, "The Grand Chasm of the Colorado River," which Congress purchased for $10,000. You can stroll short sections of the spectacular Rim Trail between scenic vistas named for Native Peoples, then catch the shuttle back to your starting point. Or you can walk it end to end. Either way, it's a refreshing path to stretch your arms and legs, marvel at the sight of White-throated swifts (*Aeronautes saxatalis*) darting through the air, picnic, and acclimate to the altitude. Watch your step, your children, and avoid during lightning storms and icy conditions.

Length	Scenic Vistas, East to West	Shuttles from Canyon View to Information Plaza
0.7 mile	Mather Point to Yavapai Observation Station (walk 0.25 mile to Mather Point)	
1.0 mile	Yavapai Observation Station to Village Transfer	Village Route Shuttle (Blue)
0.7 mile	Village Transfer to Trailview Overlook	Hermits Rest Shuttle (Red)
0.7 mile	Trailview Overlook to Maricopa Point	Hermits Rest Shuttle (Red)
0.5 mile	Maricopa Point to Powell Point	Hermits Rest Shuttle (Red)
0.3 mile	Powell Point to Hopi Point	Hermits Rest Shuttle (Red)
0.8 mile	Hopi Point to Mohave Point	Hermits Rest Shuttle (Red)
1.1 miles	Mohave Point to The Abyss	Hermits Rest Shuttle (Red)
0.9 mile	Abyss to Monument Creek Vista	Hermits Rest Shuttle (Red)
1.7 miles	Monument Creek to Pima Point	Hermits Rest Shuttle (Red)
1.1 miles	Pima Point to Hermits Rest	Hermits Rest Shuttle (Red)

Please Note: for a map of the shuttle routes, see "The Guide," available free throughout the park.

Be Careful: A twenty-two-year-old Louisiana woman disappeared on April 3, 2016. Her remains were recovered by park rangers below Pima Point on August 3, 2016. R.I.P. Diana Zacarías.

Comanche Point Trail

Landform. Named by Grand Canyon cartographer and geologist François Émile Matthes in 1902, the Palisades of the Desert is a ten-mile long, rainbow-hued wall of cliffs that stretches from the vicinity of Desert View to Cape Solitude. The imposing geological barrier soars 4,275 feet above the Colorado River and forms the East Rim of the Grand Canyon and western edge of the Painted Desert, what Spaniards call *El Desierto Pintado.*

The Comanche Point Trail, or road network, crosses the broken country behind the East Rim. Compared to the relatively carefree Rim Trail, the Comanche Point Trail is a remote track that requires route finding skills to follow the Cedar Mountain Road (closed to vehicles) across hardscrabble Toroweap stones through the corrugated, piñon-juniper (*Pinus-Juniperus*) woodlands and arid flats of the Painted Desert. The abandoned 4WD road was used by nineteenth-century Canyon visitors, cattlemen, and Navajo sheep herders to graze stock in the spectacular eastern rimlands of the Palisades of the Desert. Comanche Point was named by the U.S. Board of Geographic Names in 1906 in honor of the Southern Plains Comanche, *Nermernuh*, "the People."

From the Desert View Ranger Station, follow the Cedar Mountain Road as it descends the steep switchbacks around the bend of Tanner Canyon approximately 2.5 miles. The Old Tanner Trail, or "Horsethief Trail," enters the northeast fork of the Canyon here. Fortified stone dwellings in the vicinity offer mute testimony to the arduous rim-to-river route was used for a millennia by Ancestral Puebloans, and later by the Hopi and Navajo. Continue hiking another half mile to the Cedar Mountain Road junction. The flat-topped, 7,061-foot landmark Cedar Mountain is immediately to the east. Cedar Mountain, *Dził Łichíí'dítłoii*, is a sacred cultural landscape of the Navajo and the birthplace of Turquoise Man. Turn left (north), hike in and out of Straight Canyon, and follow the road approximately 2.5 miles toward distant 6,146-foot Cape Solitude until you come to a T-junction marked by the 6,684-foot contour line on your Desert View Quadrangle (7.5 minute) map. From the T junction, take the second left road fork and veer north/northwest for half to three-quarters of a mile toward 7,073-foot Comanche Point. En route you'll see a 1920s-era stone shelter and a tiny square icon on your topo map near the 6,684-foot contour line marks the location. Nearby is a roasting pit that was used by Ancestral Puebloans, or earlier Archaic peoples, to bake the succulent hearts of Utah agave (*Agave utahensis*) to eat. Sometimes called mescal pits, or yant ovens after the Southern Paiute word *na'anta* for agave, Major John Wesley Powell wrote of them in his ethnographic notes about the Kaibab Paiute who live to the north. If attentive, you may also see the weathered remains of a sacred tree-pole enclosure used by the Navajo (*Diné*) for sweat lodge ceremonies (*Táchééh*)—what a sublime location to cleanse the spirit. Using your map, route your way above the west side of a drainage (seasonal water can sometimes be found here), hike northwest cross-country, and climb approximately 800 vertical feet up to the serrated crest of Comanche Point.

<u>Comanche Creek, Off Route Canyoneering Report:</u> Serious canyoneers have descended to the Colorado River via Comanche Creek using the saddle between Comanche Point and BM 6841. This short, exposed, and precarious route plummets 3,600 vertical feet, involves Third and Fourth Class scrambling, and is best reconned and approached from the Beamer Trail far below near Colorado River Mile 67.3.

In his seminal 1900 book, *In and Around the Grand Canyon*, American photographer and author George Wharton James described Comanche Point as a "splendid wooded promontory." The Lincolnshire, UK-borne canyon explorer visited Comanche Point and Cape Solitude during a two-day overnight horseback trip and wrote: ". . . a wonderful view is had—down the river of the Inner Gorge . . . a strip of glistening dirty brown in the depths of the dark and forbidding granite." Peer over the edge of what James also called Bissell's Point, and you'll see the 6,800-foot high Toroweap finger of rock called Comanche Point Pinnacle, the Lost Arrow Spire of the Grand Canyon. It was first scaled by Arizona climbers Larry Trieber and Bruce Grubbs in 1975. The summit, quiet environment, and the extraordinary panorama of the Colorado River and 6,319-foot Kwagunt Butte, are the carrots that beckon free spirits to explore this isolated landscape. On occasion you may count yourself lucky—I did—to witness an American bald eagle (*Haliaeetus leucocephalus*) soaring on thermals up the dizzying cliff faces that stretch from the Colorado River to the horizon.

On September 27, 1994, *Weekly World News* ran a cover story about a reported UFO crash site at Comanche Point. The headline of the 1.2 million circulation *Lantana*, Florida weekly supermarket tabloid says it all: "4,000-year-old UFO Found in Grand Canyon! U.S. Military Rushes Alien Starship to Secret Base: Inside: Amazing Proof of Alien Colony in America—3,500 years before Columbus." Come see for yourself.

- Elevation: 7,400-feet to 6,300-feet to 7,073-feet.
- Mileage: Approximately seven miles one way.
- Vegetation: Piñon-juniper woodlands, Utah agave.
- Water: Seasonal only (see description).
- Cache Points: At T-junction, below contour line 6684.
- Seasons: Spring through fall. Wintertime may require a good mountain tent, cross-country skis, and other winter camping gear.
- Maps: Desert View Quadrangle (7.5 minute) and South Kaibab National Forest Map (visit www.fs.usda.gov/main/kaibab/maps-pubs).
- Nearest Supply Points: Desert View, Cameron, Grand Canyon Village, and Flagstaff.
- Managing Agency: Grand Canyon National Park.
- Backcountry Information Center: for information call (928) 638–7875.
- Critical Backcountry Updates: visit www.nps.gov/grca/planyourvisit/trail-closures.htm.
- NPS Grand Canyon Hiker 24-Hour Emergency Phone Number and Email
  - Phone (928) 638–7805
  - Email: grca_bic@nps.gov (Use this if the phone line is busy)

9

Bright Angel Trail: Day Hikes, Rim to River, and Rim to Rim

"This—as were all the trails from the Little Colorado River to Havasu (Cataract) Canyon—was used first long ages ago by the Havasupai Indians. . . ."

—George Wharton James, 1900, *In and Around the Grand Canyon*

LANDFORM

Among the Grand Canyon's extraordinary features is the cross-canyon Bright Angel Fault, a 150-foot slip in the earth's crust that cleaves the Canyon from the South Rim to the North Rim.

HISTORICAL OVERVIEW

Four thousand years before the Canyon's written record, Archaic people navigated the fractured rocks in yucca fiber sandals along the course of Garden Creek Canyon to Indian Garden down to the Colorado River and up Bright Angel Canyon to the North Rim. Pictographs and cultural sites discovered along the ancient path indicate the aboriginal route was also used by Ancestral Puebloans from 300 to 1300 for hunting and gathering, and as a seasonal migration corridor to farm at Indian Garden and to reach masonry homes at the confluence of Bright Angel Creek and the Colorado River. Today,

"Big Jim, Havasupai chief," 1915, Emery Kolb photo, South Rim Kolb Studio, GCNP Museum Collection

the fault line is trod by more than 100,000 American and international visitors each year. As a result, the Bright Angel Trail has become one of the planet's premier hiking trails.

The Havasupai's Trail

At one time, the peaceful Havasupai occupied 6,750 square miles of the Coconino Plateau that stretched south from the Colorado River to the San Francisco and Bill Williams Mountains, and west from the Little Colorado River to the Aubrey Cliffs. They roamed, hunted and gathered the forested plateau lands during fall and winter for antelope, mule deer, bighorn sheep, and agave, and tilled rich soils in deep canyons during spring and summer for corn, beans, squash, peaches, and melons. Nineteenth-century encroachment from neighboring tribes, miners, cattlemen, railroaders, and developers reduced their ancestral lands, and the *Havsuw' Baaja*, "People of the Blue-green Water," sought permanent refuge in the western Grand Canyon's lush oasis and riparian corridors of Cataract Creek and Havasu Creek Canyons where they had lived for 800 years. Tracing the route of Ancestral Puebloans and the *Cohonina*, the Havasupai's ancestors, along the Bright Angel Fault into the heart of the Grand Canyon, the Havasupai also found a seasonal haven to live and farm at Indian Garden. In 1900, George Wharton James described their trail and settlement at Indian Garden: ". . . in the heart of the side canyon down which the trail goes, are still to be seen the rude irrigating canals which conveyed the large volume of water that flows from a near-by spring to the so-called Indian Garden." James wasn't a rim-bound sightseer. A prolific author and photographer of a dozen books on the Southwest, James spent ten years traveling throughout the Grand Canyon region's remote chasms and plateaus, and he came to know the Native Peoples, their mesa-top pueblos, and Grand Canyon like few others. He called the Grand Canyon the "most sublime spectacle of earth."

In 1903, the Havasupai's traditional settlement at Indian Garden officially ended when President Theodore Roosevelt rode horseback down the Bright Angel Trail and, through an interpreter, told two Havasupai men living there with their families, *Gswedva* (Dangling Beard) and Captain Burro, they needed to vacate their canyon home to make way for the future. Many others had already queued up to take advantage of Roosevelt's efforts to create the Grand Canyon Game Preserve three years later.

Cameron Trail

Between 1890 and 1891, Flagstaff, Arizona, sheep men Ralph and Niles Cameron, and prospector Peter D. Berry, were among them. They forged the Havasupai's trail from the South Rim to Indian Garden into what they called the Cameron Trail. They charged tourists a dollar a head to use the signed "Bright Angel Toll Road" that provided visitors and guests with mule rides between the Cameron's trailhead hotel and their tent camp at Indian Garden. In 1902, the Camerons extended the trail to the Colorado River and filed mining claims at these strategic locations, including their Colorado River mine site called the Wizard. Coconino County wrested control of the trail from the Camerons in 1928.

Few knew what would officially become the Bright Angel Trail, and Grand Canyon National Park, better than brothers Emery C. and Ellsworth L. Kolb. They set up shop at the head of the Bright Angel Trail in 1904 and became the Grand Canyon's ex officio photographers, racing up and down the trail between Indian Garden springs and their South Rim studio darkroom to process black-and-white tourist photos. Among the visitors the Kolbs photographed sauntering on mule back up and down the hoof-beaten trail, and beyond, were Rough Rider–turned President Theodore Roosevelt, conservationist and Sierra Club founder John Muir, miner and trailblazer John Hance, missing honeymooners Glen and Bessie Hyde, river woman Georgie White, and a rogues' gallery of other canyon characters befitting the time and the place.

Bright Angel Trail

Between 1933 and 1939, Depression-era Civilian Conservation Corp crews reconstructed and widened the declivitous two-foot-wide Bright Angel Trail to four-to-six feet wide, offering comfort and safety for many visitors and flatlanders unnerved by the canyon's dizzying heights and trail exposure. The CCC's handiwork is well preserved and utilized along the trail today, from the South Rim to Phantom Ranch near the Colorado River. Day hikers, backpackers, runners, and mule riders, young and old, still welcome the CCC's shady shelters of hand-hewn wood and rock dwellings at 1.5-Mile Resthouse, Three-Mile Resthouse, Indian Garden Campground, and Colorado River Resthouse. The CCC's twenty-five-mile-long trans canyon Telephone Line also provided a vital communication link between the South Rim and the North Rim via these outposts on the Bright Angel Trail and others on the North Kaibab Trail. Taking their cue from Major John Wesley Powell's 1869 Geographic Expedition stop at Bright Angel Creek on August 16, the U.S. Board of Geographic Names officially named the trail and creek in 1937.

Directions

To reach the Bright Angel Trailhead, take the Village Route (Blue) Shuttle to the Bright Angel Lodge. Stroll a few minutes past the mule corral to the Kolb Studio and you're there. The 9.5 mile Bright Angel Trail is well-marked all the way to the Colorado River and Bright Angel Campground, though some of its highlights and challenges aren't as apparent.

Mile 0. Bright Angel Trailhead, South Rim, Elevation 6,860 feet (2,093 meters), Kaibab Limestone, Trailhead View North: Garden Creek Canyon. From the South Rim, the 9.5 mile corridor trail descends/ascends 4,380 vertical feet (1,335 m) between the Bright Angel Trailhead and the Colorado River Resthouse across the river from Bright Angel Campground near Phantom Ranch.

Mile 0.18. First Tunnel, Elevation 6,708 feet (2,045 meters), Kaibab Limestone. The trail descends into the sweeping depths of El Tovar Amphitheater and cuts through a ridge of Kaibab Limestone, the South Rim's uppermost geological layer. As you approach the First Tunnel, you'll see a beautiful window of stone on your right (downhill view) that serves as a prism for late afternoon light. Forged by the Cameron brothers with picks, shovels, and dynamite, the First Tunnel was chiseled out wide and tall enough to accommodate Cameron's mule trains. Today, wranglers adjust their riders' saddles at "Cinch Up Corner" at the first switchback below the tunnel.

Mallery's Grotto. Once you pass through the First Tunnel, stop and study the cap rock above for the pictograph panels called Mallery's Grotto. George Wharton James reported: "I first camped here with some friendly Havasupai's, nearly twenty years ago [ca. August 3, 1898], and I was then informed that some of the designs represent great hunts, in which their ancestors had been successful." Named for Yale graduate and ethnologist Garrick Mallery who wrote the "1886 Bureau of Ethnology, Fourth Annual Report, Pictographs of North American Indians," the NPS designated Class I Archaeological Site features pictograph paintings of antlered mule deer and elk, desert bighorn sheep, and symbols that were hand-painted with natural dyes and red ochre paint. These are the first of several visible rock art panels that were trail shrines, or waypoints, on the prehistoric rim-to-river route.

Mile 0.45. First Switchback, Elevation 6,560 feet (1,999 meters). Turn Around Point 1. (Use any convenient point on the Bright Angel Trail where you feel you, or your children, need to stop and turn around). If you're pushing your limit, or your knees are talking to you, this is an excellent turnaround point.

Mile 0.72. The Kolb Spring percolates to the surface from the Coconino Sandstone. An "intermittent seep," it flows at less than one liter per minute, usually between January and April.

Mile 0.75. Second Tunnel, Elevation 6,240 feet (1,902 meters), Coconino Sandstone. The Fault Switchbacks cut through the Bright Angel Fault and Toroweap Formation, then through the Coconino Sandstone and Hermit Shale.

Mile 1.6. Mile-and-a-Half Resthouse, Elevation 5,729 feet (1,748 meters), Hermit Shale. Turn Around Point 2 (introductory walk). The timber and stone CCC shelter offers shade, shelter, water (spring through fall), and a composting toilet. On occasion this is a good stretch for observing Desert bighorn sheep (*Ovis canadensis nelsoni*) once hunted by Ancestral Puebloans. In 1893, prospector Dan Hogan constructed the Battleship Trail, which left the Bright Angel Trail near here and contoured west cross-country along steep talus and hanging ledges 3.5 miles to his Orphan Lode copper and silver mine. A more direct and dangerous route to the mine located 1,000 feet below the Rim Trail's 6,995-foot Maricopa Point was the "Hummingbird Trail." Hogan was reportedly the only prospector daring enough to use the creaky metal ladders, swinging ropes, and toe holds chiseled into the rock face that miners throughout the Colorado Plateau called "Moki Steps."

Mile 2. Two-Mile Corner Switchback, Elevation 5,490 feet (1,673 meters), Hermit Shale. Turn Around Point 3 (short day hike). On the first switchback below Two Mile Corner, a second panel of pictographs can be seen beneath an overhang that dates back to AD 1300. Defaced and irreparably damaged with carved initials, the once-pristine panel includes lizards, stick figures, snakes, dots, anthropomorphic figures, shamans, and handprints, which indicate it was a sacred area for Ancestral Puebloans and, more recently, Native American canyon dwellers and pilgrims. Some elders have recounted that handprints represent hallowed ground where individuals "crossed over" to the spirit world.

The Battleship, Off Trail Hiker Report: An arduous cross-country route leaves the trail at Two Mile Corner where the first switchback makes a hard right. The six-to-eight-hour roundtrip trek and scramble follows the Hermit Shale and Supai Sandstone to the saddle of The Battleship, then northeast cross-country along a cairn-marked route up two chockstone-filled chimneys to the flat summit. The exposed 4th Class scramble up the 5,850-foot high Battleship was undoubtedly first climbed by Ancestral Puebloans long before "O. J. [indecipherable] Chadwick" carved his signature in the Esplanade Sandstone summit on April 6, 1919. The butte was named for the 1896 battleship *USS Iowa* (BB-4), and photographed in stereoscope by western photographer Frederic Hamer Maude for George Wharton James's book, *In and Around the Grand Canyon*.

Mile 3. Three-Mile Resthouse, Elevation 4,748 feet (1,449 meters), Supai Group. Turn Around Point 4 (day hike). The timber and stone CCC shelter offers shade, shelter, and water (spring through fall). No toilets. While excavating a site to install compost toilets, park archaeologists uncovered the oldest agave roasting pit in the Grand Canyon. Dating back 2,500 years, the stone hearth was used to roast Utah agave (*Agave utahensis var. kaibabensis*) for eating, which grew in abundance in the area. Below Three Mile Resthouse, you'll face the Grand Canyon's most formidable barrier for rim-to-river foot travel, the Redwall Limestone. The steep 14.85-degree descent, and return ascent, through the Redwall is made easier with "Jacob's Ladder." Named for the biblical patriarch, Jacob's Ladder switchbacks forty times through the 500-foot-thick, rust-colored Mississippian-aged cliffs, what Grand Canyon prospectors called the "blue lime" in days of old.

Mile 4.8. Indian Garden, Elevation 3,800 feet (1,160 meters). Bright Angel Shale. Turn Around Point 4 (long day hike). Indian Garden offers an NPS Ranger Station, visitor center, emergency phone, rustic wood and stone CCC-era caretaker's residence, potable water (year-round), shade, picnic tables, composting toilets, and campgrounds with fourteen tent sites (one to six hikers each) and one large tent site (seven to ten hikers). At one time, Ancestral Puebloans, and later the Havasupai, lived beneath the towering cliffs overlooking Garden Creek in ten to fifteen temporary, wikiup-type dwellings. They cached food nearby in wood-and-mud storage granaries and diverted runoff from four perennial springs to grow corn, beans, and squash. The Havasupai's simple lifestyle included mining rock salt and red ocher paint in the western Grand Canyon (used for pictographs and ceremony) they traded with the Hopi who visited them at Indian Garden. Much of Indian Garden's Native American cultural and archaeological legacy was later removed or buried by the man-made detritus of frenzied prospectors, miners, cattlemen, trailblazers, and promoters who erected a two-story photo studio, canvas-roofed stone cabins, tourist tent camps, corrals, and a moonshine still to slake their dry canyon thirst. Before Indian Garden's springs were developed, groundwater percolated through the Bright Angel Fault and created a "collection gallery" of springs in the Muav Limestone that produced 300 GPM (gallons of water per minute) that helped create a bustling way station that became the busiest, most popular destination in Grand Canyon National Park. Today, you can still savor the cool shade of Fremont cottonwood trees (*Populus fremontii*) transplanted here by Ralph Cameron from Cottonwood Canyon, Scotts Orioles and Summer Tanagers singing from the branches, and the soothing music of Garden Creek trickling beneath your feet. This verdant birder's paradise can be seen by climbers from the distant North Rim summit of 7,646-foot Shiva Temple. In this seemingly benign canyon idyll, a father and son were swept to their deaths in a deadly monsoon flashflood. The thirty-six-year-old father, Rogers Clubb, Sr., died trying to save his eight-year-old son from what *The Arizona Republic* reported in 1963 was ". . . a 10-foot wall of water swept down Indian Garden Creek, ripping out bridges and damaging other facilities . . ." Rogers was the son of Merrell D. Clubb, an English professor specializing in *Beowulf*, who became a canyon legend by climbing two of the Grand Canyon's biggest mountains: 7,721-foot Wotan's Throne (solo in 1937) and Vishnu Temple (with his son Rogers in 1945). Indian Gardens is a good introductory overnight destination, or a turnaround point for an ambitious day hike.

Plateau Point Trail Side Hike: This is a popular out-and-back side hike for visitors overnighting at Indian Garden. From the Indian Garden Ranger Station, follow the left fork of the Tonto Trail West 0.75 miles to the spur trail that leads 0.75 north across the Tonto Formation to 3,740-foot Plateau Point. Once called Angel Point, the arid promontory of blackbrush desert scrub (*Coleogyne ramosissima*) offers a spectacular view of the Colorado River swirling beneath the black basement rocks of Vishnu Schist. It also marks the vicinity of the first successful airplane landing in the Grand Canyon. On August 8, 1922, Ellsworth Kolb hired Commander R. V. Thomas of the British Royal Flying Corps to fly him in and out of the Grand Canyon to shoot the canyon's first motion pictures. Facing a precipitous drop over the edge of the South Rim, and fickle canyon winds that buffeted the deadly cliffs, the barnstormer spiraled through the sky and tail-spun into the abyss to the delight of throngs of South Rim visitors. He landed the single-engine Thomas Special fifty feet from the end of the creosote bush-strewn runway—and a 1,270-foot plummet over the edge of what *Kansas City Star* reporter, A. Gaylord, called the "Devil's Bowl." Ninety-three years later, seventy-five air miles west of Plateau Point, Australian husband and wife wingsuit pilots Glenn Singleman and Heather Swan, accompanied by Roger Hugelshofer, Vicente Cajiga, and cameraman Paul Tozer, made the first ever cross-canyon flight over the western Grand Canyon. Leaping from 30,000 feet in -50 degree temperatures, the 6.8 mile north-south, free fall flight path took seven minutes before team members pulled their rip chords and touched down in the scrubby sagebrush, piñon-juniper tribal lands of the Hualapai Nation on April 9, 2015. Commander Thomas and the Aussie team's exploits may not have been the first aerial canyon crossings and landings. A painted sign that once hung at Phantom Ranch reportedly commemorated, "'The First Balloon Crossing of the Grand Canyon,' Feb. 3rd 1879, by Capt. J. Gallagher and Mr. O'Toole, 'God Bless Ireland.'"

Old Bright Angel Trail, Off Trail Hiker Report: From Indian Garden, an increasingly popular route follows the Bright Angel Trail/Tonto Trail East approximately one mile to the first ridge east of Garden Creek. From a prow of Tapeats Sandstone, you can see the Old Bright Angel Trail descending into Garden Creek, what miners once called Bright Angel Wash. Occasionally marked by abandoned CCC telephone poles and weathered timbers, the well-marked, nonmaintained Old Bright Angel Trail leads to a cluster of Ancestral Puebloan cliff dwellings and storage granaries nestled in the Tapeats Sandstone. Below the Garden Creek dwellings, the trail joins the new Bright Angel Trail. Tread Very Lightly. This is a fragile NPS Class II Archaeological Site vulnerable to visitor impacts.

Mile 5.1 to 8. Tonto Trail Junction to the River Trail. To resume hiking down the Bright Angel Trail to Bright Angel Campground, turn right (east) at the junction and follow the Tonto Trail East 0.3 miles to a second junction. Take the left fork and follow the Bright Angel Trail down Garden Creek Canyon through the Tapeats Narrows, a charming riparian walkway lined with cottonwood trees among century plants. You'll trace remnants of the Bright Angel Fault into the head of Pipe Creek Canyon where you'll crisscross several small falls, plunge pools, and water-polished stones of Zoroaster Granite. Beyond, the steep knee-hammering switchbacks called the Devil's Corkscrew zigzag down to Columbine Springs waterfall (seasonal), through Vishnu Schist into Pipe Creek to the River Trail.

Mile 8. Colorado River Resthouse, Pipe Creek, elevation 2,480 feet (756 meters), Vishnu Schist. The timber and stone CCC shelter offers shade, shelter, emergency phone, and a compost toilet. No potable water. Pipe Creek was named by Arizona Senator Ralph Cameron and is used during the summer months by commercial river runners as an "interchange": Clients who booked the top half of a Colorado River rafting trip get out here, and hike out the Bright Angel Trail, often wishing they had booked the entire trip. Clients who booked the bottom half, hike in here, happy they're about to cool off and get really wet!

<u>Colorado River Trail.</u> From the River Rest House follow the River Trail 1.3 miles east to the silver Bright Angel Suspension Bridge. Designed by engineer W. P. Weber and landscape architect Clark Carrell, the two-mile Colorado River Trail was blasted, drilled, and chiseled through the Vishnu Schist in 1933 by Civilian Conservation Corps Company No. 818. It was described by the park as "the most difficult trail ever constructed at Grand Canyon!" The shadeless trudge over black rock through wind-scoured sand dunes might seem forlorn were it not for the proximity and microclime of cool Colorado River water flowing beneath towering ramparts of the Upper Granite Gorge and the upstream views of the 5,126-foot Sumner Butte (foreground left) and the 7,123-foot Zoroaster Temple. Avoid the hot-dry River Trail midday during summer months.

<u>Warning:</u> Do not let the Colorado River tempt you for a swim. At least a dozen people have vanished or drowned in the cold, fast-moving two-mile river stretch between Pipe Creek and Bright Angel Creek.

Mile 9.3 to 9.5. Bright Angel (Silver) Suspension Bridge to Bright Angel Campground, Elevation 2480-feet (756 meters), Vishnu Schist. Marvel at the river beneath your feet as you cross the hikers-only pedestrian bridge to reach Bright Angel Ranger Station, the next potable water stop. Started in 1965, the Bright Angel Suspension Bridge was constructed to support the 12.5 mile gravity siphon-fed Trans Canyon Pipeline from the North Rim's Roaring Springs to Indian Garden pump house to sustain the South Rim's National Park facilities, tourist concessions, lodging and services. Once you reach the Ranger Station, cross the Bright Angel Creek foot-bridge and the trail leads to the campground. Phantom Ranch is 0.4 miles beyond Bright Angel Campground.

Note: Kaibab (Black) Suspension Bridge. From the River Resthouse, the River Trail leads 2 miles (0.7 miles beyond the Bright Angel Suspension Bridge) to the Kaibab Suspension Bridge and South Kaibab Trail. Designed by engineer W. P. Weber, the 440-foot span, steel suspension bridge was built in 1928 as a trail bridge to replace Rust's Cableway across the Colorado River. The wooden-planked, five-foot-wide deck is used by hikers and mule trains destined for Bright Angel Campground, Phantom Ranch and beyond.

Mile 9.5. Bright Angel Campground, Elevation 2,480 feet (756 meters), Vishnu Schist. Nestled beneath Fremont cottonwood trees pinched between towering walls of Vishnu Schist and Bright Angel Creek, Bright Angel Campground offers an NPS Ranger Station, emergency phone, potable water (year-round), shade, picnic tables, composting toilets, and campgrounds with thirty-three tent sites (one to six hikers each) and two large tent sites (seven to eleven hikers).

(See page 224 for the North Kaibab Trail description).

Additional Considerations: If you're planning a rim-to-rim hike, (see page 56 Hiking Rim to Rim).

Indian Garden Loop Hikes/Backpacks: Two popular loop hikes lead to Indian Garden. Corridor Trail Loop Hike. The most popular Corridor Loop Hike is the 14.6 mile South Kaibab, Tonto, Indian Garden, Bright Angel Trail. Descending 4.5 miles down the South Kaibab Trail to the Tonto Trail junction, it is 4.1 miles across the Tonto Trail East to Indian Garden. (See page 202 South Kaibab Trail to Bright Angel Trail).

Wilderness Trail Loop Hike. A more challenging Wilderness Trail Loop Hike is the 24.4 mile Hermit, Tonto, Indian Garden, Bright Angel Trail. Descending 8.2 miles down the Hermit Trail to the Tonto Trail junction, it is twelve miles across the Tonto Trail West to Indian Garden. (See page 202 Bright Angel Trail to Hermit Trail).

Note: Descending either trail to reach Indian Garden is the safest option because there's always water at Indian Garden and a Ranger Station if you need help on the return hike up to the South Rim via the Bright Angel Trail.

Travel Notes

Warning Advisory: During summertime, it's imperative you be OTR (On the Trail Ready) to leave Bright Angel Campground at O'Dark-thirty to hike the River Trail and Devils Corkscrew to beat the blistering morning heat before it reaches Indian Garden. At least thirty people have died of dehydration, heat stroke, and heat-related heart attacks on the Bright Angel Trail.

- Primary Access: Bright Angel Trail: South Rim, Tonto Trail, and River Trail from Phantom Ranch.

- Elevation: 6,860-feet Bright Angel Trailhead to 2,480-feet Colorado River.
- Biotic Communities: Ponderosa pine forest, piñon-juniper woodland, Great Basin Desert scrub, and Mojave Desert scrub.
- Total Elevation Loss and Gain: 8,760 feet (4,380 vertical feet each way).
- Mileage: 19 miles (4.7 one way to Indian Garden Campground; 9.5 one way to Bright Angel Campground).
- Water: 1.5 mile Rest House and 3-mile Rest House (in summer), Indian Gardens, Pipe.
- Creek (seasonal), Colorado River (emergency), and Bright Angel Campground (year-round).
- Cache Points: Immediately below the Tonto Formation, in the shade and seclusion of Tapeats Narrows.
- Escape Routes: Bright Angel Trailhead, Indian Garden Ranger Station, or Bright Angel Ranger Station.
- Seasons: Fall and spring. Winter can be either ideal or bitterly cold. Summer, especially June, is brutally hot and the worst time to hike in and out of the Grand Canyon. July and August monsoons can pose deadly flash-flood threats in Garden Creek, Pipe Creek, Bright Angel Creek, and Phantom Creek.
- Maps: Phantom Ranch Quadrangle (7.5 minute) map.
- Camping, Corridor Trails: Indian Garden, Bright Angel, and Cottonwood Campgrounds.
- Nearest Supply Points: Grand Canyon Village, Flagstaff, Cameron, and Williams.
- Managing Agency: Grand Canyon National Park
- Backcountry Information Center: for information call (928) 638–7875.
- Critical Backcountry Updates visit www.nps.gov/grca/planyourvisit/trail-closures.htm.
- NPS Grand Canyon Hiker 24 Hour Emergency Phone Number and Email
- Phone (928) 638–7805.
- Email: grca_bic@nps.gov (Use this if the phone line is busy)

TRAIL CROSSROADS

Through the efforts of David Rust, Mary Jane Colter, and the CCC to develop the Bright Angel Creek area, it became the locus of a trail crossroads. Today, the inner canyon oasis is a staging area for short walks. (For day hikes, overnight, backpacks, canyoneering, and peak ascents via the Clear Creek Trail, Phantom Canyon, and Ribbon Falls Trail, see page 222 North Kaibab Trail).

Bright Angel Creek Walks and Points of Interest
Bright Angel Pueblo Walk

From the south end of the Bright Angel Campground, stroll 0.3 miles toward the north end of the Kaibab Suspension Bridge to the Bright Angel Pueblo Exhibit, an NPS Class I Archaeological Site. During his maiden voyage down the Colorado River in 1869, Major John Wesley Powell and his crew stopped at what Powell wrote was "a clear, beautiful creek, coming down through a gorgeous red canyon." The expedition was forced to lay-over on August 15–16 to rest and look for timbers to fashion new oars. Powell named the stream "Bright Angel" in contrast to the "Dirty Devil" Colorado River tributary he'd named far upstream in what later became Butch Cassidy and the Wild Bunch country. In Powell's expedition journal, he also wrote about the prehistoric settlement he visited near Bright Angel Creek's confluence with the Colorado River: "Late in the afternoon I return, and go up a little gulch, just above this creek . . . and discover the ruins of two or three old houses, which were originally of stone . . . It is ever a source of wonder to us why these ancient people sought such inaccessible places for their homes." Powell described what archaeologists now call Bright Angel Pueblo. Inhabited by Ancestral Puebloans between 1050 and 1140, the eight-room riverside dwelling includes a ceremonial kiva, subterranean pit house, and living and storage rooms that sheltered extended families who hunted and gathered in the area and farmed the Bright Angel Creek delta. Imagine ancestral Hopi called *Hisat.sinom*, "People Who Lived Long Ago," who lived in this sacred place interconnected by ancient trails and ritual cave shrines that served as fragile threads between canyon dwellers who once flourished at Indian Garden, Walhalla Glades on the North Rim, Unkar Delta on the Colorado River, and distant settlements throughout their canyon home.

Rusts Camp

Not far from Bright Angel Pueblo, trail builder David D. Rust established a tent camp in 1903 for hunters, prospectors, and a "few sturdy and adventurous tourists." Rust ferried his guests across the Colorado River in a 450-foot-long cable-drawn cage big and sturdy enough to carry a mule sixty feet above the river. Mouthwatering home-cooked meals at the end of the trail included venison steak, mutton, rabbit, eggs, and fresh apricots, peaches, and plums grown in Rust's orchard.

Phantom Ranch

The Fred Harvey Company and Santa Fe Railroad agreed Rusts Camp was an enchanting area for "luxury accommodations," bought the property in 1921, and hired impendent-minded, California School of Design–educated architect Mary Jane Colter to design Phantom Ranch. Among Colter's landmark buildings in the Grand Canyon region that are listed on the National Register of Historic Place—Desert Inn, Hopi

House, Desert View Watchtower, and El Tovar Hotel—Phantom Ranch stands apart. Today, the rustic, river stone and hand-hewn wooden canteen and cabins hearken modern guests back in time to a romantic, bygone era where riding saddleback still evokes memories of a Southwest brought to life in the literary works of Mary Hunter Austin, Harriet Monroe, and Zane Grey.

Civilian Conservation Corp Tent Camp

Occupying what is now Bright Angel Campground in 1936, the CCC's Company No. 818 tent camp at Phantom Ranch housed 200 men, six men per stove-warmed tent, during its heyday. Resupplied five days a week by Fort Huachica, Arizona's 7th Army Pack Team, mule teams hauled dynamite, gasoline, tools, food, and lumber down the South Kaibab Trail. Among many challenges, CCC crews faced during the 1930s in what was described as the most isolated CCC camp in the country, they dynamited the River Trail through impossibly hard Vishnu Schist, enlarged Phantom Ranch, diverted water into a hand-dug swimming pool, and constructed the 8.7-mile Clear Creek Trail. For their backbreaking efforts far from home, they received $30 a month and occasionally letters from loved ones.

An ancient split-twig figurine excavated from a remote cave, GCNP Museum Collection.

10

South Kaibab Trail: Day Hikes, Rim to River, and Rim to Rim

"The whole magnificence broke upon us. No one could be prepared for it.
The scene is to strike one dumb with awe or to unstring the nerves;
one might stand in silent astonishment, another would burst into tears. . .
It was a shock so novel that the mind, dazed, quite failed to comprehend it."

—Charles Dudley Warner, 1906
"On the Brink of the Canyon"

LANDFORM

Soaring 4,300 feet above the tributary canyons of Pipe Creek to the west and Cremation Creek to the east, Cedar Ridge extends from the Kaibab Limestone, Toroweap, and Coconino Sandstone walls of Yaki Point to The Tipoff leading into the Upper Granite Gorge of the Colorado River.

HISTORICAL OVERVIEW

Yaki Trail

Named for Sonora, Mexico's Yaqui (*Yoeme*, "The People") who were granted political asylum in the United States in 1906, the history of the "Yaki Trail" has long been associated with the Santa Fe Railroad's efforts to wrest control of Ralph Cameron's

Bright Angel Trail and the National Park's goal to build an alternate hiking trail. Under the supervision of National Park Service engineer Miner Tillotson, construction of the Yaki Trail began in December 1924. Burning dynamite fuses from both ends, Arizona Strip foreman John Brown worked his crew of fifteen Mormon men up from the Colorado River to the Tonto Formation, while Civilian Conservation Corp leader Chick Seavey worked his twenty-man crew of CCC "enrollees" down from Yaki Point to the Tonto. In little more than six months of grueling, back-breaking work, the crews had constructed an incomparably scenic, five-foot-wide, 6.5 mile long "mountain trail . . . designed for optimum sun exposure to avoid ice"—hence the virtual lack of shade on the sun-scorched trail—aided by portable jackhammers to carve steep grades through walls and cliffs. Renamed the South Kaibab Trail for the Kaibab Band of Southern Paiute, the trail crews had, as one historian summed it up, built a trail "where no trail had gone before." And that has long remained the popular conception.

Tsé'áán Ketán, "Prayer Stick Cave," Navajo (Diné)

In 1954, three men made a remarkable discovery in a Redwall limestone cave lost somewhere in the depths far below 7,300-foot Cremation Point. Quoting a brief passage from *Arizona Place Names*, Emery Kolb had conveyed to those who listened: "Here, Indians claim they used to cremate bodies and throw the ashes over the cliff." The unsubstantiated tale shrouded the hidden cave with mystery that held secrets 3,000 to 4,000 years old. The discoveries unearthed in the cave shrine named, *Tsé'áán Ketán*, to hide its location were extraordinary and conceivably alarming for the Canyon's Native Peoples. Sifting through pack rat middens that yielded arrows, chert spear points, bone fragments, and an owl roost, the speleologists and anthropologist uncovered split-twig animal figurines that resembled Desert bighorn sheep (*Ovis Canadensis*) and the skeletal remains of extinct Pleistocene-aged Harrington's mountain goats (*Oreamnos harringtoni*). Made from split, seep willow twigs (*Baccharis salicifolia*), sometimes bound with yucca and cottonwood, the hand-woven figures were pierced with small spears and arrows; others were bound with a tiny pieces of coprolite. The ancient offerings had been ritually buried beneath juniper bark and cover stones in the dark inner and outer chambers of the long, deep cavern. More compelling, perhaps, was the bundle of human hair hanging from the ceiling overhead, "wrapped with cordage and attached to two pointed pieces of wood which appear to be some sort of prayer sticks," perhaps a *k'eet'áán yálti'*, "Talking Prayer Stick" (Navajo), indicating to me the cave shrine may have also been visited by Ancestral Puebloans, or in a more recent era by the Navajo, Havasupai, or Hopi. For a millennium, the fleet-footed Hopi made salt pilgrimages on foot through the Little Colorado River Gorge near the confluence of the Colorado River where they offered sacred *paahos* (prayer sticks) and eagle feathers at *Panktupatca,* "Home of the Mountain Sheep" and *Sipàapuni,* the "hatchway where the Hopi emerged to the Fourth world." In nineteenth century ceremonies, the Hopi Mountain Sheep Clan offered prayer for their hallowed *Pañwu,* Mountain Sheep Kachina. The *bahana* (non-Hopi) cave explorers reported no cultural material link between the salt pilgrimages and cave shrine, but they speculated the split-twig bighorn sheep totems were effigies for a successful hunt, "a form of prayer or offering to ancestors at presumed entrances to the Underworld." Imagine entering a pitch black, cliff-walled sanctuary far from your mesa pueblo carrying a juniper-pitch torch to offer your prayer sticks before venturing out into the depths of a great abyss to stalk nimble-footed bighorn sheep across narrow ledges and hanging terraces with a flimsy spear in quest of food for your family and clan. (See page 296 South Canyon).

Where No Trail Had Gone Before

Years after the cave shrine discovery, serious canyoneers traced an ancient rim-to-cave "trail" from an Ancestral Puebloan storage granary perched over the edge of the South Rim and followed a faint "deer trail" through the Kaibab Limestone. Searching for a route through the precipitous maze, they detoured around the Toroweap cliffs and discovered, while looking for lines of weakness in sheer walls of Coconino Sandstone, "Anasazi hand and footholds" and "Moki steps" that had been carved into the slick rock face. They also made use of prehistoric stone steps that had been piled atop one another and weather-beaten logs that had been slotted into sinuous cracks and served as precarious ladders. Someone had been there before them, the canyoneers realized, as they worked their way through the Redwall Limestone into the subterranean cave portal. (When the researchers first probed the cave shrine, they wrote: ". . . it was very difficult to enter and required considerable mountaineering skills and equipment, including rope and pitons.") In their daring exploratory descent, the stealthy canyoneers had discovered the area's first trail "where no trail had gone before."

    Note: NPS Class IV Archaeological Sites are closed to all visitation. Visit the informative split-twig figurine exhibit at Tusayan Ruin and Museum at Desert View on the South Rim.

Directions

To reach the South Kaibab Trailhead, board the Hiker's Express Shuttle Bus at the Bright Angel Lodge. The bus departs on the hour and stops at the Backcountry Information Center, Grand Canyon Visitor Center, and South Kaibab Trailhead. (December through February the Hiker's Express departs the Bright Angel Lodge at 8 a.m. and 9 a.m.). Or you can take the Village Bus (Blue Line) to Canyon View Information Plaza and transfer to the Green Line to reach the South Kaibab Trailhead.

The 6.7-mile South Kaibab Trail is well-marked all the way to the Colorado River and Bright Angel Campground, though some of its highlights and challenges aren't as apparent.

<u>Advisory:</u> The South Kaibab Trail is primarily used as a descent trail, both for out-and-back Cedar Ridge day hikes, and as a one-way trail link to Phantom Ranch and the Tonto, River, Bright Angel, North Kaibab, and Clear Creek Trails. It's safest to return to the South Rim via the Bright Angel Trail—there's always water at Indian Garden. There is no water and little shade on the South Kaibab Trail.

Mile 0. South Kaibab Trailhead, Elevation 7,260 feet (2,213 meters), Kaibab Limestone, Trailhead View North: 6,071-foot O'Neill Butte. From the South Rim, the seven mile long corridor trail descends/ascends 4,780 vertical feet (1,457 meters) between the South Kaibab Trailhead and North Kaibab Trail Junction near Bright Angel Campground at Phantom Ranch. The heavily beaten "super highway" leaves the trailhead and passes through a forest of ponderosa pine (*Pinus ponderosa*), piñon pine (*Pinus edulis*), Utah juniper (*Juniperous osteosperma*), and Gamble oak (*Quercus Gambelii*). At first glance the scruffy forest lacks the visual appeal of spectacular South Kaibab Trail vistas, but the South Rim's woodlands and the flora and fauna it sustains offered Ancestral Puebloans a cornucopia of nutritional food. Pine seeds, piñon nuts, juniper berries, and acorns supplemented their long, stealthy journeys to hunt mule deer, elk, and Desert bighorn sheep. The bark of the drought-resistant Utah juniper, alone, was used for making medicine, cordage, sandals, sleeping mats, and cradle boards, while the strong limbs were cut and shaped for hogans, sweat lodges, and cook fires.

Mile 0.3. The Chimney. Beyond the trees, the dusty (icy in winter) trail descends through cliffs of Kaibab Limestone and ledges of Toroweap down a steep, 0.3-mile dizzying series of switchbacks into Pipe Creek called The Chimney. Carrying a day pack or backpack is challenging enough for most hikers headed down the fasted trail to Phantom Ranch. Yet, in 1928 forty-two Havasupai men did what today would seem impossible to most Grand Canyon hikers. Spaced eleven feet apart, they shouldered a 2,320 pound, 550 foot long, 1.5 inch steel cable down the cliff-hugging, serpentine switchbacks all the way to the Colorado River to help build the new Kaibab Suspension Bridge.

Mile 0.9. Ooh-Ahh Point, Elevation 6,660 feet, (2,030 meters), Coconino Sandstone. Turn Around Point 1. (Use any convenient point on the descent where you feel you, or your children, need to stop and turn around.) This breathtaking vista offers aerial panoramic views of the canyon and the South Kaibab's terracotta landmark of O'Neill Butte. The Grand Canyon's sudden exposure at this point may unnerve some with vertigo, as it did to American novelist Charles Dudley Warner: "Turning suddenly to the scene of another point of view, I experienced for a moment an indescribable terror of nature, confusion of mind, a fear to be alone in such a presence." Be Careful: A thirty-five-year-old Florida woman fell to her death while taking sunrise photos at Ooh Ahh Point on July 11, 2016. R.I.P. Colleen Burns.

Mile 1.5. Cedar Ridge, Elevation 6,120 feet (1,865 meters), Hermit-Supai. Turn Around Point 2 (day hike). Hitching post and composting toilet. The last quarter-mile along Cedar Ridge to reach this popular rest spot has been called the "Razor's Edge" because it traverses a narrow ridgeline before descending to the foot of 6,071-foot O'Neill Butte. The natural monument of Hermit Shale was named in honor of Rough Rider William Owen "Buckey" O'Neill. The former Arizona sheriff, judge, and mayor of Prescott was killed in action in Cuba on July 1, 1898, while fighting under Teddy Roosevelt in the Battle of San Juan Hill during the Spanish-American War. Cedar Ridge, *Siva tonyaha'took waio'a*, is a traditional cultural site for the Havasupai who collected piñon nuts here. From Cedar Ridge the trail heads beneath the east walls of O'Neill Butte straight to Skeleton Point.

Mile 2.9. Skeleton Point, Elevation 5,220 feet (1,591 meters), Redwall Limestone. Turn Around Point 3. (For all but experienced canyoneers, this is the last turn-around point to safely hike back up the steep, dry, shadeless trail to Yaki Point.) This landmark point was reportedly named by mule skinners for a pack string mule that slipped and fell here. Unable to retrieve the carcass, wranglers named the scenic point that was marked by sun-bleached bones for some time. The relentless switchbacks below Skeleton Point are called the "Red and Whites" for the multicolor striations the trail descends through the Redwall Formation 500 vertical feet (150 meters) to reach the Tonto Formation. Once the switchbacks bottom out on the Tonto Formation and head toward the Tonto Trail Junction, look up to your left (west/southwest). You'll be rewarded with a wonderful view of Skylight Arch beneath the rugged crest of Redwall Limestone.

Mile 4.4. Tonto Trail Junction. Elevation 4,010 feet (1,222 meters). Tonto Formation. Composting toilet. Continue straight 0.2 miles to reach the Tipoff. Turn left (west) at this junction and the Tonto Trail East leads 4.5 miles to the Bright Angel Trail and Indian Garden. Turn right (east) at the junction and the Tonto Trail East leads 21.3 miles to the Grandview Trail. (For trail descriptions see page 198 Tonto Trail.)

<u>Old Miners Trail, Off Trail Hiker Report:</u> A sketchy, abandoned route leaves the Tonto Trail five-to-ten minutes' walk west of the South Kaibab Trail. The elusive route is marked by a large cairn, but you'll have to look for and piece together the Old Miners Trail as you descend 1,200 vertical feet cross-country through the Vishnu Schist to the River Trail west of the Bright Angel Suspension Bridge. This short rugged route does not lead to a scenic ooh-aah-type vista. It's infrequently used by experienced canyoneers interested in notching off another abandoned trail.

Mile 4.6. The Tipoff, Elevation 3,870 feet (1,179 meters), Tapeats Sandstone, Shinumo Quartzite. Below this rocky aerie the South Kaibab Trail descends on average

22 percent as it traces the route of the Old Cable Trail to reach what was Rust's Cable Crossing in 1907.

Incredibly, the Havasupai reportedly made eight trips up and down the Cable/South Kaibab Trails, climbing and descending 4,780 vertical feet (1,457 meters) each way to carry eight steel cables that were needed to support the Kaibab Suspension Bridge across the Colorado River, if the report is true. From the perspective of elevation gain and loss—not altitude—that would be the equivalent of climbing from Mount Everest Base Camp at 17,598 feet (5,364 meters) to Everest's 29,029-feet (8,848 meters) summit more than three times.

Mile 5. Panorama Point, Elevation 3,620 feet (1,106 meters). Peering into the Upper Granite Gorge, you can hear and see the Colorado River before making the final 800-foot descent to the River Trail Junction.

Mile 6. Colorado River Trail Junction. Turn right and hike 0.3 miles through the 105-foot-long rock tunnel to the Kaibab (Black) Suspension Bridge. Turn west at the River Trail Junction and the River Trail leads 0.7 miles to the Bright Angel (Silver) Suspension Bridge, and another 1.3 miles to the River Resthouse and Bright Angel Trail.

Mile 6.3. Kaibab (Black) Suspension Bridge, Cross the 440-foot-long bridge and walk 0.4 miles to Bright Angel Campground.

Mile 6.7. Bright Angel Campground. Elevation 2,480 feet (756 meters). (See page 106 Bright Angel Campground).

Mile 7. South Kaibab/North Kaibab Trail junction marks the official rim-to-river length of the South Kaibab Trail from Yaki Point. The South Kaibab/North Kaibab Trails provide the cross-canyon link for the 800-mile (1,287-kilometer) Arizona National Scenic Trail.

Travel Notes

Warning Advisory: In summertime leave by dawn and hike out the Bright Angel Trail to reach Indians Gardens before midmorning. Unless you're a seasoned and acclimated canyon hiker, do not attempt hiking out the South Kaibab Trail during the hot summer months or the warm, dry months of spring and fall. If you insist, be OTR (On the Trail Ready) at dawn to reach the Tonto Trail Junction before midmorning.

- Primary Access: Kaibab Trailhead and Bright Angel Campground.
- Elevation: 7,260-feet Kaibab Trailhead to 2,450-feet Colorado River.
- Biotic Communities: Ponderosa pine forest, pinon-jumper woodland, Great Basin Desert scrub, and Mojave Desert scrub.
- Total Elevation Loss and Gain: 9,620 vertical feet (4,810 vertical feet each way)

- Mileage: Fourteen miles (6.7 one way to Bright Angel Campground; 0.3 miles to the North Kaibab Trail Junction).
- Water: There is no water between the South Kaibab Trailhead and the Colorado River.
- Hiking up, the Bright Angel Trail has water at Pipe Creek (seasonal), Indian Gardens, Three-Mile Rest House (in summer), and 1.5 Rest House (in summer).
- Cache Points: Cedar Ridge and the Tipoff.
- Seasons: Fall through spring. Summer has proven deadly.
- Escape Routes: South Kaibab Trailhead, Bright Angel Campground.
- Maps: Phantom Ranch Quadrangle (7.5 minute) map.
- Camping, Corridor Trails: Bright Angel Campground, Indian Garden.
- Nearest Supply Points: Grand Canyon Village, Flagstaff, Cameron, and Williams.
- Managing Agency: Grand Canyon National Park.
- Backcountry Information Center: for information call (928) 638–7875.
- Critical Backcountry Updates visit www.nps.gov/grca/planyourvisit/trail-closures.htm.
- NPS Grand Canyon Hiker 24 Hour Emergency Phone Number and Email
- Phone (928) 638–7805.
- Email: grca_bic@nps.gov (Use this if the phone line is busy)

Mary Jane Colter's Hermits Rest featured in a souvenir postcard, 1932, painted by Gunnar Widforss, GCNP Museum Collection.

11

Hermit Trail: Day Hikes and Rim to River

"In the morning I went out to verify the vision . . .
I climbed the steep slopes to the rocks,
crawled half prostrate to the barest and highest,
and lay there on the edge of the void,
the only living thing in some unvisited world.
For surely it was not our world . . ."

—Harriet Monroe, 1906
"Its Ineffable Beauty"

LANDFORM

Draining the forested heights of the 7,000-foot, 5,812 square mile Coconino Plateau, Hermit Canyon is a precipitously deep, tributary chasm that stretches from 6,456-foot Horsethief Tank on the South Rim to the roaring brownwater of Hermit Rapids at Mile 95 on the Colorado River. The Hermit Trail traces the eastern ledges of the gorge before switch backing into Hermit Creek.

HISTORICAL OVERVIEW

Agave roasting pits and a mystifying, butterfly-shaped, spiral maze petroglyph, or trail shrine, in Hermit Basin offer irrefutable evidence the ancient corridor was used by Archaic people, Ancestral Puebloans, and later the Havasupai, to reach reliable water at Santa María and Dripping Springs.

Architect Mary Elizabeth Jane Colter, 1892, photographer not attributed.

Prospectors, miners, and promoters traced the incipient ancestral paths that skirted the exposed rims of Hermit Canyon into Hermit Creek and Boucher Creek. Among the first was New York–born prospector and miner Daniel L. Hogan. The Rough Rider who served with Buckey O'Neill and Teddy Roosevelt during the Spanish-American War built the two-mile Waldron Trail from Horsethief Tank through Hermit Basin in 1896. It was the first leg of what became the Hermit Trail. Sixteen years later, the Atchison, Topeka, and Santa Fe Railway turned its attention to Hermit Basin and constructed what the park boasted was a "state of the art rim-to-river trail . . . to serve a luxury campsite near Hermit Creek." First proposed as the Santa María Trail and the Hermit Creek Trail, the four-to-six foot wide Hermit Trail was meticulously inlaid with native cobblestone riprap tread and included outer retaining walls to protect skittish tourists teetering atop their surefooted mules ambling along precarious points on the hand-forged trail. Santa Fe Railroad's efforts to develop the remote canyon outpost in 1912 did not stop there. Eclipsing today's controversial Grand Canyon Escalade project to build a 1.4 mile rim-to-river tramway and luxury resort at the confluence of the Colorado and Little Colorado Rivers, the Santa Fe Railroad built a 3,000-foot-long aerial tramway from 6,796-foot Pima Point to Hermit Camp to resupply the tent camp with provisions and a Model T Ford that reportedly ferried saddle-weary, joy-riding dudes on the mile-long inner canyon road. No doubt the Pima Point to Hermit Camp high wire act was inspired by the independent efforts of David Rust's cable car that ferried tourists across the Colorado River to his Bright Angel Creek camp in 1907, and William Wallace Bass's cable car that carried guests across the river to his Shinumo Camp and Garden. Seven years later the Santa Fe Railroad funded George K. Davol and his crew to survey a trans canyon aerial tramway from the South Rim's Hopi Point to the North Rim's Tiyo Point but park administrators pulled the pin on Davol's brainchild. (See page 187 Beamer's Cabin).

Directions

From Grand Canyon Village take the Hermits Rest Route (Red Route) Hermits Rest. (March 1 to November 30). Hikers with backcountry permits can drive to Hermits Rest and use an official access code to open the gate. (The gate is open December through February). The Hermit Trail begins 0.25 miles west. The rugged nonmaintained 9.7-mile Hermit Trail is well marked all the way to the Colorado River, though some of its highlights and challenges aren't as apparent.

Hermits Rest

Be sure to stop and view the native stone, rough-hewn log, and wooden roof-beamed hermitage designed by Mary Elizabeth Jane Colter. Inspired by the tales of Grand Canyon prospector Louis D. Boucher, Colter designed the West Rim retreat to resemble an eccentric folly, or abode, of a grizzled hermit who had lived on the canyon's edge since time forgot. Hermits Rest was built in 1914 by the Fred Harvey Company. The 103-year-old, "National Park Rustic"-style dwelling is a landmark in the landscape, replete with *latilla* ceilings and a cavernous, soot-stained fireplace once draped with bear skins. Hermits Rest is a classic example of Colter's extraordinary buildings that were influenced by their environmental settings, and Southwest indigenous mesa and dwellings, art, and culture. Listed on the National Register of Historic Places and National Historic Landmarks, Colter's work reflects the visions of a remarkable woman architect who challenged convention and created an enduring legacy throughout the Grand Canyon and Painted Desert region.

Mile 0. Hermit Trailhead, Elevation 6,640 feet (2,024 meters), Kaibab Limestone, Trailhead View West: Hermit Creek Canyon. Leaving the trailhead you'll descend the cobblestone staircase through the Kaibab Limestone and Toroweap 1,300 vertical feet to the Waldron Trail junction. Called the "White Zigzags," the steep, custom-forged, *Wizard of Oz* "yellow brick road"-type switchbacks bespoke the efforts the Santa Fe Railroad made to accommodate discerning tourists venturing to the bottom of the canyon to dine and sleep in cowboy comfort at Hermit Camp.

Mile 0.3. Marshal Foch Rock. A 1920s Grand Canyon National Park document reported: Marshall Foch sat here "for a half hour or more smoking his pipe December, 1921." They did not identify who the gentleman was.

Mile 0.9. Fossil Trackways. Keep your eyes peeled for fossilized lizard, salamander, and tetrapod tracks for the next quarter-mile or so. The Hermit Trail's Aeolian cross-bedded Coconino Sandstone yielded eighty-two distinct sets of trackways to paleontologists and ichnologists who recorded them. Long before Hopi guides first led Spanish conquistador, García López de Cárdenas, to the Grand Canyon in 1535, the Grand Canyon has been an open book that has touched many with its lessons. It would make an exciting journey of discovery for parents and teachers to guide their children and students down the trail to study these 260-million-year-old trace fossils.

Mile 1.5. Waldron Trail Junction, Elevation 5,400 feet (1,646 meters). Supai Formation. Turn Around Point 1. (Use any convenient point on the descent where you feel you, or your children, need to stop and turn around). From the Waldron Trail junction, turn right (north) and proceed another 0.3 mile to the Dripping Springs/Hermit Trail junction.

Waldron Trail

Elevation 6,456 feet (1,968 meters). Unconfirmed reports tell of horse thieves using the route below Horsethief Tank prior to Daniel Hogan building the trail in 1896. The two-mile Waldron Trail is a pleasant, seldom-used trail that can be day hiked four miles out-and-back, or as a four mile loop hike to Hermit's Rest (requiring a vehicle shuttle). The nonmaintained, easy-to-follow trail leads from the forested rim and signed trailhead at road's end near Horsethief Tank. Descending 976 vertical feet through the Kaibab,

Toroweap, and Coconino formations into Hermit Basin, the trail leads to the Hermits Rest trail junction near the 5,480 foot elevation contour on your Grand Canyon Quadrangle (7.5 minute) map. Turn right (east) at the wooden trail sign to hike two miles up to Hermits Rest. Or turn left (west) and hike another 0.25 miles to access the Hermit Trail/Dripping Springs-Boucher Trail junction. Directions: Use your Grand Canyon topo map to access the Rowe Well Road from Grand Canyon Village, drive 3.4 miles west on the paved, turned-to-gravel road to a secondary road junction. Turn right (north) and drive 0.5 miles to the secluded trailhead marked with a wooden sign post. (Inquire about road conditions beforehand at the Backcountry Information Center.)

Mile 1.75. Hermit/Dripping Springs Trail Junction, Elevation 5,200 feet (1,585 meters), Supai Formation. Turn Around Point 2 (day hike). Turn right (north) and follow the Hermit Trail to Santa María Springs.

Mile 2.5. Santa María Spring, Elevation 4,880 feet (1,487 meters), Esplanade Sandstone. Turn Around Point 3 (day hike). The hike down to the spring is an increasingly popular day hike that offers stunning views of the deep chasm formed by Hermit Creek. Santa Maria Spring is a seasonal spring that percolates through the Supai up to one gallon a minute. The Santa Maria Spring Resthouse was built in 1911 for tourists riding down the Hermit Trail to overnight at Hermit Camp. The rustic, hand-laid native stone and wood structures include a wooden-shingled, three-walled ramada, water trough for mules, and a scenic tin-roofed outhouse built into a boulder perched on the edge of the rim, offering stupendous views. Little else has been written about the area, including the origin of the name, Santa María, ("Holy Mary"). It may have been named by Santa Fe Railroad or National Park construction crews that were made up of Euro-American, Native American, and Mexicanos who traditionally revered Santa María.

Supai Rockslide Traverse

From Santa Maria Spring, the Hermit Trail makes a three-mile traverse through the Supai atop the Redwall Formation. For those carrying too heavy a pack, the historic, once charming tourist trail may lose its luster and romance along the boulder-strewn alleys a mile beyond, especially during the hike out. So tighten your boot laces and pack straps because you'll encounter loose rocks and avalanches of boulders you need to scramble over while lugging the dead weight of your pack around them. Look for cairns that should help you negotiate these major rockslides that buried the trail in the 1930s, in 1983, and more recently during summer monsoons that periodically spew violent torrents of brown flood water, detritus, and boulders that pulverize everything in their paths.

Mile 4. Four Mile Spring. Once a reliable water source, Four Mile Spring is reported to be dry.

Mile 4.5. Lookout Point, Elevation 4,568 feet (1,392 meters). Named by the U.S. Board of Geographic Names in 1932, the butte is an alluring vista seen trailside. Civilian Conservation Corp worker, L. C. Henley, reportedly fell 600 feet to his death at Lookout Point while hiking alone at night on August 18,1935.

Mile 5.5. Breezy Point, Elevation 4,420 feet (1,347 meters). According to *Arizona Place Names*, the vista was a descriptive name given by Emery and Ellsworth Kolb because the winds were "so strong here that it blows gravel." The U.S. Board of Geographic Names accepted the Kolb brothers' name in 1932.

Mile 5.9. Cathedral Stairs, Elevation 4,422 feet (1,348 meters), Redwall Limestone. Twenty-five switchbacks descend/ascend 400 to 500 vertical feet through the tortuous ramparts of the Redwall Formation beneath Cope Butte. Cathedral is a historic Utah place name used by early visitors, biblical pioneers, and Mormon settlers. Perhaps, it was named by one of John Brown's South Kaibab Trail Mormon crew members in 1924. Sauntering down this rock-strewn trail to the oasis of Hermit Creek on a fine spring day may seem like a stairway to heaven. Get caught at the foot of it on a hot summer day and you'll be faced with a stairway from hell.

<u>Summer Advisory:</u> Don't be caught hiking or crawling up the Cathedral Stairs midday during the summer. If for any reason you've misjudged things, count your blessings and stay near water, Hermit Creek or Santa Maria Springs, until you can get help, or walk out under your own power after the furnace cools.

From the foot of the Cathedral Stairs, the Hermit Trail angles across the Tonto Formation toward the Tonto Trail West Junction beneath the landmark 4,528-foot Cope Butte.

Mile 7. Tonto Trail West Junction, Elevation 3,210 feet (978 meters), Tonto Formation. Turn left (west) at this junction and hike 1.2 miles to Hermit Creek Campground.

Historic Hermit Camp

Not to be confused with Hermit Creek Campground, the Santa Fe Railroad's Hermit Camp was built by Fred Harvey on the hill above the Tonto Trail Junction. Depending on your water supply and your energy level, take time to explore what remains of the once-bustling tourist camp. Between 1912 and 1930, the "luxury" accommodations included eleven framed-canvas, stove-warmed tent cabins and a dining hall that catered to the wants of thirty campers long before "glamping" became fashionable. Described by the park as "the last word in gracious tourism below the rim," guests forked over $18.25 each for chef-cooked meals, a bunk, and the privilege of riding a sweaty mule. The weathered age-old camp relics include a wooden shack, timbers, stone-walled root cellar, stone mule corral, hitching rings, stone foundations, and the rusty pulleys and concrete foundation of the aerial tramway built in 1925–26.

Aerial Tramway

During the fall of 1933, geologists Ian Campbell and John H. Maxson used the now abandoned Hermit Camp as their base camp to study Archean rocks for the Carnegie

Institute. Campbell, a Caltech Professor, offered one of the few eyewitness descriptions of the aerial tramway the pair used before and after their hike down the Hermit Trail. "[We placed] all camp gear in the aerial tram car near Pima Point, rather than on one's own back or the back of a mule, constituted another propitious feature. We hiked down the Hermit Trail and arrived in time to see the cables move and the wheels start turning at the lower terminus. Presently the tram car with its load of food, instruments and other impedimenta, made a perfect landing." Wouldn't you like to have your heavy pack hauled up to the South Rim before heading back up the Cathedral Stairs and Supai Rockslides?

Mile 8.2. Hermit Creek, Elevation 2,900 feet (884 meters), Tapeats Sandstone. Located upstream in the Muav Limestone, Hermit Springs produces an estimated 210 gallons of water a minute. Hermit Creek Campground Zone BM7 offers primitive campsites nestled along the perennial creek and a protective rock overhang some hikers call the "the dormitory." Wooden shack-like composting toilets appointed with solar panels are available. Protect your food from the mice and be careful not to step on the normally timid "Grand Canyon pink" rattlesnakes (*Crotalus oreganus abyssus*).

If you're headed down to the Colorado River, follow Hermit Creek 1.5 miles to the sandy banks of the "Red River." See if you can spot Water Ouzels (*Cinclus mexicanus unicolor*), dark gray American dippers darting back and forth across the creek ahead of you.

Mile 9.7. Colorado River, Elevation 2,400 feet (732 meters), Vishnu Schist, Hermit Rapids, River Mile 95. Hermit Rapids Camp Zone BM8 offers primitive campsites on a wide riverside beach. Hermit Rapids is a roller coaster, wave train that douses thousands of river runners each year. If you're doing a summer hike during peak rafting season, chances are you can enjoy the vicarious thrill of watching screaming passengers whoop and holler through Hermit's collapsing waves. Think about being soaked to the bone with cold Colorado River while humping your load back up the Cathedral Stairs without aerial tram support.

Hermit Trail Loop Hikes/Treks
Boucher, Tonto, Hermit Wilderness Trails
The twenty-one-mile point-to-point route is the shortest, most exciting South Rim-Tonto Trail West trek. From Hermit Creek it's five miles to Boucher Creek. (See page 203 Tonto Trail West.)

Hermit, Tonto, Bright Angel Wilderness-Corridor Trails
The 24.4-mile point-to-point route is a more challenging South Rim- Tonto Trail West trek. From the Hermit-Tonto Trail West junction, it is twelve miles across the Tonto Trail to Indian Garden. (See page 202 Tonto Trail West.)

Note: If you're thinking of looping the Hermit and Boucher Trails you'll probably find it easier and safer to descend the Boucher Trail and climb out the Hermit Trail.

Travel Notes Warning Advisory: In summertime, be OTR at dawn to reach Breezy Point, or better the top of the Cathedral Stairs by mid-morning before, one grizzled Arizona cowboy told me, "it feels like someone turned on the blow torches."

- Primary Access: Hermit Trailhead.
- Elevation: 6,640-feet Hermit Trailhead to 2,400-feet Colorado River.
- Biotic Communities: Ponderosa pine forest, piñon-juniper woodland, Great Basin Desert scrub, and Mojave Desert scrub.
- Total Elevation Loss and Gain: 8,480 feet vertical feet (4,240 feet each way).
- Mileage: 9.5 miles (8.2 miles one way to Hermit Creek; 1.3 miles to the Colorado River.
- Water: Santa María Spring (don't depend on this trickle), Hermit Creek, and Colorado River.
- Cache Points: in seclusion of Dripping Springs Trail junction, top of Cathedral Stairs, and Hermit Camp—depending on hike planned.
- Seasons: Fall through spring. Summer has proven deadly.
- Escape Routes. Hermit Trailhead, Hermit Creek.
- Map: Grand Canyon Quadrangle (7.5 minute).
- Camping, Zone BM7: Designated sites at Hermit Creek, and zone BM8 beach at Hermit Rapids.
- Nearest Supply Points: Grand Canyon Village, Flagstaff, Cameron, and Williams.
- Managing Agency: Grand Canyon National Park.
- Backcountry Information Center: for information call (928) 638–7875.
- Critical Backcountry Updates visit www.nps.gov/grca/planyourvisit/trail-closures.htm.
- NPS Grand Canyon Hiker 24 Hour Emergency Phone Number and Email
  - Phone (928) 638–7805
  - Email: grca_bic@nps.gov (Use this if the phone line is busy)

12

Boucher Trail: Day Hikes and Rim to River

"He put a bell on the mule, and the tinkle could be heard for a great distance. It was an infallible sign of the approach of the Hermit with his prospector's trappings and his white beard and white mustache jogging along on his white mule. The Hermit lived in a white tent and 'told only white lies.'"

—Edwin Corle, 1946
Listen Bright Angel

LANDFORM

Draining the Douglas fir, ponderosa pine, and piñon-juniper forests of the 7,000-foot Coconino Plateau, Hermit Canyon is a deep, headwater chasm that stretches from 6,500-foot Eremita Mesa on the South Rim to Boucher Rapids at Mile 96.5 on the Colorado River. The Boucher Trail traces the western rim of the Hermit Canyon around Yuma Point before switch-backing into Travertine, Boucher, and Topaz Canyons.

HISTORY

A hidden trove of hand-painted Ancestral Puebloan ollas (pots) discovered off the Boucher Trail in 1982—and two small storage granaries—indicate Dripping Springs was a dependable water source for Ancestral Peubloans who traveled to it by way of the Hermit Basin's Waldron Trail, and from Eremita Mesa via what Louis D. Boucher developed into the Silver Bell Trail. Loosely dated from 1000 to 1100, the extraordinary cache of ollas reportedly included a "Black Mesa Black-on-white olla, Deadmans Gray

Running wild down the Boucher Trail.
Copyright © John Annerino Photography.

olla, Medicine Black-on-red seed jar, Tusayan Black-on-red bowl, Tusayan Black-on-red seed jar, and Black Mesa Black-on-white jar." There's little doubt the fleet-footed inner canyon travelers extended their hunting and gathering forays from Drippings Springs three miles north across what became the Boucher Trail to Yuma Point. Beneath this striking landmark, they could also collect seasonal water in the Esplanade Sandstone's ephemeral water pockets.

Silver Bell Trail

Described in the August 1892 edition of *Scientific American* as ". . . intelligent, obliging, and not too talkative . . ." French Canadian Louis de Bouchere migrated from Sherbrooke, Quebec, and came to the Grand Canyon in 1891 to seek his fortune mining "pay dirt." The white bearded prospector registered the "Silver Bell Trail" (Dripping Springs and Boucher Trails) in February 1902. He named the trail after his white mule, Calamity Jane, for the bell he hung around its neck. It was no easy task for Boucher to travel alone from the burgeoning Grand Canyon settlement to the largely trackless Eremita Mesa and trace the ancient passageway down to the cavernous overhang of Dripping Springs. Through grit and tough pick and shovel work, Boucher hand-forged the rugged Silver Bell Trail off the South Rim down what George Wharton James wrote during his journey with Boucher was, "a beautiful wooded canyoncito" [*sic*]. Boucher extended his miner's trail into the pristine depths of Boucher Creek to prospect for copper, but he needed to supplement his meager pickings "wrangling dudes" for fellow trailblazer John Hance on the Bright Angel and Grandview Trails. In spite of the genial social repartee Boucher enjoyed during his guiding trips, he was called "the Hermit" by the Santa Fe Land Development because he lived largely alone in his seasonal camps at Dripping Springs and Boucher Creek. The Hermit's indelible sobriquet stuck, and his "brand" was soon appropriated for architectural designs, rest stops, tourist camps, campgrounds, trails, creeks, springs, river rapids, faults, geological formations, and translated in Spanish to *Eremita* (hermit) *Mesa*.

The rugged 10.8-mile Boucher Trail to the Colorado River requires sound judgment, route finding skills, endurance, and the sure-footedness of a desert bighorn, canyon mule, or sagebrush mustang.

Mile 0. Hermit Trailhead, Elevation 6,640 feet (2,024 meters), Kaibab Limestone, Trailhead View West: Hermit Creek Canyon. Hikers often begin their 2.5-day roundtrip trek on the Boucher Trail by starting at Hermits Rest Trailhead and descending the Hermit Trail 2.7 miles to the Dripping Springs/Boucher Trail Junction.

Old Silver Bell Trail, Off Trail Report. The original, rarely used Silver Bell Trail is marked by the weathered posts of an old corral and a wooden signpost, "Dripping Springs Trail, Hiking Only." The 1.5 mile abandoned road-turned-rocky-trail heads southeast from 6,506-foot Eremita Mesa down the drainage to Eremita Tank and descends 900 vertical feet through the Kaibab Limestone, Toroweap, and Boucher's hand-laid stone staircases through precipitous ledges of Coconino Sandstone to the Dripping Springs alcove.

Directions

From Grand Canyon Village, follow the Waldron Trail driving directions to the turnoff for Horsethief Tank and the Waldron Trail. (See page 120 Waldron Trail). Use your Grand Canyon Quadrangle (7.5 minute) map and orienting skills to hike beyond the metal gate to proceed approximately a half mile west/southwest, and link the following bench marks BM 6457, BM 6372, and BM 6458 approximately 2.5 miles along abandoned roads to the signed trailhead.

Mile 1.5. Waldron Trail Junction, Elevation 5,400 feet (1,646 meters). Supai Formation. Turn Around Point 1. (Use any convenient point on the descent where you feel you, or your children, need to stop and turn around). The two-mile long Waldron Trail also provides access to the Boucher Trail. (See page 120 Waldron Trail).

Prospector Louis D. Boucher atop his white mule, "Calamity Jane," 1910, E. W. Murphy photo, GCNP Museum Collection.

Mile 1.75. Dripping Springs/Hermit Trail Junction, Elevation 5,200 feet (1,585 meters), Supai. Turn left (west) and follow the Drippings Springs Trail 0.7 miles to the Dripping Springs/Boucher Trail Junction.

Mile 2.7. Dripping Springs/Boucher Trail Junction. Elevation 5,250 Feet (1,600 meters), Supai. Turn Around Point 2 (day hike). Turn left (west) and hike 0.4 miles and climb 350 vertical feet to Dripping Springs beneath the large overhang at the foot of Coconino Sandstone.

Dripping Springs

Elevation 5,600 feet, Coconino Sandstone. Trickling down Maidenhair ferns from overhead seeps, Dripping Springs produces an estimated one gallon of water a minute. In Boucher's day, the cool delicious water splashed into a wooden mule trough swimming with goldfish he'd carried in a vial from Kansas City. The sight of goldfish delighted Boucher's guests who bunked at his tourist camp in two canvas-framed tent cabins erected end-to-end. The spacious alcove offered Boucher and his visitors shade in the summer and shelter in the winter. The stove-warmed kitchen was "as neat as wax and quite comfortably arranged," guest Margaret Armstrong wrote after her mule back journey down the Silver Bell Trail with wrangler Bill Hall. She added, "Outside near the spring, was a wooden table, and a long, low coach covered with a gay Navajo blanket." Down slope from the cabin was Boucher's corral, which penned mules, horses, and burros. By all accounts, Boucher's camp was a congenial stop on a rough lonely trail. A 1908 black and white photo shows two smiling pioneer couples embracing in front of Boucher's cook cabin, a romantic setting that undoubtedly inspired the name of Sweetheart Spring.

Sweetheart Spring Off Trail Hiker Report: Within earshot of a silver bell tinkling in Boucher's mule corral, canyoneers discovered the hidden, seldom visited Sweetheart Spring beneath the towering walls of Coconino Sandstone. An historic, hand-laid stone dwelling and hand-carved inscription "Harry Kislingbury [18]89" will also reward keen-eyed canyon sleuths who find the hidden spot.

Mile 2.7. Boucher Trail Junction, Elevation 5,250 Feet (1,600 meters), Esplanade Sandstone. Follow the Boucher Trail north through rockslides and drainages across the spectacularly exposed rim of Esplanade Sandstone to Yuma Point. Not for the faint of heart, the edge-of-the-rim footing and aerial views offer some of the most exciting hiking in the Grand Canyon, but it has proved unnerving and dangerous. While guiding a challenge discovery natural history group across the snow-covered slickrock trail one winter, I turned around to check their progress. I slipped and fell headlong toward a free fall into Hermit Canyon. At the time, I'd carried an old wooden ice axe for hiking canyon trails. Without thinking, I self-arrested and managed to stop in the rocky snow. I crawled on my hands and knees, anchoring the pick with each knee-step until I reached my students standing back from the narrow sandstone catwalk. Shaken by the fall, I mustered on, leading my students cross-country whenever the trail skirted too closely to the abyss's icy precipice.

Mile 5.2. Yuma Point Crossover, Elevation 5,429 feet (655 meters), Esplanade Sandstone. 6,840-foot Yuma Point looms over the Boucher Trail and the landmark 4,514-foot Columbus Point is seen below the trail. Yuma Point was named for the historic Yuma Crossing and was used by Spanish conquistadors, missionary explorers, indigenous *Quechan*, and California 49ers to cross the lower Colorado River. Yuma Point makes a great lunch stop, camping area, cache point, and seasonal water stop. Summer monsoons, winter ice and snow, and spring rain recharge the shallow sandstone depressions and water pockets with sweet water that shimmers in the sunlight. Yuma Point offers what George Wharton James wrote: ". . . forms one of the noblest of all panoramas of the Canyon my eye has ever rested upon."

Supai Descent to Travertine Canyon, 1.5 miles: From Yuma Point, the Boucher Trail circles around the base of the point and traverses straight across the Supai rim until it begins a 1,000 vertical foot descent through breaks, cliffs, and ledges rife with small stones called "ball bearings," loose rocks, and boulders that must be carefully negotiated without slipping and falling, or toppling head over heels with a heavy pack. If need be, take off your pack and carefully scout the perilous breaks and chutes in the Supai cliffs below the 5,400 feet elevation contour. At times this precarious stretch of Boucher's mule trail—reclaimed here and there by nature, rain, and freeze-thaw erosion—has required some hikers who may have been off route to use their hands, feet, and nylon cordage to lower their packs. Take your time—going down you can see the route—and carefully gauge your line of travel into the Redwall Limestone creek bed of Travertine Canyon near the 4,400 foot level. This is no place to twist an ankle. From Travertine Creek, the next 0.75 mile section of trail only climbs 233 feet to reach Whites Butte Pass.

Dragon Corridor

Hikers have complained about the drone of air tour helicopters and fixed wing aircraft flying over Yuma Point disrupting the natural acoustics, song birds, and wilderness values of the Grand Canyon hiking experience. The park pointed out: "This area is directly below the Dragon Corridor; between 8 and 5, the constant drone of sightseeing over flights can be a major distraction." One veteran canyoneer-turned-blogger wrote: "I would be interested in funding an anti-aircraft battery located out on Yuma Point."

Mile 7.6. Whites Butte Pass, Elevation 4,633 feet (1,412 meters), Supai Formation. The saddle between Whites Butte and Cocopah Point makes another good rest stop, cache point, camp, and opportunity to scout the hiker's gap in the Redwall Limestone rim. From the notch on the north side of the pass, the Boucher Trail plummets 1,533 vertical feet in 1.3 miles through the Redwall Limestone, down, down, steep, sharp limestone scree through a narrow, cliff-walled canyon bottoming out on rocky talus slopes leading to the Tonto Trail West Junction. This is no place to be caught in a "gulley washer," 'er flashflood. Some hikers have called this Redwall stretch "brutal." Depending on your level of fitness, weight carried, and the season, that description can be used to describe any rim-to-river trail.

<u>Whites Butte, (once called Bunker Hill Monument)</u>
A short hike and a Third to Fourth Class scramble from Whites Butte Pass leads up to the 4,850 foot summit of the Supai butte named for horse thief James White. One of the Grand Canyon's most colorful and controversial characters, White claimed to have survived running the wild Colorado River on a hastily made log raft on September 7,1867. If White's tale was true—Congress concurred it was—he would have been the first to navigate the Colorado River two years before Major John Wesley Powell's "maiden voyage" down the Colorado River in 1869.

<u>Cocopah Point</u>
The 6,620-foot Point was named for the Cocopah, or *Cocopá*, who live along the lower Colorado River in Arizona and Sonora, Mexico. They call themselves *Xawill kwñcha-waay*, meaning "Those Who Live on the River," and they plied the fickle Colorado River currents and the Sea of Cortés' deadly tidal bores in flimsy reed rafts for hundreds of years before Spanish conquistador Hernado de Alarcón first made contact with them in 1540. During the Kolb brothers' epic Colorado River journey, described in their book *Through the Grand Canyon from Wyoming to Mexico*, Emery boated alone all the way to tidewater in the Sea of Cortés circa May 31, 1913. In the book, Emery briefly mentioned his impressions of the indigenous river runners: "Here too was the track of a barefooted Cocopah, a tribe noted for its men of gigantic build . . . These Indians have lived in these mud bottoms so long, crossing the streams on rafts made of bundles of tules . . ."

Mile 8.9. Tonto Trail West Junction, Elevation 3,100 feet (945 meters), Tonto Formation. From the Tonto Trail Junction, the Boucher Trail descends into Boucher Creek.

Mile 9.3. Boucher Creek, Elevation 2,760 feet (841 meters). To reach the Colorado River, follow Boucher Creek downstream to the confluence of Topaz Creek, which enters from the left (southwest).

Boucher Camp

Scout around a bit and you'll see the stone walls of Boucher's Cabin and his copper vein prospects dug and built within sight and sound of melodious Boucher

Creek. During his nineteenth-century pack trip with Boucher, George Wharton James counted seventy-five trees Boucher had planted in his orchard that bore ". . . oranges, figs, peaches, pears, apricots, apples, nectarines, and pomegranates," and a garden flush with ". . . melons, cantaloupes, beets, onions, tomatoes, chili, carrots, cucumbers, parsnips." Boucher supplemented his cornucopia of fresh fruit and vegetables with mule deer and desert bighorn sheep he hunted near Dripping Springs, perhaps with a lever-action carbine reminiscent of the Winchester Model 1873 .44–40 caliber reportedly given to a Sioux chief that was inscribed on the left plate, "Chief Spotted Tail/from/Louis Boucher." Boucher caught fish from the Colorado River 1.5 miles below his small stone cabin that James also described: "As to fishing, Louis Boucher caught and took to El Tovar a silver salmon, two feet eight inches in length, sixteen inches in circumference, and weighing eleven and a half pounds," (Colorado pikeminnow, *Ptychocheilus lucius*, now extirpated from the Grand Canyon). Sadly, Boucher's era came to an end in 1909 when the Santa Fe Railroad and Fred Harvey Company bought out his holdings. The tinkle from Calamity Jane's silver bell fell silent, and the little known, unassuming prospector disappeared from the Grand Canyon as quietly and mysteriously as he first appeared from his travels among the Oglala Sioux. One of the lasting impressions of the "elaborately courteous" trail blazer, entrepreneur, and some inferred a gun runner for the Oglala Sioux, is a telling black and white photo of Boucher sporting a neatly-trimmed white beard and moustache, proudly sitting in the saddle atop his white mule, a carbine cradled upside down in a leather rifle scabbard tucked beneath his right leg and a long lariat.

Mile 9.7. Topaz Canyon, Turn right (northeast) at the confluence of Topaz Creek and continue boulder dancing down Boucher Creek to the Colorado River. Topaz Canyon takes its name from semi-precious stones and the series of Colorado River Rapids called "The Gems." Beginning three miles below Boucher Creek, they are Agate, Sapphire, Turquoise, Emerald, and Ruby Rapids.

Mile 10.8. Colorado River, Elevation 2,325 feet (709 meters), Vishnu Schist, Boucher Rapids, River Mile 96.5. End of the trail.

Boucher Trail Loop Hikes/Treks
Boucher, Tonto Trail West, Hermit Wilderness Trails
The twenty-one-mile point-to-point route is the shortest, most exciting South Rim-West Tonto trek. From Boucher Creek it's five miles to Hermit Creek. (See page 203 Tonto Trail West.)

Boucher, Tonto Trail West, South Bass Wilderness Trails

The forty-five-mile point-to-point route is long, remote, and requires situational awareness and careful route planning from one perennial and seasonal water source to the next.

Travel Notes

- Warning Advisory: During summertime, be OTR to leave Boucher Creek at dawn to reach Yuma Point before midmorning.
- Primary Access: Hermit Trailhead; secondary access Waldron Trailhead; primitive access Silver Bell Trailhead.
- Elevation: 6,640-feet Hermits Rest to 2,325-feet Colorado River.
- Biotic Communities: Ponderosa pine forest, pinon-jumper woodland, Great Basin Desert scrub, and Mojave Desert scrub.
- Total Elevation Loss and Gain: 8,630 feet (4,315 vertical each way).
- Mileage: 21.6 miles (9.3 miles one way to Boucher Creek; 10.8 miles one way to the Colorado River.
- Water: Dripping Springs (sporadic), Yuma Point water pockets (seasonal) Boucher Creek, Colorado River.
- Cache Points: Dripping Springs area, Yuma Point, and Whites Butte Pass.
- Escape Routes: Hermit Trailhead.
- Seasons: Spring and fall. Winter can be treacherous along the exposed sections of Supai and summers can be unkind.
- Map: Grand Canyon Quadrangle (7.5 minute).
- Camping: Zone BN9: At-large low impact camping on Yuma Point Crossover, Whites Butte Pass, Boucher Creek, and Colorado River.
- Nearest Supply Points: Grand Canyon Village, Flagstaff, Cameron, and Williams.
- Managing Agency: Grand Canyon National Park
- Backcountry Information Center: for information call (928) 638–7875.
- Critical Backcountry Updates visit www.nps.gov/grca/planyourvisit/trail-closures.htm.
- NPS Grand Canyon Hiker 24 Hour Emergency Phone Number and Email.
  - Phone (928) 638–7805
  - Email: grca_bic@nps.gov (Use this if the phone line is busy)

Thilwisa, "Captain Burro," ca. 1900, Fredrick H. Maude hand-colored lantern slide, GCNP Museum Collection

13

South Bass Trail: Day Hikes and Rim to River

"Billy, you give me a sack of flour and half of beef, and I show you my spring, and you can always use it for yourself and your horses."

— *Thilwisa*, "Captain Burro," Havasupai, 1898, to his friend William Wallace Bass

LANDFORM

Stretching from an ancient rimtop lookout at the remote BM 6,646 point on the western South Rim, the primitive trail traces breaks in the stair-step cliffs of the Kaibab Limestone, Toroweap Formation, and Coconino Sandstone and crosses a north-trending Esplanade Sandstone bench before descending the Redwall Limestone into Bass Canyon at its confluence with the Colorado River at Mile 107.5.

HISTORY

The crumbling remains of a timber beam–roofed, masonry cliff dwelling and a well-preserved storage granary perched atop the Coconino Sandstone mark the rugged, relatively short prehistoric route that was used by Ancestral Puebloans, or perhaps earlier by Archaic peoples, to travel between the plateau and the inner canyon seep at Mystic Spring. In the shadow of Mount Huethawali, the freshet spring and the Esplanade Sandstone's ephemeral water pockets supported a small settlement of canyon dwellers, and later the Havasupai, who lived in wickiup-type dwellings, cached food, seeds, and water in granaries, and pit-roasted agave. From this seasonal camp, it was easy to follow the age-old, rim-to-river-to-rim route down Bass Canyon to ford the Colorado River on driftwood logs or rafts and use the well-established route up Shinumo Creek—still marked by cliff-side storage granaries—to reach seasonal hunting and gathering grounds in the sub-alpine forests on the North Rim and Powell Plateau.

Mystic Spring Trail

The Ancestral Puebloan route dated 600 was later used by the Havasupai to reach sacred ground and seasonal camps encircling *Huethawali*, "White Rock Mountain." In 1883 the Havasupai guided former Erie Railroad train conductor William Wallace Bass from Williams, Arizona, to the South Rim near 6,678-foot Havasupai Point. One look into the Grand Canyon, and there was no turning back for the homesteader, prospector, road builder, entrepreneur, and trailblazer who started building the trail in 1884. Few other canyon visionaries personally did more to develop the area, and establish long-lasting, friendly relations with the Havasupai, than Bass. He came out West for his health, later married one of his guests, music teacher Ada Diefendorf, raised four children—the first family on the South Rim—and didn't succumb to ill health until he was eighty-four. During his forty years at the canyon, the tireless Bass delivered mail and medicine from Grand Canyon Village to Havasupai, traveled to Washington, D.C., to drum up congressional support to build the first school in Havasupai, prospected more than twenty-five mining claims for gold, copper, and asbestos, led the first cross-canyon tourist treks, and built fifty miles of rugged canyon trails. Among those was the Mystic Spring Trail Bass developed with the help of two Havasupai men. The trio and others extended the trail down to the Colorado River at Bass Rapids in 1891, a year before Bass lead the first tourists to Mystic Spring. Bass's trail later became popularly known as the South Bass Trail.

Driving Directions

To reach the South Bass Trailhead, use your South Kaibab National Forest map and drive thirty-one miles west via the Rowe Well Road, Forest Road 328, and Pasture Wash Road, where you'll stop at the Havasupai Indian Reservation ranger station to pay a $25 entrance fee. Pasture Wash, *Ma ten yo'a*, is a cultural landscape and winter camp of the Havasupai.

The rugged and remote 7.8 South Bass Trail to the Colorado River requires sound judgment, route finding skills, endurance, and mental awareness—you're hiking far from the nearest help if anything goes awry.

Bass Camp Stone Ruins

Between 1885 and 1923, Bass Camp offered rustic accommodations, incomparable views, and canyon trail adventures for an estimated 3,000 to 5,000 visitors who traveled by horse, buckboard, and stage coach on Bass's dusty seventy-three-mile stage road from Ashfork, Arizona, to stay overnight on the South Rim. Many took Bass's guided day and overnight trips down the Mystic Spring Trail to visit what was then a popular inner canyon spring and overnight camp. Today, little remains of the once bustling Bass Camp on the rim that included a main building with a kitchen, dining room, and bedrooms for the lucky few. They may have been reserved for registered guests like painter Thomas Moran, conservationist John Muir, and novelist Zane Grey. Everyone else ponied up $2.50 a night to bed down in canvas-framed tent houses and tents not far from the wranglers' bunkhouse, tack room, and hitching posts. Bass also built a wooden hunting cabin near 6,678-foot Havasupai Point for guests and Havasupai guide Chickapanagi who hunted mule deer with Bass on the North Rim. The stone remnants of this bygone era at the head of the South Bass Trail is now part of the Bass Camp and Trails Historic District.

Mile 0. South Bass Trailhead, Elevation 6,646 feet (2,026 meters), Kaibab Limestone, Trailhead View North: 6,281-foot Mount Huethawali. The rocky, serpentine trail descends the Kaibab Limestone and Toroweap Formation, crosses a dry creek, and switchbacks through the Coconino Sandstone in and out of a Garnet Canyon tributary drainage en route to the Esplanade Trail Junction. Near the top of the Coconino, look for the Ancestral Puebloan cliff dwelling and storage granary.

Bass Camp Darkroom

As you start the descent, keep your eyes peeled for the historic easy-to-miss masonry darkroom the enterprising Bass built between ledges near the top of the trail. Many noted landscape and cultural photographers rode horses or burros down the South Bass Trail to photograph canyon vistas from Darwin Plateau, Spencer Terrace, and Huxley Terrace. Among the lens men who used the crude stone shelter to process their stereoscopes and large format, black and white images were Frederick H. Maude, known for photographing the Hopi Snake Dance and the Grand Canyon region; Henry G. Peabody, who was a National Park Service Eminent Photographer; John R. Putnam and Carlton Valentine, who were based at the South Rim and contributed to the Fred Harvey Collection; and, of course, George Wharton James, who's still well known among canyon aficionados, researchers, and canyoneers for his Grand Canyon and Painted Desert books.

Mile 1.45. Esplanade Trail Junction, Elevation 5,400 feet (1,646 meters), Esplanade Sandstone. Turn Around Point 1. (Use any convenient point on the descent where you feel you, or your children, need to stop and turn around). Continue straight (north) across the Esplanade. The left (west) fork follows the narrow, cliff-hugging Apache Trail eighteen miles to 6,322-foot Apache Point. (See page 207 Apache Trail.) Some canyoneers use the Apache Trail to gain access to the upper route to Royal Arch 12.6 miles distant.

Mile 2. Garnet Canyon/Bass Canyon Divide, Elevation 5,300 feet (1,615 meters), Esplanade Sandstone. Turn Around Point 2 (day hike). On your left (west) Garnet Canyon drains into the Colorado River at Mile 114.5. To your right (east) Bass Canyon drains into the Colorado River and Bass Rapids at Mile 107.5. Turn Around Point 2 (day hike).

Note: Few people drive thirty-one miles across the Coconino Plateau to day hike the South Bass Trail. Those who do are often headed to search for Mystic Spring or climb Mount Huethawali.

Mile 2.5. Bass Canyon Descent. Elevation 5,371 feet (1,637 meters), Supai. Turn Around Point 3 (day hike). This is a good spot to cache food and water. From BM 5371 marked on your Havasupai Point Quadrangle (7.5 minute) map, the trail continues north a short distance through the Supai cliffs down the southeast fork of Bass Canyon, what used to be called Trail Canyon. The trail doubles back south into the head of Bass Canyon and tumbles down a narrow cliff-walled break in the Redwall Limestone into the creek bed where it turns northeast. The cairned route and trail weave in and out of the creek bed on the east side en route to Bedrock Tanks and the West Tonto Trail Junction. Compared to other Southwest water pockets, potholes and, on the border, *tinajas* (rain catchments), Bedrock Tank's unique appearance stands out. The deep, white-rimmed waterhole has been eroded, perhaps enlarged by Ancestral Puebloans, in black Hakatai Shale. The seasonal pothole and others en route to the Colorado River were so reliable during spring snowmelt and summer monsoons Bass built Rock Camp beneath an overhang a mile up from the Colorado River.

Mount Huethawali, "White Rock Mountain"

Sometime in August 1898, Bill Bass guided George Wharton James up the mythical peak, and made what by all published accounts was the first recorded ascent of the 6,281-foot summit. James also called it Mount Observation. White Rock Mountain was undoubtedly first climbed by the Havasupai for its spiritual significance, and perhaps earlier by Ancestral Puebloans, for the extraordinary view the aerie would have afforded them, as well. During one of his many trips to the area, James often retreated to his cave office to work on his first canyon book, *In and Around the Grand Canyon*. An 1898-era black and white photo shows the bearded author sitting at a manuscript-cluttered wooden desk. From his "Author Amphitheater," James wrote the inspiring panorama he gazed upon included Mystic Spring Plateau, Powell Arch, and Mount Huethawali, a siren that may have beckoned the intrepid canyon explorer to climb it.

Directions

From the Bass Canyon Descent, marked by BM 5371 on your topo map, hike west cross-country over the Darwin Plateau along the south side of Mount Huethawali to scramble up a Third Class route that ascends the steep talus, Coconino Sandstone, and Toroweap Formation. Note: When you're walking cross-country, stay on the slick rock sandstone. "Don't Bust the Crust" by walking on fragile cryptobiotic soil that grows in Esplanade Sandstone depressions. The living soil takes fifty to 250 years to recover from a single footprint.

Mystic Spring, the Spring Unseen

Those lucky enough to visit the secret spring were guided there by the Havasupai's ancestral knowledge. After failed attempts to locate it, William Wallace Bass traded a sack of flour and a half-side of beef to his Havasupai friend *Thilwisa*, "Captain Burro," to show him the spring. In turn, George Wharton James and visiting tourists were guided there by Bass. And after five frustrating attempts to locate the peek-a-boo rock features that shielded the spring, one of the Canyon's renowned hikers needed James's historic photographs to successfully locate it. In the 1940 book, *Arizona, The Grand Canyon State*, an unaccredited author working for the WPA Writer's Project of America wrote ". . . the springs are revered by the Havasupai." Vital to the Havasupai whose spiritual connection to the spring extended to Mount Huethawali, Mystic Spring had curative powers and was said to ooze out of solid rock, then disappear and reappear without explanation. The mysterious spring discharged enough water for Bass to quench the thirst of guides, wranglers, horses, and burros, and an estimated 1,000 or more tourists who visited the Mount Huethawali area between 1885 and 1923. Mystic Spring reportedly dried up three months before the great San Francisco earthquake when a magnitude 6.2 earthquake rocked Flagstaff, Arizona, on January 25, 1906, and reverberated through parts of the Grand Canyon. You'll need to use your own canyon sleuthing skills to locate the dry seeps near curious rocks.

Directions

From the Bass Canyon Descent, marked by BM 5371 on your topo map, hike north across the Darwin Plateau and circle around the north side of Mount Huethawali to start your search. Good luck.

Conquistador Mystery Trail

Assuming you locate the Mystic Spring X that no longer appears on any maps, the real unsolved mystery in the vicinity is the Spanish inscription, *Monte Video*. Loosely translated, it means "Mountain View." Some believe the inscription dates back to sixteenth-century conquistador Francisco Vásquez de Coronado, who ordered García López de Cárdenas and twelve men to find the "big river." Obliging the Spaniards, the Hopi reportedly guided Cárdenas and his men to the South Rim in September 1540. Many historians concurred the expedition's "first view" of the Colorado River was located between the South Rim's Desert View and Moran Point because the area fit the post expedition chronicler's vague description, [it was] ". . . elevated and full of low twisted pines, very cold, and lying open to the north." George Wharton James, a former Methodist minister, contested the canyon gospel and wrote the Hopi "had no use for the Spaniards," and led them on futile twenty day trek west along Hopi trails "over which they habitually traveled, which brought them to *Hue-tha-wa-li,* the White Rock Mountain—opposite Bass Camp,—and on to the Havasupai Villages." A geologist working in the area during the 1990s located the captivating *Monte Video* inscription. It measured thirty-five inches long, four inches wide, and ¼-inch deep. Based on meticulous research, since debunked by Grand Canyon pundits, the professor compared the stylistic calligraphy with sixteenth-century Spanish documents, studied historic trails, and surmised the inscription marked the vista where the Spaniards first viewed the Colorado River. It also fit the chronicler's description. Moreover, he suggested the Hopi would have diverted the expedition away from Desert View where hidden trails lead to their sacred salt mines and *Sípàapuni,* the "hatchway where the Hopi emerged to the Fourth world." Imagine, then, three trail weary Spaniards sitting on the edge of the rim rock, gazing down far below at the *Río del Tizón,* "Firebrand River," they had failed to reach after three days. Nothing to show for the pitiless journey through the arid canyon lands, one man decided to leave his mark. Unsheathing his dagger or rapier, he carefully incised rectilinear letters in the soft stone with the pointed steel blade. Occasionally, he looked up across the canyon at the looming 7,661-foot Powell Plateau, which may have resembled Madrid, Spain's, 11,411-foot Sierra Nevada in the Castilian's eyes, then he continued carving *Monte Video.* Or was it, as pundits concluded, the handiwork of one of Bass's clients? They didn't suggest who. Was there a Spanish-speaking furrier and master calligrapher, or a headstone engraver among his tourists who'd grown weary of chiseling *Que en paz descanse,* "Rest in Peace," on his countryman's tombstones who'd lugged along his hammer and chisel on vacation, and described his own impression of the extraordinary view?

Mile 5.9. Tonto Trail West Junction, Elevation 3,200 feet (975 meters), Tonto Formation. Go straight. The left fork is the Tonto Trail West that leads 11.6 miles to Garnet Canyon where it officially dead ends 267 feet above the Colorado River at Mile 114.5. From the dead end switchbacks, a wild cat trail follows the left bank of the Colorado River. (See page 202 Tonto Trail West).

Mile 6. South Bass/Tonto Trail West Junction East, Elevation 3,150 feet (960 meters), Tonto Formation. Take the left fork (west) and continue hiking down Bass

Canyon toward the geological landmark called the Wheeler Fold. The right (east) fork is the Tonto Trail West that leads forty-five miles east to Boucher Creek. (See page 133 Tonto Trail West.)

Mile 6.8. Rock Camp, Elevation 2,837 feet (865 meters), Bass Limestone. Marked by the word "Spring" opposite BM 2837 on your topo map, Rock Camp is tucked beneath a shaded overhang near a series of seasonal potholes. Bass and his family camped here during the winter to escape the cold and snow at Bass Camp. His cowboy guide Bert Lauzon used the sheltered alcove as a rest stop and camp for guests and as storage cache for provisions and mining equipment.)

Mile 7.8. Colorado River, Elevation 2,250 feet (686 meters), Vishnu Schist, Bass Rapids and Beach, River Mile 107.5. End of the trail. On your way down to Bass Beach skirt around the pour off on the left (west) side of the canyon, and look for the steel hull of the Ross Wheeler, a looted artifact abandoned by river runners in 1915. When you get back home, try asking your sweetheart if they can do a little three-day errand and load up the packhorse or burro with dirty laundry, ride it down the trail you'd just hiked out, and do the family wash in the muddy Colorado River . . . That's what I thought. But that's exactly what Ada Bass did when Bass was away prospecting, trail building, gallivanting with important guests, or engineering his cable car across the Colorado River to reach the North Bass Trail. (See page 24 North Bass Trail.)

Additional Considerations:
Reaching the Remote Trailhead

Before driving out to the trailhead, inquire about current road conditions at the Back-country Information Center. High-clearance 4WD vehicles are recommended. Order your South Kaibab National Forest map beforehand by visiting www.fs.usda.gov/main/kaibab/maps-pubs.

Rim-to-River-to-Rim

If you're planning a rim-to-rim hike consider hiking down the North Bass Trail and out the South Bass Trail. If you haven't hiked the North Bass Trail before you may find it easier to come down—and stay oriented—on the rugged and elusive trail. Next to the Nankoweap Trail, it is the most difficult rim-to-river trail or route described in this guide. (See page 157.)

River Crossing

Seasoned canyoneers commonly cross the slow water between Bass Rapids and Shinumo Rapids without incident. But this is a serious, personal safety issue you should strongly consider before embarking on a rim-to-rim hike via the Bass Trails in either direction. (See page 57 River Crossings.)

Wilderness Trail Loop and Trek

The forty-five-mile Boucher, Tonto, and South Bass trail loop can also be hiked west to east, using the South Bass Trail as the first leg. Because of the South Bass Trailhead's remote location and unpredictable road conditions, you may find it safer to descend the South Bass Trail, cross the Tonto Plateau, then hike out the more accessible Boucher Trail or Hermit Trail to Hermits Rest. (See page 133 Tonto Trail West.)

Travel Notes

- Warning Advisory: During summertime, it's imperative you leave your Colorado River camp at dawn to hike up Bass Canyon in order to reach the Esplanade Sandstone before the morning heat smothers the landscape.
- Primary Access: South Bass Trailhead.
- Elevation: 6,646-feet South Bass Trailhead to 2,250-feet Colorado River.
- Biotic Communities: Ponderosa pine, piñon-jumper woodland, Great Basin Desert scrub, and Mojave Desert scrub.
- Total Elevation Loss and Gain: 8,792 feet (4,396 vertical feet each way).
- Mileage: 15.6 miles (7.8 miles one way to the Colorado River).
- Water: Esplanade Sandstone ephemeral water pockets (seasonal), Bedrock Tanks (seasonal), and the Colorado River.
- Cache Points: Esplanade Sandstone, Bass Canyon, and Tonto Plateau.
- Escape Routes: South Bass Trailhead, or Colorado River.
- Seasons: Spring and fall. Summertime it's hot and there are no perennial water sources between the trailhead and the Colorado River. Wintertime and summer monsoon weather can make the access road impassable.
- Map: Havasupai Point Quadrangle (7.5 minute) and South Kaibab National Forest.
- Camping. Zone BQ9: At-large, low-impact camping on the Esplanade Sandstone, Tonto Formation, and Bass Beach on the Colorado River.
- Nearest Supply Points: Grand Canyon Village, Williams, and Flagstaff, Arizona.
- Managing Agency: Grand Canyon National Park.
- Backcountry Information Center: for information call (928) 638–7875.
- Critical Backcountry Updates visit www.nps.gov/grca/planyourvisit/trail-closures. htm.
- NPS Grand Canyon Hiker 24 Hour Emergency Phone Number and Email

- Phone (928) 638–7805
- Email: grca_bic@nps.gov (Use this if the phone line is busy)

Ancestral Puebloan Tusayan black on red bowl, 1050–1150 AD, GCNP Museum Collection.

14

Grandview Trail: Day Hikes, Rim to Mesa, and Beyond

"A man on foot cannot walk down without digging his heels deep into the loose earth and steadying himself by clinging to the rocky walls; and to that wall all timid ones are glued by the horror that rises from the fathomless depths into which a false step, or the slipping of rock might drop the trembling traveler."

—Elias Burton Holmes, 1901
"The Grand View Trail"

LANDFORM

From the east-facing cliffs and amphitheaters of 7,410-foot Grandview Point's Kaibab, Toroweap, and Coconino formations, 5,246-foot Horseshoe Mesa thrusts two narrow, pincer-shaped arms into the canyon 1,300 feet above the Tonto Platform. The scorpion-shaped limestone terrace is drained by the deep Colorado River tributaries of Hance Creek on the east and Cottonwood Creek on the west.

HISTORY

Long before Peter D. Berry forged a new trail along the precipitous Ancestral Puebloan foot path and discovered an oval, cradleboard-sized water olla in a remote prehistoric cave, the Hopi traveled a hundred miles across the Painted Desert to Horseshoe Mesa to gather *saqwa*, copper ore (blue azurite and green malachite). The colorful stones were ground, mixed with corn meal and water, and used for ceremonial face and body paint and sacred prayer sticks called *paahos*. They reverently daubed the *paahos* with yucca fiber brushes and placed them as offerings at trail shrines, sacred mountains and springs, and kiva altars. Imagine the long journey on foot the Hopi once made from their distant mesa pueblos in quest of the hallowed pigment in the depths of what they, the Hopituh Shi-nu-mu, "The Peaceful People," revered as Öngtupqa, "Salt Canyon." Grandview Point, *Wikatata*, is also a sacred cultural landscape for the Havasupai and their "Origin Tale."

Grandview Trail

Hailing from the mining boomtowns and disease-laden tunnels of Colorado's "Silver Rush," Peter D. Berry moved to Flagstaff, Arizona, and opened the San Juan Saloon in 1883. His eye still on the prize of finding the mother lode, Berry started prospecting in the Grand Canyon with brothers Ralph and Niles Cameron and filed mining claims on Horseshoe Mesa. One included the Last Chance Mine, a name that reflected the "boom or bust-fever" that drove many canyon prospectors. Before long, the trio found color and hit "pay dirt." When they did, Berry started rebuilding the old trail with hand-laid native cobblestones in the blistering heat of June 1892 and drove the first pack strings 3.5 miles up the icy, snow-bound trail in February 1893. Loaded down with 200 pounds each, eight to ten mules per pack train hauled the rich copper ore out to Grandview Point on a daily basis. But the tough canyon mules were no match for the 600-pound copper "nugget" that was discovered and winched out of the mine. In a plan that would have tested the mythical strength of Paul Bunyon and his Blue Ox, six men were faced with the Sisyphean task of lugging the "precious gem" out of the canyon in 1893. Using cables, and block and tackle, they harnessed and hauled the unwieldy boulder inch-by-inch over the raspy stones and trail timbers for six grueling days until they'd managed to move it 2,500 tortuous feet up to Grandview Point. Think about that when you carry your pack back up to the South Rim. The copper stone was transported by rail to the Chicago Field Museum, assayed at 70 percent copper carbonate, awarded top honors, and was acquired by the museum for $600 ($1 a pound), $16,300.00 by today's estimates. As rich as the Last Chance Mine's ore was worth, it wasn't Berry's "pot of gold at the end of the rainbow." It was a money pit in a deep hole in the middle of the Grand Canyon. Berry, like other canyon prospectors, discovered tourism. He and his wife, Martha, built a large multistory log lodge called the Grandview Hotel and did a booming business until the Santa Fe Railroad realigned its track to service the Grand Canyon Village area to the west. The prospector, saloon keeper, miner, hotelier, and canyon trailblazer sold out his interests to the Canyon Copper Company, which was later acquired by American newspaper publisher and politician William Randolph Hearst. At the end of his trail, Berry was buried alongside Martha in the Grand Canyon Pioneer Cemetery among many other canyon legends.

Directions

From Grand Canyon Village drive twelve miles east on Desert View Drive to Grandview Point and the trailhead.

The rugged, narrow three- to 11.4-mile long Grandview Trail requires sure-footedness and calm nerves to traverse dangerously exposed sections of the Kaibab Limestone, Toroweap Formation, Coconino Sandstone, and Redwall Limestone—and endurance if you're headed all the way to the Colorado River.

Mile 0. Grandview Trailhead, Elevation 7,410 feet (2,258.5 meters), Kaibab Limestone, Trailhead View North: 5,246-foot Horseshoe Mesa. The frequently exposed, rocky and rickety, juniper log gangways—clinging to steel roads bored into the cliff face, and shored up with riprap—can be unnerving for hikers balancing down the 45-degree gangways through the Kaibab Limestone and Toroweap Formation.

Mile 1.1. Coconino Saddle, Elevation 6,235 feet (1,900 meters), Coconino Sandstone. Turn Around Point 1. (Use any convenient point on the descent where you feel you, or your children, need to stop and turn around). Carefully descend the steep cobblestone and interlaid slab switchbacks, a testament to Berry's handiwork that has endured for over a century.

Mile 3. Horseshoe Mesa, Elevation 4,900 feet (1,493 meters), Supai Group and Redwall Limestone. Turn Around Point 2 (day hike). There is no shade, shelter, or water. Three small group campsites, one large group site, and two open air outhouses are available in Zone BF5. The Last Chance Mine's six-foot high, stone-laid-in-adobe cook house walls, crumbling fireplace, and chimney are relics of the small mining camp that included bunkhouse shanties (six beds to a room), mule corral, and tunnels and shafts operated by Canyon Copper Company.

From this Horseshoe Mesa trail crossroads, there is a spider web of spur trails, wilderness trails, and routes that offer memorable day hikes and challenging, overnight rim-to-river routes.

Grandview Trail

Horseback tourists, photographers, and travel writers visiting the Last Chance Mine sometimes ventured north across Horseshoe Mesa with guides who led them to Cave of the Domes or down the Tonto Trail where they dismounted to rest and picnic. Some continued on foot and followed the Old Grandview Trail, scrambling down cliffs and steep ravines to the Colorado River. It's an arduous trek along an elusive route that still tests the nerves and skills of canyoneers.

Cave of the Domes

From the Last Chance Mine, the Grandview Trail leads a half-mile north and contours along the west side of 5,246-foot Horseshoe Mesa Butte toward the western arm of the mesa. A spur trail branches off the Grandview Trail and leads west into a drainage through a break in the Redwall Limestone. A short exposed path follows a narrow ledge to two cave openings. (The first cave is closed due to the White Nose Syndrome that infects bats). Head to the second cave opening nearby, and maneuver through the crawl space that enters the dry, dusty cave. When you stand up, focus your headlamp overhead and you'll see a conical ceiling scrawled with the signatures of 1900s New York and San Francisco tourists. In the hundred-foot-long solution cavern beyond, you can marvel at columns, calcareous curtains, stalactites, and stalagmites. Some of the latter were said to have walked out of here and mysteriously showed up at the Grandview Hotel among its array of deer hides, Navajo blankets, Hopi art, and Ancestral Puebloan ollas. Cave of the Domes was reportedly first discovered in 1897 by Joseph Gildner, the camp cook for Canyon Copper Company. It's one of 335 recorded caves of the Grand Canyon's estimated 1,000 subterranean chambers. Bring three sources of light and don't touch the fragile formations.

Grandview Trail, Tonto Trail East

From the Last Chance Mine, you can also hike the Grandview Trail north to the Tonto Trail East via the same trail that leads to the Cave of the Domes spur trail. From the Last Chance Mine, hike approximately one mile north, contour west of Horseshoe Mesa Butte, and follow the trail toward the unnamed 4,800-foot saddle beneath point 4923 on your Cape Royal Quadrangle (7.5 minute) map. A shade south of the saddle, the Grandview Trail heads northeast into a drainage and switchbacks 900 vertical feet down to the creek bed at the 3,900 feet Tonto East Trail Junction. Turn right (east) and it's 1.5 miles to Miners (Page) Spring. Turn left (west) and it's 1.5 miles to Cottonwood Creek.

Old Grandview Trail (route), Off Trail Canyoneeers Report

To reach the start of what's still called the Old Grandview Trail, turn left (west) on the Tonto Trail East and hike 1.5 miles west to Cottonwood Creek. From Cottonwood Creek, trace the Tonto Trail a mile or more to the most prominent east-trending cliff point between Cottonwood Creek and Grapevine Creek. A cross-country route leads north from the Tonto Trail to a large cairn that marks the descent route of Old Grandview Trail.

Caution: for Serious Canyoneers Only. Make sure you eyeball a safe passage down the incredibly steep route through the Tapeats Sandstone and the Vishnu Schist cliffs and ravines piece-by-piece to the river. The route is occasionally marked by the old trail, cairns, and faint bighorn sheep trails. Photographer and travelogue writer Burton Holmes wrote: "[Berry] built the Grand View Trail and made it possible for travelers to reach the river at a point where there is no chance of anti-climax, for this trail winds down into the depths of the black archean inner cañon where we may see the river slowly carving out its pathway in the resistant but never vanquished granite." Holmes illustrated his adventure with the black and white photo, "At the Foot of the Grand View Trail," showing two party members standing in a massive boulder slide on the south bank of the Colorado River.

Note: The following trail and route descriptions below Horseshoe Mesa are divided into East Horseshoe Mesa Trail (Miners (Page) Spring), and West East Horseshoe Mesa Trail (Cottonwood Creek).

East Horseshoe Mesa Trail

Mile 3. East Horseshoe Mesa (Miners (Page) Spring) Trail junction. Elevation 4,860 feet (1,481 meters), Redwall Limestone. From the Last Chance Mine area, the East Horseshoe Mesa Trail leads 0.7 miles to Miners (Page) Spring. Caution. The "trail" through the Redwall is steep, narrow, and exposed. A misstep with a heavy pack along some stretches would be fatal.

Mile 3.7, from the Grandview Trailhead. Miners (Page) Spring, Elevation 4,400 feet (1,341 meters), Redwall Limestone. A short spur trail leads to the perennial, fern-draped seeps that drip from an overhang into a welcome pool of refreshing water. Miners (Page) Spring is also used by hikers replenishing their water supply for camping overnight atop Horseshoe Mesa and for hiking back out to the South Rim.

Mile 4.8, from the trailhead. Tonto Trail East/East Horseshoe Mesa Trail junction, Elevation 3,760 feet (1,146 meters), Tonto Formation. Turn right (north, then southeast), and its 0.8 miles to Hance Creek. Turn left (north) and the Tonto Trail East leads three miles west around Horseshoe Mesa to the Cottonwood Creek.

Mile 5.6, from the Trailhead. Hance Creek/Tonto Trail East, Elevation 3,700 feet (1146 meters). At-large, low-impact camping and perennial water in Hance Creek in Zone BE9. From Hance Creek, the 2.8-mile Tonto Trail East traverses beneath the looming Redwall Limestone prow of 4,961-foot Ayer Point, switchbacks into Mineral Canyon and contours its east slopes before turning east to Hance Rapids. Hiking this stretch in either direction during warm spring or fall days can make for a long slog across hot stones to reach water and shade.

Ayers Point, Pioneer Ascent

The remote 4,961-foot Ayer Point was named after author Emma Burbank Ayer ". . . the first white woman who is known to have made the descent to the river at this point [Hance Rapids]." Incredibly, the difficult to reach canyon vista was reportedly climbed by two of John Hance's tourists on August 21,1895. In Hance's guest book, the tough city slickers matter-of-factly noted their unprecedented ascent:

> We made this day the ascent of Ayer's Peak. A flag was placed on the northern peak, one on the southern, and a monument reared on the middle one. Ayer's Peak occupies a central position in the Grand Cañon from which are revealed such a touch of immensity and grandeur as to produce an indelible impression. Chas A. Bailey, Oakland Cal., W. M. C. Vaughn, Chicago, Ill.

Note: Their brief three-summit entry is more descriptive of Coronado Butte near the New Hance Trail. (see page 155)

Hance Canyon Route, Off Trail Canyoneers Report

A four-mile-long route follows the boulder-strewn streambed and cliff-walled narrows of Hance Creek to Sockdolager Rapid, Mile 78.5, Colorado River, Elevation 2,525 feet (770 meters). Three serious obstacles, waterfalls, pour offs and cliffs must be climbed around that require nimble footedness and honed inner canyon route finding skills.

Mile 11.4, from the Trailhead. Hance Rapids, Mile 76.5, Colorado River, Elevation 2,608 Feet (795 meters), Vishnu Schist. The Tonto Trail ends (or begins) at the confluence of Red Canyon at the foot of the New Hance Trail. At-large, low-impact camping, perennial water at the Colorado River in Zone BD9.

West Horseshoe Mesa Trail

Mile 3.15. West Horseshoe Mesa (Cottonwood Creek) Trail junction, Elevation 3,900 (1189 meters), Redwall Limestone. From Horseshoe Mesa, the West Horseshoe Mesa Trail leads 1.5 miles down short, steep, scree-covered switchbacks through, the Redwall to Cottonwood Creek.

Mile 4.5. Cottonwood Creek, Tonto Trail East. Elevation 3,690 feet (1,125 meters), Tapeats Sandstone. At-large, low-impact camping, seasonal water only at Cottonwood Creek, Zone BG9, and a spring in the southwest fork. Turn right (north) and the Tonto Trail East leads three miles east around Horseshoe Mesa to the Miner Page Springs Trail Junction. Look for the cairns that will guide you out of the Cottonwood Creek. Turn left (north) and the Tonto Trail East leads 3.5 miles west to Grapevine Creek. It also provides access to the Old Grandview Trail. (See page 147.)

Additional Considerations

If you're day hiking to Horseshoe Mesa, or camping overnight, make sure you carry enough water for your stay and roundtrip hike back up to the South Rim. Otherwise, you'll need to make what some hikers consider a dangerous 1.4 mile roundtrip detour off Horseshoe Mesa to replenish your water supply at Miner Springs.

Travel Notes

- Warning Advisory. Leave early to beat the heat with enough water to enjoy the hike out.
- Primary Access: Grandview Trailhead.
- Elevation: 7,410-feet Grandview Trailhead, 4,900-feet Horseshoe Mesa, 2,608-feet Colorado River.
- Biotic Communities: Ponderosa pine, piñon-jumper woodland, Great Basin Desert scrub, and Sonoran Desert.
- Total Elevation Loss and Gain: Horseshoe Mesa 5,020 feet (2,510 vertical feet each way); Colorado River 9,604 vertical feet (4,802 vertical feet each way).
- Mileage, Rim to Mesa: Six miles (three miles one way to Horseshoe Mesa).
- Mileage, Rim to River: 22.8 miles (11.4 miles one way to the Colorado River).
- Water: Miners (Page) Spring, Hance Creek, Cottonwood Creek and springs (seasonal), Colorado River.
- Cache Points: Horseshoe Mesa.
- Escape Routes: Grandview Trailhead.
- Seasons: Spring and fall. Summertime is hot and there is no water on Horseshoe Mesa. Wintertime is treacherous when snow and ice accumulate on the upper trail, riprap, and gangways.
- Maps: Cape Royal and Grandview Point Quadrangles (7.5 minute).
- Camping: Horseshoe Mesa BF5, four sites; at-large, low-impact camping at Hance Creek BE9, Cottonwood Creek BG9, and the Colorado River BD9.
- Nearest Supply Points: Grand Canyon Village, Williams, and Flagstaff, Arizona.
- Managing Agency: Grand Canyon National Park.
- Backcountry Information Center: for information call (928) 638–7875.
- Critical Backcountry Updates visit www.nps.gov/grca/planyourvisit/trail-closures.htm
- NPS Grand Canyon Hiker 24 Hour Emergency Phone Number and Email.
  - Phone (928) 638–7805
  - Email: grca_bic@nps.gov (Use this if the phone line is busy)

Tonto Trail Loop Hikes/Treks

Grandview, Tonto Trail East, New Hance Trailhead

The 17.9-mile point-to-point route is a thorough multiday introduction to the rigors and rewards of trans-canyoneering.

Grandview, Tonto Trail East, South Kaibab Trailhead

The 24.9-mile point-to-point route is rigorous trek in and out of four intervening canyons that are normally dry. Careful seasonal planning is required to assure the availability of reliable drinking water. (See Tonto Trail East page 200.)

Souvenir "Burrometer" weather postcard, 1951, GCNP Museum Collection.

15

Hance Trail: Day Hikes and Rim to River

"God made the cañon,
John Hance the trails.
Without the other,
neither would be complete."

—Wm. O. "Buckey" O'Neill
25 January 1893

LANDFORM

Red Canyon is a deep tributary chasm that drains the forested heights and ramparts of the Coconino Plateau between 7,141-foot Moran Point on the east and 7,162-foot Coronado Butte on the west that flows into the Colorado River at Mile 76.5.

HISTORY

A mano, metate, and "swallow nest" cliff dwelling perched beneath the 7,344-foot summit of the Sinking Ship overlooks the rock slide–covered path leading off the rim to hidden wonders. The phantom trail was first trod by Ancestral Puebloans, and later by the Havasupai who were reported to have used the secret track "for untold centuries."

When conservationist John Muir first journeyed down the route he took note and reflected that most of the canyon's ruins were built on ". . . the brink of the wildest, giddiest precipices, sites evidently chosen for safety from enemies, and seemingly accessible only to the birds of the air . . . Many caves were also used as dwelling-places, as were mere seams on cliff-fronts . . . some of them were covered with colored pictures of animals." Who on God's green earth would try building a trail to such places?

"Captain" John Hance

A Civil War veteran who survived the battlefield ravages between the Union and Confederacy, the steely-eyed prospector and raconteur headed West to seek his fortune in a canyon he would tell tourists he'd dug himself. It probably seemed like it. In 1884 the bearded, Tennessee-born Hance forged a steep, narrow—one to two feet wide—dangerous trail with pick, shovel, crow bar and dynamite down the "giddiest precipices," cliffs, and hanging terraces that his tourist-ferrying mules negotiated with the nimble-footedness of a canyon bighorn sheep. One of his first clients was Massachusetts-born Emma Augusta Burbank Ayer. Educated at Benedict and Shatterlee's College, the world traveler, adventurer and author who would later become famous for photographing and coauthoring the exotic travel book, *A Motor Flight through Algeria and Tunisia* (1911), Mrs. Ayer became the first known woman to journey into the depths of the Grand Canyon. With the help of Captain Hance. In 1894, landslides buried the Old Hance Trail, and Hance went to work building the New Hance Trail for tourists and his asbestos mining interests.

New Hance Trail

Word got out about the Grand Canyon—and John Hance. "Anyone who comes to the Grand Cañon, and fails to meet Captain John Hance, will miss half the show," T. C. Poling wrote in Hance's guestbook on July 2, 1897. People came by rail, stage coach, horseback, and bicycle to lodge at Hance's rustic log cabin, tent camp, and ranch in the ponderosa pine forest at the trailhead. Among myriad guests who enjoyed his hospitality, listened to his yarns, and depended on his trail guiding expertise was gun-toting naturalist C. Hart Merriam. The Yale- and Columbia-educated scientist arrived at the South Rim on September 10, 1889, after a two-day horseback ride from his Flagstaff, Arizona, base camp. For months "Hart," as his field colleagues called him, had been studying the biogeography extending from the of 12,633-foot sub-alpine tundra-covered summit of the San Francisco Mountains to the arid reaches of the Painted Desert where he nearly died of thirst when a Hopi man saved him. The last stop on Merriam's scientific quest to establish his Life Zones of North America concept was to journey to the Sonoran Desert life zone at the bottom of Grand Canyon. From the trailhead Hance led the way down to the Colorado River, while Merriam and his associate stopped to study a wide diversity of plant and animal species during their natural history trek (see page 73 Biogeography).

At the height of his trail guiding business, Hance had guided hundreds of tourists into the Grand Canyon on foot, mule, and horseback, including John Muir, George Wharton James, Pulitzer-prize-winning author Hannibal Hamlin Garland, and photographer and travelogue writer Elias Burton Holmes. Of the scores of guest book entries that praised Hance over the years, Holmes' trail description stands out, sometimes reflecting the modern hiker's perception of what the park calls a primitive trail: "I say that I descended sections of the trail on foot. "On foot," however, does not express it, but on heels and toes, on hands and knees, and sometimes in the posture assumed by children when they come bumping down the stairs; thus did I glissade around "Cape Horn," and past a dozen other places, where neither the mocking laughter of men nor the bitter words of the brave Amazon could tempt me to forget that my supremest duty was to live to give a lecture on the cañon."

Homes was talking about the "new" trail, not the "old" trail Emma Augusta Burbank Ayer had braved.

The 6.5-mile New Hance Trail is considered the South Rim's most difficult rim-to-river trail and requires nerves, off trail canyon hiking experience, honed route finding skills, and endurance.

Directions

Drive sixteen miles east on the Desert View Drive to Moran Point, park, and walk one mile west to the pull off marked by "No Parking Signs." The 0.25-mile dirt path leads to the New Hance Trailhead.

Mile 0. Hance Trailhead, Elevation 6,960 feet (2,121 meters), Kaibab Limestone, Trailhead View North/NW: 7,162-foot Coronado Butte. The two-foot-wide, scree-covered trail descends through the piñon and juniper and plunges down an accordion of steep switchbacks, made more difficult by boulder-blocking passages and the trail's knee-wrenching "Mother May I?!" giant steps you need to take descending through the Kaibab Limestone and Toroweap Formation. The steep grade eases on the rubble-strewn trail through the Coconino Sandstone that's crisscrossed with sometimes gnarly juniper log waterbars held in place with rusty bolts. Take your time with a heavy pack. You may need an hour to safely negotiate your way down to Coronado Butte Saddle.

Mile 1. Coronado Butte Saddle, Elevation 6,040 feet (1,841 meters), Hermit Shale. From the saddle the trail descends a thousand feet down the rugged drainage beneath Coronado Butte through broken Supai ledges, chutes, and falls you need to climb down to reach the top of the Redwall Limestone. In the distance you can see the North Rim's 7533-foot Vishnu Temple, one of the biggest and most dramatic mountains in the Grand Canyon first climbed by Merrill D. Clubb and his son Roger on July 13, 1945 (see page 103).

Coronado Butte, Pioneer Ascent

Named for Spanish conquistador Francisco Vásquez de Coronado, 7,162-foot Coronado Butte was believed to be climbed by Archaic peoples, and later by Ancestral Puebloans. The Kaibab Limestone and Toroweap Formation butte was reportedly first climbed by Hance and a tourist prior to 1900. From their August 21, 1895, guestbook entry, that may have been Chas A. Bailey and W. M. C. Vaughn who might have mistakenly called Coronado Butte "Ayer's Peak." (See page 149 Grandview Trail.) From Coronado Butte Saddle, a two-mile roundtrip, cross-country trek and exposed 3rd Class scramble leads to the isolated summit.

Mile 2. Red Canyon Overlook, drop off. Elevation 5,000 feet (1,524 meters), Redwall Limestone. From the overlook turn right (east), then turn northeast and begin the sketchy mile-long traverse atop the Redwall. Stay focused—one hiker slipped and almost died on this stretch—and take care on the pebbly and stony footing as you wind around and skirt the crumbling ledges atop the ragged buttresses and edges of the Redwall Limestone. The trail, 'er route, has been washed out by flashfloods in some places, and blocked by boulder slides in other places, that need to be carefully negotiated. During September 1927, Grand Canyon ranger S. B. Jones reported seeing an American bald eagle (*Haliaeetus leucocephalus*) frolicking in a water pocket on a Redwall ledge. In the park's *Nature Notes*, Jones reported, ". . . this is the first definite record we have of our National bird in the Grand Canyon."

Mile 3. Redwall Descent, Elevation 4,949 feet (1,509 meters), Redwall Limestone. BM 4949 marker. Consult your Cape Royal Quadrangle (7.5 minute) map to follow the USGS benchmarks in this description. A large boulder, etched with indecipherable names and numbers, marks the point where the route turns west and begins the tough, steep descent through the loose, friable, sometimes frightening Redwall. Cairns mark the point where the route turns north to BM 4286. From this point the route contours into a steep side drainage that courses to BM 3659 where the trail turns northeast and descends to the streambed of Red Canyon. En route you can see a verdant grove of cottonwood trees (*Populus fremontii*) that indicate the seasonal streambed spring may be flowing when you reach it.

Mile 4.9. Red Canyon creek bed, Elevation 3,250 feet (991 meters), Hakatai Shale. The seasonal streambed spring is a pleasant place for a snack or rest stop, assuming it's not flash flood season. It also provides an emergency water source if you've miscalculated your water requirements.

Caution: The Park advises the springs' arsenic levels may exceed municipal qualities. Red Canyon takes its name from canyon's brilliant Hakatai Shale. Relatively easy walking down the streambed leads to BM 2993 where the ever widening streambed turns north toward the Colorado River. Stop, look around and savor this canyon idyll. Author Hamlin Garland described Hance's balmy winter retreat: ". . . when the cold winds threaten and snow begins to slide along the high plateau, John mounts his

favorite mule, and driving all his cattle before him, descends 6,000 feet and finds per-
petual summer. On the sage-green bushes, 1,000 feet above the river, his cattle feed. In
his tent among the mesquite trees, the old pioneer lives, while far above him the harsh
winds howl and the whirling snow falls foot by foot . . . He knows that in the midst of
these overawing immensities there are grassy nooks where the ferns grow and water falls
with merry gurgle. . .He knows, too, the cliff-dwellers' houses, mere swallow nests in the
unscalable cliffs, and he muses upon the antiquity of man."

Mile 6.49. Tonto Trail Start/End, Elevation 2,608 feet (795 meters), Vishnu
Schist. The 121.4 mile Tonto Trail begins at Hance Rapids and ends at Garnet Canyon
(see page 198 Tonto Trail East). Turn left (west) and it's 11.4 miles to the Grandview Trailhead. One of the more memorable historic treks along this route was made
by Emery Kolb from August 16–18, 1923. Emery worked as chief boatman for Col.
Claude H. Birdseye expedition. Their work on the Colorado River mapping the proposed dam sites for the U.S. Geological Survey proceeded more quickly that they'd
planned, and they beached their boats at the foot of the Hance Trail a week before the
expedition's resupplies would arrive by mules. Emery, accompanied by boatmen Leigh
B. Lint and Elwyn Blake, went into action, left their river camp at 3:00 PM—too late,
and too hot in the day—and trudged over eleven miles to Grandview Point. Carrying
little more than film and mail, the exhausted trio didn't arrive at Grandview Point until
midnight. Two days later, they accompanied the pack string back down the trail to the
river, this time ferrying Emery's sixteen-year daughter, Edith, who wanted to watch the
expedition run legendary Hance Rapids.

Mile 6.5. Colorado River, Elevation 2,548 feet (780 meters), Hakatai Shale, Hance
Rapids, River Mile 76.5, Hance Rapids Camp BD9 offers primitive campsites on a
wide riverside beach. One look at the Colorado River was all it took, and the inde-
pendent-minded Edith "nagged" her father until he agreed to let her run the muddy,
flood-swollen rapids with the handsome, chiseled-jawed Lint. Lint shoved off into "one
of the worst" rapids on the Colorado River. Wielding heavy wooden oars, the rough
water boatman careened toward a fifteen foot collapsing back-wave and deep hole, running a half-mile down the churning waters. The fifteen-minute journey earned Edith a
sweet spot in Lint's heart and a place in the history books. Edith Kolb became the first
woman in history to run a dangerous Grand Canyon rapid.

Primitive Trail Loop Trek
New Hance, Tonto Trail East, and Grandview Trailhead
The 17.9-mile point-to-point route may be safer and less confusing for you if you
descend the New Hance Trail and ascend the Grandview Trail via Miners (Page) Spring.

Additional Considerations: If you're day hiking, or camping overnight, make sure you carry enough water for your roundtrip hike back to the New Hance Trailhead.

Travel Notes

- Warning Advisory: Don't hike the New Hance Trail in the summer. If you do, it's imperative you leave camp at dawn to reach the top of the Redwall before late morning.
- Primary Access: New Hance Trailhead.
- Elevation: 6,982-feet New Hance Trailhead to 2,548-feet Colorado River.
- Biotic Communities: Ponderosa pine, piñon jumper woodland, and Sonoran Desert.
- Total Elevation Loss and Gain: 8,868 vertical feet (4,434 feet each way).
- Maps: Grandview Point and Cape Royal Quadrangles (7.5 minute).
- Mileage: 6.5 miles to the Colorado River.
- Water: Colorado River, Red Canyon (seasonal springs).
- Cache Points: Coronado Butte Saddle, top of the Redwall, Red Canyon.
- Seasons: Fall and spring. Upper sections can be treacherous in winter snow. Summertime can be unforgiving.
- Escape Routes: New Hance Trailhead, Colorado River.
- Camping: At large, low impact camping Red Canyon BD9, and the Colorado River BD9.
- Nearest Supply Points: Grand Canyon Village, Williams, and Flagstaff, Arizona.
- Managing Agency: Grand Canyon National Park.
- Backcountry Information Center: for information call (928) 638–7875.
- Critical Backcountry Updates visit www.nps.gov/grca/planyourvisit/trail-closures.htm
- NPS Grand Canyon Hiker 24 Hour Emergency Phone Number and Email
  - Phone (928) 638–7805
  - Email: grca_bic@nps.gov (Use this if the phone line is busy)

View of Comanche Point Pinnacle near the foot of the Tanner Trail.

16

Tanner Trail: Day Hikes and Rim to River

"The Holy Young Woman walks far around
On the blue mountains, she walks far around.
Far spreads the land. It seems not far.
Far spreads the land. It seems not dim."

—The Mountain Chant, 1887
A Navajo Ceremony

LANDFORM

Tanner Canyon, and its braided forks, form a deep tributary chasm that drains the east rim of the Painted Desert and Coconino Plateau between 7,073-foot Comanche Point and 7,380-foot Lipan Point that flows into the Colorado River at Mile 68.5.

HISTORY

Steeped in Old West tales of horse thieves, moon shiners, and lost gold, the saga of the Tanner Trail celebrates the colorful exploits of Seth Benjamin Tanner, a hardy Mormon pioneer who homesteaded the Little Colorado River in 1876 at what later became known as Tanner Crossing. Seldom seen fortified cliff dwellings, ceremonial sites, storage granaries, and agave roasting pits unveil the hidden Native American legacy of Tanner Canyon and its environs. Threads of ancient foot paths that cross the historic Tanner Trail were used by canyon dwellers dating back to Archaic people 4,000 years ago, and later by Ancestral Puebloans, *Hisat.sinom*, "People Who Lived Long Ago," and

Anaasází, "Enemy Ancestors." Perhaps, no other trail in the Grand Canyon embodies the multilingual cultural diversity of the Tanner Trail.

Hopi Trails

In September 1540, Hopi guides led Spanish-speaking García López de Cárdenas and twelve men to an area most historians concluded was located near the head of Tanner Canyon between Desert View and Moran Point. Under the orders of conquistador Francisco Vásquez de Coronado, Cárdenas and his men spent three days searching for a way down to the "large river" they'd learned about from the Zuni. Dispatched by Cárdenas, Captain Malgosa, Juan Galeras, and an unidentified soldier struggled to find passage through impossible cliffs that were reported to be higher than the 323-foot tall bell tower of *La Giralada,* "the great tower of Seville," Spain. But their efforts were futile, and expedition chronicler Pedro de Castañeda de Nájera later wrote: "What appeared to be easy from above was not so, but instead very hard and difficult." It's a mantra that's been repeated by canyon hikers to this day.

Some *Pahaanna* (non-Hopi) profess the Hopi used the east fork of Tanner Canyon as an alternate route to the sacred trail they traditionally used on pilgrimages down the Little Colorado River Gorge to their salt mines in *Öngtupqa,* "Salt Canyon." If so, why didn't the Hopi lead the *Kastíila,* meaning "Spanish," down Tanner Canyon to the Colorado River? Lips are sealed. Contrary to what the Hopi told George Wharton James, some theorize the Hopi didn't want to guide the Spaniards anywhere near the gorge's hallowed *Sípàapuni,* the "hatchway where the Hopi emerged to the Fourth world." As a result, they believe the Hopi led the Spaniards on a roundabout twenty-day trek west where Cárdenas "discovered" the Grand Canyon. (See page 139 South Bass Trail.)

Navajo Trails

The Navajo knew well the trails leading to the Little Colorado River Gorge they called *Tólchí'-íkooh,* "Red Water Canyon," and the Redwall water pockets in Tanner Canyon that sustained them. On their journeys down *Áshįįh ha'atiin,* "Salt Trail out of Canyon," they offered corn pollen to Salt Woman. They would need her protection. Between September 1863 and January 1864 "great numbers of Navajo" fled Colonel Christopher "Kit" Carson's deadly scorched earth campaign and sought sanctuary in the depths of the Grand Canyon. Not far from where the Female Mountaintop Ceremony, *Dzilk'ijí Bi'áádjí,* was held near Desert View in 1862, the Navajo escaped down Tanner Canyon, the traditional route they traveled to reach their salt deposits and ceremonial water they collected in the Little Colorado River Gorge. For a time, they remained beyond reach of the ruthless frontiersman who orchestrated the "Long Walk" from Navajo homelands to Fort Sumner, New Mexico. Two hundred Navajo perished during Carson's brutal eighteen-day, 300-mile forced march.

Tanner French Trail

Seth B. Tanner, a scout, prospector, and Indian trader, was known for his friendly dealings with the Hopi and the Navajo who called him *Hastiin Shush*, "Mr. Bear." Perhaps he'd heard stories from the Navajo, or Mormon pioneers who traveled the Honeymoon Trail via Tanner Crossing, but Tanner ventured from his remote cabin in the Painted Desert and headed down the rugged route in quest of the mother lode that had eluded him in the California gold fields. Convinced he'd found rich copper beneath the soaring walls of Palisades of the Desert, Tanner filed the Tanner Ledge mining claim in 1877. Within three years Tanner organized the Little Colorado Mining District and, together with his partner Franklin French, started building the trail between their Lava Canyon and Palisades Creek diggings and the distant South Rim. "We called it a trail," French, a Civil War veteran told George Wharton James, "but it was only a roughly marked out suggestion of where a trail ought to be." French was married to Emma Louise Batchelor Lee, a handcart Mormon pioneer who pushed her own cart 1,400 miles from Nauvoo, Illinois to Salt Lake City, Utah. She was also the widow of John D. Lee, a tough as nails Mormon cattleman and settler who was executed by a firing squad for his alleged role in the Mountain Meadows Massacre. Before he professed his innocence to his last breath and was riddled with bullets, Lee gave his eighteenth wife Emma two coffee cans filled with gold dust. But there was more—or so everyone believed. Rumors flew: "John D. Lee had buried seven cans of almost pure native gold near the mouth of the Little Colorado River." The trove was never found, and Tanner gave up the ghost for the same reason nearly every other canyon prospector turned to "dude wrangling." His claims were taken over by Ohio-born George W. McCormick, son of a reputed horse thief who was said to have used the Tanner Trail.

Horse Thief Trail

In March 1886, another colorful tale was spun. As told to George Wharton James, William Wallace Bass also got a hankering to find John D. Lee's hidden cache of gold. Early one morning Bass and two companions scrambled down the east fork of Tanner Canyon and discovered an abandoned campsite, James wrote, that was "evidently vacated but a short time before by its owners, for there were five rolls of bedding, left just as the sleepers had tumbled out of them, five Winchester rifles, five six-shooters, five saddles, and so on. Knowing the owners could not be far away, Bass and his companions passed on, and, on reaching Rock Tanks, in the gorge below, were not surprised to find five men busily engaged in watering eighteen horses, which, it required no expert to discern, had just undergone the suspicious operation of "changing the brands."

Historic artifacts reportedly discovered by canyoneers, and a father-son confession, infer there may be a kernel of truth regarding the Grand Canyon's own "wild bunch" who may have spurred their mounts riding hell-for-leather across the canyon's Butte Fault between House Rock Valley and Flagstaff, Arizona. But don't bet a rusty coffee can full of John D. Lee's gold dust on it.

Directions

From the junction of State Highway 64 and Village Route Drive, drive 19.7 miles east on Desert View (East Rim) Drive to Lipan Point. The signed Tanner Trailhead is east of the point.

The primitive nine-mile Tanner Trail is the South Rim's longest and driest rim-to-river trail, and one of its toughest. It requires nerves, honed route-finding skills, endurance, and good judgment to cache water on the descent for the long, frequently shadeless climb back out to the trailhead.

Mile 0. Tanner Trailhead, Elevation 7,380 feet (2,249 meters), Kaibab Limestone, Trailhead View North (south of the Colorado River): 6,586-foot Escalante Butte, 6,281-foot Cardenas Butte, Colorado River, Palisades of the Desert, and Desert Façade. Desert View near the head of Tanner Canyon is a sacred cultural site of the Navajo where they once performed the *Diné yázhí ba'íítá,* Enemy Way healing ceremony. Go slow, and take care where you place your feet and hiking poles, if you're using them, descending what some hikers call the South Rim's "toughest first mile." From the trailhead "walk the plank" east before the trail plummets 1,700 vertical feet through scruffy stands of piñon and white fir and slaloms through loose dirt, scree, shattered stones, and boulders poised to trip or waylay pack-heavy hikers on the ragged descent the trail makes through the Kaibab, Toroweap, Coconino, and Hermit formations. If you fall, fall up hill on your back side. Many hikers complain about the "upper Tanner." Alongside the Boucher Trail, the Tanner Trail was one of my students' oft-repeated favorite Grand Canyon treks when I taught and guided outdoor education treks. At a careful pace, it takes about an hour to reach Seventy-five Mile Saddle.

Mile 1.9. Seventy-five Mile Saddle, Elevation 5,640 feet (1,719 meters), Esplanade Sandstone. Turn Around Point 1. (Use any convenient point on the descent where you feel you, or your children, need to stop and turn around.) This spectacular high-back ridge is the dividing line between Seventy-five Mile Creek on your left (west) and Tanner Canyon on your right (east). Seventy-five Mile takes its name from the fact the creek's confluence with the Colorado River is located seventy-five river miles downstream from Lees Ferry at River Mile 0. The trailside, overhead Supai boulders, some call Stegosaurus Rocks, is a great place to snack or lunch. It offers shade in hot weather, windbreaks in cold weather, and rim-top views of Mary Jane Colter's seventy-foot tall Desert View Watchtower that was inspired by Utah's Hovenweep Castle. The saddle is a pivotal area to cache water for the long waterless climb back out of the canyon.

In December 1924, cowboy and game warden Jack Fuss's pack horse slid off the snow-covered trail and broke its neck near here during a daunting cross-canyon trail ride, Colorado River ford, and calf-skin kyacking [sic] adventure Fuss, his men and twenty-seven horses and mules endured to reach the North Rim via the trail less Horsethief Trail to resupply and join in the snow-stormed "Great Kaibab Deer Drive." (See Nankoweap Trail page 248.)

From Seventy-five Mile Saddle, the 2.1-mile romp across the Esplanade, what some call the "Supai Traverse," is a breeze as it contours around the base of 6,529-foot Escalante Butte and 6,269-foot Cardenas Butte all the way to the Redwall Descent. You should find the mesmerizing scenery and gentle rolling trail across the Esplanade through piñon and juniper a welcome respite and chance to work out the kinks from the steep descent off the South Rim.

Mile 3.1. Escalante/Cardenas Basin, Elevation 5,500 feet (1,676 meters), Esplanade Sandstone. This is an excellent area to cache water and offers at-large, low-impact camping. Navajos on the run down Tanner Canyon from Kit Carson's 1st Regiment New Mexico Volunteer Cavalry, one ethnographer reported, "stopped to rest and camp on a wide shelf, where they were attacked by a band of Navajo renegades. After considerable fighting the renegades were ambushed and killed." This basin is the widest shelf along the Tanner Trail. After the deadly skirmish, the Navajo left the camp and moved deeper into the canyon where they were tracked down by Round Moccasin, Carson's envoy. The Navajo tracker offered them protection and food. Most accepted and joined the Long Walk. Others stayed and descended deeper into the canyon.

Ancient Pass

An Ancestral Puebloan path, once marked by pottery sherds, led west from the modern Tanner Trail, crossed over the pass between Escalante and Cardenas Buttes, and descended into Escalante Creek.

Backstory: During a formative multiday trans canyon journey run below the South Rim one spring, I stopped to rest somewhere along the Esplanade bench. I took off my small pack, and two bota bags of water, and sat down on a flat rock. I bent over to rest my head on my knees, but laying on the ground beneath me was a yucca fiber sandal. What! I picked up the delicate sole, but I didn't know what to make of it at first. I started to wonder, *Who had worn it*? Then, I suddenly realized I should hide it out of sight and put it back where it had evidently been washed out from. I feared it would end up on someone's trophy wall. I looked around to make sure no one was coming, laid down on the ground, then slid the ancient relic beneath the stone as far back as I could reach and covered it with powdery red sand. I got up and started running again, my spirit lifted I might have found the path of ancient runners and traders I had hoped to find during my weeklong journey run. I never went back to that terra cotta stone, or told anyone where it was.

From Escalante/Cardenas Basin you can make enjoyable off-trail scrambles up Escalante and Cardenas Buttes by hiking up to the small terraced knob located in the pass informally known as Escaldenas Butte. From the 5,920-foot Supai landmark you can traverse the ridge south to reach Escalante Butte, or you can traverse the ridge north to reach Cardenas Butte. They both offer the best panoramic views on the Tanner Trail.

Don't bust the fragile cyptobiotic crust.

6,586-foot Escalante Butte

A cross-country scramble up steep talus and ledges strewn with boulders leads to the Class III Coconino Sandstone summit block. If the exposure doesn't unnerve you, you can make an airy jump (or step) across the three-foot wide crevice that splits the summit block to reach the true summit. The butte was named for Spanish missionary explorer Silvestre Vélez de Escalante who, together with Mexican padre Francisco Atanasio Domínguez, embarked on an epic 1,700-mile journey in 1776 to explore a new route from Santa Fe, New Mexico, to the Spanish presidio in Monterey, California.

6,281-foot Cardenas Butte, Supai Sandstone

A scramble up steep boulder-strewn talus and ledges leads to the Class III chimneys and cracks to the Supai summit. The butte was named for Coronado's point man, Don García López de Cárdenas.

Mile 4. Redwall Descent, Elevation 5,600 feet (1,707 meters), Esplanade Sandstone, Redwall Limestone. Fifty yards northwest of the descent, a secondary trail leads to the Redwall Overlook's sweeping vistas of Comanche Point, Palisades of the Desert, and the Colorado River. Popular at-large, low-impact campsites are located at this aerie. From the Redwall Descent, the broken trail and switchbacks trace the Butte Fault through the Redwall 740 vertical feet down to an unnamed saddle. A slip on the exposed, narrow, ball-bearing covered sections can be fatal. Imagine Navajo men, women, and children herding goats and sheep down the treacherous Redwall, Muav, and Tapeats cliffs and breaks to reach the Colorado River.

Mile 4.6. Unnamed Saddle, beneath Peak 4873. From the foot of the Redwall, the trail descends through the Bright Angel Shale and wanders northwest-to-northeast to a narrow Tapeats Sandstone ridge.

Mile 6. Tapeats Catwalk, Elevation 4,600 feet (1,402 meters), Tapeats Sandstone. The trail traverses this spectacular ridge for nearly a mile before it reaches a tip-off.

Mile 7. Tapeats Tip-off. Elevation 4,200 feet (1,280 meters), Dox Sandstone. The trail tips off the right (north) side and contours beneath the ridge line on the west side of Tanner Canyon and glides downhill. This section of the Tanner is enjoyable because you feel like you're flying across the Dox Sandstone all the way to Tanner Canyon.

Mile 8.5. Tanner Canyon, Elevation 2,720 feet (823 meters), Dox Sandstone. The trail descends into the creek bed and follows it to the *Río Colorado*, "Red River."

Mile 9. Colorado River, Elevation 2,680 feet (817 meters), Dox Sandstone, Tanner Rapids, River Mile 68.5. Tanner Beach. Zone BB9 offers primitive campsites on a wide riverside beach and a composting toilet. If you reach the river during white water rafting season, you may find a group of river runners camped near the mouth of Tanner Creek, but the area is such a large one, there's no reason to feel crowded. Just head west along the sand dunes and you should find the solitude you came to enjoy.

The Navajo Trail to Indian Garden

From Tanner Rapids, the Navajo's forced exodus from *Dinétah*, "Navajoland," via their escape route down Tanner Canyon, continued fifty miles west through unknown country all the way to Indian Garden where they used handmade yucca fiber ropes to haul their goats and sheep up the precipitous Bright Angel Fault. Imagine, if you will, the courage and skill it took Navajo families to route-find their way on foot in flimsy moccasins across the stony banks and trail less "benches and breakers" of what's been erroneously named the Escalante Route to the Tonto Platform. "Far spreads the land. It seems not far. Far spreads the land. It seems not dim," from the Navajo Mountain Chant.

Look then at the swift moving currents of the Colorado River. The Navajo's extraordinary journey was made a full five years before Major John Wesley Powell and his surviving crew members were hailed as heroes for navigating what they feared as the "Great Unknown" in wooden boats. Judging from Powell's Geographic Expedition diary entry for August 11, 1869 at the confluence of the Colorado and Little Colorado Rivers, the "great unknown" was devoid of any semblance of human life but their own at the time: "I walk down the gorge to the left at the foot of the cliff, climb to a bench, and discover a trail, deeply worn in the rock," Powell wrote. "Where it crosses the side gulches, in some places, steps have been cut I can see no evidence of its having been traveled for a long time. It was doubtless a path used by the people who inhabited this country anterior to the present Indian races."

Medicine Man Trail

East of Tanner Canyon, the traditional river path was still being used by medicine men nearly a century after Powell's diary entry. Undoubtedly, it still is. With great sadness to

"A Navaho shaman," John K. Hillers albumen silver print, 1879, Library of Congress.

the Diné, seventy-two-year-old Bennie Tohe, a Navajo *ha'athali*, "singer," from Chinle, Arizona, died on June 30, 1960, near a ritual prayer stop at *Tsétáťah ha'atiin* (Palisades Creek) beneath the towering rim of the Painted Desert and 6,146-foot Cape Solitude, *Tsin dah shijaa' bidáá'*, where the healing ceremony, *Hozhooji*, or Blessingway Ceremony, was traditionally performed. In spite of the medicine man's age, the extreme heat, and the distance he traveled alone on foot to cross and recross the perilous sandstone ledges of the Beamer Trail that early Navajo medicine men and salt pilgrims first called the *Tsétáťah ha'atiin*, "Trap Trail," or "Rock Ledge Trail," he had the vision and endurance to journey all the way across *Áshįįh ha'atiin*, "Salt Trail out of Canyon," on a sacred pilgrimage to *Áshįįh Asdáá*, "Salt Woman," at *Tooh Ahidiilíní*, the hallowed confluence of the Colorado and Little Colorado Rivers. If the elder's journey isn't a testament to the sanctity of the Grand Canyon for its Native Peoples, what is? One wonders how many other canyon trails were followed with such reverence as the medicine man's spirit trail. (See page 185 Beamer Trail, and page 296 South Canyon.)

PRIMITIVE TRAIL CROSSROADS

Escalante Route/Blessingway Trail

The ten-mile point-to-point route leads west along the Colorado River and Escalante Route to the foot of the Hance Trail. The route should be renamed the Navajo Trail or Blessingway Trail to honor the brave elders, men, women, and children who first trod it. As inspiring as Domínguez and Escalante expedition was their distant route, now part of the Old Spanish National Historic Trail, gave the Grand Canyon a wide berth along the Arizona/Utah border. (See page 183 Trans Canyon Trails and Routes.)

Beamer Trail

The 8.5-mile point-to-point route leads east along the Colorado River and Beamer trail to the confluence of the Colorado and Little Colorado Rivers. (See page 185 Beamer Trail.)

Additional Considerations:

- Warning Advisory: Do not hike the Tanner Trail in the summer. If you do, it's imperative:
  1. You cache a minimum two to three quarts of water for every 1,500 vertical feet on you descend for the climb back out;
  2. You leave the Colorado River at O'Dark-thirty to reach the top of the Redwall before mid-morning.

- Primary Access: Tanner Trailhead, Lipan Point.
- Elevation: 7,380-feet to 2,650-feet.
- Biotic Communities: Ponderosa pine, piñon jumper woodland, and Sonoran Desert.
- Total Elevation Loss and Gain: 9,460 vertical feet (4,730 feet each way).
- Map: Desert View Quadrangle (7.5 minute).
- Mileage: Eighteen miles (nine miles one way to the Colorado River).
- Water: Colorado River only.
- Cache Points: Seventy-five Mile Saddle, Escalante/Cardenas Basin, top of the Redwall. Descent, along the Tapeats Catwalk or below.
- Seasons: Fall through spring. Summers are hot and have proved to be deadly. No water, little shade.
- Escape Routes: Tanner Trailhead, Colorado River.
- Camping: At large, low impact Camping Zone (BB9) in Seventy-five Mile Saddle, trailside along the Esplanade, above the Redwall Descent, in the Tapeats, and Colorado River beach east Tanner Creek (composting toilet).
- Nearest Supply Points: Flagstaff, Grand Canyon Village, Desert View, and Cameron.
- Managing Agency: Grand Canyon National Park.
- Backcountry Information Center: for information call (928) 638–7875.
- Critical Backcountry Updates visit www.nps.gov/grca/planyourvisit/trail-closures.htm.
- NPS Grand Canyon Hiker 24 Hour Emergency Phone Number and Email
  - Phone (928) 638–7805.
  - Email: grca_bic@nps.gov (Use this if the phone line is busy)

17

Hualapai (Havasupai) Trail: Rim to Waterfalls

"I had to remain five days; during which
They waited upon me, and regaled me
with flesh of deer and of cow, with
maize, beans, *quelítes*, and mescal, with
all of which were they well provided."

—Padre Francisco Tomás Garcés, 1776
Havasupai Creek

LANDFORM

From the forested heights of 9,256-foot Bill Williams Mountain, Cataract Canyon drains an estimated 3,000 square miles of the Coconino Plateau and carved the deep sinuous tributaries of Hualapai and Havasu Canyons. Havasu Canyon flows into the Colorado River at Mile 156.5.

HISTORY

The Havasupai's ancestral canyon and plateau lands were inhabited by the Cohonina people from 600 to 1050. What little is known about the *Cohonina*, their name is reportedly derived from the ". . . Hopi word *Co'onín*, whose meaning refers to being

Havasu Falls, the other side of *Havasuw Hagjahgeevma*.
Copyright © John Annerino Photography.

guardians of the sacred canyon." The Havasupai are linguistically related to Northern Baja, Mexico's Paipai, and Arizona's Yavapai and Hualapai. Since migrating from the Coconino Plateau in AD 1050 the Havasupai, *Havsuw' Baaja*, "People of the Blue-green Water," have remained guardians of what by all appearances is a canyon Eden nestled among the verdant water courses of Cataract Creek and Havasu Creek Canyons. During times of drought and summer heat the sweet springs and emerald waters formed the lifeblood of their existence in the arid, red desert chasms. During times of winter rains and summer monsoons they formed a deadly threat the Havasupai faced from disastrous flash floods that roared through their beautiful village and destroyed their community, homes, livestock, crops, and pushed them to the edge of survival. Except for Hopi traders, Hualapai neighbors, Yavapai raiders, and the distant Mojave, few had ventured into the remote corner of the western Grand Canyon before June 20, 1776. That's when Spanish missionary explorer Francisco Hermenegildo Tomás Garcés was led by Mojave and Hualapai guides to a *ranchería*, Garcés wrote, "which is on the Río Jabesúa [Cataract Creek]."

When word of the secret canyon got out, it traveled far and wide by foot, mule, pony express, stagecoach, railroad, and transcontinental telegraph, enticing explorers, missionaries, fugitives, prospectors, steamboat captains, generals, creationists, postbellum authors, Indian fighters, and pioneer photographers. Following the ancient paths of plateau, canyon and desert dwellers who proceeded them, the new strangers traced the long serpentine trails in deep redrock gorges through the Havasupai's heartland to the fabled waterfalls and dreams of souls, silver, conquest, and discovery they envisioned awaited them at journey's end. (See "Old Trails to Havasupai" in this section.)

Hualapai (Havasupai) Trail, Hualapai Canyon

Foremost among the trails that lead to Supai was the Hualapai Trail used by Franciscan missionary Francisco Tomás Garcés who on June 20, 1776, made the first recorded descent of the now popular hiking and bridle trail and is credited with being the first non-Native to reach the bottom of the Grand Canyon. Incredibly, botanist and explorer Lieutenant Joseph Christmas Ives later followed the padre's path to Supai from his Colorado River paddle-wheeler. Assigned by the War Department to explore the head of steamboat navigation from the Colorado River Delta from the Sea of Cortés in Sonora, Mexico to northern Arizona, Ives' steel-hulled *Explorer* ran aground in Black Canyon far short of his impossible goal to navigate the Colorado River upstream through the Grand Canyon. Ives pushed on nonetheless, lead overland by Ireteba, a Mojave scout and two Hualapais. In descending the perilous trail to Havasupai the Ives expedition made the second recorded descent of the trail on April 13, 1858. Ives described Hualapai Canyon in his *Report Upon the Colorado River of the West*: "We were deeper in the bowels of the earth than we had ever been before, and surrounded by walls and towers of such imposing dimensions that it would be useless to attempt to described them."

Directions

To reach the trailhead at 5,200-foot Hualapai Hilltop, drive thirty-four miles west of Seligman, Arizona, or seven miles east of Peach Springs, on U.S. 66 to the Supai turnoff, and follow Indian Route 18. The paved sixty-two-mile road heads across the Blue Mountains, Aubrey Cliffs, and Coconino Plateau to Hualapai Hilltop. There are no services on this road or at Hualapai Hilltop.

One of the most celebrated hikes in the world, the eight-mile-long Hualapai (Havasupai) Trail leads to what's been called the "Shangri-La of Shangri Las." The well-worn trail is easy to follow from one wooden milepost to the next all the way to Supai and Havasu Campgrounds. The trail requires less physical effort than the Grand Canyon's rim-to-river trails, unless you're hiking beyond Mooney Falls to the Colorado River.

Mile 0. Hualapai Hilltop, Elevation 5,197 feet (1,584 meters), Toroweap Formation, Trailhead View West: Hualapai Canyon and 5,674-foot Long Mesa. The end-of-the-road view is commanding. But the spectacular canyon point serves as a parking lot, heliport, and staging area for sight seers, hikers, helicopters tours and services, and Havasupai wranglers leading pack strings of horses and mules ferrying tourists, supplies, and mail in and out of the beautiful desert canyon. Be prepared for the traffic on the dusty, heavily beaten trail as it quickly descends steep switchbacks down the east fork of Hualapai Canyon through cross-bedded Coconino Sandstone and rust-colored Hermit Shale 1,110 vertical feet to the floor of Hualapai Canyon. When Padre Garcés faced this descent, he wrote: ". . . on one side is a very lofty cliff, and on the other a horrible abyss (*voladéro*). This difficult road passed, there presented itself another and a worse one, which obliged us to leave, I my mule and they their horses, in order that we might climb down a wooden ladder."

Mile 1.5. Hualapai Canyon, Elevation 4,087 feet (1,246 meters), Esplanade Sandstone. From the main trail to Supai, the mile-long Willow Spring horse trail forks left (southwest) and climbs 200 vertical feet up the west fork of Hualapai Canyon to the seasonal spring. Stay on the Hualapai Trail and follow it north as it descends narrow clefts of Esplanade and Supai Sandstone walls that loom increasingly higher the further you descend. The trail stays in the canyon streambed weaving in out of the sun and welcome shaded overhangs 4.5 miles to its confluence with Havasu Canyon. There is no perennial water along this stretch. Flashflood Warning signs along the trail should be taken seriously. Violent flashfloods have thundered down Cataract, Hualapai, and Havasu Canyons since the nineteenth century. An account in the October 7, 1899, edition of the *Arizona Graphic* reported Cataract Canyon's near Biblical flooding: "Sometime in the past a great flood in the canyon destroyed all their granaries and killed many of the tribe. The balance all but starved before another crop was produced, and since then a year's crop is always kept stored in caves, high up in the rock walls of the canyon." A twenty-foot wall of water engulfed a family of three along this stretch in 2001, killing the father, mother, and their two-year son. The family's three other children who were hiking ahead of them survived.

En route to the confluence of Havasu Canyon, hoof and boot prints, weathered mileposts, old land line telephone wires, and historic ore carts mark the trail until you reach a switchback about Mile 5.5 that contours right (east) around a pour over to safely regain the canyon floor.

Mile 6. Hualapai Canyon/Havasu (*Havsuwa*) Canyon Confluence, Elevation 3,280 feet (1,000 meters), Supai Sandstone. From the Fremont cottonwood tree-shaded confluence the character of the trail changes from a dry desert canyon to a lush riparian corridor sprouting from freshwater springs and rivulets of Havasu and Cataract Canyons that begin in Williams, Arizona, eighty miles south. The confluence also serves as a trail junction. Turn left (north) and keep hiking to Havasupai. Turn right (southeast) and the trail leads 0.25 miles upstream to Havasu Springs. Special permission is required to hike to Havasu Springs or beyond through Cataract Canyon. From the confluence, continue hiking another two miles down canyon along the left (west) side of the streambed to Havasupai.

The "Old Trails to Havasupai" feathered down Cataract Canyon (*Wigasiyáva*) and joined Havasupai Creek at the confluence. Perhaps no trail embodies the reverence the Havasupai have for their traditional lands better the *Tovokyóva* (precipice), or Topocoba Trail. When Frank Hamilton Cushing rode past the mouth of Lee Canyon in 1882 for his two-part *Atlantic Monthly Magazine* feature, "The Nation of Willows," he described the Havasupai's Cataract Canyon shrine and medicine man: "A resounding cave, the walls of which were painted with emblems, and whose rocks were hunting shrines of the strange inhabitants . . . Here, seated on the ground, the worshipper blows smoke to the north, west, south, and east, upward and downwards; then says in a low voice a simple prayer." Cushing may have witnessed Havasupai medicine man, Rock Jones, or one of his descendants. The Topocoba Trail is a sacred cultural landscape of the Havasupai and for the Hopi who call it *Potavey'taqa*.

Mile 8. Supai, Elevation 3,157 feet (962 meters), Supai Sandstone. Located near the confluence of Havasu and Schoolhouse Canyons, Supai is located in a verdant U-shaped canyon of terra cotta cliffs that tower over cottonwood trees, willows, and mesquite, alfalfa pastures with grazing horses and cattle, peach orchards, and fields of corn, beans, squash, melons, and sunflower. Since time forgot, the twin Supai Sandstone spires popularly known as *Wigleeva* have watched over the Havasupai people, their hidden paradise, and canyon home.

Havasupai horseman, *Hamteq,* "Nighthawk," 1899, Henry G. Peabody photo,
GCNP Museum Collection.

Wig-Li-I-Wa Spiritual Landmark

Nineteenth-century photographer Henry Greenwood Peabody photographed the sacred sandstone hoodoos, and noted in pencil on the back of the landscape photograph, "Wig-Li-I-Wa columns, revered as gods. Havasu Canyon, September 1899, H. G. Peabody." A year earlier Charles C. Pierce photographed a mustached tourist, saddled white burro, and Havasupai woman and child in front of mythical landmark and wrote along the bottom of his black and white image, "Cataract Canyon, YavaSupai Gods." The Havasupai's original story has been lost over time and through translation, but it's believed one stone totem is male, the other female. During his earlier visit to Supai, George Wharton James wrote: "On the summit of the wall on the other side of the canyon from the *Hue-gli-i-wa* are two stone objects, one named *Hue-a-pa-a*, and the one farther down the canyon, *Hue-pu-keh-i*. These are great objects of reverence, for they represent the ancestors of the Havasupai race."

Modern Supai

After walking eight miles down the Hualapai (Havasupai) Trail, it might seem a bit out of sorts that you've walked through a canyon idyll into a bustling Native American community and tourist haven, replete with heliport, mule and horse corrals, lodge, trading post, café, store, clinic, school, bible church, telephones, WiFi, and trail crossroads. All hikers must check in at the Havasupai Tourist Office. Navajo Falls is 1.25 miles beyond.

Canyon Oasis

Supai thrives in the arid desert canyons from snowmelt and winter and summer rains, which recharge aquifers with water said to be 30,000 years old. The runoff feeds the perennial course of Havasu Creek, 130 miles of ephemeral streams, springs such as Moqui Spring, Topocoba Spring, Hilltop Spring. Havasu Springs, Fern Springs, and countless seeps. Leached from Redwall Limestone and funneled through a deep narrow canyon over dramatic rust-colored cliffs, the tropical blue waters formed from calcium carbonate produce soft tufa that recrystallizes and produces travertine deposits that create Havasu's fairy tale waterfalls, hanging bridal veils, and terrace-rimmed plunge pools.

Mile 9.25. Navajo Falls. Named in honor of Captain Navajo, a Havasupai *Kohot*, "chief," seventy-five-foot Navajo Falls was destroyed and rerouted by an August 17, 2008, flashflood that created the new fifty-foot Upper Navajo Falls and the thirty-foot Lower Navajo Falls.

Mile 10. Havasupai Campground, Elevation 2,758 feet (841 meters), Redwall Limestone.

The cottonwood tree-shaded campground among the willows offers 200 at-large tent sites, picnic tables, and composting toilets. Campfires are not permitted. Freshwater Fern Spring is located on the west side of Havasu Creek. Havasupai flying squirrels are creatures to be reckoned with. No, they don't actually fly, but they make four- and five-foot leaps into backpacks that unwary hikers have carefully suspended from tree limbs with cordage, textbook-fashion.

Havasu Falls (*Havasuw Hagjahgeevma*)

Located at the confluence of Carbonate Canyon, the twin cascades of Havasu Falls spew 100 feet over the Redwall Limestone travertine into a plunge pool. Early visitors likened the falls to a bridal veil and during the nineteenth century it was commonly called Bridal Veil Falls.

Mile 10.25. Mooney Falls. The 190-foot high falls was named for Prescott, Arizona, prospector D. W. Mooney who fell to his death in 1882 while climbing down a short rope. It was impossible for party members to retrieve Mooney's body until they returned a year later, widened the natural travertine caves, and bolted a ladder to the travertine in order to climb down to the foot of the falls. When they reached Mooney's travertine-encrusted body they buried him at the foot of his namesake falls. But his body later disappeared in a flash flood.

Reaching the foot of Mooney Falls is still dangerous and requires you to climb down a steep and exposed travertine stepway while hanging onto hand-polished chains bolted to the friable travertine.

Ghost Canyon

At one time Havasupai elders encountered apparitions upstream in Cataract Canyon called *amíye* "short and like a shadow." The tributary near the foot of the Mooney Falls is called "Ghost Canyon" because the Havasupai reportedly cremated and buried the dead there in days of old. William Wallace Bass's daughter, Edith, recalled: "My Dad was down in Havasu Canyon one time when one of the Indians, old Tom, died. And the Supais had to burn him, as was their custom, and burn everything with him. All his possessions." According to pioneer photographer Ben Wittick, Captain Tom was an English-speaking Havasupai sub-chief, ". . . the "Boss" really." Ethnographer Leslie Spier visited the Havasupai twice and wrote of their custom: "Formerly, the body was placed on a pyre at some distance from the camp . . . Cremation began to go out of use sixty years ago, the last body being burned twenty-five years back. The change was not suggested nor enforced by the whites. "We wanted to change: we thought burning was not a good way."

DAY HIKES (OVERNIGHT HIKING BELOW MOONEY FALLS IS NOT PERMITTED)

Mile 13.5. Beaver Falls, Beaver Canyon/Havasu Canyon Confluence. The hike downstream from Mooney to Beaver Falls requires route-finding skills to trace the primitive use trail through hanging vines of wild grapes (*Vitis Arizonica*) as it winds around the travertine cliffs on the east side of Havasu Creek above Beaver Falls. This is a popular day hike for rafters hiking up from the Colorado River to view the forty-foot-high falls, swim in the travertine plunge pool, and explore in a single-breath the subterranean solution cave beneath the falls.

Pioneer Photographer

During a side trip to Cataract Canyon in 1885, Civil War veteran and documentary photographer George Ben Wittick packed in his camera, wet plates, and equipment down to Havasupai and photographed Bridal Veil and Mooney Falls, then trekked all the way to Beaver Falls to photograph the charming cascade.

Mile 18. Colorado River. The hike downstream from Beaver Falls to the Colorado River also requires route finding, but the river runners' trail makes it easier to follow, and cairns often mark the numerous thigh-to-waist deep Havasu Creek crossings.

Havasupai sweat bath, Cataract Canyon, Robert L. Carson photo, 1924, Doheny Scientific Expedition.

Caution: Unless you've packed along a Type III or V PFD (Personal Flotation Device), don't plan on replenishing your drinking water from the Colorado River. Scrambling around the slick exposed Muav Limestone ledges near the river is dangerous. Four hikers have fallen and drowned or disappeared in the benign-looking Havasu Rapids.

Old Trails to Havasupai

Listed in ascending order up-canyon (south) from Supai I've included these long-forgotten trails to Supai for travelers, Native Peoples, armchair adventurers, and aficionados interested in pursuing the faded paths, historical threads, and broadening their insight into the Grand Canyon's first and only remaining canyon dwellers.

Topocoba (*Tovokyóva*) Trail, Lee Canyon/Havasu Canyon

Mormon missionary explorer Jacob Vernon Hamblin first visited the Havasupai on April 7, 1863, and tried proselytizing to them, but the "Buckskin Apostle" and his party were cast out, told not to return "under penalty of death," and after "Assuring the Hava-Supai they would send no enemies into their secret valley, Hamblin led his party to the eastward, up the Tope-Kobe trail to the plateau." It's not widely known if Hamblin crossed paths with Mormon fugitive John D. Lee who fled down his namesake canyon that same year, perhaps surviving at Burro Springs, to escape retribution for his alleged role in the Mountain Meadows Massacre. "Lee, while subsisting upon seeds and desert plants," George Wharton James wrote, "was found by the Havasupais, and by them secretly taken into the depths of their canyon home. Here for nearly three years he remained, teaching them improved methods of irrigation, fruit culture, vegetable raising, etc."

Sixteen years later Edward L. Doheny led a group of prospectors down the Topocoba Trail and discovered a "dinosaur" petroglyph pecked into the wall of Lee Canyon. Many years later, the prospector-turned-oil-magnate and creationist organized the "Doheny Scientific Expedition to the Hava Supai Canyon," and returned in the fall of 1924 to photograph the dinosaur etching. Expedition members built a fifteen-foot tall wooden platform they called "The Parallel" to precisely document the 11 x 7 inch long-necked figure they believed resembled a Jurassic-aged Diplodocus. Dinosaur tracks they visited in the Painted Desert 100 miles east convinced the expedition members they'd made an earth shattering discovery. Debunked in the halls of academia, expedition director Samuel Hubbard protested and wrote: "The fact that some prehistoric man made a pictograph of a dinosaur on the walls of this canyon upsets completely all of our theories regarding the antiquity of man."

Moqui (*Móka*) Trail, Moqui Trail Canyon/Cataract Canyon

When Padre Garcés left Havasupai on May 25, 1776 after his five-day *visita* he was guided up the Móka Trail, a Havasupai name for the fleet-footed Hopi who traveled the long trail across the Painted Desert and Coconino Plateau to trade with the Havasupai. Over a century later, the Hopi guided anthropologist Frank Hamilton Cushing down the precipitous trail for his two-part 1882 account of the Havasupai, "Nation of Willows," he wrote for *The Atlantic Monthly* magazine. In part, Cushing described the trail I later followed on foot during a week-long journey run from the Hopi pueblo of Oraibi to Havasupai: "Even the entrances to that tremendous chasm can scarcely be pictured." The Pennsylvania-born ethnologist used the buckskin fringe of his leather jacket to knot and count the trail's "forty-three abrupt turns . . . each one deeper, each turn narrowing the vision. . . [until] only a narrow strip of sky could be seen from our pathway." Navajo traders also used the Moqui Trail, and they called it *Gohniinii Ha'atiin*.

Black Tank Trail, Black Tank Wash/Cataract Canyon

J. W. McKinney made one of the first recorded ascents of the Havasupai's horse trail to Williams, Arizona, sometime during September 8–13, 1884. Little else is known about the lightly clad tinhorn, other than he wore a gold watch, carried $400 in cash, and abandoned William Wallace Bass one night during a punishing three day pack trip to Havasupai with the seasoned trailblazer. Bass returned to Williams and formed a search party to look for McKinney that included a Doctor Mason and a Justice of the Peace named Scott who was going to perform an autopsy if they found McKinney's body. The pair suspected Bass killed McKinney for his loot, and the townsfolk were hankering for an old fashioned "neck-tie party." Incensed when he got wind of their suspicions, Bass pushed on and discovered that his Havasupai friends found McKinney when he was mad with thirst. The friendly Havasupai hosted McKinney during his three-day recovery, then loaned him a horse and blanket and gave him food before they sent him—and two other prospectors who were poking their noses, picks, and shovels into places they shouldn't be digging—back to Williams up the Black Tank Trail. The Havasupai used the trail for their traditional winter camp.

Kla-la-Pa Trail, Cataract Canyon

Ordered to survey new reservation boundaries for the Havasupai, the U.S. Army 6th Cavalry first used the remote trail on June 10, 1881 to meet with Havasupai Captain Navajo. Accompanying the contingent was Pai-speaking interpreter Charles Spencer and Army surgeon, historian and author Elliot Coues. Coues was studying the area for his book, *On the Trail of the Spanish Pioneer*, a milestone translation of Padre Garcés's diary of his journey to Havasupai. "Three sleeps" after the 6th Cavalry sent a message to Captain Navajo (*Wasakwívamgn),* he waited for them at the foot of the trail 2,500 vertical feet below. According to Lieutenant Colonel W. M. Redwood Price's July 1, 1881, report, it was a "very steep, zigzag, rocky, hazardous trail over a mile long which consumed an hour in descending brought us to the bed of the canyon and we were soon joined by Navajo and several of his people." Captain Navajo led the contingent to Supai where he learned of the 6th Cavalry's dire recommendations to reduce the Havasupai's vast ancestral canyon and plateau lands. Under Executive order dated March 3, 1882, President Chester A. Arthur confined the Havasupai to 516 acres of what once encompassed their 6,750 square mile homeland on the Coconino Plateau.

Pack-a-the-true-ye-ba Trail, Cataract Canyon

U.S. Army General George Crook rode down the slippery trail on November 9, 1884, with diarist Captain John Gregory Bourke and a small contingent of soldiers and packers. Bourke wrote: "There is a trail descending the Cataract Cañon so narrow and dangerous that pack trains rarely get to the bottom without accidents. . . . One of our mules was pushed off the trail by another mule crowding up against it, and was hurled over the precipice and dashed into a pulp on the rocks a thousand feet below." Known to the Chiricahua Apache as *Nantan Lupan,* "Grey Wolf," for hunting Geronimo, General Crook advised the Havasupai they could still hunt on the plateau as they'd done for centuries. Crook's advice, swept up in the tides of Manifest Destiny, the Homestead Act, and Indian Removal Act, reached deep into the heart of the Grand Canyon and did not bode well for the Havasupai. In an impassioned dispatch sent to the Commissioner of Indian Affairs on September 25, 1915, Havasupai Captain Jim wrote: "A long time ago the Gods gave the deer to the Indian for himself. The women and children all like deer meat very much. The Indian men like buckskins to trade for grub, saddles, horses, saddles, blankets, and money. A long time ago … the Indians all go out on the plateau and hunt deer for two or three months and then all come back to Supai to stay."

Hiker Use is restricted to the Hualapai (Havasupai) Trail. Special permission must be obtained from the Havasupai Tribe to trek any of the Old Trails to Havasupai. Permission to use the Topocoba Trail must also be obtained from the Backcountry Information Center at Grand Canyon National Park.

Additional Considerations

- Warning Advisory: Do not hike the Hualapai (Havasupai) Trail, or below Supai, during July-August monsoon weather, or during flash flood weather or warnings any time of the year. Check local weather updates (Williams, Arizona) beforehand. During summertime it's important to leave Havasupai Campground at dawn—don't delay in Supai—to beat the heat to Hualapai Hilltop.

- Primary Access: Hualapai (Havasupai) Trail.
- Elevation: 5,200-feet Hualapai Trailhead, 3,157-feet Supai, 1,800-feet Colorado River.
- Biotic Communities: Piñon juniper woodland, Upper Sonoran, and deciduous riparian.
- Total Elevation Loss and Gain: Supai 4,086 feet (2,043 vertical feet each way); Colorado River 6,600 feet (3,400 vertical feet each way).
- Maps: Supai, Havasu Falls, and S. B. Point Quadrangles (7.5 minute).
- Mileage, Rim to Supai: 16 miles (8 miles one way to Supai).
- Mileage, Rim to Campground: 20 miles (10 miles one way to campground).
- Mileage, Rim to Beaver Falls: 27 miles (13.5 miles one way to Beaver Falls).
- Mileage, Rim to Colorado River: 36 Miles (18 miles one way to Havasu Rapids).
- Water: Supai and Fern Spring.
- Cache Points: Secluded areas of Hualapai Canyon.
- Seasons: Spring, fall, and warm days of winter. June can be a scorcher, and July and August monsoons pose serious flash flood dangers.
- Escape Routes: Hualapai Hilltop, Supai.
- Camping: Havasupai Campground only.
- Nearest Supply Points: Williams, Seligman, Peach Springs, Kingman, and Supai.
- NPS Grand Canyon Hiker 24 Hour Emergency Phone Number and Email
  - Phone (928) 638–7805
    - Email: grca_bic@nps.gov (Use this if the phone line is busy)

Managing Agency:

Havasupai Tribe
P. O. Box 10, Supai, Arizona 86435
Phone (928) 448–2731
Fax (928) 448–2551
Visit: www.havasupai-nsn.gov/

Havasupai Tourist Office
Advance reservation required
Entry and Camping Permits
Phone: (928) 448–2121
Visit: www.httourism0@havasupai-nsn.gov

Havasupai Lodge
Phone: (928) 448–2111
Visit: www.htlodge0@havasupai-nsn.gov

Havasupai Trading Post
Phone: (928) 448–2951
Visit: www.htstore0@havasupai-nsn.gov

18

Trans Canyon Trails and Routes: Point-to-Point Hikes and Treks

"Lonesome? Not when you get used to it."

—Ben Beamer, Prospector, July 17, 1892

LANDFORM

Beginning at the confluence of the Colorado and Little Colorado Rivers, the Colorado River corridor beneath the South Rim offers a natural pedestrian inner-canyon walkway that follows the banks, benches, ledges, hanging terraces, and plateaus through the Grand Canyon's geological stratigraphy and the Life Zones of North America's plants, animals, birds, and invertebrates all the way to Cataract Canyon—and beyond in the chasm's western reaches.

HISTORY

Archeological evidence indicates much of this rugged and remote trans canyon route was traveled by Archaic peoples 4,000 years ago; later by Ancestral Puebloans and Native Peoples, including the Hopi, Navajo, Paiute, Havasupai, and Yavapai, and in historic times by explorers, surveyors, prospectors, miners, trailblazers, guides, and intrepid tourists.

Hopi Clans and Salt Trail Shrine, *Tutuventiwngwu*, "Place of the Clan Rocks," Willow Springs.

The ancient thoroughfare opens many doors for hikers, canyoneers, and naturalists keen on extending their canyon forays beyond the canyon's characteristic rim-to-river trails to include multiday rim-to-river loop hikes and multiday to week-long point-to-point treks that traverse the heart of the inner Canyon.

From the confluence of the Colorado and Little Colorado Rivers, these primitive trans canyon trails and routes lead 126.85 miles west to 6,322-foot Apache Point near Havasupai Tribal lands. Tracing them requires stamina, good judgment, route-finding skills, and the ability to travel confidently and safely off the grid far from help.

<u>Note:</u> Except for the Beamer Trail, which is typically accessed from the Tanner Trail, each of these trails and routes is described sequentially east-to-west.

Beamer Trail

The trail begins—and ends—at the foot of the Tanner Trail near Tanner Rapids on the Colorado River at Mile 68.5, Elevation 2,650 feet (808 meters), Dox Sandstone. Named for prospector and pioneer Ben Beamer, the primitive 8.5-mile point-to-point trail courses east along the Colorado River and Beamer Trail to the Little Colorado River confluence. From Tanner Canyon delta, follow the east bank of the Colorado River 2.9 miles through sand, invasive stands of tamarisk (*Tamarix ramosissima*), and Dox Sandstone boulders past Comanche Creek and Espejo Creek to Palisades Creek. (At Comanche Creek an exposed Third and Fourth Class route leads 3,600 vertical feet to Comanche Point saddle on the rim of the Palisades of the Desert.) Seth B. Tanner filed the Tanner Ledge mining claim at Palisades Creek in 1877. The claim was later developed by George W. McCormick, who called it the Copper Blossom Mine. Tailings, toxic-air mine tunnels, and odd bits of equipment are still evident from the diggings-to-bust enterprise. Tanner and his partner Franklin French developed this leg of what's officially called the Beamer Trail, a path that has long been used by the Navajo from Tanner Canyon, and the Hopi from Salt Trail Canyon, to reach their sacred salt deposits.

From the mouth of Palisades Creek, the Beamer Trail makes an abrupt 250 vertical foot ascent through the Dox Sandstone, loose talus, and boulders to the top of the Tapeats Sandstone. Once you've topped out on this Tapeats bench, the narrow, dangerously exposed Beamer Trail courses along the outer rim of the Tapeats offering dizzying and distracting views of the Colorado River and 6,394-foot Chuar Butte across the river. The trail is neither flat nor straight. It contours in and out of drainages cut by headward erosion, frequently descending fifty to 100 vertical feet into each drainage before climbing out the opposite side. Make sure you eyeball the hide-and-seek trail and cairns on the opposite sides of each of these minor drainages before descending into them and you'll save time and unnecessary scrambling on this 5.6-mile stretch.

Chasm view, Little Colorado River Gorge.
Copyright © John Annerino Photography.

Navajo medicine men and salt pilgrims who first used the trail to reach their salt mines from Tanner Canyon before Ben Beamer crossed the Tapeats Sandstone ledges called it the *Tsétátʼah haʼatiin,* "Trap Trail," or "Rock Ledge Trail." When Grand Canyon explorers and photographers Emery and Ellsworth Kolb traced the Beamer Trail with their provision-laden burro, Jennie, for the August 1914 *National Geographic* magazine feature, "Experiences in the Grand Canyon," they wrote: "A test of nerve. From this point on to the mouth of the Little Colorado, we slowly worked our way over one of the worst trails we had ever seen." Pay attention. A gust of wind, or one misstep, at the wrong spot can send you hurtling over the edge. Imagine leading a stubborn skittish burro along this narrow precipice.

From the northeast end of the Tapeats bench, the Beamer Trail descends a well-worn route to Beamers Cabin. When the Kolb brothers finally reached the confluence after their perilous crossing of the Beamer Trail, they exclaimed: "Imagine living in such a place!" And they added: "Still it is not unusual to find men in these out-of-the-way corners of the West, happy and contented with their lot, diligently searching for the fortune which they feel sure they will find before another week has passed."

Beamers Cabin

Ben Beamer lived in one of those "out-of-the-way corners of the West." And his back story is as mysterious as prospector Louis D. Boucher's. In a rare interview Beamer gave for the July 17, 1892, *Denver Republican,* he described his life in the canyon: "I never saw a human being until this spring, when line surveyors of the Atlantic and Pacific Railroad, with a guide, made their way into the cañon. I took up a ranch at the mouth of the Little Colorado, where there are about ten acres of cultivable land, built me a cabin and went about my own business of prospecting for the precious metals . . . How do I live? Well, as all prospectors do, only I get plenty of fish and wild goat [bighorn sheep], and there are some otter. After the snow melts the Colorado backs up into some of those small cañons and the fish come in millions to feed on a vegetable that grows on the rocks. They are so thick that you can lean over the water's edge and pull them out by the tail two at a time."

Beamer may have been catching Colorado pikeminnow (*Ptychocheilus lucius*) now extirpated from the Grand Canyon.

Beamer lived in a hand-laid stone dwelling nestled beneath wind-sculpted ledges of Tapeats Sandstone overlooking the loamy delta he farmed at the confluence of the Colorado and Little Colorado Rivers.

Colorado and Little Colorado Rivers

Pictographs, potsherds, and lithic scatters indicate Beamer reconstructed his "cabin" from a cliff dwelling that dated back 4,000 years. Beamer's view of the Little Colorado River's turquoise waters surging with the Colorado River's muddy red waters was mesmerizing, set against the backdrop of towering three-thousand-foot high bronze cliffs and walls and powder blue skies. For good reason the Confluence, as it's known to many Native Peoples and eleven culturally affiliated tribes, is still held sacrosanct:

The Hopi, *Hopitu Shinumu,* made dangerous pilgrimages on foot across *Tutskwa,* "Hopi land," on the Salt Pilgrimage Trail, *Homvi'kya* to *Tutuventiwngwu,* "Place of the Clan Rocks" through the Little Colorado River Gorge, *Öngtupqa,* "Salt Canyon," and offered eagle-feathered, corn pollen-dusted praye sticks, *paahos,* at sacred trail shrines and their place of emergence, *Sípàapuni,* before painting their clan symbols and collecting salt at *Öönga.*

The Navajo, *Diné,* journeyed on foot across *Dinétah,* "Navajo land," down Tanner Canyon, *Áshįįh ha'atiin,* "Salt Trail out of Canyon," across the *Tsétát'ah ha'atiin,* "Trap Trail," or "Rock Ledge Trail" to the Confluence, *Tooh Ahidiiliníand,* where they made offerings to Salt Woman, *Áshįjh Asdáá,* in the Little Colorado River Gorge before collecting sacred salt at *'Ashiih* in *Tólchí'-íkooh,* "Red Water Canyon," and ceremonial water from Blue Springs, *Tó dootł'izh.*

The Havasupai, *Havsuw' Baaja,* traveled along the rim the Coconino Plateau, far beyond their sacred canyon home totems of *Wig-Li-I-Wa* and their cultural Grand Canyon landscape of *Wikatata,* "Origin Tale," and descended into the Little Colorado River Gorge, *Hak tha e 'la,* to gather agave near the Confluence at *Kwantupe,* "Agave Roasting-place," within sight of the Hopi shrine, *Panktupatca,* "Home of the Mountain Sheep."

The Kaibab Paiute, *Kaipa'pici,* journeyed from their forested homelands of the Kaibab Plateau, *Kaivavic,* "Mountain Lying Down," across the Grand Canyon, *Piapaxa 'Uipi,* "Big River Canyon," to the Little Colorado River, *Oavaxa,* which they also revere as *Puaxantu Tuvip,* "holy land." They gathered "salt called *timpi-oavi* (rock salt)" from a sacred "cave where the water dripped all the time." A supernatural being *anungwuts,* "salt person," showed the San Juan Paiute the trail to the salt cave.

The Zuni, *A:shiwi,* sacred place of emergence is Ribbon Falls on Bright Angel Creek, *Thmik'yana'kya,* and they journeyed across the Grand Canyon, *Chimik'yana'kya dey'a,* from trail shrine to trail shrine through the Confluence and Little Colorado River Gorge on their ritual migration route, *Chimik'yanakona penane,* that crossed the Painted Desert to reach *Idiwana'a,* "Middle Place," near Zuni Pueblo, New Mexico.

In this extraordinary natural setting and hallowed ground and waters of the Colorado and Little Colorado Rivers, at the foot of the eagle's perch atop the soaring cliffs of *Tsin dah shijaa' bidáá',* 6,146-foot Cape Solitude, where for epochs the Diné have traditionally performed their visionary healing *Hozhooji*, "Blessingway Ceremony," developers envision building a luxury resort and a 1.4-mile rim-to-river tramway to reach the confluence that can be seen from Beamer's front window, a pristine view first seen by the indigenous canyon dwellers who built Beamers Cabin 4,000 years ago.

The current developers weren't the first, nor are they likely to be the last, who envisioned tapping the wild revenue stream of tourists and pay dirt in the depths of the Grand Canyon in ways unimagined by the Grand Canyon's first caretakers, its Native Peoples.

SKYWALKS, SKYWIRES, AERIAL TRAMS, CABLE CARS, NARROW BRIDGES, AND BRAIDED ROPES

"Leave it as it is. You can not improve on it.
The ages have been at work on it, and man can only mar it."

—President Theodore Roosevelt, May 6, 1903
South Rim, Grand Canyon Game Preserve

By the time the forty-three-year old Republican president gave his historic speech at the Grand Canyon on May 6,1903, the genie had already been let out of the bottle with the General Mining Act of 1872: "The mineral lands of the public domain, both surveyed and unsurveyed, are hereby declared to be free and open to exploration and occupation by all citizens of the United States . . ." Prospectors, followed by miners, cattleman, timber companies, and the "iron horse," were already deeply entrenched at the Grand Canyon, and there was no putting the genie back into its brass bottle in spite of President Roosevelt's impassioned speech. No one seemed to listen. Most everyone wanted their slice of the pie: builders, contractors, miners, loggers, hoteliers, concessionaires, the National Park Service, and the Santa Fe Railroad built and maintained the roads, railroad lines, lodges, trails, concessions, and infrastructure vital to the unbridled commercial development of Grand Canyon National Park, what the late Edward Abbey called "industrial tourism." It was the accepted norm. But a fire storm ignited with the proposed Grand Canyon Escalade development at the confluence of the Colorado and Little Colorado Rivers. In spite of my personal view that development would desecrate a hallowed area revered by indigenous canyon dwellers for a thousand years, the development and aerial tramway is the latest in a series of stepping stones first explored, surveyed, or built by the Grand Canyon's "colorful and historic" figures under the auspices of independent, corporate, national park, and tribal interests.

1907. Rusts Cable Crossing

Entrepreneur Edwin D. "Uncle Dee" Woolley forms the Grand Canyon Transportation Company and, with his son-in-law David R. Rust, builds the Grand Canyon's first cable crossing using a mule-sized cage to ferry tourists and their mounts traveling between the North Rim and the South Rim, via the old Bright Angel Canyon Trail, Rust's Tent Camp on the Colorado River, and the Bright Angel Trail.

1908. Bass's Cable Crossing

Trailblazer and promoter William Wallace Bass constructs his own cable car crossing for tourists traveling between the South Rim and North Rim via the South Bass Trail, Shinumo Garden and Camp near the Colorado River, and the North Bass Trail. It was also pivotal for transporting Bass's mining equipment to, and ore from, his asbestos and silver mine (and mining claims) that grossed a reported $25,000, valued at $330,342.18 today.

1919. Grand Canyon Cableway

Engineer George K. Davol and his survey crew explore the inner canyon for his proposed cross canyon, temple-hopping cableway that would carry tourists between the South Rim and the North Rim, via the 7,066-foot Hopi Point terminal down to the 5,031-foot Dana Butte tower, soar over the Colorado River, and climb up and link the summit towers atop 6,012-foot Tower of Set, 6,613-foot Osiris Temple, and 7,646-foot Shiva Temple, and terminate at the North Rim's 7,766-foot Tiyo Point. The project is vetoed by millionaire (20 Mule Team Borax), industrialist, conservationist, and Sierra Club vice president, National Park Service Director Stephen Tyng Mather when Grand Canyon National Park was established in 1920 because it was ". . . too costly, and damaging to the canyon's ecology."

1925. Hermit Camp Tramway

The Santa Fe Railroad builds a 6,300 foot long aerial tramway—"the longest single-span cable tram in the United States"—between the South Rim and the Tonto Plateau to carry supplies from 6,799-foot Pima Point to Hermit Camp for Santa Fe Railroad's "luxury" tourist accommodations at Hermit Camp for an undisclosed cost. The Hermit Camp and Hermit Trail were built for $100,000, a princely sum duing the 1920s.

1930. Cheyava Falls

Grand Canyon explorers and photographers Emery and Ellsworth Kolb erect a timber boom and block and tackle threaded with 600 feet of rope to photograph their daring attempt to descend the North Rim's 700-foot tall Cheyava Falls. (See Clear Creek Trail page 281.)

1949–51. Marble Canyon Dam Cable Car

The U.S. Bureau of Reclamation constructed a 3,400-foot-long aerial tram from the 5,702-foot rim of Tatahatso Point nicknamed "Henry Lane's Elevator" to ferry men and equipment down to the Colorado River at the Mile 39.5 survey site to drill, blast, test, and explore the feasibility of building the dam. Allison Steel Manufacturing Company, of Phoenix, offered a $23,000 bid to build what the *Arizona Republic* headlined, "Marble Canyon Dam Site Line is World's Longest," in the Phoenix newspaper's June 25, 1950, edition. The Bureau of Reclamation decided to the build the cableway themselves, though it was a fraction of their 1963 estimated cost of $144 million to complete what was also called the Redwall Dam. (See page 229 Colorado River.)

1956. Orphan Lode Mine Cable Tram

The Golden Crown Mining and Western Gold and Uranium consortium constructs an 1,800-foot-long cable tram from the South Rim to reach Dan Hogan's historic Orphan Lode Mine site below the South Rim's Hopi Point to transport miners to the site and to haul out 800-pound bucket loads of rich uranium ore that yielded 13 million pounds valued at $40 million between 1956 and 1969.

1957. Bat Cave Tramway

The Consolidated Western Steel, U.S. Steel, and U.S. Guano Corporation consortium constructs an 9,400-foot aerial tramway from the South Rim, across the Colorado River, to the mine site below the North Rim in order to vacuum-mine nitrogen-rich, carbon-dated 12,000-year-old bat guano for lawn and patio fertilizer. Built at the cost of $680,000, the mine was a bust netting approximately $100,000 (1,000 tons of guano at $100 a ton). What some viewed as an engineering feat, construction of the tram was more of helicopter-flying marvel by pilot Buzz Westcott, who reportedly made 3,000 flights to the Colorado River Mile 266 construction site to haul 115 tons of equipment, concrete mix, and steel, and string 11,500 feet of aviation cable through three steel towers.

1966. Trans Canyon Pipeline

Under the direction of the National Park Service, Halvorson Construction Company builds a 12.4-mile pipeline at a cost of $2 million, but a devastating fifteen-inch rain destroyed sections of pipeline shortly after completion and the project repairs push the final cost to $6 million. The gravity-fed siphon pipeline pumps 500,000 gallons of water a day from Roaring Springs on the North Kaibab Trail, across the Colorado River beneath the Bright Angel Suspension Bridge, and up the Bright Angel Trail to 8,576-acre Grand Canyon Village to develop and sustain park operations, visitor services, and infrastructure, as well as the needs of commercial concessions and interests to accommodate more than five million visitors a year. The cost to replace the aging but critical water pipeline is estimated to be $100 million to $150 million.

2001. Journey into Amazing Caves

Funded in part by the National Science Foundation, MacGillivray Freeman Films produce a thirty-nine-minute IMAX film featuring Greenland's glacial ice caves, Mexico's Mayan *cenotes*, and the Grand Canyon's "never explored" Redwall Limestone cave 700 feet above the Little Colorado River Gorge. Helicopters shoot Space Cam aerials of the gorge and transport the thirty-person crew to and from the undisclosed Navajo Nation Tribal Park location each day on what appears to be the northeastern point of 5,680-foot Palisades of the Desert plateau opposite the Little Colorado River Gorge's Big Canyon. The production's 3.5 tons of equipment includes a twenty-foot winch-powered, guy wire-anchored truss that carried the cave characters, crew, and seventy-pound cameras down and up the 300-foot wall to the cave entrance each day. The gross box office receipts go north of $51 million.

2007. Grand Canyon Skywalk

Envisioned by developer David Jin, the Hualapai Tribe constructs the Grand Canyon Skywalk on the South Rim of the western Grand Canyon to offer tourists window-floor views of the Colorado River through a U-shaped glass promenade that juts seventy feet out from the canyon rim. The $30 million cantilevered walkway lures 370,000 visitors a year and is the cornerstone of the Hualapai's future commercial development of the 9,000-acre site near what some tribal elders consider the Hualapai's sacred rim of Eagle Rock.

2013. Skywire Live

Seventh-generation tight rope walker Nik Wallenda of The Flying Wallendas fame completes what Reuters headlined was the first "historic high-wire walk. . . over the Grand Canyon." The event was seen by thirteen million viewers worldwide on primetime television and generated untold millions in advertising revenue. The 1,400-foot crossing on a two-inch cable bolted between opposite rims 895 vertical feet above Little Colorado River Gorge was made 45.5 miles distant upstream from its confluence with the Colorado River in Grand Canyon National Park.

2014. Grand Canyon Escalade Project

Confluence Partners, LLC, has proposed a 420-acre resort complex on the 6,061-foot west rim of the Painted Desert Façade on Navajo Nation lands near the east rim of

Grand Canyon National Park. Perched 2,690 vertical feet above the confluence of the Colorado and Little Colorado Rivers, Sundt Construction would build out the $1 billion travel resort and tourist destination that, according to the feasibility study, would include eight-person gondola rides on a 1.4-mile rim-to-river tramway that would ferry upward of an estimated 10,000 tourists a day from the rim of the Desert Facade to the restaurant and gift shop overlooking the Confluence, and the elevated Colorado Riverside walkway and amphitheater. What would follow? A cross-canyon Tianmenshan, China-style glass bottomed bridge to 6,146-foot Cape Solitude, a cliff hanging El Caminito del Rey, Spain-inspired walkway to Blue Springs, a river skimming Vortex, Ohio-modeled hill lift terrain roller coaster roaring alongside the Colorado River, a Vegas-styled Egyptian pyramid and sphinx rim rock retreat, and a spider web of "eco-adventure" zip lining, rappelling, and B&B cliff camping in hanging, glass-windowed portaledges?

Additional Considerations

The Beamer Trail is most often trekked out-and-back from the Tanner Trail. Few venture fifty-seven miles down the Little Colorado River Gorge from Cameron, Arizona, to reach the Confluence. (See page 159 Tanner Trail.)

Travel Notes

- Warning Advisory: Do not hike the Beamer and Tanner Trail in the summer.
- Primary Access: Tanner Trail, Colorado River (river runner side hike).
- Elevation: 2,650-feet to 2,722-feet at Colorado River level.
- Biotic Communities: Sonoran Desert.
- Total Elevation Loss and Gain: Approximately 500 vertical feet each way.
- Maps: Desert View and Cape Solitude Quadrangles (7.5 minute).
- Mileage: Seventeen miles (8.5 miles one way to the Confluence).
- Water: Colorado River only.
- Cache Points: Tanner Canyon delta, Palisades Creek.
- Seasons: Fall through spring. Summer heat can be deadly, and hot upstream winds can make exposed sections of the Beamer Trail especially dangerous.
- Escape Routes: Tanner Trailhead, Colorado River.
- Camping: No camping within 0.25 miles of the Confluence. At-large, low-impact camping at Tanner Beach Zone BB9, Palisades Creek Zone BA9, and bivouac cubby holes in between.

"Navajo brave and his mother," Timothy H. O'Sullivan stereoview, 1873, Library of Congress.

The Escalante Route/Blessingway Trail

The Escalante Route begins at the foot of the Tanner Trail near Tanner Rapids on the Colorado River at Mile 68.5, Elevation 2,650 feet (808 meters), Dox Sandstone. Named for Spanish missionary explorer Silvestre Vélez de Escalante, the ten-mile point-to-point route leads west along the Colorado River and Escalante Route to the foot of the Hance Trail. On the run from Colonel Christopher "Kit" Carson's merciless Long Walk campaign, Navajo elders, men, women, and children—herding goats and sheep—first used this remote route that should be renamed the Navajo Trail or Blessingway Trail to reach the safety of Indian Garden in 1864. (See page 165 Tanner Trail.)

Tanner Canyon to Red Canyon

At one time the three-mile stretch between the mouth of Tanner Canyon and Cardenas Creek was a faint path. But so many river runners have hiked it over the years, it is now a distinct trail. From Tanner Canyon the trail heads west along the bench above the river to Cardenas Creek. Summertime temperatures along this stretch have been recorded reaching 140 degrees Fahrenheit, resulting in the name "Furnace Flats." From Cardenas Creek bed (normally dry), follow the mile-long river runner's trail 400 vertical feet up to Cardenas Hilltop Ruin. Civil engineer–turned-boatman Robert Brewster Stanton thought he first discovered the stone masonry dwelling on January 23, 1890, during his second disaster-plagued Denver, Colorado, Canyon and Pacific Railroad expedition through the Grand Canyon. So the Mississippi-born river man called it "Stanton's Fort." But two of Major John Wesley Powell's 1871–72 Second Expedition members first noted the dwelling eight years earlier. On August 27, Walter Powell and Almon H. Thompson reportedly ". . . climbed a peak about 500 feet high . . . Found an old stone house evidently built by the Sto-ce nee nas [Cosninas]." Judging from its commanding 360-degree view, some profess the Ancestral Puebloan dwelling was a place of vision quest. But the late anthropologist Robert C. Euler suggested it ". . . lies on what probably was a cross-canyon trail from the Pueblo villages in the Unkar [Delta] vicinity up to the South Rim of the canyon . . . and about 1100–1150 and [it] may have been a "lookout" if not a defensive unit."

If you lie on your stomach you'll get a head-spinning, raptor's view of Unkar Rapids 337 vertical feet below. When Welshman Colin Fletcher first backpacked this route in 1966 during the first modern trans canyon crossing of the Grand Canyon for his book *The Man Who Walked Through Time*, the Colorado River was a veritable trickle at 1,260 cfs (cubic feet per second). The flow was low enough for him to walk along the east bank of Unkar Rapids at river level. But chances are the Colorado River won't be low enough to walk the riverside stretch if you were thinking about retracing Fletcher's route. The river flow wasn't low enough when I first trod the route. From the Unkar overlook, I followed a faint trail up a ridge of Dox Sandstone until I eyeballed a route down into the head of the first major unnamed drainage west of the Cardenas Creek.

On site, at the time, it didn't seem practical to follow what looked like the Escalante Route's long circuitous detour. So I picked my way down to the Colorado River without encountering any difficult obstacles and followed a route on site along the river to Red Canyon at Hance Rapids. (Note: *From Unkar overlook, the established "high route" of the Escalante Route stays high, climbs into the head of Escalante Creek, and winds in and around Seventy-five Mile Creek, before descending to the river at Nevills Rapid. Cairns and boot traffic reportedly mark the increasingly popular High Route.*) Assuming the Colorado River isn't rumbling along at 25,000 to 30,000 cfs, you can follow the River Route along the left-hand (southeast) side of the river through irritating stands of tamarisk, along upward-sloping steps of Hakatai Shale to Escalante Creek. If high water has covered the River Route, or you encounter any problems, back track to the High Route. I'm fairly certain the 1864 Navajo refugees pioneered the upper Escalante Route to avoid losing their goats and sheep along the river. (Call the Backcountry Information Center beforehand for current river flows.)

Continuing along the River Route, the bed of Escalante Creek drops off near the Colorado River. Cairns once marked the way through a series of three pour offs between the beaches on the west side below them. If for some reason you can't find the cairns, follow the easiest and safest path of least resistance to the west and follow the beach at Escalante Creek to Papago Creek.

If you study the next section carefully, there is a line that climbs out of the mouth of Papago Creek and traverses the sandstone ledges above it. It has a tendency to diagonal up and west to the top of the rockslide facing downstream, which is your descent route back down to river level. From the bottom of this rockslide, it's a thirty-minute hike along the beach to Hance Rapids, the foot of the New Hance Trail, and the start of the Tonto Trail East.

<u>Note:</u> I wore a light deflated CO_2-charged scuba diver vest for safety while following the River Route.

Additional Considerations:

If you're planning to hike the Escalante Route, you may find it safer and easier to descend the Tanner Trail, traverse the Escalante Route, then hike out the New Hance Trail or the Grandview Trail (see page 156).

Travel Notes

- Warning Advisory: Do not hike the Escalante Route in the summer.
- Primary Access Trails: Tanner Trail, New Hance Trail, and East Tonto Trail via the Grandview Trail.

- Elevation: 2,650-feet to 2,548-feet at the Colorado River.
- Biotic Communities: Sonoran Desert.
- Total Elevation Loss and Gain: Approximately 1,000 vertical for the route described.
- Maps: Desert View and Cape Royal Quadrangles (7.5 minute).
- Mileage: Ten miles one way.
- Water: Colorado River.
- Cache Points: None on this point-to-point hike.
- Seasons: Fall through spring. Furnace Flats is no place to backpack during the summer. It's one thing for veteran river guides to beach their rafts at Cardenas Creek and scamper up to Hilltop Ruin in their flip flops. It's quite another to backpack down the Tanner Trail across Furnace Flats to reach it.
- Escape Routes: Tanner Trailhead, Colorado River.
- Camping: At-large low-impact camping at Cardenas Creek, Escalante Creek, Seventy-five Mile Creek, and Papago Creek Zones BC9; and Red Canyon Zone BD9.

The Tonto Trail

The Tonto Trail begins at the foot of the New Hance Trail and dead ends in Garnet Canyon 121.4 miles west. The trail was named for the Tonto band of Western Apache—a disparaging Spanish term—who are known as *Dilzhę'é*, "People with High Pitched Voices." During the 1880s–1890s, prospectors and miners William Wallace Bass, John Hance, Peter D. Berry, Louis D. Boucher, Ralph and Niles Cameron, and Daniel L. Hogan reconstructed the ancient trail atop the Tonto Platform from Red Canyon all the way to the South Bass Trail, which interlinked seven of the South Rim's eight rim-to-river trails. George Wharton James wrote of the trail's origin in 1899: "The trail made centuries ago by mountain sheep, small bands of which are still to be found in the remoter corners of the Canyon—then followed by the Indians, whose moccasin feet made less impression upon it than did the hoofs of the sheep." The old trail traverses the Tonto Plateau, the broadest terrace coursing east-to-west through the Grand Canyon. This "plateau" may look flat when viewed from the lofty scenic vistas of the South and North Rims, but don't be fooled. The rugged nonmaintained trail that snakes its way across the Tonto Plateau is circuitous and undulating, making abrupt ascents and descents in and out of each and every single tributary drainage, creek and canyon cut by headward erosion that drain into the Colorado River.

Tonto Trail East

The Tonto Trail East begins at foot of the New Hance Trail near Hance Rapids on the Colorado River at Mile 76.5, Elevation 2,548 feet (780 meters), Vishnu Schist. From Hance Rapids, the Tonto Trail East leads thirty-six miles west to Indian Garden on the Bright Angel Trail.

Red Canyon to Hance Creek

From the sand dunes at the mouth of Red Canyon, the 2.8-mile Tonto Trail climbs a steep, rocky stretch of Hakatai Shale up through slumps, landslides, and rock falls 850 vertical feet along the east side of Mineral Canyon. At the 3,400-foot elevation contour on your Cape Royal Quadrangle (7.5 minute) map, the trail crosses the creek bed of Mineral Canyon (watch for cairns) and winds around into the unnamed canyon between Mineral Creek and Hance Creek to Shady Overhang. This welcome shelter is a great spot for a water break, rest, and snack stop.

From Shady Overhang, the trail climbs through the Tapeats Sandstone and tops out on the Tonto Plateau below 4,961-foot Ayer Point. The point was named for Emma Augustus Burbank Ayer "the first white woman" to journey to the bottom of the Grand Canyon via the Old Hance Trail in 1885. Ayer was noted for coauthoring the travel book *A Motor Flight through Algeria and Tunisia* (1911) and for translating the New Mexico diary of seventeenth-century Portuguese-speaking, Franciscan missionary Alonso de Benavides. From Ayer Point, the trail contours around the promontory and skirts the Tapeats Sandstone along the east side of Hance Creek until you cross the creek bed where you'll find perennial water, shade, and primitive camp sites. Hike out of Hance Creek on the west side, and a half-mile beyond you'll reach the Hance Creek/East Tonto Trail junction, Elevation 3,780 feet (1,149 meters).

Travel Notes

- Warning Advisory: Do not hike this section of the Tonto Trail East during the summer.
- Primary Access Trails and Routes: Tanner Trail, Escalante Route, New Hance Trail, and Grandview Trail.
- Elevation: 2,548-feet Hance Rapids to 3,780-feet East Tonto Trail junction.
- Biotic Communities: Sonoran Desert.
- Total Elevation Gain: 1,250+ vertical feet.
- Map: Cape Royal Quadrangle (7.5 minute).
- Mileage: 2.8 miles one way.
- Water: Colorado River, Hance Creek, and Page Springs (Miner Springs) in the west arm of Hance Creek below Horseshoe Mesa.

- Cache Points: None on this point-to-point hike
- Seasons: Fall through spring. Hiking uphill in the summer heat from Hance Rapids may be worse than Furnace Flats.
- Escape Routes: Grandview Trail, Colorado River.
- Camping: At large, low-impact camping at Hance Rapids Zone BD9, and Hance Creek Zone BE9.

Tonto Trail East/Hance Creek/Cottonwood Creek

From the Hance Creek/ Tonto Trail East junction, Elevation 3,780 feet (1,149 meters), Tapeats Sandstone, the three-mile Tonto Trail East loops around the base and twin arms of 5,246-foot Horseshoe Mesa to the Cottonwood Creek/ Tonto Trail East junction, Elevation 3,690 feet (1,125 meters), Tapeats Sandstone. The easy to follow trail traces the 3,700-foot elevation contour on your Cape Royal Quadrangle (7.5 minute) map.

The Tonto Trail was not always so easy to follow. At the turn of the last century when the "color" played out, and pay dirt proved too expensive to haul out, prospectors tuned lose their lovable burros. For years the beasts of burden, made popular in the children's book, *Brighty of the Grand Canyon*, (1953) had faithfully carried provisions, camp equipage, picks, shovels, and dynamite, and offered companionship to prospectors like Louis D. Boucher, John Hance, and William Wallace Bass. The Grand Canyon proved to be a perfect breeding ground for *Equus asinus*, and hundreds of feral burros created a maze of trails wherever they roamed and foraged that were often indecipherable from the Tonto Trail. Their presence threatened the native, more timid Desert bighorn sheep (*Ovis canadensis nelsoni*), destroying its habitat and depleting ephemeral water sources. Intent on restoring the canyon's ecological balance, park rangers killed 2,608 feral burros between 1924 and 1968. The public outcry over Brighty's kin being slaughtered in the nation's "Crown Jewel of National Parks" echoed far and wide. And the park responded. Between 1981 and 1982 Park Rangers airlifted 577 burros to safety, restoring the canyon's natural order and wilderness values many felt had been disrupted by the legendary symbol of lonely prospectors and the Old West.

Additional Considerations:

This section of the Tonto Trail East is most frequently done as a loop hike, (see page 144 Grandview Trail).

Travel Notes

- Primary Access: Grandview Trail.
- Elevation: 3,780-feet Hance Creek to 3,750-feet Cottonwood Creek.

- Biotic Communities: Sonoran Desert.
- Total Elevation Gain and Gain: Approximately 200 vertical feet.
- Mileage: Three miles one way.
- Water: Miner (Page) Springs, Cottonwood Creek southern spring (seasonal).
- Cache Points: None on this point-to-point hike.
- Seasons: Fall through spring. Summer's a scorcher on the Tonto Trail.
- Map: Cape Royal Quadrangle (7.5 minute).
- Escape Routes: Grandview Trail, Colorado River.
- Camping: At large, low impact camping Hance Creek and Cottonwood Creek Zone BG9.

Cottonwood Creek/Tonto Trail East/South Kaibab Trail

Assuming an old feral burro trail doesn't lead you off on a dead end scenic tour through a sea of Black Brush (*Coleogyne ramosissima Torr*), it is 19.8 miles from Cottonwood Creek to the South Kaibab Trail/East Tonto Trail junction. Compared to the 39.5-mile stretch of the Tonto Trail between the Hermit and South Bass Trails, this popular stretch is relatively easy to follow, though care is required traversing several exposed catwalks. The point-to-point route is a rigorous trek across a remote trail in and out of five intervening canyons that are normally dry. Careful seasonal planning is needed to assure the availability of reliable drinking water.

From the Cottonwood Creek/Tonto Trail East junction, Elevation 3,690 feet (1,125 meters), Tapeats Sandstone, the 5.5-mile Tonto Trail East heads out of Cottonwood Creek, skirts the precipitous edge of the Upper Granite Gorge and, like the fate-tempting Beamer Trail, winds along the outer rim of the Tonto Plateau as it heads past ephemeral Grapevine Springs (above the trail on east) into Grapevine Creek (perennial water), Elevation 3550 feet (1,082 meters), Tapeats Sandstone. Grapevine Creek is the longest tributary canyon on this stretch of the Tonto Trail East, and it can be debilitating to walk from one side of Grapevine Creek to the other at the end of a weary day. Don't expect to dash in and out of Grapevine Creek because it is farther than it looks. Grapevine Creek is also the only perennial water source on this stretch of the Tonto Trail East. And the head of the creek is a good place to camp and replenish your water supply the next morning before heading across the largely waterless desert plateau beyond.

From the Grapevine Creek, Elevation 3,680 feet (1,122 meters), the 8.7-mile Tonto Trail East makes the long haul out of Grapevine Creek to a spectacular upstream view of Grapevine Rapids a thousand feet below, and contours in and out of Boulder Creek (ephemeral springs) across the sagebrush flats to Lone Tree Canyon (slick rock ephemeral springs), Elevation 3,680 feet (1,122 meters), Tapeats Sandstone. The landmark 5,315-foot Pattie Butte towers over Lone Tree Canyon and was named in honor of

American pathfinder and fur trapper James Ohio Pattie. The Kentucky-born mountain man explored the Grand Canyon's *terra incógnita*, "unknown country," between March 28 and April 12, 1826. What little is known about Pattie's route, he noted in his diary: "April 10th, we arrived where the river emerges from these horrid mountains, which so cage it up, as to deprive all human beings of the ability to descend to its banks, and make use of its waters. No mortal has the power of describing the pleasure I felt, when I could once again reach the banks of the river."

From Lone Tree Canyon, Elevation 3,680 feet (1,122 meters), the 3.5-mile Tonto Trail East crosses a largely featureless and shade less expanse of desert scrub to the gravel streambed of Cremation Creek, Elevation 3,650 feet (1,113 meters), Tonto Formation. "Wait-a-minute" catclaw acacia (*Acacia greggii*) overhang Cremation Creek, along with tamarisk that managed to gain a toehold in this sere expanse of the Sonoran Desert. Cremation Creek has long been said to be a burial ground for "Indians" who reportedly cremated their dead on the South Rim and hurled the ashes into the abyss. The only grain of truth I've uncovered regarding the tale may be linked to American anthropologist Leslie Spier's 1928 *Havasupai Ethnography*, which reported that cremation was a death custom among the Havasupai during the late 1800s, but it was not a location specific citing. (See page 176 Ghost Canyon.)

From Cremation Creek, Elevation 3,650 feet (1,113 meters), the rocky and meandering 2.1 mile Tonto Trail East climbs up to the South Kaibab/Tonto Trail Junction, Elevation 4,010 feet (1,222 meters), Tonto Formation. Turn right (south) and it's 2.1 miles past the Tipoff (scenic vista and composting toilet) to the Bright Angel Campground and water. Turn left (south) and it's a dry, shadeless 4.4 miles and a 2,590-vertical-foot climb to the South Kaibab Trailhead (see page 110).

Additional Considerations

It's imperative you plan your trek along the Tonto Trail East to coincide with reliable seasonal water sources.

Travel Notes

- Primary Access: Grandview Trail, South Kaibab Trail.
- Elevation: 3,690-feet Cottonwood Creek to 4,100-feet South Kaibab Trail.
- Biotic Communities: Sonoran Desert.
- Total Elevation Loss and Gain: Approximately 1,000 vertical feet one way.
- Mileage: 19.8 miles one way.
- Water: Grapevine Creek, Cottonwood Creek (seasonal), Boulder Creek (seasonal), and Lone Tree Canyon (seasonal).

- Cache Points: None on this point-to-point hike.
- Seasons: Fall through spring. Summer has proven deadly in Cremation Canyon and elsewhere.
- Maps: Grandview Point, Cape Royal, and Phantom Ranch Quadrangles (7.5 minute).
- Escape Routes: Grandview Trail, Bright Angel Campground.
- Camping: At large, low-impact camping in Grapevine Creek and Boulder Creek Zone BH9, Lone Tree Canyon and Cremation Creek Zone BJ9; and Bright Angel Campground.

South Kaibab Trail/Tonto Trail East/Bright Angel Trail

From the South Kaibab/Tonto Trail East junction, Elevation 4,010 feet (1,222 meters), Tonto Formation, the nonmaintained, easy-to-follow 4.5 mile Tonto Trail East contours west into Pipe Creek past the shady grove of Burro Springs (perennial) to Indian Garden Campground, Elevation 3,860 feet (1,177 meters), Bright Angel Shale (see page 104 Bright Angel Trail).

Tonto Trail West

The Tonto Trail West begins near Indian Garden Campground on the Bright Angel Trail, leads west to the South Bass Trail, and dead ends in Garnet Canyon 85.4 miles west of Indian Garden.

Bright Angel Trail/Tonto Trail West/Hermit Trail

From Indian Garden Campground, Elevation 3,860 feet (1,177 meters), Bright Angel Shale, the popular, easy-to-follow 13.3 mile trail leads to the Hermit Trail/Tonto Trail West/Boucher Trail junction, Elevation 3,210 feet (978 meters), Tonto Formation. From this trail junction it's 1.2 miles to Hermit Creek Campground and water. (See page 122 Hermit Trail.)

Mileages, Water Sources, and Trail Landmarks

- 2.5 miles to Horn Creek, Elevation 3,550 feet (1,082 meters), seasonal water (radioactive)
  - Landmark: 5,031-foot Dana Butte
- 4.8 miles to Salt Creek, Elevation 3,550 feet (1,082 meters), seasonal water (mineralized)
  - Landmark: 5,810-foot The Alligator
- 3.4 miles to Monument Creek, Elevation 2995 elevation, (913 meters), perennial water

- Landmark: 4,528-foot Cope Butte
- 2.3 miles to the Hermit Trail/Tonto Trail West junction, Elevation 3,210 feet (978 meters)
  - Landmark: 6,640-foot Yuma Point. From this trail junction, it's 1.2 miles to Hermit Creek. Elevation 2,900 feet (884 meters), perennial water

Additional Considerations

This is the most popular multiday loop hike in Grand Canyon National Park. Summer is too hot for most. But a well-conditioned young family of four, with two smiling pre-teen girls, spent five days hiking down the Hermit Trail, across the Tonto Trail West, and out the Bright Angel Trail in June 2003 for their blog, "Summer in the Grand." Visit talusfield.net/.

Travel Notes

- Primary Access: Bright Angel Trail via Indian Garden and Hermit Trail.
- Elevation: 3,860-feet Indian Garden to 2,900-feet Hermit Creek.
- Biotic Communities: Sonoran Desert.
- Total Elevation Loss and Gain: Approximately 1,000 feet one way.
- Mileage: 14.5 miles one way to Hermit Creek.
- Water: Indian Garden, Monument Creek, Hermit Creek, Colorado River.
- Cache Points: None on this point-to-point hike.
- Seasons: Fall through spring. Summer's too hot for most. The basin in Salt Creek is named The Inferno, and should be a telling reminder the Tonto Trail West isn't the best place for most hikers to trek during the summer.
- Maps: Phantom Ranch and Grand Canyon Quadrangles (7.5 minute).
- Cache Points: None on this point-to-point hike.
- Escape Routes: Bright Angel Trail, Hermit Trail, Colorado River.
- Camping: At large, low-impact camping at designated campsites in Horn Creek Zone BL4, Salt Creek Zone BL5, and Monument Creek and Hermit Creek Zone BM7.

Hermit Creek/Tonto Trail West/Boucher Trail

From the Hermit Trail/ Tonto Trail West junction, Elevation 3,210 feet (978 m), Tonto Formation, the popular 5.1-mile Tonto Trail West leads west from the base of 4,528-foot Cope Butte, contours into Hermit Creek beneath 4,514-foot Columbus Point, snakes along the outer rim of Yuma Point overlooking Hermit Rapids, winds in and out of rocky and rugged Travertine Canyon beneath 4,860-foot Whites Butte, and descends to the Boucher Trail/Tonto Trail West Junction, Elevation 3,120 feet (951 meters), Tonto Formation. From this junction follow the switchbacks 0.4 miles down to Boucher Creek, Elevation 2,760 feet (841 meters), Vishnu Schist, Boucher Cabin. (See page 131 Boucher Trail.)

Additional Considerations

This is shortest, most exciting Tonto Trail West trek. It's frequently done as a twenty-one-mile point-to-point loop hike by descending the Boucher Trail, crossing the Tonto Trail West, and hiking up the Hermit Trail—primarily because most hikers find it easier to climb out the more popular Hermit Trail than the less frequently used Boucher Trail. Knowledgeable canyoneers hike it both ways.

Travel Notes

- Primary Access: Hermit Trail and Boucher Trail.
- Elevation: 3,210-feet Hermit Trail junction to 3,120-feet Boucher Trail junction.
- Biotic Communities: Sonoran Desert.
- Total Elevation Loss and Gain: Approximately 300 vertical feet one way.
- Mileage: 5.1 miles one way.
- Water: Hermit Creek, Boucher Creek, and Colorado River.
- Cache Points: None on this point-to-point hike.
- Seasons: Fall through spring. Summer can be unforgiving.
- Map: Grand Canyon Quadrangle (7.5 minute).
- Escape Routes: Hermit Trail via Hermit Creek, Colorado River, Boucher Trail.
- Camping: At large, low-impact camping at designated campsites in Hermit Creek Zone BM7 and Boucher Creek Zone BN9.

Boucher Trail/Tonto Trail West/South Bass Trail

West of the Boucher Trail is the kind of country medieval cartographers might have scribed on their parchment maps with quill pens, "Here be the dragons." Spanish conquistadors who explored the Southwest during the sixteenth century would have described it as a *despoblado*, "uninhabited country" in their diaries had they ventured across it. And pioneers, cattlemen, and cowboys who followed would have cursed it as *mal país*, "bad country," had they survived it. Once you leave Boucher Creek, you're on your own with more room to roam than you might anticipate or desire, and fewer water sources you might end up praying for. The 28.4-mile back of beyond point-to-point trail is remote and requires stamina and situational awareness of where you are and careful route planning from one perennial and seasonal water source to the next. When the trail becomes faint—and it will—look for cairns that often mark the rocky, boulder-strewn sections. But understand that cairns are often camouflaged by their color because they've often been stacked from the same rocks the primitive trails pass through. If you get in trouble, you'll need a satellite phone or messenger, or need to be able to walk or crawl out under your own power, or have a reliable companion to send for help. Seasoned canyoneers are rewarded with solitude, freedom, and the opportunity to experience the canyon's natural rhythms for days at a time.

From Boucher Creek, Elevation 2,760 feet (841 meters), follow the creek downstream 0.36 miles to the confluence of Topaz Creek, which enters from the left (southwest). Cross the creek and trek 0.25 miles up toward 4,721-foot Marsh Butte. The trail switchbacks up through the Tapeats Sandstone to the 3,000 foot elevation contour on your Grand Canyon Quadrangle (7.5 minute) map, and regains the Tonto Trail West at the unnamed point 3171. From the point, the faint 5.25-mile Tonto Trail West from Boucher Creek traces the 3,200 elevation contour around Marsh Butte a long way into Slate Creek, Elevation 3,100 feet (945 meters), Tapeats Sandstone. There's seasonal water in the streambed, and a spring below the trail where it crosses Slate Creek. This is the point where you might feel you've just entered no-man's land. Marsh Butte was named in honor of American paleontologist Othniel Charles Marsh who competed with rival paleontologist Edward Drinker Cope during the "Bone Wars," or "Dinosaur Gold Rush," to discover new dinosaur species in the American West between 1877 and 1892.

Mile 5.25. From Slate Creek, Elevation 3,100 feet (945 meters), Tapeats Sandstone. It's 9.3 miles to Turquoise Canyon, Elevation 2,950 feet (899 meters), Tapeats Sandstone.

Mileages, Water Sources, and Trail Landmarks

- 4.5 miles to Agate Canyon, Elevation 3,160 feet (963 meters), Tapeats Sandstone, no water.
  - Landmarks: 5,005 foot Geikie Peak, 3,844 foot Scylla Butte and, 1,000 feet below the Tonto Trail West, Crystal Rapids, Colorado River Mile 98.
- 2.05 miles to Sapphire Canyon, Elevation 3,240 feet (988 meters), Tapeats Sandstone, seasonal streambed water and potholes.
  - Landmark (across the river): 5,832-foot Scorpion Ridge, a descriptive name for the arachnid-shaped terrace.
- 2.72 miles to Turquoise Canyon, Elevation 3,150 feet (960 meters), Tapeats Sandstone, seasonal water Upper Turquoise Spring 100 yards upstream from the trail and Lower Turquoise Spring 0.25 miles downstream. Tapeats Sandstone overhangs provide shade, shelter, and bivouac sites.

- ◆ Landmark: 6,718-foot Walapai Point, South Rim.
- 2.4 miles to Jasper Canyon, Elevation 3,120 feet (951 meters), Tapeats Sandstone, no water.

From Turquoise Canyon the trail crosses the Shaler Plateau and contours into Jasper Canyon, an unofficial river runner's name not marked on your Grand Canyon Quadrangle (7.5 minute) map.

- 0.73 miles to Jade Canyon, Elevation 3,160 feet (963 meters), Tapeats Sandstone, no water.

From Jasper Canyon the trail crosses the La Conte Plateau and contours into Jade Canyon, an unofficial river runner's name who refer to the five-and-a-half-mile stretch of the Colorado River in Granite Gorge as the "gems": Agate, Sapphire, Turquoise, Jasper, Jade, Ruby, Quartz, Emerald, and Serpentine.

- 2.3 miles to Ruby Canyon, Elevation 3,110 feet (948 meters), Tapeats Sandstone, seasonal streambed water. En route to Serpentine Canyon, the Tonto Trail West contours in and out of two unnamed tributaries, unofficially called Quartz Canyon and Emerald Canyon, before descending into Serpentine Canyon, Tread Lightly. The area was utilized by Ancestral Puebloans to harvest and roast Utah agave (*Agave utahensis*).
- ◆ Landmark: 6,141-foot Havasupai Point.
- 4.8 miles, Serpentine Canyon, Elevation 3,100 feet (945 meters), Tapeats Sandstone, seasonal streambed water, slick rock campsite.
- ◆ Landmark: 5,667-foot Grand Scenic Divide.
- 3.8 miles, South Bass/Tonto Trail West junction, Elevation 3,150 feet (960 meters), Tonto Formation, seasonal spring water down canyon at Bedrock Tanks.
- ◆ Landmarks: 5,630-foot Huxley Terrace and 5,209-foot Wallace Butte. (See page 141 Bass Trail.)

South Bass/Colorado River

To reach the Colorado River, take the first right fork (northeast) and hike 1.8 miles down to Bass Rapids and Beach, Elevation 2,250 feet (686 meters), Vishnu Schist, River Mile 107.5.

South Bass Trail/Tonto Trail West/Garnet Canyon

To reach the end of the 121.4-mile Tonto Trail, hike 200 yards up the South Bass Trail, and take the right fork (northeast) and the Tonto Trail West leads 11.6 miles to Garnet Canyon where it officially dead ends 267 feet above the Colorado River at Mile 114.5. From the dead end switchbacks, a wild cat trail leads down to the left bank of the Colorado River.

South Bass, South Bass Trailhead

To reach the South Bass Trailhead, continue hiking up the South Bass Trail 5.9 miles to the rim at Elevation 6,646 feet (2,026 meters). (See page 137 South Bass Trail.)

Travel Notes

- Primary Access: South Bass Trail and Boucher Trail.
- Elevation: 2,760-feet Boucher Creek to 3,200-feet South Bass Trail.
- Biotic Communities: Upper Sonoran Desert.
- Total Elevation Loss and Gain: Approximately 2,000 vertical feet one way across the West Tonto Trail.
- Mileage: 28.4 miles one way from Boucher Creek.
- Water: Boucher Creek, Colorado River; Turquoise Canyon (seasonal Upper and Lower Turquoise Springs); Slate Creek and Sapphire, Ruby, and Serpentine Canyons (seasonal streambed water).
- Cache Points: None on this point-to-point hike
- Seasons: Fall and spring. Summer can be deadly; summer monsoons and winter snow often prevent access to South Bass Trailhead.
- Maps: Grand Canyon, Shiva Temple, and Havasupai Point Quadrangles (7.5 minute).
- Escape Routes: Boucher Trail, Colorado River, South Bass Trail.
- Camping: At large, low-impact camping at Boucher Creek Zone BN9, Slate Creek and Turquoise Canyon Zone BO9, Ruby Canyon and Serpentine Canyon Zone BP9, and Bass Canyon Zone BQ9.

South Bass Trail, Apache Trail, Apache Point

To reach the Apache Trail, hike 4.5 miles up the South Bass Trail (or 1.45 miles down the South Bass Trail from the South Rim trailhead) to the Esplanade Trail Junction, Elevation 5,400 feet (1,646 meters), Esplanade Sandstone. Turn west and you're on the Apache Trail, what the park calls the Esplanade Route.

Apache Trail

Pictographs, petroglyphs, Moqui steps, and a tree log-ladder indicate the Apache Trail was used by Ancestral Puebloans, or perhaps earlier by archaic peoples 4,000 years ago. A fortified ruin atop the isolated 6,295-foot summit opposite 6,322-foot Apache Point offers mute testimony the Havasupai were also on the lookout to defend themselves from marauders bent on sacking their vulnerable canyon home. Anthropologist Leslie Spier recorded one raid during the 1860s, "when about two hundred of the enemy . . . came from the south straight across the plateau, from the Moki trail to the rim of Grand Canyon at Apache point . . ." Apache Point takes its name from the Northeastern Yavapai band, *Wiipukepaya,* "People from the Foot of the Red Rock," who intermarried and raided with the Northern Tonto Apache band, *Tsé Hichii Indee,* "Horizontal Red Rock People."As a result they were commonly called "Apache" by the Havasupai, pioneers, and writers. After interviewing the Havasupai in 1899, James Wharton James, an ordained minister, wrote graphically about the point: "The name Apache Point was given . . . because it is singularly and tragically connected with the Apaches and Havasupais . . . whenever the hated Apaches entered Havasu Canyon on their depredatory or murdering excursions, and happened to be caught by those whom they came to slay or plunder, no mercy was shown to them. They were put to the torture and slain cruelly, and one method of killing them was to bring them out to Apache Point, where there is a frightful precipice, and there, one man holding the prisoner by the hair and the other by his feet, calling upon all the evil powers that are supposed to lurk in and about *Chic-a-mi-mi Hack-a-tai-a* (Grand Canyon), the unhappy wretch was swung to and fro over that awful precipice until he showed certain signs of fear. Then, with a wild yell of triumph, giving him a fierce swing outward, both captors loosed their hold and he dropped a thousand or more feet, to be mashed to a jelly on the rugged rocks beneath. A terrible way of punishing their hated and dreaded foes, and yet, the only way to inspire with wholesome fear such a tribe."

At one time the Apache Trail traversed the Esplanade Sandstone about 1,500-vertical-feet below the western South Rim, and it reportedly provided the Havasupai and trailblazer William Wallace Bass with another means of traversing the hanging terrace from east to west.

What once existed on the ground, and what still exists on many topographical maps, rarely exists *in situ* today. The seldom traveled, foot-wide, eighteen-mile point-to-point Apache Trail requires as much care and route-finding skill as any primitive route in the Grand Canyon. From the South Bass Trail, the route clings to the steep talus of Hermit Shale and traces the 5,500-foot elevation contour on your King Arthur Castle Quadrangle (7.5 minute) map around 6,600-foot Chemehuevi Point overlooking the Drummond Plateau. Look for the natural arch on the northwest wall between Chemehuevi Point and 6,580-foot Toltec Point. The only water source on this first stretch is the seasonal Seep Spring located in the first drainage west of Chemehuevi Point. If the seep isn't flowing across the route, and you need water, you'll need to scramble 560 vertical feet up to it to see if it's trickling enough to replenish your water.

As you contour above the Aztec Amphitheater around 6,408-foot Montezuma Point, the trail drops back down to the Esplanade Sandstone for about half a mile, then climbs back up to the Hermit Shale until you reach 6,421-foot Point Huitzil, where it descends back down to the Esplanade. The South Bass to Point Huitzil leg is physically the most demanding stretch of the Apache Trail, and the route-finding challenge isn't over until you reach Apache Point.

West of Point Huitzil, an Ancestral Puebloan route climbs up to the South Rim. It's marked by a tree log crevice-ladder, hand-carved Moqui foot and handholds, red ochre paint daubed pictographs, and mystifying hand-pecked petroglyhs of a warrior, shaman, spirit beings, giant spider, and trail map. The Apache Trail stays on the Esplanade as it contours around 6,283-foot Point Centeotl and 6,357-foot Point Quetzal. The Esplanade Formation is often devoid of the trail, so look for phantom traces and cairns that indicate you're on the historic course of the foot and pack trail. Stay on the Esplanade until you reach the first major drainage southeast of Apache Point. The route climbs up this steep drainage, regains the Hermit Shale, climbs through the Coconino Sandstone, and completely encircles the floating 6,295 foot summit opposite Apache Point counterclockwise through the Toroweap Formation until it leads through breaks in the Kaibab Limestone to Apache Point. Rim View North: 4,940 Apache Terrace, and Colorado River in Conquistador Aisle.

Additional Considerations

This remote route requires careful planning, good physical conditioning, and skilled route finding. Unless the Havasupai Tribe permits you with overland access to Apache Point (see page 181 Havasupai Tribe), you'll need to trek the Apache Trail out-and-back from the South Bass Trail, in which case your mileage doubles, or you have the option of hiking out-and-back say part way to or from Montezuma Point, or another geographical point on your topo maps. The Apache Trail is sometimes used in part by canyoneers descending the upper Royal Arch Route from Montezuma Point into an eastern arm of upper Royal Arch Canyon. (Note: I have not followed that route, so I can't provide a first-person description. I used the lower Royal Arch Route from the Colorado River.)

- Primary Access: South Bass Trail and Apache Point.
- Elevation: 5,400-feet South Bass Trail to 6,322-feet Apache Point.
- Biotic Communities: Piñon juniper woodlands.
- Total Elevation Loss and Gain: Approximately 2,000 vertical feet one way.
- Mileage: Approximately eighteen miles one way.
- Water: Seasonal Seep Springs and water pockets on the Esplanade Sandstone.
- Cache Points: None on this point-to-point route.
- Seasons: Spring and fall. Winter snow and summer monsoons can make the South Bass Trailhead inaccessible. Hauling water across the Apache Trail during dry summer heat may prove unwieldy in many stretches that require keen balance and sure-footedness.

- Maps: Havasupai Point and Explorers Monument Quadrangles (7.5 minute).
- Escape Route: South Bass Trail.
- Camping: At large, low-impact camping at designated campsites South Bass Trail Zone BQ9.
- Managing Agency: Grand Canyon National Park.
- Backcountry Information Center: for information call (928) 638–7875.
- Critical Backcountry Updates visit www.nps.gov/grca/planyourvisit/trail-closures.htm
- NPS Grand Canyon Hiker 24 Hour Emergency Phone Number and Email
  - Phone (928) 638–7805
  - Email: grca_bic@nps.gov (Use this if the phone line is busy)

19

North Rim: Rim Trails

Some of the most overlooked and rewarding hiking opportunities in Grand Canyon National Park are the rim bound trails that probe the secret sub-alpine forests of the North Rim. When summertime temperatures turn the inner Canyon into a furnace—and hikers who've survived it into the limping wounded—there are few more beautiful places to hike and explore than the 9,200-foot high Kaibab Plateau's cool forests of Engelmann spruce, Douglas fir, quaking aspen, ponderosa pine, and lush mountain meadows called "parks." Ancestral Puebloans made seasonal migrations from their

North Rim, in the canyon of stone and light. Copyright © John Annerino Photography.

Colorado River delta pueblos to the lofty heights of the North Rim long before the surface temperature of the inner canyon's basement rocks became too hot to touch. You would do well to follow their seasonal lead and seek cooler climes during hot weather. If your vacation time is limited to summer months, you should find it more enjoyable to focus your Grand Canyon hiking in the supernal reaches of the North Rim than the teeming South Rim. The North Rim offers a diverse variety of forest and rim trails that can keep novice and avid hikers busy for a week. The trails include everything from the paved half-mile stroll to Bright Angel Point to half-day forest fire lookout walks and day-long hikes to 8,819-foot Point Imperial on the east to day-long and overnight hikes on the 7,761-foot Powell Plateau on the west.

Directions

To reach the North Rim Entrance Station from Jacob Lake at the US Highway 89A and AZ Highway 67 crossroads, drive thirty-one miles south on State Highway 67 through beautiful forests and meadows that lead to Highway 67 being designated the Kaibab Plateau–North Rim Scenic Byway and the National Forest Scenic Byway. From the North Rim Entrance Station continue driving 12.5 miles south to the North Rim Visitor Center.

RIM TRAILS

Bright Angel Point Trail

From the Grand Canyon Lodge, or North Rim Visitor Center, the self-guiding half-mile round-trip hike on the paved Bright Angel Point Trail leads to spectacular views from 8,255-foot Bright Angel Point. Seen from the Kaibab Limestone promontory, the vista includes the majestic Coconino Sandstone monuments of 7,363-foot Deva, 7,651-foot Brahma, and 7,123-foot Zoroaster Temples, and the 4,000-foot-deep chasms of Bright Angel Canyon on your east and The Transept on your west. During the 1920s, adventurous tourists traveled by horseback across the Grand Canyon and rode up the Bright Angel Canyon Trail to lodge at Wylie Way Camp on Bright Angel Point for $6 a night. Accommodations included: ". . . a central dining tent and comfortable sleeping tents; everything is spotlessly clean. Camp opens about June 20 and closes about October 1. There are accommodations for about 25 people."

Transept Trail

This well-marked 1.5-mile-long trail is one of the real rewards for staying in what becomes a bustling summer campground. The 8,226-foot high trail starts west of the North Rim Campground and contours southwest along the edge of The Transept to the Grand Canyon Lodge. En route you may see a 900-year-old Ancestral Puebloan surface dwelling that also offered its canyon dwellers views as spectacular as any secluded vista in the Grand Canyon. Look for 8,068 foot Oza Butte across the chasm on the west rim of The Transept. The flat-topped Kaibab Limestone butte takes its name from the Southern Paiute word, *ottsa*, for a pine-pitched sealed water basket. Oza Butte can be climbed via a short rugged cross-country forest trek from the Widforss Trailhead using the Bright Angel Point Quadrangle (7.5 minute) map. (See page 215.)

RIM TRAILS EAST

Uncle Jim Trail

The pedestrian and mule trail was named for Texan James T. "Uncle Jim" Owens, who was appointed game warden for the Grand Canyon Game Reserve in 1906. Based out of his rustic North Rim log cabin, the famous lion hunter was equipped with nine horses, a mule, eleven hounds, and an Airedale, and hunted lions with President Theodore Roosevelt and Western novelist Zane Grey. During his tenure, Uncle Jim and his outfit tracked, treed, and shot 532 mountain lions on the North Rim—forever compromising the tenuous ecological balance between the North Kaibab mule deer (*Odocoileus hemionus*) and the rim rock lairs of predatory mountain lion (*Felis concolor*).

Uncle Jim Trailhead, Elevation 8,250 feet (2,515 meters), Kaibab Limestone. The first mile of the well-marked five-mile loop trail also serves as the first mile of the Ken Patrick Trail. The Uncle Jim Trail skirts the rim of Roaring Springs Canyon, drops into and climbs out of its headwater drainage, and offers splendid views en route to its junction with the Ken Patrick Trail. A weathered wooden sign post at the junction reads ←Ken Patrick Trail, Uncle Jim Trail→. Turn right (south), and the Uncle Jim Trail beelines 1.2 miles through the woods to the picnic-style scenic vista at 8,402-foot Uncle Jim Point. Look to the west and you can see the North Kaibab Trail switchback into Roaring Springs Canyon. Return the way you came, or follow the 2.8-mile east leg of the Uncle Jim Trail along the rim of Bright Angel Canyon to point 8427 on your Bight Angel Point Quadrangle (7.5 minute) map where it loops northwest back to the junction and trailhead.

Ken Patrick Trail

The Ken Patrick Trail was named in honor of Grand Canyon National Park Ranger Kenneth Carmel Patrick. His watch ended on August 5, 1973, when he was gunned down during a traffic stop at Point Reyes National Seashore, California. A bronze gravestone epitaph in the Grand Canyon Pioneer Cemetery commemorates Patrick's short life. The ten-mile point-to-point trek along his namesake trail leads to 8,819-foot Point Imperial. Bring your Bright Angel topo map, and wear long pants, because this route is more of a rugged and scenic orienteering course than a well-marked trail hike.

From its junction with the Uncle Jim Trail at Mile 1, the Ken Patrick Trail contours the southeast slope of the Roaring Springs headwater drainage. At point 8529 on your Bright Angel topo, the trail drops into and climbs out of the drainage and continues uphill to the Old Bright Angel Trail junction at Mile 3.5. The junction is located approximately one-quarter mile south of point 8665 on your topo map. Stay on the Ken Patrick Trail, which veers northeast and becomes more difficult to follow 2.9 wherever-you-can-find-the-best-route miles to reach the paved Cape Royal Road. Progress en route is impeded by the moonscape of forest fire scars and hand-dug fire breaks from the 2000 Cutlet Fire, the never-friendly New Mexico locust, and "widow makers," blow-down, timber, and snags that must be detoured around or climbed over and crawled under. From point 8665, I followed the path of least resistance north, crossed the paved Cape Royal Road near the roadside "Picnic Area" marked on the Bright Angel topo to Point 8732. From that point I dead reckoned east cross-country, and crossed the Cape Royal Road a second time to pick up the well-marked 2.6-mile Ken Patrick Trail along the east rim to Point Imperial. This scenic stretch of the seldom explored, corrugated terrain below the east rim of the Grand Canyon, along with stunning views of the iconic Coconino Sandstone temples of 8,321-foot Sullivan Peak and 8,362-foot Mount Hayden, are the carrots at the end of this elusive trail.

Directions
The Uncle Jim Trail and the Ken Patrick Trail begin near the North Kaibab Trailhead 1.5 miles north of Grand Canyon Lodge at Bright Angel Point. It's a half-mile walk from the North Rim Campground.

Cape Royal Trail
Look south from the Cape Royal parking lot and the wooded sky island of 7,669-foot Wotans Throne commands your attention. A surface dwelling and an agave roasting pit discovered atop the 135-square-acre *mesita*, "little mesa," indicates Ancestral Puebloans negotiated the serrated ridge from the North Rim out to Wotans Throne and climbed it a half a millennia before the 1937 American Museum of Natural History-sponsored expedition claimed the first ascent of the North Rim's Shiva Temple, that was secretly climbed twice by Emery Kolb—so he wouldn't lose the Kolb Studio concession to the Park, which supported the "scientific expedition"—the first time in August with his daughter Edith Kolb, Gordon Berger, and Ralph White.

From the Cape Royal parking lot, the 0.6-mile round-trip walk on the paved Cape Royal Trail leads past natural history interpretive signs to scenic views of the Angels Window and the Colorado River. Through the heavenly prism of Kaibab Limestone, or the aerie atop it, you can trace the remarkable seasonal migration route that Ancestral

Puebloans once made from their Colorado River pueblo at Unkar Creek delta 5,354 vertical feet up through Unkar Creek and its dangerous cliffs and headwalls to their rim top dwellings at Walhalla Glades. (Look for the signed access off the Cape Royal Road.)

Directions

The Cape Royal Trail is located twenty-three miles from the Visitor Center via the paved Cape Royal Road.

RIM TRAILS WEST

Widforss Trail

Named for 1920s Swedish American painter Gunnar Mauritz Widforss, the ten-mile out-and-back trail is an enjoyable and enchanting forest and canyon hike. It's well marked all the way out to 7,822-foot Widforss Point, has gentle gradients, and makes one of the best day hikes on the North Rim. From the parking area, the trail climbs gently, skirts the north and northeastern arms of The Transept, then heads south through the woods, terminating near the head of Haunted Canyon. Widforss Point is as captivating a vista and lunch spot as any on the North Rim, with a raven's views of 7,184-foot Manu Temple and 7,212-foot Buddha Temple. One can only imagine Widforss, known at the time as the "Painter of National Parks," sitting at this inspiring point deftly brushing the canyon's ever-changing hues and fall leaves of quaking aspen with his palette of water colors.

Directions

One quarter-mile south of the Highway 67/Cape Royal Road junction, turn left (west), and drive one mile on the dirt road through charming North Rim country to reach the Widforss Trailhead. Nestled in the aspen grove on the far side of the meadow is the one-room hand-laid stone-enclosed Uncle Jim's Cave that was undoubtedly used by Ancestral Puebloans long before Owens used it as a staging area for horseback tourist trips.

Powell Plateau, Isthmus in the Sky

One of the most appealing aspects of the North Rim is that it drains and erodes into the Grand Canyon, compared to the South Rim, which characteristically drains away from the canyon. The resulting erosion and fault block uplifting has created eight of northern Arizona's remarkably diverse plateaus. From west to east they are Shivwits, Uinkaret, Kanab, Paria, and Kaibab Plateaus, which comprise most of the North Rim. Extending south from the Kaibab Plateau are three subsidiary plateaus: Fishtail, Powell, and Walhalla. Of the three, I find the Powell Plateau the most appealing to explore on foot. It's remote, scenic, seldom traveled, and situated at over 7,661 feet in elevation.

Powell Plateau Trail, Remote Trail

Mile 0. Swamp Point, Elevation 7,565 feet (2,306 meters), Kaibab Limestone, no water. From Swamp Point, the well-marked, rocky trail offers distant views of 7, 410-foot Steamboat Mountain as it switchbacks down through the treeless landscape 854 vertical feet through the Kaibab Limestone, Toroweap Formation, and Coconino Sandstone to Mile 1. Muav Saddle, Elevation 6,711 feet (2,046 meters), Coconino Sandstone. The Powell Plateau Trail/North Bass (Shinumo) Trail junction is located in Muav Saddle. The trail to the left (east) leads 0.25 miles to the seasonally reliable Muav Saddle Spring, also called Queen Anne Spring, and the rim-to-river North Bass Trail. The use trail to the right (north) leads 100 yards to the rickety, two-room wooden "Muav Saddle Snowshoe Cabin." Muav Saddle Cabin was one of three patrol cabins built by the National Park Service in 1925 that included Muav Saddle, Kanabonitz [sic] Spring, and Greenland Seep cabins. Crews used the Muav cabin to improve the trail between Swamp Point and Powell Plateau, and to fight forest fires atop the lightning-prone tablelands. Muav Saddle Cabin was nicknamed "Teddy's Cabin" because Rough Rider Theodore Roosevelt reportedly camped nearby while hunting lions with "Uncle Jim" Owens. Beyond Muav Saddle Cabin to the north is the Saddle Canyon Route to Thunder River (see page 228). To explore the Powell Plateau continue straight (west) and climb the 1930s Civilian Conservation Corp-improved 1.5 mile long trail as it switchbacks through dense manzanita overgrowth 950 vertical feet to the plateau's northern high point at Mile 2.5. Powell Plateau, Elevation 7,661 feet (2,335 meters), Ponderosa pine forest, no water.

Until recent forest fires, the northern third of Powell Plateau was covered with one of the most impressive old growth forests of Ponderosa pine on the heavily logged North Rim. A black and white photo taken during the 1900s shows William Wallace Bass and his friend Chickapanagi standing in the virgin forest over two black-tailed mule deer they'd hunted after traveling on foot and horseback all the way from Bass Camp on the South Rim to the Powell Plateau. Bass's daughter Edith recalled: "Chickapanagi was my father's favorite friend among the Havasupai. My dad often took him to hunt on the north rim. He would give Chickapanagi his rifle and three shells, and Chick would come back with three deer." The Powell Plateau was also fertile hunting grounds for lion hunter "Uncle Jim" Owens and Zane Grey. This was the little-known location where Grey observed cowboy, hunter, and frontiersman Charles Jesse "Buffalo" Jones climb a tall ponderosa pine tree and lasso a mountain lion treed by Uncle Jim's hounds. Hog tied, claws clipped, jaws muzzled, and slung over the back of a saddle, the horseback party transported the suffering catamount across the Grand Canyon to the South Rim where the lion was chained to a wooden post at El Tovar Lodge for tourists to marvel at during cocktail hour.

From point 7661, what remains of the trail from this point on is marked by metal blaze tags nailed to trees that were not destroyed by forest fires. The trail marked on your King Arthur Castle Quadrangle (7.5 minute) map disappears. The blaze marks become less frequent, and you'll have to hike at-large and look for trail remnants if you want to follow the historic course of the trail. From point 7661, the popular option is to hike 3.2 miles of relatively easy cross-country walking and follow the high ground south along the east rim of the plateau past point 7,659, descend into and climb out of Dutton Canyon, and hike past point 7,561 to reach 7,553 foot Dutton Point. Located at the southeastern tip of the Powell Plateau, the point was named in honor of eminent Grand Canyon geologist Clarence Edward Dutton who surveyed the region—and Powell Plateau—during the summer of 1880 for Major John Wesley Powell's, *United States Geographical and Geological Survey of the Rocky Mountain Region.*

Given the isolated plateau's paucity of water it's remarkable that eighty-five Ancestral Puebloan surface dwellings were recorded on Powell Plateau that were inhabited between 1050 and 1150. According to the study, *Archaeology of the Powell Plateau*, Robert C. Euler and his field team estimated the average density of thirty-three dwelling sites was seventy-one rooms per square mile. Euler, Richard W. Effland, Jr., and A. Trinkle Jones estimated "there were 650 to 700 rooms used by prehistoric people living on the plateau." Which begs the question, where did they get the water? It could only come from ephemeral water pockets recharged by winter rain, spring snowmelt, and summer monsoons, seasonal springs below Muav Saddle, or the perennial flows of the more distant Saddle Canyon and Muav Canyon carried atop the plateau in large tumpline water ollas. Do not disturb any of these cultural sites if you happen upon them.

You can spend a several days exploring and camping atop this incredible 9.6-square-mile isthmus that reaches deep into the heart of the Grand Canyon overlooking the Colorado River and experience an altogether different natural world.

Directions

From AZ Highway 67, located one mile south of the North Rim Country Store, (Milepost 605), it's eighteen miles of rutted, high-clearance roads to Swamp Point via the "Swamp Ridge Road." Take USFS Road 422 to USFS Road 270 and turn left (south). Follow USFS Road 270 to USFS Road 223, turn right (west), and take 223 to USFS Road 268B. Road 268B will eventually take you out to Swamp Point.

Additional Considerations

On your drive to the Grand Canyon's North Rim Entrance Station, stop at the Kaibab Plateau Visitor Center, junction US Highway 89A and AZ Highway 67, Jacob Lake, AZ

86022, Phone (928) 643–7298. Get up-to-date travel conditions and a North Kaibab Forest Road map you should consult on the drive out to Swamp Point.

Visit www.fs.usda.gov/recarea/kaibab/recarea/?recid=11698.

Hiking Smart

Depending on the weather and your conditioning you should be able to hike the 5.7 miles from Swamp Point to Dutton Point and camp nearby with enough water to safely return to the trailhead if you cache a *minimum* of two quarts of water at Teddy's Cabin, two quarts at Point 7,661, and carry one gallon of water to your Dutton Point area camp. Weighing in unforeseen risk factors, I would suggest carrying and caching 2.5 to three gallons of water.

Travel Notes

- Primary Access: Swamp Point; secondary, rarely used access via the North Bass Trail (from the Colorado River), Saddle Canyon route (from Thunder River).
- Elevation: 7,565-foot Swamp Point to 6,711-foot Muav Saddle to 7,661-foot Powell Plateau to 7,553-foot Dutton Point.
- Biotic Communities: Ponderosa pine and Piñon juniper woodlands.
- Total Elevation Loss and Gain: 3,588+ vertical feet (1,794+ feet each way).
- Map: King Arthur Castle Quadrangle (7.5 minute).
- Mileage: Five to 11.4 miles (2.5 miles one way to Point 7,661; 3.2 miles one way to Dutton Point).
- Water: Muav Saddle Spring (Queen Anne Spring), seasonal, 0.25 mile below Muav Saddle), remote Cougar Spring in Dutton Canyon. If you want to camp atop Powell Plateau, you need to carry and cache two gallons of water from Swamp Point to Point 7,661.
- Cache Points: Muav Saddle, and Point 7,661, and beyond if you're exploring Dutton or 6,600-foot Ives Point in the vicinity of Cougar Spring.
- Seasons: Spring through fall. Summer monsoons and winter snow can make the roads impassable. (For winter access see page 236 North Kaibab Trail).
- Escape Routes: Swamp Point; emergency shelter Teddy's Cabin, Muav Saddle (double check accessibility during your hike in).
- Camping: At large, low-impact camping in Zone AS9.
- Nearest Supply Points (for all North Rim trails): Jacob Lake Store, junction US Highway 89A and AZ Highway 67; North Rim Country Store, Highway 67, (Milepost 605); General Store, North Rim Campground; and Fredonia, Arizona, and Kanab, Utah.

- Managing Agency: Grand Canyon National Park.
- Backcountry Information Center: for information call (928) 638–7875.
- Critical Backcountry Updates visit //www.nps.gov/grca/planyourvisit/trail-closures.htm
- NPS Grand Canyon Hiker 24 Hour Emergency Phone Number and Email
  - Phone (928) 638–7805
  - Email: grca_bic@nps.gov (Use this if the phone line is busy)

FOREST FIRE LOOKOUT WALKS AND RAMBLES

> "The fire. The odor of burning juniper is the sweetest fragrance
> on the face of the earth, in my honest judgment . . . One breath
> of juniper smoke, like the perfume of sagebrush after rain,
> evokes in magical catalysis, like certain music, the space and
> light and clarity and piercing strangeness of the American West."
>
> —Edward Abbey, 1968
> *Desert Solitaire*

Environmental essayist Edward Abbey devoted far more time than most canyon travelers contemplating the fragrance of smoke. He spent four seasons in the hundred-foot tall, steel eagle's nest in the Jacobs Lake Lookout searching for the slightest hint of smoke wafting up from the emerald green, old growth forests of the nine thousand foot high Kaibab Plateau. Abbey's decade-long tenure as a fire lookout stretched from the Canadian border to the Mexican border, and it included posts in the stone and timber Mount Harkness Lookout in Lassen Volcanic National Park, California, the wooden ground house of Atascosa Lookout on the Arizona/Sonora border, the two-story Numa Ridge Lookout in Glacier National Park, Montana, the steel cage Aztec Peak Lookout overlooking the Sierra Ancha Wilderness, and the towering Jacobs Lake Lookout, Arizona. With birds eye window views from the Jacobs Lake Lookout of the Southwest's finest remaining old growth forest, Abbey wrote passionately of his fire seasons in the wilderness in essays and novels that fueled the environmental movement, including *Fire on the Mountain* (1962), *Black Sun* (1971), *The Journey Home* (1977), *Abbey's Road* (1979), among other literary works. It's not widely known if Abbey ever visited or climbed to the dizzying heights of the Kaibab Plateau's Forest Lookout Trees.

Forest Lookout Trees

Home to the beautiful imperiled raptor Northern goshawk (*Accipiter gentilis*) and the bushy-tailed Kaibab squirrel (*Sciurus kaibabensis*), old-growth Ponderosa pines (*Pinus ponderosa*) range from 300 to 600 years old, stand ninety to 130 feet tall, and measure thirty to fifty inches in diameter. Between 1905 and 1940, foresters and firefighters utilized towering Ponderosa pine trees, and White fir (*Abies concolor*), for thirty-three rudimentary Forest Lookout Trees they used for fire detection on the Kaibab Plateau. To reach their lookout perches, firefighters lag-bolted, spiked, or nailed twelve-to-fourteen-foot-long sections of wooden two-by-four ladders to the trunks of the rust, black, and white barked Lookout Trees.

Every Tree Tells a Story

Dating back 929 years to the world's oldest Ponderosa pine tree discovered in Utah's Wah Wah Mountains, the Kaibab Plateau's old growth giants were also nurtured from pinecone seeds that took root in the moist, needle-covered forest floor and became seedlings reaching out toward sunny and stormy skies. Growing at the rate of two to three feet a year, one seedling had matured into a 57.5-foot-tall Ponderosa pine when the Hopi led Spanish conquistador García López de Cárdenas and twelve men to the South Rim in 1540.

By the time Franciscan missionary explorers Francisco Atanasio Domínguez and Silvestre Vélez de Escalante skirted the Kaibab Plateau south of the Wah Wah Mountains led by *Timpanogos* Shoshone guides in 1776, the tree had become a 110-foot-tall, three-foot-diameter forest canopy giant. When foresters first used the still-standing forest lookout tree, their twelve-inch lag bolts were hammered through wooden ladders and tree bark that bored through tree rings revealing forest fire scars, drought, and climate change over the span of several hundred years. What the tree rings don't tell is the significance the old growth trees may have held for the Southern Paiute, and the Grand Canyon's neighboring Native Peoples. The Hualapai take their name from Ponderosa pine trees, *Hwalbáy*, "People of the Tall Pines," as does the Uinkaret Paiute name for 8,029-foot Mount Trumbull, *Yipinkatiti*, "Ponderosa Pine Peak." Ponderosa pine tree limbs were used to build hogans, cliff ladders, foot bridges, and sweat lodges, as well as cook fires and ceremonial fires, such as the Fire Dance held on the final night of the Navajo's 9 day *Kieje Hatal*, (Night Chant). Burning pine boughs provided the healing smoke for sweat lodge ceremonies. Pine pitch was used for torch lights, sealing hand woven water baskets, and as a soothing ointment for pain. Pine bark was used for infant cradles, sleeping ground covers, snowshoes, and roofing. Pine needles provided insulation and reduced fevers. And pines seeds were gathered for food. The Kaibab Plateau was the homeland of the Kaibab Paiute, and their traditional and pilgrimage trails stretched from Deer Creek and Toroweap on the west to Nankoweap Creek on the east. Had *Puha'gants*, "shamans," stopped and made offerings of sacred water and blue stone at "shrine trees" during their pilgrimages for *puha*, or "power?" Were the great trees *tututuguuvi*, "spirit helpers," who aided them on their spirit quest? We don't know for certain, and we may never will. The 500-year-old giant stands hidden among 55,000 younger old growth tress slated for the sawmill.

In Search of Fire Lookouts and Hidden Lookout Trees

When geologist Clarence E. Dutton explored the Kaibab Plateau during the summer of 1882, he wrote:

> In the Kaibab the forest reaches to the sharp edge of the cliff and the pine trees shed their cones into the fathomless depths below. The great trees grow chiefly upon the main platform. . . It is difficult to say precisely wherein the charm of the sylvan scenery of the Kaibab consists. We, who through successive summers have wandered through its forests and parks, have come to regard it as the most enchanting region it has ever been our privilege to visit. Surely there is no lack of beautiful or grand forest scenery in America . . . The trees are large and noble . . .

Follow the charming forest roads and seldom used trails to these hidden lookouts, and you'll be awestruck standing in the presence these noble old growth Ponderosas. Many Forest Lookout Trees that remain are listed on the National Register of Historic Places, and they offer enticing destinations and places of contemplation for canyon and forest sleuths who can see the forest lookouts from the trees. The following list includes well-known Forest Lookout Towers, as well as the names of Forest Lookout Trees and a few clues to their whereabouts for those who savor the art of discovery.

Forest Lookout Towers/North Rim/Kaibab Plateau/North Kaibab Forest

- Big Springs Lookout, Elevation 7,900 feet, Tower Height 100 feet, 7 x 7 foot cab, Year 1934, Access: Big Springs Point.
- Dry Park Lookout, Elevation 8,710 feet, Tower Height 120 Feet, ground house, Year 1944, Access: Dry Park.
- Jacobs Lake Lookout, Elevation 8,161 feet, Tower Height 100 feet, 7 x 7 foot cab, Year 1934, Access: Jacobs Lake, Highway 67. Manned by Edward Abbey during the 1969–1971 fire seasons.
- Kanabownitz Lookout, Elevation 8,241 feet, Tower Height 82.6 feet, 7 x 7 foot cab, Year 1940, Access: Kanabownitz Canyon, Kanabownitz Lookout Tower Road.

- North Rim Lookout (moved from Bright Angel Point 1928), Elevation 9,165 feet, Tower Height 75 feet, 7 x 7 foot cab, Year 1933, Access: Highway 67, Lookout Tower Road.

Forest Fire Lookout Trees/North Rim/Kaibab Plateau

- Cooper Ridge Lookout Tree, Ponderosa pine ladder lookout, Elevation 7,850 feet, Tree Height seventy-five feet (five wooden ladders), Diameter four feet, Year 1920s to 1960s, Access: North of Highway 67, Moquitch Canyon. Condition: Still standing, good condition.
- Corral Lake Lookout Tree, Ponderosa pine ladder lookout, Elevation 8,132 feet, Tree Height seventy-five feet (four wooden ladders sixty feet tall), Diameter thirty inches, Year 1920s to 1960s, Access: Highway 67, Moquitch Canyon. Condition: Still standing, good condition.
- Fracas Lookout Tree, Ponderosa pine ladder lookout, Elevation 8,160 feet, Tree Height 100 feet (seven wooden ladders, bottom ladder removed), Diameter three feet, Year 1905–1937, Access: Fracas Ridge and Warm Springs Canyon. Condition: Still standing, good condition.
- Little Mountain Lookout Tree, Ponderosa pine ladder lookout, Tree Height 110 feet (five wooden ladders sixty feet tall), Diameter 3.5 feet, Year 1905–1940, Access: Little Mountain and Big Springs. Condition: Still standing, good condition.
- Murray Lookout Tree, Ponderosa pine ladder lookout, Tree height n/a, Diameter three feet, Year 1905–1940, Access: Murray Ridge, FS Road 225. Condition: Still standing, poor condition, treetop broken snag and ladder.
- Tater Point Lookout Tree, Ponderosa pine platform lookout, Elevation 8,000 feet, Tree Height 100 feet (eight wooden ladders seventy feet tall), Diameter three feet, Year 1905–1940, Access: Tater Ridge. Condition: Still standing, good condition.
- Telephone Hill Lookout Tree, White fir platform lookout, Elevation 8,910 feet, Tree Height 110 feet (four wooden ladders, bottom ladder removed), Diameter four feet, Year 1905–1937, Access: Telephone Hill, Highway 67. Still standing, good condition.
- Tipover Lookout Tree, White fir platform lookout, Elevation 9,160 feet, Tree Height seventy-five feet (two wooden ladders, bottom ladder removed), Diameter three feet, Year 1905–1940, Access: Bear and Wall Lakes, Demotte Park. Condition: Still standing, good condition.

Forest Lookout Towers/South Rim/Coconino Plateau/South Kaibab Forest

- Grandview Lookout, Elevation 7,531 feet, Tower Height eighty feet, 7 x 7 feet cab, Year 1936, Access: East Rim Drive, Grandview Road. First built in 1909 in Grand Canyon National Monument.
- Hopi Lookout, Elevation 7,140 feet, Tower Height twenty-four feet, 12 x 12 foot cab, Year 1953, Access: Hermit Road. First built in 1909, Hopi Point Lookout Tree, treetop platform lookout.
- Signal Hill Lookout, Elevation 6,780 feet, Tower Height thirty-five feet, 7 x 7 foot cab, Year 1929. Access: Pasture Wash Road.

Forest Fire Lookout Trees/South Rim/Coconino Plateau

- Grandview Lookout Tree, Ponderosa pine platform lookout, Elevation 7,240 feet, Tree Height seventy feet (two rows of lag bolts, one wooden ladder five feet tall), Diameter thirty-five inches, Year *circa* 1916, Access: Grandview Point. Condition: Still standing, poor condition, dead snag.
- Hull Tank Lookout Tree, Ponderosa pine platform lookout, Elevation 7,400 feet, Tree Height sixty-five feet (two rows of lag bolts two feet apart), Diameter thirty-two inches, Year *circa* 1916, Access: south of Grandview Point. Condition: Still standing, "excellent" condition.
- Tusayan Lookout Tree, Ponderosa pine platform lookout, Elevation 6,650 feet, Tree Height fifty feet (wooden ladders missing), Diameter two feet, Year *circa* 1925 or earlier, Access: Tusayan, FR Road 2607. Condition: Still standing, good condition.

Backstory

My two seasons in northwest fire lookouts paled in comparison to Abbey's, but I developed an affinity for the panoramic landscapes until I was drawn to the front lines of wildfire suppression as a helitack crew leader. Chasing—and eating—smokes took me from helicopter drop points, spike camps, helibases, and project fires in Alaska's Kenai Peninsula and Washington's North Cascades National Park to Montana's Pasayten Wilderness. Never in those wanderings did I ever see or hear anything like the Kaibab Plateau's mysterious-sounding Lookout Trees until I returned home to the Grand Canyon State to fight fires with the White Mountain Apache. The quest to find the Kaibab Plateau's Lookout Trees reminds me of the poem "The Explorer" (1898), in which Rudyard Kipling wrote: "Something hidden. Go and find it. Go and look behind the Ranges—Something lost behind the Ranges. Lost and waiting for you. Go!"

20

North Kaibab Trail: Day Hikes, Rim to River, and Rim to Rim

"We found ourselves face to face with a barrier more formidable than the Rocky Mountains, —an abyss 280 miles long containing an unbridged, unfordable, dangerous river. . .we cast longing glances up Bright Angel Canyon . . . But Bright Angel Canyon, we were told, afforded no practical route for pack animals, and might be impassible even to the foot of man."

—François Emile Matthes, Cartographer, 1902
Breaking a Trail through Bright Angel Canyon

LANDFORM

From its headwaters at 9,002 feet in the sub-alpine forests of the Kaibab Plateau, Bright Angel Creek follows the cross-canyon Bright Angel Fault from the North Rim to the Colorado River and up Garden Creek to the South Rim of the Coconino Plateau.

HISTORICAL OVERVIEW

Cliff and riverside dwellings, water diversion ditches, farmed terraces, and storage granaries at Bright Angel Canyon, Ribbon Falls, Bright Angel Creek, Clear Creek, Unkar Creek, and Walhalla Glades indicate Ancestral Puebloans followed precariously exposed and dangerous rim-to-river routes between seasonal hunting and gathering camps on the North Rim and riverine pueblos along the Colorado River to farm Bright Angel Creek and Unkar Creek Deltas. Based upon historic and oral accounts of the Kaibab band of Southern Paiute, their ancestors the *Mukwic*, "those we never saw," undoubtedly used these same perilous rim-to-river routes.

The North Kaibab Trail takes its name from the Kaibab Paiute's ancestral lands on the Kaibab Plateau in northern Arizona and the Kaiparowits Plateau in southern Utah. The Paiute identify both as *Kaivavic*, "Mountain Lying Down." The Kaibab Paiute's lifeways were so inextricably linked with the forested tablelands and sprawling valleys in between they called themselves *Kaipa'pici*, "Mountain Lying Down People." Today, they still know the Grand Canyon as *Piapaxa 'Uipi*, "Big River Canyon." They revere the plateaus, canyons, waterfalls, creeks, springs, and Colorado River as *Puaxantu Tuvip*, "sacred land," or "powerful land." Even stone-lined depressions they used for roasting Utah agave, *yaant*, are considered "highly sacred" for the lifesaving bounty of food they provided the Paiute and the ceremonies held at each location. It's little wonder that the Kaibab's trails that crisscrossed the Kaibab Plateau were used by Native Peoples, explorers, Mormon pioneers, and trappers who often called it Buckskin Mountain for the bounty of deer hides they obtained from the plateau's abundance of mule deer.

Foremost among the missionaries, topographers, surveyors, scientists, geologists, pioneer photographers, and river explorers who were guided by the Kaibab, Shivwits, Uinkaret, and San Juan bands of Southern Paiutes were men attached to John Wesley Powell's second Colorado River expedition in 1871–72. Their notes, journals, and published books document the Southern Paiute's ancestral lands, sacred landmarks, plateau and canyon trails, hunting and gathering grounds, and summer and winter camps. Among Powell's ten-man roster was brother-in-law Almon Harris "Prof" Thompson. The Civil War veteran, explorer, and topographer kept a telling diary of Powell's river expedition and his own overland and inner canyon travels with the Southern Paiute. On October 22, 1872, Thompson made what in all probability was the first recorded descent of Bright Angel Canyon (not to be confused with the South Rim's Bright Angel Trail). Led to the chasm by Kaibab Paiute guides, Thompson wrote:

> Went south to the cañon and then west. The valley we are in drains into Bright Angel Creek . . .There is a big spring, as the Indians say, at the head of one branch [Roaring Springs]. Small springs in others. The Indians call the creek 'Pounc-a-gunt' or 'Beaver Creek' and say a long time ago the beavers lived in it, but that they are all killed. Can see the granite [Vishnu Schist] along the creek and the granite capped by limestone on the [Colorado] river.

Thompson wasn't the only intrepid traveler who got wind of beaver in Bright Angel Creek. In a December 10, 1927, letter to Grand Canyon Park Naturalist Glen E. Sturtevant, prospector L. L. Sydney Ferrall wrote:

> A year previous to [Jim] Murray (now dead) and myself making this trip [in November 1902] Wash Henry and Porter Guffey with pack burros spent two or three months in Bright Angel creek trapping beaver, they went from the South rim and through to the North rim and returned to Flagstaff by way of Lees Ferry. Guffey wrote me from Flagstaff telling me of their success and it is my recollection that they got between thirty and forty beaver in the creek.

Ferrall and Murray were the two men cartographer François Émile Matthes met before descending into Bright Angel Canyon on November 7, 1902, and had written about: "On the very day when we started to examine this route, by a remarkable coincidence, there emerged from the head of Bright Angel Canyon two haggard men and a weary burro. These men, Sidney Ferrall and Jim Murray, had explored up through the Canyon and finally had fought their way up along the fault zone." It long has been popularly believed Matthes made the first recorded rim-to-rim canyon crossing via Bright Angel Canyon. Unless the report that prospectors Daniel L. Hogan's and Henry Ward's little known rim-to-rim crossing in 1891 can be substantiated, that distinction may well go to trappers Wash Henry and Porter Guffey.

The "first" does not detract from the Matthes efforts during his party's first canyon crossing—down the South Bass Trail, swimming the Colorado River with their horses, riding, pushing, and pulling their mounts up the North Bass Trail, and overland travel—to reach the head Bright Angel Canyon where the party began building the trail to survey Matthes' topographic masterpiece and first map of the Grand Canyon, *Bright Angel Quadrangle.* "By noon the bottom of Bright Angel Canyon was reached," Matthes wrote, "and then the party threaded its way down along the bouldery creek, crossing and recrossing it to knee-depth, no less than 94 times. Camp was made a short distance above the boxed-in lower part of the canyon [The Box], and a large bonfire was lit so that the people on the South Rim might see that we had successfully reached that point." The Dutch born Matthes also wrote: "The next year, when the survey was extended eastward, Bright Angel Canyon became our regular route of travel across the Grand Canyon, both northward and southward, although the trail remained as rough as ever."

Indian hunter Edwin D. "Uncle Dee" Woolley picked up where Matthes' U.S. Geological Survey party's rudimentary trail construction began. The Mormon stake president formed the Grand Canyon Transportation Company and, together with his son-in-law David R. Rust, hand forged a tourist trail down Bright Angel Canyon past

Ancestral Puebloan cliff dwellings to Rust's Tent Camp and Cable Crossing near Bright Angel Creek in 1907.

By 1928, National Park Service construction of the new rerouted North Kaibab Trail down Roaring Springs Canyon was completed, according the same meticulous specifications as the South Kaibab Trail to carry what promoters envisioned would be heavy tourist and mule traffic from the South Rim to the Colorado River to North Rim at a cost of $147,500. The Bright Angel Canyon leg of the original eighteen-mile-long trail was reclaimed by nature and returned to the same rugged Paiute trail the Kaibab first showed Almon Harris Thompson a half century earlier.

Directions

The North Kaibab Trailhead is 1.5 miles north of Grand Canyon Lodge at Bright Angel Point. It's a half-mile walk from the North Rim Campground.

The maintained 14.2-mile North Kaibab Corridor Trail is the only maintained trail on the North Rim. It's well marked and it includes ten steel-beam pedestrian and equestrian footbridges between the trailhead and the Colorado River below Bright Angel Campground. Mule-riding concessions also use this trail and have the right-of-way.

Mile 0. North Kaibab Trailhead, Elevation 8,241 feet (2,513 meters), Kaibab Limestone, Trailhead View South/SW: Roaring Springs Canyon. The steep trail switchbacks quickly down through ramparts of Kaibab Limestone and Toroweap Formation to the Coconino Overlook.

Mile 0.7. Coconino Overlook, Elevation 7,450 feet (2,270 meters), Coconino Sandstone, no water. Turn Around Point 1. (Use any convenient point on the Bright Angel Trail where you feel you, or your children, need to stop and turn around). A wooden sign marks the slickrock sandstone perch atop the continuous, five hundred foot high, band of white cliffs with views into the maw of Roaring Springs Canyon between 8,250 feet Uncle Jim Point to the east and 8,255-foot Bright Angel Point to the south.

The rim rock, sheer cliffs, and isolated tributary canyons is perfect mountain lion country. When author Charles Bowden hiked the Grand Canyon rim-to-rim for *Arizona Highways,* he wrote:

> First clouds roll in, then the thunder and lightning begin, and a spate of showers. The temperature sinks below freezing, and the rain goes to ice, the ice to snow. I listen to the tent shift under the fists of wind and finally let sleep take me. At 12:49 A.M. a slash of lightning followed instantly by a clap of thunder pulls me from my dreams. I look out the tent door at moonglow caressing the fresh snow. Two screams shred the night air. A lion moves along the Rim to my left.

Mile 1.7. Supai Tunnel, Elevation 6,800 feet (2,073 meters), Esplanade Sandstone, water (mid-May to mid-October), and composting toilet. Turn Around Point 2, (short day hike). The trail switchbacks down to the Redwall Foot Bridge, the first of ten bridges that span Roaring Springs and Bright Angel Creeks. The twenty-foot-long, hole-in-the-wall tunnel brings to mind the 1890s heyday of train and bank robbers Butch Cassidy and the Wild Bunch who were hell-bent, out-riding lawmen and Pinkerton Detectives, to their hideout at Hole-in-the-Wall, Wyoming. During the 1930s, Civilian Conservation Corp trail crews maintained the North Kaibab Trail to keep it free from seasonal landslides that often pulverized and buried the trail with boulders, rubble, and huge broken timbers all the way from the rimtop switchbacks, Supai Tunnel and Roaring Springs, to The Box above Phantom Ranch.

Mile 2.6. Redwall Bridge, Elevation 6,100 feet (1,860 meters), Redwall Limestone, no water. Turn Around Point 3 (day hike). Hanging from colorful 500-foot-high Redwall Limestone cliffs on the west side of Roaring Springs Canyon, the North Kaibab Trail, like its South Rim counterpart, is more of a 1920s-era engineering marvel than a natural indigenous route that followed paths of least resistance through the breaks, fault lines and creeks in the imposing stair step canyonscape. Using dynamite, portable jack hammers, and drills to blast and gouge out the dizzying stretch of the precipitous trail, park crews described it as a "half tunnel." It's just that, much like the stone "dug way" Mormon pioneers made with rudimentary picks, shovels, and black powder to blast a wagon route 2,000 feet down the fissure at Hole in the Rock, Utah, during the 1880s. The North Kaibab Trail clings to the Redwall on one side and catwalks above sheer cliffs on the other side where one misstep would be the last.

Mile 3.6. Eye of the Needle, Elevation 5,850 feet (1,780 meters), Redwall Limestone/Temple Butte, no water at this iconic trailside landmark pinnacle.

Mile 4.7. Roaring Springs 5,200 feet (1,585 meters), Muav Limestone/Bright Angel Shale contact point, water (mid-May to mid-October), emergency phone, composting toilet. Turn Around Point 4 (long day hike). Roaring Springs Canyon ends at this confluence where Bright Angel Canyon continues its headlong descent to the Colorado River. The quarter-mile downhill detour leads past the confluence of Bright Angel Creek to a verdant picnic area in the cool micro clime beneath the cavernous falls. Roaring Springs spews 500,000 gallons of water a day into the 12.4 mile gravity-fed-siphon Trans Canyon Pipeline to Indian Garden to sustain Phantom Ranch and the South Rim. A separate pipeline carries pump-fed water up to the North Rim. Roaring Springs is the only municipal water supply for Grand Canyon National Park and the burgeoning commercial concessions and developments that now lure more than 5 million visitors annually. It begs the question: What if the 100-year drought cycle, El Niño, and global warming persists? Lake Mead on the western edge of the Grand Canyon is a glaring warning sign. Surface water levels have sunk to historic record lows, revealing the Mormon pioneer ghost town of St. Thomas, a World War II–era B-29 Super Fortress bomber (Serial No. 45–21847), and threatening Las Vegas, Nevada's, drinking water supply.

Old Bright Angel Trail

The rugged and rocky sixteen-mile loop hike and trek starts near the North Kaibab Trail parking area. Follow the Ken Patrick Trail (see page 213) 3.5 miles east to the Old Bright Angel Trail. Descend into brush-choked head of Bright Angel Creek, and contour above the creek beneath difficult-to-see Ancestral Puebloan dwellings to its confluence with Roaring Spring Canyon. Follow the Roaring Springs side trail up to the North Kaibab Trail and make the steep climb back out to the North Rim.

Mile 5.4. Pump House Ranger Station, Elevation 4,560 feet (1,390 meters), Tapeats Sandstone/Dox Sandstone, water (mid-May to mid-October), emergency phone, composting toilet. The Ranger Station, heliport, and foot bridges are located at the confluence of Bright Angel and Manzanita Creeks. The Ranger Station is the former home of pump house operator–turned-Grand Canyon painter Bruce Aiken, his wife Mary Katherine, and three home-schooled children who once sold cold lemonade from a trailside stand to thirsty hikers. They lived in this canyon outpost for thirty years. The stone pump house and Manzanita Creek Bridge below their home were demolished on December 3, 1996, when a "1,000 year flood" swept down Bright Angel Creek at 4,000 CFS (cubic feet per second).

Mile 6.8. Cottonwood Campground, Elevation 4,080 feet (1,240 meters), Vishnu Schist, water (mid-May to mid-October), seasonal Ranger Station, emergency phone, campground, and composting toilet. Located a quarter-mile below the confluence of Bright Angel Creek and The Transept, the campground has eleven small group sites, and one large site. A half-mile south of the campground, Wall Creek enters Bright Angel Canyon from the left (east).

Mile 8.4. Ribbon Falls, Elevation 3,720 feet (1,130 meters), Vishnu Schist, no potable water. The quarter-mile (day use only) hike down the CCC built trail leads to the cool side-canyon travertine altar and cascade of Ribbon Falls. Depending on the stream flow, lower Ribbon Falls has been estimated to be between eighty and 148 feet high.

Tread lightly. It was recently brought to light that Ribbon Falls is the Zuni peoples' "origin place," called *Chimik'yana'kya dey'a*. One Zuni elder recounted: "The Zuni or *A:shiwi* as we call ourselves came into first light of the Sun Father at a beautiful spot called Ribbon Falls." From their sacred place of emergence, the Zuni's ancient migration route reportedly traced Bright Angel Creek to the Colorado River below Bright Angel Pueblo, and coursed east along the river (North Tonto bench) to Unkar Delta, where it continued beyond to the confluence of the Colorado and Little Colorado Rivers. From

"Zuni girl," 1903, Edward S. Curtis photogravure, Library of Congress.

the Confluence the migration route coursed through the rugged Little Colorado River Gorge from trail shrine to trail shrine and crossed the Painted Desert to Zuni Pueblo, New Mexico more than 200 miles east. The Zuni place of emergence, *Chimik'yana'kya dey'a*, Ribbon Falls, the traditional migration route, trail shrines, burial sites, and all of the Grand Canyon are sacred to the Zuni. Contrary to Zuni and Hopi spiritual beliefs, which may or may not have been known to cultural historians at the time, archaeologists excavated a burial site at Bright Angel Pueblo (see page 108) and unearthed the remains of a woman and an infant.

The middle-aged women reportedly showed signs of "*metate* elbow" from the repetitive daily work of using a *mano* and *metate* (mealing stones) to grind seeds, mesquite beans, and maize. The child was wearing an olivella shell (*Olivella biplacata*) and siltstone bead bracelet on her left wrist. Olivella shells are reportedly used in sacred Zuni ceremonies. Olivella shells were also excavated at Unkar Delta and at burial sites along the Zuni migration route. Archaeologists concluded, "They are but one material reminder that these people once lived in the Grand Canyon." The precious sea shells were gathered along the Pacific Coast and carried overland on foot through the San Gabriel Mountains, across the Mojave Desert, along the Hopi Havasupai Trail, and passed from hand to hand from one indigenous trader to the next until the shells reached the Zuni.

From Ribbon Falls, the North Kaibab Trail enters The Box, a 7.2-mile stretch beneath thousand foot high walls of Vishnu Schist to Bright Angel Campground. It's not a "box canyon" in the sense of outlaws corralling rustled cattle in the Old West, but a narrow corridor that becomes insufferable for many hikers when extreme summer heat combined with dry air, scorching ground temperatures, and direct sunlight refracting off the dark canyon walls produces a pedestrian oven that can melt the unwary. The last 2.5 mile stretch of The Box above (north) of Phantom Ranch narrows to forty-feet. On March 5, 1995, a fifteen-foot-deep flash flood rumbled through the gorge that took out the Trans Canyon Pipeline and washed out the North Kaibab Trail.

Mile 12. Phantom Canyon Confluence, Elevation 2,760 feet (841 meters), Vishnu Schist, no faucet water. Phantom Canyon is normally accessed from Bright Angel Campground. So this entry is described south-to-north. Two miles north of Bright Angel Campground, Phantom Canyon enters from the left (west). To access the mouth of the beautiful, flood prone canyon, hikers cross the second footbridge and ford Bright Angel Creek to enter Phantom Canyon. It offers an unspoiled canyoneering outing up the narrow gorge as far as your experience and skills will allow.

Warning: It's imperative you check the Bright Angel Creek water level and regional weather at the Bright Angel Ranger Station before embarking on this scenic journey that has claimed the lives of two canyoneers.

Mile 13.5. Clear Creek Trail Junction, Elevation 2,640 feet (805 meters), Vishnu Schist, no water. The nine-mile point-to-point Clear Creek Trail is normally accessed from Bright Angel Campground. This entry is also described from south-to-north. A half-mile north of Bright Angel Campground is the North Kaibab Trail/Clear Creek Trail junction. Turn right (east) on the Clear Creek Trail and the 0.75-mile trail climbs 854 vertical feet to two stone benches at the 3,400-foot Phantom Ranch Overlook. Sumner Wash at Mile 2 offers access through the Redwall Limestone headwall to the Fourth Class climb of 7,551-foot Brahma Temple; at Mile 9 secluded Clear Creek Canyon is reached. (See page 281 Clear Creek Trail.)

Mile 13.8. Phantom Ranch Elevation 2,546 feet (776 meters), Vishnu Schist, water, shade, food, and lodging.

Phantom Ranch

The Fred Harvey Company and Santa Fe Railroad envisioned "luxury accommodations" in this canyon idyll, bought Rust's Tent Camp from trailblazer David R. Rust, and hired California School of Design educated architect Mary Jane Colter to design Phantom Ranch. Today, the rustic, river stone and hand-hewn wooden timber canteen and cabins harkens modern guests back in time to a romantic bygone era where riding saddleback still evokes memories of a Southwest brought life in the literary works of Mary Hunter Austin, Harriet Monroe, and Zane Grey (see page 119 Hermits Rest).

Mile 14. Bright Angel Campground, Elevation 2,480 feet (756 meters), Vishnu Schist. The established campground offers an NPS Ranger Station, water (year-round), shade, emergency phone, picnic tables, composting toilets, and campgrounds with thirty-three tent sites (one to six hikers each) and two large tent sites (seven to eleven hikers).

Mile 14.2. Colorado River, Elevation 2,400 feet (730 meters), Vishnu Schist.

Warning: Do not let the Colorado River tempt you for a swim. At least a dozen people have vanished or drowned in the cold, fast-moving two-mile river stretch between Bright Angel Creek and Pipe Creek.

Trail Crossroads

Today, the inner canyon oasis of Bright Angel Campground (formerly the Civilian Conservation Corp Tent Camp) and Phantom Ranch is a staging area for day hikes, overnight backpacks, canyoneering, and peak ascents via the Clear Creek Trail, Phantom Canyon, and Ribbon Falls Trail. It's also an ideal spot for short walks to Bright Angel Pueblo, Rusts Camp, and Phantom Ranch Overlook (see 108 Bright Angel Creek Walks).

Additional Considerations: Hiking Rim-to-Rim: (See page 57)
Trans Canyon Shuttle

The private shuttle offers transportation between the North Rim and South Rim. Call for reservations, fees, and departure and arrival times. Phone (928) 638–2820, visit www.trans-canyonshuttle.com/.

Travel Notes

- Warning Advisory:
  - North Rim: During summer, it's imperative you be OTR to hike back up the North Kaibab Trail through The Box to beat the morning heat before it reaches the Pump House Ranger Station.
  - South Rim: During summer, it's imperative you be OTR to hike the River Trail and Devils Corkscrew to beat the morning heat on the Bright Angel Trail before it reaches Indian Garden. At least thirty people have died of dehydration, heat stroke, and heat-related heart attacks on the Bright Angel Trail.
- Rim-to-Rim: Summertime, do not hike out the South Kaibab Trail. It's steep, hot, and climbs nearly a vertical mile through a virtually shadeless desert.
- Primary Access: North Kaibab Trail; South Rim Bright Angel and South Kaibab Trails.
- Elevation: 8,241-feet North Kaibab Trailhead to 2,480-feet Colorado River
- Biotic Communities: C. Hart Merriam's Life Zones: Canadian Zone, Neutral or Pine Zone, Piñon Zone, and Desert Area Zone. (See page 73 Biogeography.)
- Total Elevation Loss and Gain: 11,522 feet round-trip (5,761 vertical feet one way)
- Total Elevation Loss and Gain: Rim-to-River-to-Rim via the North Kaibab, Bright Angel Suspension Bridge (Silver Bridge), and Bright Angel Trails: 10,141 feet point-to-point
- Mileage: 28.4 miles roundtrip (14.2 miles one way to the Colorado River).
- Mileage, Rim-to-River-to-Rim via the North Kaibab, Bright Angel Suspension Bridge (Silver Bridge), and Bright Angel Trails: 23.7 miles.
  - Note: Don't let the shorter mileage deceive you into embarking on a grueling rim-to-rim crossing that's tested and exceeded the limits of many hikers who just weren't physically or psychologically prepared for it.
- Water: Year-round at Bright Angel Campground and Phantom Ranch; mid-May to mid-October at Supai Tunnel, Roaring Springs, Pump House Ranger Station, and Cottonwood Campground; emergency at Roaring Springs and

Bright Angel Creek (be careful on the slippery footing obtaining water creek-side and when they are flood swollen).

- Cache Points, Out-and-Back from North Rim: Secluded areas near any of the mileposts you think are best for your short hike, day hike, or overnight hike down to Cottonwood Campground or Bright Angel Campground.
- Escape Routes: North Kaibab Trailhead, Pump House Ranger Station, or Bright Angel Ranger Station, whichever is easiest and safest to reach; and seasonal Cottonwood Ranger Station if it's staffed at the time of your hike.
- Seasons: Fall and spring. North Rim roads are closed during the fall after the first snow. Summer, especially June, is brutally hot and the worst time to hike in and out of the Grand Canyon. Winter through spring rain, and July August monsoons pose deadly flash flood threats in The Transept, Roaring Springs Canyon, Bright Angel Canyon, The Box, and Phantom Canyon.
- Maps: Phantom Ranch and Bright Angel Point Quadrangles (7.5 minute).
- Camping, Corridor Trails: Cottonwood, Bright Angel, and Indian Garden Campgrounds only.
- Nearest Supply Points:
  - North Rim: Jacob Lake Store, junction US Highway 89A and AZ Highway 67; North Rim Country Store, Highway 67, (Milepost 605); General Store, North Rim Campground Store; and Fredonia, Arizona, and Kanab, Utah.
  - South Rim: Grand Canyon Village, Tusayan, Flagstaff, Cameron, and Williams, Arizona.
- Managing Agency: Grand Canyon National Park.
- Backcountry Information Center: for information call (928) 638–7875.
- Critical Backcountry Updates visit http://www.nps.gov/grca/planyourvisit/trail-closures.htm
- NPS Grand Canyon Hiker 24 Hour Emergency Phone Number and Email
  - Phone (928) 638–7805
  - Email: grca_bic@nps.gov (Use this if the phone line is busy)
- Winter Access: Average winter snowfall on the North Rim is fifteen to 100 inches and scenic Highway 67 and the North Rim park road are locked.
- Road Closures:
  - Grand Canyon National Park October 31 through May 15.
  - Highway 67 south of Jacob Lake December 1 (often sooner) through May 15.

A cross-country skier stops for a quiet respite in the deep forest.
Copyright © John Annerino Photography.

North Kaibab National Forest Road Access

The North Rim is not always buried in snow. What I call "false springs" occasionally open up bright windows of sunshine from one to two weeks or more at a time. During one of those optimal windows, two climbing companions and I drove backcountry forest roads to reach 7,766-foot Tiyo Point in order to hike and climb 7,646-foot Shiva Temple. We spent two balmy days and nights camping, exploring, and sunbathing atop the remote mesa-like summit. We also encountered three other like-minded canyoneers crossing Shiva's summit to climb 6,982-foot Claude Birdseye Point and 6,613-foot Osiris Temple.

Follow the weather forecasts. If the window opens for you, study your North Kaibab National Forest Road Map. From Jacobs Lake, weather and conditions permitting, you can drive eight miles northwest on US Highway 89A and turn left on Forest Road 422A and drive nine miles southwest to Forest Road 22. Drive south on Forest Road 22 past Big Springs to the road sign crossroads of Forest Road 425 and Forest Road 22. Reference your North Kaibab road map and follow the best route to your objective, that is, Crazy Jug Point, Indian Hollow Campground and Thunder River Trailhead, Muav Point and the Powell Plateau and North Bass Trailhead, and so on. East of Jacobs Lake on US 89A, backcountry forest roads lead south to the Nankoweap Trailhead, Point Imperial, Ken Patrick Trail.

Cross-Country Skiing

During ideal winter snow conditions, you can cross-country ski from Jacobs Lake forty-four miles to the National Park Service's North Rim Yurt fifteen minutes from the North Kaibab Trailhead from December 2 to April 14. Contact the Backcountry Information Center for reservations and full details.

21

Nankoweap (Route) Trail: Day Hikes and Rim to River

"On my left, the canyon wall juts upward, a wind-polished sheet of rock. There are no jagged outcroppings, no sturdy trees or bushes that might serve as handholds if I begin to fall . . . One misstep, one careless bump against the canyon wall could end me falling toward eternity. I dare not even look because I know I will be overcome with fear. . . ."

—Gail Dudley, 1996, "Grand Canyon's Scariest Trail"

There are three nonmaintained rim-to-river trails and routes on the North Rim that see occasional to regular use: Thunder River (Bill Hall) Trail, North Bass (Shinumo) Trail, and Nankoweap Trail (route). Compared to most of the South Rim's wilderness trails that offer relatively easy access on paved roads, the North Rim's wilderness trails require long drives over secondary and high-clearance dirt roads to reach their remote trailheads. For the most part, the North Rim Trails are longer and have a greater elevation loss and gain than South Rim Trails. They also visit seldom-explored areas of Grand Canyon National Park where the consequences of poor planning, insufficient canyoneering experience, or an error in judgment can have disastrous consequences. If you've recently hiked and trekked the South Rim's wilderness trails, you should be prepared for the Thunder River Trail. Avoid the North Bass and Nankoweap Trails until you gain sufficient experience.

Distant views of the Desert Façade and Palisades of the Desert can be seen from the North Rim's trails and routes. Copyright © John Annerino Photography.

LANDFORM

From its headwaters in the sub-alpine forests of the 8,848-foot East Rim of the Kaibab Plateau, the north fork of Nankoweap Canyon drains the rugged corrugated terrain of the eastern Grand Canyon into the main stem of Nankoweap Canyon and Creek, which flows into Nankoweap Rapids at Mile 52 on the Colorado River.

HISTORICAL OVERVIEW

Seven hundred fifty feet above the Colorado River a well-preserved, cliff-side row of four masonry storage granaries had been mortared together by ancient hands end-to-end in a Redwall Limestone alcove. Down by the river, these same practiced hands chiseled petropglyphs, shaped and fired a Tsegi Orange Ware pitcher, roasted agave, ground maize with *manos* and *metates*, and built a ceremonial kiva and thirty-four, multiroom dwellings along the banks of the timeless river. They were Ancestral Puebloans, and they trod what became known as the Nankoweap Trail in yucca fiber sandals and deerskin moccasins to farm the alluvial creek delta between 1050 and 1150.

The Nankoweap Trail takes its name from the Kaibab Paiute term, *Nananku 'uip*, that elders stated means "Fighting River." Others used the term, *Nunku 'uip*, which loosely translates into "Burial Canyon." Both relate to an incident at Big Saddle that took place long ago when, as one ethnographer related, "Apache marauders forded the Colorado River and came upon a Kaibab Camp at night. They hit each sleeping Indian on the head, killing all but one woman who escaped . . ." The Kaibab Paiute reportedly used their moccasin path from Saddle Mountain to reach Nankoweap and Little Nankoweap Creeks on a seasonal basis to farm, hunt and gather, trade, and for ceremony.

In the rim-to-river canyons and valleys south of Nankoweap Canyon, Major John Wesley Powell named one such valley Kwagunt, for *Kwaganti*, "quiet man," an Uninkarets Paiute nick-named "Indian Ben." The Paiute, in turn, called the one-armed explorer *Kapurats*, "arm off." Frederick S. Dellenbaugh was a member of Powell's 1871–72 United States Colorado River Expedition, and he briefly noted both canyons during the river voyage on August 27, 1872: "On the right were two minor valleys within the canyon called Nancoweap and Kwagunt, named by Powell after the Pai Utes, who have trails coming down [from the East Rim] into them. . . Kwagunt was the name of a Pai Ute who said he owned this valley—that his father, who used to live there, had given it to him." Few places in the eastern Grand Canyon are more difficult to reach on foot than Kwagunt Valley. Kwaganti's probable route crossed Saddle Mountain Saddle, descended the Nankoweap Trail and, from Nankoweap Creek, followed the rugged Butte Fault south to Kwagunt Creek. Imagine tracing Kwaganti's little-used trail beyond after you've finally reached water and shade in Nankoweap Creek ten miles below the East Rim.

On November 17, 1872, paleontologist and geologist Charles Doolittle Walcott met Major Powell at Saddle Mountain Saddle to begin building a horse trail down what was then called Nun-ko-weap Valley for the U.S. Geological Survey. Doolittle wrote: "Reached camp at 10 a.m. and found Major Powell and party. [I'm] Half sick with cold. Stormy day." Provisioned with nine pack mules, food, and equipment, Doolittle's party spent the next seventy-two days during the winter of 1872–73 cleaving a trail out of the Kaibab Paiute route down to Nankoweap Creek and beyond. Incredibly, the trail-blazing geologist pushed across the incomparably rugged Butte Fault to the Colorado River in order to continue studying the eastern Grand Canyon's little known geology and stratigraphy of the Unkar and Chuar series of rock layers in what Powell called the Grand Cañon Group. Throughout the expedition, members grew lonely, climbed out of the Canyon, and headed back home to Kanab, Utah. The indefatigable Walcott wrote of the loss of one member: "Illness brot on by homesickness rendered him unfit for work. This is a very lonely, quiet place. No life & nothing but cliffs & cañons. Rocks-rocks-rocks. . .I was left with but one man for two weeks, and was obliged to undertake many dangerous climbs on the cañon walls alone."

The most controversial and audacious story about the Nankoweap Trail had its beginnings with Lone Star cowboy and mountain lion hunter James T. "Uncle Jim" Owens. Born in San Antonio, Texas, Owens punched cattle for legendary cattleman

Charles Goodnight on the Goodnight Loving Trail before heading west, where he was appointed game warden on the Kaibab Plateau for the Grand Canyon Game Reserve in 1906. That was akin to hiring a fox to guard the hen house. "Uncle Jim" built a log cabin as his home base, hung a sign inside that read, "Lions Caught to Order, Reasonable Rates," and entertained famous guests like Zane Grey and Teddy Roosevelt. Cowboy and hunter Charles Jesse "Buffalo" Jones showed Grey how to rope mountain lions for his book, *Roping Lions in the Grand Canyon* (1924), and Roosevelt who wrote his own account of hunting lions with Jones for his travel book, *A Book-Lover's Holidays in the Open* (1916). Owen's game warden responsibilities were two-pronged: protect the mule deer (*Odocoileus hemionus*) population and thin out mountain lions (*Felis concolor*) that preyed on Kaibab Plateau deer herds. With his pack of baying hounds, Owens hunted, tracked, treed, shot, trapped, and poisoned lions throughout the forests and rim rock of the 1,200 square mile Kaibab Plateau, from the Powell Plateau on the west to the Walhalla Plateau on the east. By all accounts, Owens killed over 532 lions with his favorite hound, Pot, who reportedly wore a silver collar that read: "I Have Been at the Death of More Than 600 Cougars." Smithsonian Institution paleontologist Charles E. Resser reported a death toll even higher during his 1930 geological expedition down the Nankoweap Trail: ". . . some of the claws of the 2,200 cougars he [Owens] is said to have killed are still seen tacked to the barn." Though Owens raised a hound-friendly three-month old mountain lion kitten, the famous lion hunter was not on any conservation groups' short list to be a key note speaker on wildlife conservation. Between 1906 and 1939, Owens, along U.S. Bureau of Biological Survey predator eradication hunters, and Euro-American settlers, had "produced an ecological calamity" by slaughtering 816 mountain lions, thirty wolves (*Canis lupis*), 863 bobcats (*Lynx rufus*), 7,388 coyotes (*Canis latrans*), and all the deer venison that hunters, poachers, and hounds could eat that was 'harvested' from the Kaibab Plateau. During Owen's reign, mountain lions were viewed as a scourge, not as a magnificent natural predator that kept the Kaibab Plateau deer population's delicate balance in check. Of one hunt, Roosevelt wrote: there ". . . stood the big horse-killing cat, the destroyer of the deer, the lord of stealthy murder, facing his doom with a heart both craven and cruel." It's a description that some conservationists might find more fitting for Owens, himself.

As a result of such drastic measures, the Kaibab mule deer population grew unchecked to an estimated 26,000 deer by 1924. Pitched by Copper Blossom Mine prospector and rumored horse thief, George W. McCormack, Arizona governor George W. P. Hunt agreed to pay McCormack $2.50 a head for 5,000 to 10,000 deer for each animal his party successfully herded across the Grand Canyon to restock the South Rim's forests with surplus deer. Zane Grey offered $5,000 for the film rights, and Hollywood motion picture director D. W. Griffith showed up on location with a film crew ready to roll. Meanwhile cowboy and game warden Jack Fuss and six mounted men leading twenty-seven pack horses and mules loaded with provisions and kayaks crossed the Grand Canyon and Colorado River and met the roundup at the South Canyon "corral" six miles north of Saddle Mountain.

The skeleton crew of twenty-five mounted cowboys, Gray Hat Charlie, and seventy-two fellow Navajos ["200 Indians" according to Jack Fuss] ringing bells on foot had no chance of herding ten wild, half-starved mule deer in a snowstorm, let alone a thousand. Jack Fuss knew the scheme was preposterous even before he lost two pack mules crossing the canyon with McCormick. Not long after Fuss arrived at the South Canyon ranger station, he told everyone gathered: ". . . there's no way under God's sun that you could herd 'em." In the end, McCormick didn't receive a Buffalo or Indian Head nickel of the $2,000 for film rights he was promised by the Lasky Motion Picture Corporation if they got the film in the can; locals were out $2,250 the Bureau of Indian Affairs insisted they pay the Navajos in advance; and no one had their "million dollar movie" of "Indians" riding mule deer swimming across the Colorado River. Nevertheless, Grey didn't let the facts stand in the way of a good story when he wrote of the disastrous roundup: "I saw thousands of deer [200 according to Jack Fuss], most of which ran in small bands. The ringing of bells, the yelling of the Indians did not seem to frighten them, but the approach of riders on horseback, trying to herd them, brought swift flight."

News of what promoters had called the "Great Kaibab Deer Roundup" was headlined on page one of the Thursday morning, December 18, 1924, issue of the *Arizona Republican*: "Kaibab Dear Drive is Called Off. Snowstorm Ends Plans of McCormick. Motion Picture Men Return to Flagstaff in Blinding Snowstorm; Deer Scatter Widely."

Directions

From AZ Highway 67, located one mile south of the North Rim Country Store, or 4.6 miles north of the North Rim Entrance Station, drive east on Forest Road 610 some 13.6 miles to the Nankoweap Trailhead (East Rim) at the road's end.

Warning: STOP. Do not hike the Nankoweap Trail unless you're a skilled and seasoned Grand Canyon hiker. The primitive fourteen-mile Nankoweap Trail is actually a route Grand Canyon National Park considers its "most difficult" named trail. The largely shadeless, rugged, exposed, and incipient path is one of the canyon's longest and perhaps most dangerous.

The historic route requires nerves, honed route finding skills, endurance, situational awareness of your location—and the consequences of poor judgment or one misstep on what hikers call "scary spots," "fall to your death places," and "ledges of death" (a term usually reserved for the eastern Grand Canyon's Buckfarm Canyon/Eminence Break route). The Nankoweap Trail also requires strategic planning caching water and food on the descent for the long, sketchy, and precipitous climb back out to the trailhead.

Mile 0. Nankoweap Trailhead, Elevation 8,848 feet (2,697 meters), Kaibab Limestone, Trailhead View East: 8,424 foot Saddle Mountain and Nankoweap Creek Canyon. The trailhead is located on the border of the Kaibab National Forest (north), Grand Canyon National Park (south), and the Saddle Mountain Wilderness (east). From the beautiful aspen groves on the East Rim, the cairned Nankoweap Trail (Forest Trail #57) descends 350 vertical feet through Douglas fir, Ponderosa pine, and thick stands of Manzanita (*Arctostaphylos pungens Kunth*) that may inspire other names if you happen to be wearing walking shorts instead of long pants. Continue following the trail where it reveals itself along the Forest/Park boundary, and climb 381 vertical feet to the twin summit of Two Small Hills at 8,881 feet on your Nankoweap Quadrangle (7.5 minute) map.

Mile 0.7. Two Small Hills, Elevation 8,881 feet (2,707 meters), Toroweap Formation. The trail descends to level ground on what some hikers call Manzanita Park. East-southeast from the manzanita-choked hilltop, you can look south and view two distinct landmarks rising up from the labyrinth: 6,680-foot Seiber [sic] Point was named, and misspelled by the U.S. Board of Geographic Names on January 1, 1932, for Civil War veteran, prospector, and Army "Chief of Scouts," Al Sieber. The frontier scout was wounded 28 times during Major General George Crook's war against the Chiricahua Apache—and hunt for Geronimo—during the 1880s. (The three historical figures were memorialized in the 1993 Walter Hill film, *Geronimo: An American Legend*, starring Wes Studi as Geronimo, Robert Duvall as Sieber, and Gene Hackman as Crook). The 6,545-foot Bourke Point was named for Captain John Gregory Bourke who rode with General Crook the Chiricahua Apache called *Nantan Lupan,* "Grey Wolf," and penned his biography, *On the Border with Crook.*

Mile 1.3. Manzanita Park, Elevation 8,450 feet (2,576 meters), Coconino Sandstone. Turn Around Point 1. (Use any convenient point on the descent where you feel you, or your children, need to stop and turn around. Most hikers don't drive all the way out to the Nankoweap Trailhead to day hike). The trail courses northeast across forest fire-ravaged open ground atop the Coconino Sandstone, through aspen, tenacious clusters of manzanita, lone ponderosa pine trees, and towering Ponderosa pine snags firefighters call "widow makers." Stay alert, especially if fall winds are howling south across House Rock Valley when these deadwood totems often topple. You don't want to be in their fall line, whether you're married or not. From the northeast rim of Manzanita Park, the rocky trail snakes through the Coconino Sandstone down a northeast-trending ridgeline to the saddle on the west side of 8,424-foot Saddle Mountain, high point of the 40,610-acre Saddle Mountain Wilderness.

Mile 2.7. Saddle Mountain Saddle, Elevation 7,540 feet (2,298 meters), Esplanade Sandstone. Turn Around Point 2. The Nankoweap Trail/Saddle Mountain Trail junction is located in this saddle beneath the Coconino Sandstone prow of Saddle Mountain.

Both Forest Service trails are named Trail #57. To simplify matters for this description, Saddle Mountain Trail comes in from the south end of the House Rock Valley Road on your left (north) and joins the Nankoweap Trail you descended from the East Rim.

Supai Traverse

From the saddle, the Nankoweap Trail descends a rocky chute through the Esplanade Sandstone and courses southeast on ledges beneath seventy-five-foot tall Supai Sandstone cliffs four miles to the tip of 6,961-foot Marion Point. The meandering, roller coaster traverse is generally easy to follow, but there are no guarantees you're going to make it across safely. It's exposed, narrows to a footprint-wide, and creeps across steep slippery talus with drops of one hundred to a thousand feet or more into the abyss. Some call these "Death Zones." All of the frightening descriptions apply. It's puzzling why National Park trail crews and/or National Forest fire crews haven't widened these perilous sections on the Supai Traverse and Tilted Mesa with Pulaskis, McLeods, and shovels. It'd be easy enough to set up a three-to-five day spike camp on Saddle Mountain Saddle, protect crew members by clipping them into fixed 9-mm perlon climbing ropes, and keep them on the clock reforging a safer hiker's route while waiting for the next wild land fire call out.

Death Zones

Carefully consider each of these exposed sections on the Supai Traverse. You lose nothing if you turn around where there's room enough to do so safely *before* committing yourself to the first fate-temping stretch. Don't let anyone push you into "walking the plank" on one of these highline phantom tracks. This forsaken trail is not worth your life. You can always spend a beautiful evening camping under heavenly stars at Saddle Mountain Saddle or Manzanita Park instead of taking a shortcut to the hereafter.

During an oral history interview with Susan L. Rogers on November 25, 1975, Jack Fuss told of a mule he lost on one of these stretches while leading his pack string up to Saddle Mountain for the 1924 deer roundup: "You couldn't look down, it would scare you to death. And we all just creeped along, holding on to our horses coming along behind us . . . We made the north side where it was cold and it was all ice, as slick as a goose. And then when we got around to the south side it was all mud. Same condition only mud, five-hundred feet, six-hundred feet down. Straight down. You couldn't see. You couldn't get out and look. Just like going off of an airplane, and that was the trail . . . I don't know what ever made him do it, but he turned the horse around with his rump out and the horse's hind feet went off the rock . . . That horse lit, honest to God, from me to you, right on the back of his head in front of me, and you never heard such a noise and such a crunchin'. It was the most horrible noise I ever heard. And he made one bounce and plooey! Couldn't even see where it went. Never seen where it went at all. Just disappeared entirely."

Mile 4.6. Marion Point, Elevation 6,961 feet (2,122 meters), Supai Sandstone. Four tan-and-terra cotta stone hoodoos mark the small rough camp in the wild, wind-bent stands of piñon trees and tree skeletons on the southeastern tip of Marion Point. The distinctive Coconino Sandstone caprock mortared atop blocks of Hermit Shale aren't as dramatic as the Goblins at Devils Garden in Grand Staircase-Escalante National Monument, Utah, but they're a welcome trailside landmark along the "look alike" hanging ledges of the Supai Traverse.

Mile 6.5. Supai Traverse End, Elevation 6,440 feet (1,963 meters), Supai Sandstone. After crossing the frightening traverse with writer Gail Dudley for their *Arizona Highways Magazine* feature, Grand Canyon Park Ranger and photographer Richard Danley told his hiking companion: "You made it! That's the point where the Sierra Club turned back." Given the Sierra Club's legacy of hiking conservationist John Muir's trails through California's high sierra, and repeating legendary climber Norman Clyde's first ascents of the Sierra Nevada's highest peaks, it's a wonder they turned back unless someone just had an off-day and the party did the right thing and stayed together for the hike out. At this beautiful and largely barren southern point beneath the long line of Supai cliffs, the Supai Traverse is behind you, and the cairned descent notch hikers call the "Gate of Hell" marks the stony breach that looks like a step into oblivion. The trail angles southeast down a ridgeline south of point 6088 on your Nankoweap map to 5,888-foot Tilted Mesa.

Mile 6.8. Tilted Mesa Saddle, Elevation 5,930 feet (1,807 meters), Redwall Limestone. At the first unnamed saddle beneath point 6088, the trail switchbacks off the southeast side of Tilted Mesa through boulders and ragged ledges of crumbly Redwall Limestone and the steep exposed talus and scree sliding through the Muav Limestone. Leading his pack string up toward the Supai ledges, Jack Fuss described this slippery stretch: "Well, you couldn't stand up on it. You couldn't walk around on it. But we had to get around it, so old George [McCormick] and Lou Wesley and Johnny, all of us took George's mining picks and one thing or another that he had and picked toe holds about the size of a saucer, or so, around in this shale so this old mule could make the first steps around. Then all the rest of the horses, of course, they followed along."

Mile 8.4. Muav Shelf, Elevation 4,920 feet (1,500 meters), Muav Limestone. From this rocky shelf, the trail angles through the black bush across what feels and looks like an isolated swatch of the Tonto Formation, and heads for the unnamed saddle on the northwest side of point 4154 on your Nankoweap topo. Descend the drainage from the saddle through the Galeros Formation and follow the trail to the cottonwood trees beckoning you from Nankoweap Creek.

View: To the east you can see 4,697-foot Barbencita Butte, named for Barbencito, *Hashké yich'i' Dahilwo'*, "he is anxious to run at warriors." Barbencito was a Navajo warrior and spokesmen who helped broker a treaty with General William T. Sherman and Col. Samuel F. Tappan at Fort Sumner, New Mexico, on June 1, 1868, for the Navajo to safely return to their homelands, *Dinétah*, after the terrifying Long Walk to Bosque Redondo that killed 323 innocent men, women, and children.

Mile 11. Nankoweap Creek, Elevation 3,280 feet (1,000 meters), Tapeats Sandstone-Muav Limestone. The gravel and boulder-hopping streambed route traces the course of the perennial, spring-fed Nankoweap Creek three miles to the Colorado River. The trickling sound of running water in the desert, the breezy shade of cottonwood trees, and the solitude is an ideal spot for rest and contemplation. Before climbing up the Nankoweap Trail at the end of his unprecedented trans canyon crossing of the Grand Canyon, Colin Fletcher touched upon his feelings in his 1967 book, *The Man Who Walked Through Time*: "For a long time I stayed sitting there beside the creek letting the sun dry me off (it was over 100 degrees now, even in the shade), and I found myself beginning to list. . .The things I had gained from the journey. . .the journey had conferred upon me a rare but simple gift: an almost perfect confluence of what I thought and what I felt. Had offered me, that is, the key to contentment."

Butte Fault/Horse Thief Trail

Almost directly across the creek 100 yards south of where the Nankoweap Trail reaches the canyon bottom is the wild eyed, tale of a trail called the Horse Thief Trail that follows the Butte Fault south to the Colorado River. (See page 271 North Trans Canyon Routes and Trails.)

Mile 14. Colorado River, Elevation 2,802 feet (854 meters), Redwall Limestone, Nankoweap Rapids, River Mile 52. Camping at large, low-impact campsites on a wide riverside alluvial delta formed by Nankoweap Creek in Zone AE9.

Nankoweap Granaries Trail

The steep, popular river runners trail switchbacks from the river 750 vertical feet up to the cliff-side Ancestral Puebloan storage granaries and a stunning downstream view of the Colorado River and Marble Canyon.

Additional Considerations

Wherever you travel between the Nankoweap Trailhead and perennial Nankoweap Creek you need to carry, consume, and cache water. This is a critical consideration whether you plan on hiking rim-to-river-and-back in three or four days. The delicate balance is to carry sufficient water between the cache points suggested (below) to stay hydrated, but not to carry so much water that it's going to be dangerously unwieldy climbing up Tilted Mesa and tip-toeing across the Supai Traverse or elsewhere.

Travel Notes

- Warning Advisory: Do not hike the Nankoweap Trail during the summer.
- Primary Access: Nankoweap Trail (#57) from the East Rim, Saddle Mountain Trail (#57) from House Rock Valley; secondary access from the Colorado River.
- Elevation: 8,848-feet Nankoweap Trailhead (East Rim) to 2,802-feet Colorado River
- Biotic Communities: Sub-alpine forests to the Sonoran Desert.
- Total Elevation Loss and Gain: 12,092 feet (6,046 vertical feet each way)
- Mileage: Twenty-eight miles roundtrip (14 miles one way to the Colorado River).
- Water: Nankoweap Creek, Colorado River; Marion Point (tricky-to-locate seasonal seep, don't bet your life on it).
- Cache Points: Manzanita Park, Saddle Mountain Saddle, Marion Point, Tilted Mesa, and Nankoweap Creek.
- Escape Routes: You're on your own. Nankoweap Trail (#57), Saddle Mountain Trail (#57), Colorado River—whichever trail you judge offers the best chance for survival. A Boy Scout died of dehydration just short of the Colorado River in spite of an EMT's efforts to rehydrate and save him.
- Seasons: Fall before the snow flies, and spring after the snowmelt and the mud dries. Summers have proven deadly, and winter access can be difficult and treacherous.
- Maps: Nankoweap Quadrangle (7.5 minute), North Kaibab National Forest Road Map.
- Camping: At large, low-impact camping at Manzanita Park, Saddle Mountain Saddle, Marion Point, Tilted Mesa, Nankoweap Creek terraces, and Colorado River Zone AE9.
- Nearest Supply Points: Jacob Lake Store, Cliff Dwellers Lodge, and Vermilion Cliffs Lodge on U. S. Highway 89A; Fredonia, Arizona, and Kanab, Utah.
- Managing Agency: Grand Canyon National Park.
- Backcountry Information Center: for information call (928) 638–7875.
- Critical Backcountry Updates visit www.nps.gov/grca/planyourvisit/trail-closures.htm.
- NPS Grand Canyon Hiker 24 Hour Emergency Phone Number and Email
  - Phone (928) 638–7805
  - Email: grca_bic@nps.gov (Use this if the phone line is busy)

Saddle Mountain Trail and Winter Access

For canyoneers interested in hiking the Saddle Mountain Trail, and cross-country skiers keen on exploring the eastern Grand Canyon after winter snows have buried U.S. Forest Road 610, check weather conditions and forecasts beforehand to access the Saddle Mountain Trail (#57) by driving 42.6 miles south of U.S. Highway 89A via Forest Road 8910 to the trailhead at road's end. The steep three mile Trail #57 climbs 350 vertical feet, then descends 399 vertical feet, and climbs another 1,125 vertical feet to reach the Saddle Mountain Saddle trail junction.

High above the Tonto Route North, a climber approaches the summit of 6,761-foot Angels Gate. Copyright © John Annerino Photography.

22

North Bass Trail: Day Hikes and Rim to River

"For many years I have been hearing of the beauty of the Shinumo, the purity of its waters, the charm of its willow-fringed creek, the interest of its cliff dwellings and prehistoric irrigating ditches and gardens, and the fascinating but repulsive stories of human selfishness, murder, and cannibalism that have desecrated its beauties and native sanctity."

—George Wharton James, 1899,
Shinumo Creek, North Bass Trail

LANDFORM

From its headwaters formed by the amphitheater between 7,549-foot Dutton Point on the Powell Plateau, 7,569-foot Swamp Point on Swamp Ridge, and 7,560-foot Emerald Point on the Rainbow Plateau, Muav Canyon drains the sub-alpine forests of the Kaibab Plateau and flows into Shinumo Canyon en route to Bass Rapids at Mile 108.5 on the Colorado River.

HISTORICAL OVERVIEW

Here, and elsewhere throughout the mythical canyons, mesas, and painted deserts of the Colorado Plateau, the sacred landscape-inspired Native People to build captivating cliff dwellings and lookouts from timber, stone, and mud, cowboy archaeologists who "discovered" troves of forbidden treasures, and all manner of explorers, surveyors, scientists, anthropologists, writers, and photographers who stood humbled in their presence. The Pueblo people's natural environment, culture, dwellings, and lifeways had also inspired Mary J. Colter's visionary architecture and traditional interior designs she emulated in her extraordinary buildings and native stone monuments throughout the Grand Canyon and Painted Desert region. If Colter had visited the North Bass Trail she would have undoubtedly been enlightened to see, and immerse herself in, this isolated wilderness of water, stone, and light hidden within the Grand Canyon. She would have noted White and Shinumo Creeks' cliff dwellings, creek side masonry homes, storage granaries crafted from stone and mud, beautiful hand-smoothened ollas, sacred agave roasting hearths, flint-napped stone blades used to skin deer hides, stone-worn *manos* and *metates*, and incised ditches that diverted sweet water to hand-tilled plots of corn, beans squash. She would have understood that the Ancestral Puebloans who dwelled along the perennial creeks between 1100 and 1150, and perhaps earlier by Archaic peoples, traveled seasonally to the forested Powell Plateau, where they lived in harmony with the land, seasonal seeps, and supplemented their natural diet with mule deer, antelope, and bighorn sheep they hunted with bows and arrows, and piñon nuts, pine seeds, juniper berries, and acorns they gathered by hand.

It is doubtful America's most celebrated woman architect would have bought into the volatile conjecture that peaceful Ancestral Puebloans had resorted to anthropophagy George Wharton James wrote he had heard about, and modern archaeologists who have publicly espoused at great harm to Native Peoples. In the American Southwest, the concept of eating "man corn" dates back to 900 at the trade crossroads of Chaco Canyon, New Mexico, where several archaeologists later excavated human remains they reported showed signs of cannibalism: disarticulated bones, cut marks, breakage, burning, pot polishing, and missing vertebrae. Ancestral Puebloans living in lofty caves and cliff dwellings along White and Shinumo Creeks between the Kaibab Plateau and Colorado River had everything they needed to sustain their lives, culture, and spiritual beliefs.

There was no need to resort to the desperate practice American pioneers had when forty-seven members of the snowbound Donner Party faced starvation in California's Sierra Nevada during the winter of 1846–47. Like Chaco Canyon, there was no physical evidence discovered anywhere near the Grand Canyon, or among its Native Peoples—no skull racks, pictographs, or mass burials associated with the macabre ritual practice—that would substantiate the claims associated with "Mesoamerican Toltec warrior-cultists" who were said to rule Chaco and the advanced culture that built its "Great Houses." Visit the Mayan center of Chichén Itzá in southern Mexico today, and you can still see *Plataforma de los Cráneos*, "Platform of the Skulls," and the haunting wall engravings of machete-wielding warriors carrying the heads of their human sacrifices. The defense positions of the Ancestral Puebloans' difficult-to-reach cave and cliff dwellings in Muav and Shinumo Canyons, and elsewhere throughout the region, suggest they fortified themselves against marauding enemies, much the same way the peaceful cave, canyon, and mesa dwelling Tarahumara (*Rarámuri*, "Foot Runners"), in

Mexico's Sierra Madre, had when they fled from the neighboring Tobosos who hunted them for food and ritual.

Shinumo Trail/White Trail

The trail, canyon, creek, and altar take their name from the Paiute word, *Shinumo*, which loosely translates into "ancient people," or "cliff dwellers," for the ancestral Paiute who lived in and traveled through Muav and Shinumo Canyons. Little is known about a man named White (not to be confused with 1860s-era horse thief James White), who reportedly first built the upper North Bass Trail sometime during the 1880s. In his 1933 report, "On Canyon Trails," Grand Canyon National Park Naturalist Edwin D. McGee wrote: "Information obtained from Mr. Bass before his death [March 7, 1933] indicates that some of the northern part of this trans-canyon route was first developed by a prospector from the North Rim area named White, the man after whom White Creek received its name." White rebuilt the Paiute foot trail through White and Shinumo Creeks sometime after Powell expedition topographer Almon Harris Thompson and his party started rebuilding the Paiute trail down Bright Angel Creek during its first recorded descent in 1872. Around 1887, William Wallace Bass began reforging White's trail into a tourist and bridle trail so that guests who stayed at his Shinumo Camp and Garden could visit the beautiful, yet remote, North Rim where Bass and his Havasupai friend Chickapanagi traveled to hunt mule deer on the Powell Plateau.

North Bass Trail

Intriguing tales first lured George Wharton James up the North Bass Trail in 1899, two years before Bass finished it: "Several years ago," James wrote, "an Indian brought out from one of the cliff dwellings an exquisitely shaped large olla, fashioned exactly after one of the common oriental patterns. It was perfect in every way." The promise of discovery enticed James to take a pack trip with Bass on the Grand Canyon's first cross-canyon trail system, and first rim-to-river-to-rim tourist crossing he described, in part: "Another two or three weeks' delightful experience can be gained by arranging to go down Bass's Trail [South Bass], cross on his cable ferry, go up the Shinumo Trail to Powell Plateau, watch herds of protected and preserved deer and antelope . . . and pleasantly saunter [eighteen miles] along out to Point Sublime." The 7,458-foot Point Sublime, *Potavey'taqa*, is a cultural landscape of the Hopi.

    The primitive nonmaintained 13.5-mile long North Bass Trail requires keen judgment, honed route finding skills, endurance, and, if you insist on wading through manzanita stands instead of bypassing them, farmer's overalls or cowboy chaps to trace the brushy, boulder-strewn, and declivitous course to the Colorado River.

Directions

To reach the North Bass Trailhead at Swamp Point from AZ Highway 67, see page 217 Powell Plateau Trail.

Mile 0. Swamp Point, Elevation 7,565 feet (2,306 meters), Kaibab Limestone, no water, Trailhead View West: 7,661 foot Powell Plateau. From Swamp Point, follow the well-marked, rocky trail and switchbacks one mile down to Muav Saddle (see page 216 Powell Plateau Trail). Eminent geologist Clarence E. Dutton surveyed the North Rim during the summer of 1880 for his U.S. Geological Survey Monograph, *Tertiary History of the Grand Canyon*, and described the trail leading to Muav Saddle that still holds true today: "The descent into the Muav Saddle is very steep, and, though hardly dangerous, requires caution and the steadiest and best trained pack animals to go safely past some points. At the bottom a fine camp may be made beneath the yellow pines, and good water may be obtained from a spring about a quarter of a mile away, issuing from a ledge of the lower Aubrey sandstone."

Mile 1. Muav Saddle, Elevation 6,711 feet (2,046 meters), Coconino Sandstone, no water. Turn Around Point 1. (Use any convenient point on the descent where you feel you, or your children, need to stop and turn around. Most hikers don't drive all the way out to Swamp Point to day hike). From Muav Saddle, turn left (east) and follow the North Bass Trail along the base of the Coconino Sandstone to the secondary trail that leads to seasonal Muav Saddle Spring (Queen Anne Spring), the headwaters of White Creek, which flows down Muav Canyon.

Mile 1.25. Muav Saddle Spring, Elevation 6,740 feet (2,054 meters), Supai Sandstone, (Dutton's "lower Aubrey sandstone"). Turn Around Point 2. Top off your water bottle, reverse the secondary trail, and continue down the rim-to-river trail to the Colorado River, or your destination of choice in between. A hike down the North Bass Trail isn't much different today than it was in Bass's era nearly a century-and-a-half ago. It's remote, difficult, and wildly beautiful. From Muav Saddle all the way to the Colorado River it follows the course of White Creek and Shinumo Creek—rarely exposing itself to the breadth of the Canyon itself. A trek down the North Bass is more akin to exploring a distinct wilderness within the Grand Canyon—a seldom-trod, undiscovered wild land that heeds its own primeval laws and offers its own sublime rewards.

Mile 2.25. White Creek Benchmark, Elevation 5,692 feet (1,735 meters), Supai Sandstone. From Muav Saddle Spring at the foot of the towering Coconino Sandstone, the steep trail descends past an historic masonry structure through dense stands of manzanita and loose Hermit Shale to the Supai Waterfall. Park Service trail crews realigned the historic course of this stretch in 2005.

Mile 2.5. Supai Waterfall, Elevation 5,640 feet (1,719 meters), Supai Sandstone. The short charming single-rivulet falls is located in a corner of Supai Sandstone. Muav Canyon takes its name from the Paiute elder *Muavigaipi*, "Mosquito Man," or word, *moavi*, for the pests that swarm its springs and creeks during warm weather. In his book, *Beyond the Hundredth Meridian*, Wallace Stegner described Clarence Dutton as the "*genius loci* of the Grand Canyon region." The Yale-educated geologist was the quintessential Grand Canyon sightseer, describing its points, promontories, plateaus, terraces, temples, canyons, gorges, bays, and amphitheaters, often in literary and poetic terms. When Dutton viewed Muav Canyon, he wrote: ". . . look into the great gorge which has received the name of Muav Cañon. The Muav is relatively only a little nook—a mere detail like scores of others, which open directly into the chasm itself. Yet as we view it apart from the whole we are still oppressed with its magnitude. Its walls are a mile in height and . . . the trees dwindle to shrubs and then to minute flecks; the fallen blocks, as big as cottages, fade away . . . and far down in the lower depths the eye can recognize nothing but a playground for the imagination."

Mile 3.1. Redwall Gorge Gateway, Elevation 5,175 feet (1,577 meters), Redwall Limestone. A slot canyon groove at the head of Muav Canyon marks the beginning of the Redwall Gorge Traverse along the right (west) side of the hard-scrabble broken rim.

Mile 3.25. Natural Bridge, Elevation 5,160 feet (1,573 meters), Redwall Limestone. Located on the east side of the gorge, partially obscured by brush, is the forty-foot span and difficult-and-dangerous-to-view-from-below natural bridge. The collapsed cave doline was discovered by William Wallace Bass before 1900 and later rediscovered by pioneer Grand Canyon climber Merrell D. Clubb. Stay on the traverse and carefully trace the exposed rimrock beyond.

Mile 4.5. Redwall Rim Descent Benchmark, Elevation 5,007 feet (1,522 meters), Redwall Limestone. The Redwall Gorge Traverse ends. From the rim, the trail switchbacks more than 900 vertical feet down to White Creek in the bottom of Muav Canyon. Follow the course of White Creek downstream along benches of Bright Angel Shale to the canyon slot that marks White Creek Falls. At the height of summer when the merciless morning sun beats down, and the afternoon skies turn dark and ominous, and the heavens unload with thunder, lighting, and torrential rains, when rocks, boulders, and mud slides spew from looming cliffs and Muav and Shinumo Canyons roar with flashfloods too deep and violent to ford, the Grand Canyon's greatest map maker, François Émile Matthes, was faced with a difficult choice. How to lead his survey party and pack string rim-to-river-to-rim down the South Bass Trail, and across the Colorado River, and up the Shinumo Trail to reach 7,468-foot Point Sublime to continue his work on the canyon's first topographical map, *Bright Angel Quadrangle*. Matthes tapped a rock with a stick and the monsoon heavens parted for his mid-August crossing in 1902. He wrote: "There was but one other choice . . . climb out on the north side through Shinumo and Muav canyons. The crossing was known to be dangerous . . . and the Shinumo Trail was little more than a faint track, seldom used. Yet this was the route we finally selected. It took us a day and a half of arduous, exhausting work to gain the top, and the entire trip to Point Sublime, where the mapping operations were resumed, consumed six days." It took six days to ride, lead, and push and pull the weary, heavily laden horses and mules—via the rim rock of the Redwall Gorge Traverse—thirty-one miles across the canyon wilderness. Don't overload your backpack.

Mile 5.8. White Creek Falls Benchmark, Elevation 4,001 feet (1,220 meters), Bright Angel Shale. From the pour off, follow the benches of Bright Angel Shale along the right (west) side of White Creek for a half-mile until it crosses a slip of Tonto Formation and descends back into the creek bed. Continue downstream to BM 3480 on your King Arthur Castle Quadrangle (7.5 minute) map. Approximately 250 yards southeast, is the Tapeats Narrows/Tonto Bypass Trail junction. If there is no chance of flash floods you can discover the magic and beauty of Tapeats Narrows—and the challenges of streambed boulder hopping—as you follow the corridor downstream to the confluence of Shinumo Creek. But if there's any chance of a flash flood turn right (west), climb the stony switchbacks out of White Creek, and follow the Tonto Bypass Trail toward BM 3602 opposite Holy Grail Temple.

Note: Some canyoneers prefer to rappel down the pour off and explore Tapeats Narrows from its head.

Mile 7.9. Bass Tomb Memorial Point, Elevation 3,602 feet (1,098 meters), Bright Angel Shale. From the desert expanse among bayonet yucca and prickly pear cacti, the trail continues south along the Tonto Formation on the right (west) side of White Creek toward its confluence with Shinumo Creek. Before you head south, stop for a moment and gaze high above the soaring walls of Redwall Canyon on your left (east) at 6,711-foot Holy Grail Temple. Your King Arthur Castle map pinpoints the landmark. After William Wallace Bass's death in 1933, the trailblazer's ashes were scattered from an airplane atop the peak that was renamed Bass Tomb by Virginia Dox, the first woman Bass guided on the trail. Forty-three years later Arizona climbers Larry Trieber and Bruce Grubbs made a white-knuckle ascent of the difficult-to-reach Coconino Sandstone temple on October 23, 1976. Before he crossed over, Trieber was a dedicated and prolific rock climber who left his mark climbing remote Grand Canyon temples no one had ever trod before, where there was no room for error, and little chance of being rescued. While climbing the last pitch of Holy Grail Temple, Trieber reportedly pulled on a chock stone that was the keystone for the deadly rubble of stones that cascaded beneath him as he clung terrified, spread-eagle with his hands and feet tenuously counterbalanced against slick sandstone walls. Trieber was *this* close to having Bass Tomb renamed after him.

Mile 9. White Creek Descent, Elevation 3,460 feet (1,055 meters), Bright Angel Shale. From this point southeast of BM 3450, the trail crosses through a low saddle, descends into White Creek, and follows it to the confluence of Shinumo Creek. Shinumo Creek flows in part from Abyss River Cave. The hidden cave springs was discovered by Grand Canyon climber Merrell D. Clubb and first explored by Arthur L. Lange and Thomas J. Aley in July–August 1959 during a North Rim cave reconnaissance. During that same reconnaissance Lange, Aley, and fellow caver George Mowat were shaken by an "awesome rumble" deep inside distant Silent River Cave by a Richter Magnitude 5 earthquake that reverberated sixty miles south from its epicenter in Fredonia, Arizona, on July 21.

From its headwaters in the lofty untracked wilderness of the Shinumo Amphitheater, Abyss River Cave was reported to carry "a volume of water equal to that of Roaring Springs Cave" on the North Kaibab Trail, which may be a stretch.

Mile 10.3. Shinumo Creek/White Creek Confluence, Elevation 2,680 feet (817 meters), Dox Sandstone. From the confluence, follow the course of Shinumo Creek downstream through its flash flood swept narrows to Shinumo Camp.

Mile 12.0. Shinumo Camp and Garden, Elevation 2,468 feet (752 meters), Supergroup. From Shinumo Camp, the trail climbs 449 vertical feet out of Shinumo Canyon, contours south over the notch between BM 2917 and BM 2996, and switchbacks 749 vertical feet down to the Colorado River.

During his maiden 1869 Geographic Expedition down the Colorado River, Major John Wesley Powell and his crew stopped near Shinumo Creek on August 20, 1869.

Historical remains of William Wallace Bass's Shinumo Camp and Garden.
Copyright © John Annerino Photography.

Powell tersely noted: "Found remains of old Moquis village on bank, stone houses and pottery." During Powell's Second Colorado River Expedition of 1871–72 two years later Powell stopped at Shinumo Creek again. On September 3, 1872, Powell used even fewer words to note: "Camped for dinner at the Shinumo Ruins above the deep side gulch." William Wallace Bass was so enamored with the Ancestral Puebloan winter refuge Powell was credited with discovering, he extended the South Bass Trail down to the river, and erected a cable crossing to ferry mules, burros, provisions, mining equipment, farm tools, a cast iron stove, and tourists across the Colorado River he guided to his tent camp. Bass squatted his camp near ancient farm terraces he also tilled with the Ancestral Puebloan triumvirate of corn, beans, squash, as well as melons, cantaloupes, onions, radishes, and peaches.

In his self-published booklet extolling the virtues of his rim and river camps, Bass wrote: "The Shinumo Camp and Garden are on the other side of the river, beautifully enclosed in the grand, rugged and sublime Shinumo Canyon. Here one may spend a week, or a month, bathing in the creek, climbing the canyon walls, exploring side canyons and gorges, and during the whole time, in the proper season, eat daily of fresh fruit and vegetables gathered in the garden close by, which Mr. Bass planted years ago and irrigates with water from the Shinumo." Bass's canyon oasis beckoned many.

What looks like a tall Coconino headstone below Shinumo Camp bears the neatly chiseled inscription, W. L. VAUGHN CLAUDE, TEX 7–11–1912. Above the block letter signature is a bar Y-cattle brand. Near as a feller can figure, a bar Y brand was used by Mary Ann "Molly" Goodnight. She was the wife of legendary Texas Panhandle cattleman Charles Goodnight. Goodnight, his partner Oliver Loving, and eighteen brush-popping cowhands drove 2,000 Texas longhorns north on the Goodnight-Loving Trail from Fort Belknap, Texas, to Fort Sumner, New Mexico. The herd was purchased for $12,000 in gold to feed 9,000 Navajos held captive at Bosque Redondo after the merciless Long Walk. (The Goodnight-Loving Trail cattle drives later inspired Larry McMurtry's Pulitzer Prize–winning novel, *Lonesome Dove* (1985), and the epic award-winning TV miniseries of the same name starring Robert Duvall, Tommy Lee Jones, Diane Lane, and Danny Glover). The Palo Duro Canyon cowboy, Goodnight, invented the chuck wagon and bred "cattalo" from buffalo and polled Angus cattle. After meeting with the onetime Texas Ranger, Charles Jesse "Buffalo" Jones was inspired by Goodnight's efforts to breed his own cattalo in House Rock Valley, Arizona. You can still view descendants of Buffalo Jones' herd grazing in the verdant parks and meadows along Highway 67 on your drive into the North Bass Trailhead. Vaughn, and his partner T. W. Lynch, who inscribed his moniker and hometown name "Claude" on a small wooden plank outside Shinumo Camp, heard the call of the canyon. Talk of hitting the mother lode near Bass's diggings no doubt loomed large in their eyes and campfire tales while punching cattle in the Texas Panhandle for $45 a month.

Mile 13.5. Colorado River, Elevation 2,198 feet (670 meters), Vishnu Schist, Bass Rapids, Mile 108.5, Camp Zone AS9 along mile-long river terrace.

Additional Considerations
Reaching the Remote Trailhead
Before driving out to the trailhead, inquire about current road conditions at the Backcountry Information Center. High-clearance 4WD vehicles are recommended. Get a North Kaibab National Forest map beforehand by visiting www.fs.usda.gov/main/kaibab/maps-pubs.

Out-and-Back
If you're hiking the North Bass Trail out-and-back from Swamp Point, take time to familiarize yourself with the terrain on the descent by stopping every so often to turn around and take a mental picture of the rugged landscape you'll be climbing back up through.

Rim-to-River-to-Rim: (See page 135 South Bass Trail.)

River Crossing: (See page 57 River Crossings.)

Travel Notes

- Warning: Do not hike the North Bass Trail in the summer. The heat can be deadly. And July–August monsoon pose serious threats in the Tapeats Narrows and Shinumo Narrows.
- Primary Access Trails: North Bass Trail.
- Elevation: 7,565-feet Swamp Point to 2,198-feet Colorado River.
- Biotic Communities: Douglas fir, aspen, Ponderosa pine, piñon juniper woodland, Great Basin Desert scrub, and Mojave Desert scrub.
- Total Elevation Loss and Gain: 10,734 feet (5,367 vertical feet each way).
- Mileage: 27 miles (13.5 miles one way to the Colorado River).
- Water: Muav Creek, Shinumo Creek, Colorado River; Muav Saddle Spring (seasonal, fairly reliable).
- Cache Points: Muav Saddle, head of Muav Canyon, head of the Redwall Gorge, Tonto crossover.
- Escape Routes: North Bass Trail, or Colorado River. Remember the North Bass and South Bass Trailheads are perhaps the two most remote interconnecting trailheads in the Grand Canyon.

- Seasons: Late spring and early fall. Deep snow, mud, and tree blow-down can make winter access from the North and South Rims difficult to impossible. Spring and summer monsoon runoff can make Tapeats Narrows deadly, and fording Shinumo Creek dangerous to impossible without a seasoned skill set of using dead Century plant pole vaults or stringing Tyrolean traverses.
- Maps: King Arthur Castle and Havasupai Point quadrangles (7.5 minute).
- Camping: At-large, low-impact camping near water sources and caches listed above in Zone AS9.
- Nearest Supply Points: Jacob Lake Store, junction US Highway 89A and AZ Highway 67; North Rim Country Store, Highway 67, (Milepost 605); General Store, North Rim Campground; and Fredonia, Arizona, and Kanab, Utah.
- Managing Agency: Grand Canyon National Park.
- Backcountry Information Center: for information call (928) 638–7875.
- Critical Backcountry Updates visit http://www.nps.gov/grca/planyourvisit/trail-closures.htm
- NPS Grand Canyon Hiker 24 Hour Emergency Phone Number and Email
  - Phone (928) 638–7805
  - Email: grca_bic@nps.gov (Use this if the phone line is busy)

23

Thunder River Trail: Rim to Falls and Rim to River

"In the year 1876 a rumor was circulated that gold had been found in the sands of the river, and it gained credence enough to attract a number of the restless people who tramp the deserts of the far west in pursuit of—they know not what. With considerable labor and danger this trail was built and used long enough to satisfy those who went there that they had been deceived."

—Clarence E. Dutton, Summer 1880
Sev-tun-kat, Tapeats Creek

LANDFORM

On the west, Deer Creek Canyon drains the Kaibab Plateau between 6,240-foot Little Saddle and 7,166-foot Monument Point, courses through Surprise Valley, and tumbles down a narrow fissure over Deer Creek Falls into the Colorado River at Mile 136. On the east Tapeats Creek drains the Tapeats Amphitheater between Monument Point and 7,443-foot Crazy Jug Point and flows downstream past the white water confluence of Thunder River into the Colorado River at Mile 133.5.

HISTORICAL OVERVIEW

Ghostly pictographs of eagle-feathered shamans, crescent moon spirals, hematite-daubed red handprints where some "crossed over" to the spirit world, river and creekside masonry dwellings, and agave roasting pits still trace phantom paths that once whispered through the red rock desert and primeval rim-to-river creek corridors running with the lifeblood of the primordial canyon lands that sang out to Virgin Ancestral Puebloans from 1100 to 1150.

Paiute Spirit Trail

Two men unwittingly traced Southern Paiute spirit trails into Deer Creek and Tapeats Creek. Both were attached to Major John Wesley Powell's Colorado River Geographical Expedition in 1869 and the US Geological Survey (and second river journey) in 1871–72. Photographer E. O. Beaman was first among the pair that included geologist Clarence E. Dutton. Each made immutable discoveries in faraway canyons were few white men had ventured before, but neither reported visiting a remote cave shrine with stone altars of split-twig figurines offered by Archaic peoples as sacred totems for successful mountain sheep and mule deer hunts.

While reveling at a New Year's foot-stomping, hand-clapping ball in the Mormon hamlet of Kanab, Utah, on January 1, 1872, Salt Lake City photographer E. O. Beaman overheard news from Powell's Kanab Wash prospecting party that one of the men "claimed to have discovered gold in paying quantities within the distance" of the Colorado River. The news traveled like brushfire and by March of that year five hundred prospectors, tinhorns, gadabouts, and hungry and desperate men journeyed down the incomparably rugged Kanab Creek Canyon to work placer diggings downstream to the banks of the Colorado River. Beaman was among the miners who traveled sixty stone bruising miles down the 3,500-foot deep gorge, but he went to photograph their wild-eyed discoveries, not to reap the prospect of filling his own saddle bags with heavy nuggets.

Kanab Creek has long been a traditional Kaibab Paiute travel corridor they used to trade with the Havasupai and Hualapai on the south side of the Colorado River. The Kaibab Paiute tilled corn and squash along the life-sustaining creek they called *Kanav 'uip*, "Willow Canyon," and they recorded their history and spiritual myths along the canyon's stone canvasses. Beaman hadn't traveled far down the Kaibab Paiute's ancestral gorge when he made his first discovery in Snake Gulch. "The walls in many places," Beaman wrote, "are carved [and painted] with strange figures and signs . . . The Utes state in their traditions that the hieroglyphics upon these cañon-walls have existed for many hundreds of moons." The eight-mile-long tributary gulch Beaman visited was adorned with mysterious and colorful pictographs of anthropomorphic figures, shamans, ghost dancers, hunters, trails, springs, and animals. They were hand painted with yucca fiber brushes daubed with sacred *ompi*, "red paint," white clay, black charcoal, blue azurite, and yellow limonite that dated to 500 BC. It was one of the Colorado Plateau's exemplary prehistoric rock art sites that men from Powell's Survey would visit and note.

When Beaman and his assistant finally reached the confluence of the Colorado River after their weary journey, they were surprised to learn they had missed the swarm of prospectors lured by the gold rush. In a March 21, 1872, letter to the *Chicago Tribune*, Powell's cousin, Walter Clement Powell, wrote, "After prospecting for a time, and getting but a few fine grains of gold, provisions run out, hopes fall, starvation stares them in the face." Hearing of a dreamy waterfall beyond, Beaman turned his attention upstream along the Colorado River and, with his assistant, struggled seven grueling boulder-strewn miles across the merciless stones to the foot of a rainbow-misted 190-foot tall riverside waterfall. He named it "Buckskin Cascade," after Buckskin Mountain (Kaibab Plateau), which bore the name for the abundance of mule deer hides the Kaibab Paiute cured, wore and traded. Wielding their alpenstocks and ropes, the pair made the precipitous climb to the headwaters of the falls, where Beaman exclaimed ". . . we found ourselves in the heart of the American Alps." Beaman was about to make yet another discovery in the deep dark fissure on a narrow footstep-wide ledge cribbed with ancient stones and mortar. Above the muffled roar of the chasm falls that threatened to sweep them over the edge, Beaman braced himself, then noticed a hand print on the red wall. "In one place the impress of a beautiful feminine hand graced the wall," he wrote. "This hand was like a dark blood-stain in color, and was neither carved nor laid on with any material that chemicals would act on. Could it be that this was the mausoleum of some long-extinct race, and this hand so symmetrical and womanly reached out from the external rocks to tell the tale of its ossification?" Beaman had unknowingly pieced together a Southern Paiute spirit trail that led from the shaman pictographs he'd seen in Snake Gulch to the sacred *Ompi* hand pictograph he viewed in Deer Creek that were said to ward off evil spirits. Beaman had entered the heart of the Kaibab Paiute's "holy lands" they revere as *Puaxant Tuvip*, "power land."

One mystifying pictograph remained hidden from Beaman's Deer Creek journey, and conceivably it linked the Southern Paiute spirit trail between Snake Gulch, Deer Creek, and beyond. It may have been painted by the *Mukwic*, (ancestral Paiute), or perhaps later during the Ghost Dance movement. It seemed likely that geologist Clarence Dutton would discover it during his journey eight years later.

During a solar eclipse one extraordinary day on January 1, 1889, *Wovoka*, a Northern Paiute shaman, was touched with a vision: "When the sun died, I went up to heaven," Wovoka recounted, "and I saw God and all the people who had died a long time ago. God told me to come back and tell my people they must be good and love one another, and not fight, or steal, or lie. He gave me this dance to give my people."

Wovoka, Ghost Dance shaman, circa 1890, photographer not
attributed, perhaps Lorenzo D. Creel.

Wovaka's transformative, five-day ceremony spread throughout the West and Great Plains, from the Oglala Lakota Sioux to the Comanche, the Northern Paiute to the Pai peoples. Wovaka, or Jack Nelson as he was known by whites, reportedly met with the Kaibab Paiute on several occasions. As a result of his efforts and Ghost Dance apostles, the Ghost Dance crossed the Grand Canyon from the west where it was practiced by the desert dwelling Chemehuevi and the Mojave, and from the north where the Kaibab Paiute traveled south and forded the Colorado River to reach the Havasupai via Kanab Creek and Cataract Creeks, and the Hualapai via Toroweap Valley and Prospect Canyon. Captain Navajo, a Ghost Dance apostle, held the ceremony at Havasupai. As did the neighboring Hualapai who performed it while an outsider was in attendance: "The dance place was a circular piece of ground . . . and surrounded by high mountain walls of granite, which reflected the light from a half-dozen fires blazing within the circle. The dancers, to the number of 200, clad in white robes . . . Their faces and hair painted white in various decorative designs, moved slowly in a circle, keeping rhythm with a wild chant." The sacred white pigment that adorned the dancers may have been quarried from a seam in Snake Gulch where the Kaibab Paiute held their own Ghost Dance ceremony. Who carried the sacred paint to the ghost mural between Snake Gulch and Deer Creek Narrows?'

Clarence Dutton was headed in that direction during the summer of 1880:

> With one man to pull on the halter and two to push each animal [mule] may be launched on its adventurous journey . . . As it is the trail needed in many places to be built up to give a narrow tread along some projecting shoulder, where the packs brush the rocks as the mules pass by. At length it becomes steeper, the ledges more frequent and higher, and the way grows somewhat alarming. A single inadvertence, the slightest accident, sends man or beast to the great unknown." Of his trusty mules, Dutton later reported, ". . . how high and steep and rough a hill a mule can roll down without getting killed.

Dutton had descended into the canyon from the Kaibab Paiute's Parrissawampitts Spring, (*Pa-rish-u-um,* "gurgling water"), in order to survey *Sev-tun-kat,* "Tapeats Creek." From Tapeats Creek Dutton ventured over the bench Beaman called "Surprise Valley" that stretched between the Tapeats Creek and Deer Creek, but he reportedly never saw the hidden ghost mural. It may have been seen by miners who built the trail across Surprise Valley in the eight intervening years between Beaman's and Dutton's visits so they could prospect for gold down Tapeats Creek to the Colorado River. But their efforts did not pan out. Could one of the grizzled old prospectors "who tramp the deserts of the far west" have seen the ghost mural and inscribed the date of his visit in charcoal, "Jan 16, 1905"? More likely it was the mark of Arizona Strip cowboys ranging cattle across the Esplanade. Or perhaps the "ghost dancers" were painted by a Kaibab Paiute medicine men or shaman, a *Puha'gants*," one who has sacred power,"who knew the secret spirit trail from Snake Gulch and was accompanied by a young novice he was teaching to acquire *utu'xuxuan* (supernatural spirit), or *puha*, "power." Conceivably, they may have made a ritual pilgrimage to offer tobacco, prayer, and white paint at the *Tumpituxwinap*, "Storied Rock," either before or after the last recorded Ghost Dance was performed by the Havasupai in 1901.

(Spirit trails and song lines were a concept practiced by fleet-footed Chemehuevi runner-hunters who sang their mythic Mountain Sheep songs and offered gifts to the mountain spirits during long distance journeys across the Mojave Desert from one spiritual landmark to the next all the way to their bighorn sheep hunting grounds in Death Valley. The Kaibab Paiute, Chemehuevi, and many other tribes had joined together with five hundred people at the Hualapai's first Ghost Dance held at *Tanyika Ha'a*, "Grass Springs," Arizona in May 1899.)

Except for Dutton's poetic accounts of Tapeats Amphitheater—he apparently missed Thunder River altogether or he would have provided a grandiose description—his biggest discovery may have been Parusiwompats Spring from his exploration of the Powell Plateau. "Beneath a clump of spruces the spring sends forth a slender thread of clear pure water, almost icy cold," Dutton wrote. "If anyone would know how great a luxury pure cold water is, let him drink of Parusiwompats, and afterwards pitch his tent by the water-pockets of the Kanab and Uinkaret deserts." Or the desert in Surprise Valley.

DIRECTIONS

Thunder River Trailhead

From Highway 67 one mile south of the North Rim Country Store, turn west on Forest Road 422, and drive eighteen miles to the junction of FR 425. Turn left (south) on FR 425 and drive ten miles to the junction of Forest Road 232. Indian Hollow Campground trailhead is at the end of FR 232.

For Bill Hall Trailhead, stay on Forest Road 425, turn right on FR 292, and make another right onto FR 292A and follow it to the Monument Point Trailhead. See Bill Hall Trail.

The rugged nonmaintained 13.8 mile Thunder River Trail from Indian Hollow is easy to follow all the way to the Colorado River, and requires sure footing, stamina, good judgment, and situational awareness. The rustic canyon trail leads to three of the most beautiful, aquifer-fed cataracts on the Colorado Plateau: Deer Creek Falls, Tapeats Creek Springs, and Thunder River Falls.

Mile 0. Indian Hollow, Elevation 6,240 feet (1,902 meters), Kaibab Limestone, Trailhead View South/SW: Deer Creek Canyon. From Indian Hollow Creek, the Thunder River Trail traverses west beneath the rim toward Little Saddle and switchbacks through the Toroweap Formation and Coconino Sandstone to the Hermit Shale where the old cowboy trail courses east across the Esplanade Sandstone to the north fork of Deer Creek at Benchmark 5029 on your Tapeats Amphitheater Quadrangle (7.5 minute) map.

Mile 1.9. North Fork Deer Creek, Elevation 5,029 feet (1,533 meters), Esplanade Sandstone. From this unnamed creek fork, the trail continues southeast across the high red desert, contours the main fork of Deer Creek at point 4–128 on your Tapeats Amphitheater map, and turns south to the Bill Hall Trail Junction. Some distance below the North Fork is the difficult to reach Vaughn Spring in the Supai Sandstone-Redwall Limestone contact. The intermittent spring was named after Bob Vaughn, a 1940s cowboy who hailed from Texas Panhandle country of Charlie Goodnight with Uncle Jim Owens. Vaughn grazed cattle and buffalo on the Arizona Strip with colorfully-nicknamed, living legends of their day: Walapai Johnny, Hades Church, Cowhide Adams, Bullhide Woolley, and cattleman and rodeo cowboy Johnny Schoppmann. During the 1960s, Vaughn and cattleman Rell Little reportedly rounded up the last of the maverick cattle that still grazed the hardscrabble Esplanade by baiting the mavericks with two cows. Trailing the heifers, Vaughn and Little herded the mavericks up the Thunder River Trail to Indian Hollow, put them on a truck, and drove them straight to the slaughter house to pick up their payout. It was one of the Grand Canyon's last round-ups. And Zane Grey missed it. . .

Mile 5. Bill Hall Trail Junction, Elevation 5,420 feet (1,652 meters), Esplanade Sandstone. (From 7,155 foot Monument Point, the Bill Hall Trail descends 2.6 miles to this junction). Somewhere in the lost horizon of tawny slickrock desert hoodoos, ghost white shamans dance in a summer mirage of shimmering heat waves calling out to the Great Spirit from smoky walls: "The Father will descend, The earth will tremble, Everybody will arise, Stretch out your hands." Listen for the phantom whispers of the Ghost Dance traveling aloft in the scorched and hypnotizing evening breeze as you stride through the crimson glow of twilight.

Mile 6.1. Bridgers Knoll View Point, Elevation 5,340 feet (1,628 meters), Esplanade Sandstone. Less than a half-mile due east is landmark 6,602-foot Bridgers Knoll. It was named for western mountain man and trapper James "Jim" Felix Bridger. Among his infamous exploits, Bridger left legendary mountain man Hugh Glass for dead after he was savagely attacked by a grizzly bear on the forks of the Grand River, South Dakota, in August 1823. Glass survived his incredible ordeal (featured in the Oscar winning movie *The Revenant*), but he did not shoot the repentant frontiersman. During the winter of 1824–25, Bridger led his trapping expedition through Sylvan Pass to the Grand Canyon of the Yellowstone River, not the Grand Canyon of the Colorado River, or Thunder River.

Mile 8.1. South Rim Surprise Valley/Redwall Descent, Elevation 5,240 feet (1,597 meters), Supai Sandstone. From the rim, the trail switchbacks 1,460 vertical feet down through the Redwall Limestone to the Surprise Valley trail junction. Cowboys, cattlemen, and Park Ranger Ed Laws reportedly built and blasted this steep, loose, and rocky trail through the Supai and Redwall from 1925–26.

Mile 9.5. Surprise Valley Trail Junction, Elevation 3,780 feet (1,152 meters), Tonto Formation. Camp Zone AM9. Turn left (south) to hike east across Surprise Valley to the Thunder River Trail. Turn right (south) to hike west across Surprise Valley to the Deer Creek Trail.

East Fork/Thunder River Trail

Mile 10.7. Thunder River Overlook, Elevation 3,845 feet (1,172 meters), Tonto Formation. From the Surprise Valley trail junction hike past the head of Bonita Creek 1.3 miles east across Surprise Valley to the Thunder River overlook. Percolating through the forest floor and the underlying 250-million-year-old seabed of Kaibab Limestone, rain and snowmelt pool up in subterranean aquifers and form underground streams that explode through twin fissures from the canyon's Muav Limestone walls, creating Thunder River—the shortest river in the world. The cottonwood tree-shrouded whitewater river tumbles a half-mile into Tapeats Creek, 1,045 vertical feet below. The Arizona landmark was reportedly the late Senator Barry M. Goldwater's favorite spot in his home state.

Mile 11. Thunder River Spring and Cave, Elevation 3,490 feet (1,064 meters), Muav Limestone. Thunder River's high flow spring discharge was estimated to be twenty-one million gallons of water per day. During their Easter break in 1960, cave adventurers George Beck and Peter Huntoon used surplus fighter jet one-man rafts to explore and paddle through the cold dark subterranean Thunder River Cave they called a "Kaibab stream cave" for three-quarters of a mile behind the falls.

Mile 11.35. Thunder River/Tapeats Creek Confluence, Elevation 2,445 feet (745 meters), Muav Limestone-Tapeats Sandstone. From the confluence, you can travel east upstream cross-country along the north side of Tapeats Creek to the mouth of Tapeats Falls. At BM 2817 on your map, the route turns left (north) and climbs 915 vertical feet up to where you can view Tapeats Falls and Cave at BM 3732. Tapeats Spring's high flow spring discharge was estimated to be forty-eight million gallons of water per day. In 1963, cavers Beck and Huntoon returned to the area to explore Tapeats Cave with dry suits. They reportedly explored 1.1 miles of the dark frigid passage.

Mile 11.6. Upper Tapeats Camp, Elevation 2,460 feet (750 meters), Muav Limestone-Tapeats Sandstone. Upper Tapeats Camp was established on an Ancestral Puebloan site that was later used by cowboys, trail builders, and guides who kept Cove Camp stocked with cooking utensils and supplies. Camp Zone AW7. *Warning*: Do not attempt to ford, or follow, Tapeats Creek during high spring runoff, or flashflood potential at any time of the year. The 2.2-mile long stretch from Tapeats Camp to the Colorado River is a continuation of the Miner Trail scratched out and dynamited across Surprise Valley from Deer Creek. The modern trail still shows its rustic and dangerous origins tracing precipitous and exposed ledges, terraces and steep talus past Ancestral Puebloan masonry dwellings you'll see if attentive. Stay focused on the trail. The trail crosses Tapeats Creek approximately one hundred yards below camp and traces the east side of the creek for about 1.5 miles where it again crosses the creek and follows the west side of Tapeats Creek to the Colorado River. If you're hiking the trail during spring, you may have to follow the more rugged and exposed west side trail. Bring a short twenty-five-foot length of six mm or larger perlon cordage to lower packs and for protection.

Major John Wesley Powell named Tapeats Creek after his young Shivwits Paiute guide, *Ta-peats*, "Small Rocks," who showed Powell the creek he said he owned. When explorer Frederick Dellenbaugh climbed up Tapeats Creek from the Colorado River on September 6, 1872, during Powell's second river journey, he wrote from the expedition camp: "A morning was spent at Tapeats Creek for examinations, and we found there some ancient house ruins not far up the side canyon." The late anthropologist, Robert C. Euler, who devoted much of his scholarly field work in the Grand Canyon, corrected Dellenbaugh's observations and pointed out the trailside "ancient house ruins" dated from 1100 to 1150 and were built above the box canyon at the mouth of Tapeats Creek three-quarters of a mile from the expedition's Colorado River camp.

Mile 13.8. Tapeats Creek/Colorado River Confluence, Elevation 2,003 feet (611 meters), Vishnu Schist, Tapeats Rapids, River Mile 133.5, Lower Tapeats Camp Zone AW8. A mile-and-a-half downstream from the confluence, the Colorado River flows through a seventy-six foot wide portal in Granite Narrows, the narrowest river passage the Colorado River makes through the Grand Canyon. During the 1923 U.S. Geological Survey Expedition, leader Claude H. Birdseye was inspired to name the gorge on September 10: "At the entrance to this short granite gorge the walls are only 75 feet apart. We name this point Granite Narrows." Four months earlier Major Edward Alphonso Goldman, an esteemed mammalogist for the U.S. Bureau of Biological Survey, stocked Thunder River with trout. On May 23, 1923, the *Kane County Standard* wrote: "Major Goldman arrived in Kanab last week with 10,000 trout fry to be placed in Thunder River Canyon won't it be great to hop into Thunder river and get a fry for breakfast. If they live they will grow to be an enormous size." Ever since, back country fisherman have been making the long trek down the Thunder River Trail to fish for "monster trout" at the confluence. Perhaps they'd read George Wharton James' account of the two feet eight inch long, eleven and a half pound "silver salmon" (Colorado pikeminnow, *Ptychocheilus lucius*, now extirpated from the Grand Canyon) prospector Louis D. Boucher caught at Boucher Creek and hauled up to the El Tovar Hotel. Bring a big stove, frying pan, and all the fixin's. Or a block and tackle and dry ice to pack out your catch.

West Fork/Deer Creek Trail

Deer Creek is a wonderful, easy-to-follow Miner's Trail that leads through the Kaibab Paiute's holy ground, *Puaxant Tuvip*, "power land." This was the route of Ancestral Puebloans, Kaibab Paiutes, E. O. Beaman, Clarence E. Dutton, gold rush miners, and cowboys.

Mile 10.2. Cogswell Butte Saddle, Elevation 3,725 feet (1,135 meters), Tonto Formation. From the Surprise Valley Trail Junction, hike 0.7 miles west across Surprise Valley to Cogswell Butte Saddle. From this low saddle, you'll see 4,545-foot Cogswell Butte a half-mile south. Named for Raymond Austin Cogswell, he was the expedition photographer for the 1909 Nathaniel Galloway and Julius F. Stone Colorado River Expedition that journeyed from Green River, Wyoming to The Needles, California. Stone's brother-in-law reportedly took 2,000 black and white photographs during the three-month-long expedition. The summit of Cogswell Butte can be reached from this saddle via a rugged Third class scramble 820 vertical feet up to the 360 degree lookout atop the Supai Sandstone perch that offers spectacular summit-to-river views of the western Grand Canyon: 7,661-foot Powell Plateau to the southeast, 6,524-foot Great Thumb Mesa to the west; 6,125-foot Fishtail Mesa to the northwest, and 6,240-foot Indian Hollow and 6,602-foot Bridgers Knoll to the north.

Mile 10.9. Deer Creek Canyon Descent, Elevation 3,240 feet (988 meters), Temple Butte Formation. Watch out for loose rocks and boulders.

Mile 11.2. Deer Creek Springs, Elevation 2,760 feet (841 meters), Muav Limestone. After crossing the shadeless desert of the Tonto Formation, you'll be delighted by the charming cascade and cool water of Deer Creek Springs streaming out of the canyon wall in the morning shade of what hikers call the Throne Room.

Mile 11.9. Deer Creek Campground, Elevation 2,360 feet (719 meters), Muav Limestone-Tapeats Sandstone. The designated cottonwood tree-shaded backcountry campground offers camping and an outhouse in Zone AX7.

Mile 12. Deer Creek Narrows, Elevation 2,320 feet (707 meters), Tapeats Sandstone.

Tread lightly as you stroll through the hallowed chamber echoing mesmerizing sounds of running water, and gaze upon the mythical handprints of ancestral Kaibab Paiutes whose descendants still make pilgrimages to this pulsing sacred heart of stone. It's a place of great power for the Kaibab Paiute and others. When I asked a Paiute woman elder in Cannonville, Utah, about the handprints, she said they symbolized where "some crossed over" to the spirit world. Another Kaibab Paiute elder recounted, "Our Creation place is near Deer Creek along the Colorado River." *Note*: Rappelling, bouldering, and canyoneering, with or without ropes, in Deer Creek Narrows is prohibited. Watch out for poison ivy on the steep descent to the foot of mist-shrouded Deer Creek Falls at the Colorado River.

Mile 12.6. Deer Creek/Colorado River Confluence, Elevation 1,936 feet (590 meters), Tapeats Sandstone, Deer Creek Falls, River Mile 136. When Raymond Cogswell photographed Deer Creek Falls on November 9, 1909, thirty-seven years after John K. "Jack" Hillers took the first recorded image, expedition leader Julius Stone wrote: "We passed a beautiful waterfall, possibly one hundred feet high, above Kanab Wash. It comes from Surprise Valley on the north, there being many crevices in the wall which is free flowing. Vegetation has made the most of this opportunity, the result being a vertical flower garden of rare beauty."

Bill Hall Trail

From the west end of the Monument Point parking spot, the nonmaintained 2.6-mile trail contours southwest along the rim past Millet 7206 on your topo map for a half-mile to the southern tip of 7,166-foot Monument Point. The trail turns left (south) at this point and switchbacks through the Kaibab Limestone and Toroweap Formation to point 6,520 on your map. The airy trail turns abruptly right (northwest) and courses atop the Coconino Sandstone before steep switchbacks lead through the broken cross-bedded sandstone to the Esplanade Sandstone and the Thunder River Trail junction. The Bill Hall trail descends 1,786 vertical feet. You may need a twenty-five-foot length of six mm perlon cord to lower your pack/s on a short stretch between the Coconino and Esplanade Sandstone.

Additional Considerations

Be prepared, and stay alert. This is a remote location, even for skilled Nellis Air Force Base, Nevada Blackhawk helicopter pilots who rescued an injured hiker from Tapeats Creek.

Travel Notes

- Warning: High spring runoff and periodic flashfloods can make Tapeats Creek extremely dangerous or impossible to cross on foot. Don't underestimate the summer heat on the high desert trails crossing the Esplanade and Surprise Valley.
- Primary Access: Thunder River Trail, Bill Hall Trail; secondary access Colorado River via Tapeats and Deer Creeks.
- Elevation:

- Thunder River Trail: 6,240 feet Indian Hollow to 2,003 feet Colorado River.
- Deer Creek Trail: 6,240 feet Indian Hollow to 1,936 feet Colorado River.
- Biotic Communities: Ponderosa pine, piñon-juniper woodland, Great Basin Desert scrub, and Mojave Desert scrub.
- Total Elevation Loss and Gain:
  - Thunder River Trail: 8,474 feet (4,237 vertical feet each way).
  - Deer Creek Trail: 8,606 feet (4,304 vertical feet each way).
- Mileage:
  - Thunder River Trail: 27.6 miles (13.8 miles one way to the Colorado River).
  - Deer Creek Trail: 25.2 miles (12.6 miles one way to the Colorado River).
- Water: Thunder River, Tapeats Creek, Deer Creek, Colorado River; Deer Creek Springs (seasonal), and ephemeral water pockets on the Esplanade Sandstone after spring snowmelt, summer monsoons, and rain anytime of the year.
- Cache Points: Esplanade Sandstone, Surprise Valley, and any other shaded and secluded spot near the mile posts highlighted in this section.
- Escape Routes: Thunder River Trail, Bill Hall Trail, and the Colorado River at Tapeats Creek and Deer Creek. Remember nine months out of the year (fall-through-spring) the remote Thunder River and Bill Hall trailheads, and Colorado River, are often secluded. Three months out of the year (summer months) the trailheads and Colorado River receive hikers and river runners who may or may not be able to help during an emergency.
- Seasons: Spring and fall. Winter snow and mud can make access difficult to impossible.
- Summer heat has proven unbearable to many. Summer monsoon and seasonal runoff can make Tapeats Creek extremely dangerous or impossible to cross on foot.
- Maps: Tapeats Amphitheater, Fishtail Mesa Quadrangles (7.5 minute), and North Kaibab National Forest Road Map.
- Closures:
  - Deer Creek Narrows: The Kaibab Paiute's Deer Creek Narrows sacred site is closed to canyoneering, with or without ropes, from the "Patio" atop the falls to the bottom of Deer Creek Falls.
  - Thunder River Cave and Tapeats Cave: Closed to visitation. (See page 22 Caving, Inside Earth, Speleology.)
- Camping: Camping near perennial water sources available in designated campsites at Upper Tapeats Camp Zone AW7 (outhouse), Lower Tapeats Camp Zone AW8, and in designated campsites at Deer Creek Camp Zone AX7

(toilet); at-large, low-impact camping on the Esplanade Formation Zone AY9 and in Surprise Valley Zone AM9.

- Nearest Supply Points: Jacob Lake Store, junction US Highway 89A and AZ Highway 67; North Rim Country Store, Highway 67, (Milepost 605); General Store, North Rim Campground; and Fredonia, Arizona, and Kanab, Utah.
- Managing Agency: Grand Canyon National Park.
- Backcountry Information Center: for information call (928) 638–7875.
- Critical Backcountry Updates, visit www.nps.gov/grca/planyourvisit/trail-closures.htm
- NPS Grand Canyon Hiker 24 Hour Emergency Phone Number and Email
  - Phone (928) 638–7805
  - Email: grca_bic@nps.gov (Use this if the phone line is busy)

Maj. J. W. Powell Expedition Journal, April 21, 1871, GCNP Museum Collection.

24

North Trans Canyon Trails and Routes: Point-to-Point Hikes and Treks

"Cutting the bloody cord, that's what we feel, the delirious exhilaration of independence, a rebirth backward in time, and into primeval liberty, into freedom."

—Edward Abbey, 1968
Desert Solitaire

INTRODUCTION

The largely trailless North Trans Canyon Trails and Routes is a natural history journey of adventure and discovery that lures seasoned canyoneers off the grid to explore the inner canyon below the North Rim, sometimes from one end of the Grand Canyon to the other. These primitive trails and routes require canyon-specific skills, knowledge, the ability to trek and scramble for days on end over precipitous terrain with tenuous footing, on-site route finding through waterless, uncompromising topography, and, if something goes awry, survival and self-rescue skills. In many sections this trans canyon route is comparable in difficulty to the cliff-hugging Nankoweap Trail you need to descend just to reach the start of the Butte Fault/Horsethief Trail. Whatever you've hiked below the relatively accessible South Rim may pale in comparison to the

An Ancestral Puebloan storage granary remains hidden in a North Rim canyon gorge. Copyright © John Annerino Photography.

hazards and rewards of trekking this remote, seldom-explored country. An accident in this inner canyon frontier might prove akin to stepping off the face of the earth. Aerial searches by Blackhawk helicopter pilots, and ground searching rescue teams, trackers, and bloodhounds would prove difficult locating you in what amounts to a modern no man's land before you succumbed to the elements, thirst, or injury. If you undertake this trek in whole or part—and exercise good judgment—you may have the rare opportunity of experiencing "a rebirth backward in time, and into primeval beauty, into freedom."

The North Trans Canyon Trails and Routes below the Kaibab Plateau courses south from the Nankoweap Trail then west all the way to the Thunder River Trail within the original 1926 Grand Canyon National Park boundaries. (Welshman Colin Fletcher used these boundaries when he made the first trans canyon backpack crossing in 1966. I followed this North Rim route when I made my last trans canyon journey run crossing within the same boundaries). All mileages are approximate, except for the Clear Creek Trail. Elevation losses and gains are minimums. Each section of this daunting route is described east-to-west and links one section to the next.

BUTTE FAULT/HORSE THIEF TRAIL

"The superb horsemanship of . . . Butch Cassidy's Wild Bunch must always be kept in mind. They could outride any sheriff's posses, skimming the rail fences like fox hunters. And of course if they wanted to go on living they had to be expert judges of horse flesh."

—James David Horan, 1949
Desperate Men

Landform

Paralleling the Colorado River on the west, the cross canyon Butte Fault is a north/south trending tectonic fracture in the earth crust that collided with the East Kaibab Monocline 800 to 742 million years ago. It produced a cataclysmic upheaval of rock layers called the Grand Canyon Super Group you'll need to negotiate while trekking the fault line. It offers rugged passage across the grain of the corrugated east-trending terrain of deep rugged tributary canyons that drain into the Colorado River. The North Rim of the Kaibab Plateau drains into the Grand Canyon whereas the Coconino Plateau slopes away from the South Rim. As a result, the North Rim's tributary canyons are generally longer, steeper, and more rugged, including those traversed by the Butte Fault.

Historical Overview

Creekside dwellings, pictographs and petroglyphs, *manos* and *metates*, ollas and hand-painted pot shards clearly establish the Butte Fault—and the creeks and canyons it descends into and climbs out of—was traversed by Archaic peoples, Ancestral Puebloans, and Kaibab Paiute wearing little more than yucca fiber sandals and buckskin moccasins. Their ancient paths were later developed by geologist Charles D. Walcott for the U.S. Geological Survey. This route was long rumored to have been used by horse thieves. A romantic tale ripped out of the real life exploits of Butch Cassidy, the Sundance Kid, and the Wild Bunch, Grand Canyon horse thieves were said to have stolen Mormon horses in southern Utah, drove them down the Nankoweap Trail, across the Butte Fault, swam the horses across the Colorado River at low water, pushed them up Tanner Canyon, and then sold the cold-rebranded mounts in Flagstaff, Arizona. William Wallace Bass first reported his encounter with canyon "horse thieves" to George Wharton James in March 1886. (See page 161 Tanner Trail.) The only physical evidence that supports the colorful as-told-to-story comes from the rusty horse shoe, tin cans, and old coffee pot canyoneers found in Malgosa Canyon and on the Kwagunt Butte divide in 1977. As enticing a dime novel saga as it is, I believe the historic artifacts either came from one of Walcott's documented campsites on the Butte Fault during the winter of 1882–83, or they were dropped in December 1924 when cowboy Jack Fuss and his outfit drove tweny-seven noisy, pan-banging, supply-laden horses and mules across the Butte Fault to support the "Great Kaibab Deer Drive."

The Butte Fault/Horsethief Trail isn't a trail any more than the Nankoweap Trail is. The ancient route and historic trail traces the Butte Fault southeast/south to the Colorado River. If horse thieves actually made the crossing, riding, climbing, slipping, and sliding with stolen mounts across the eastern Grand Canyon—I'd love to believe the tale—they were extraordinary horsemen. Once you trek out of Nankoweap Creek and climb nearly fifteen hundred vertical feet up to Nankoweap Saddle you'll realize that even Zorro—Joaquin Murrieta, legendary horse thief, Mexican Robin Hood, and avenger of his wife's brutal murder during the California Gold Rush—would have dismounted and used geologist Clarence E. Dutton's "one man to pull on the halter and two to push" the mule from behind technique.

Directions

Hike fourteen miles down the Nankoweap Trail to reach the north end of the Butte Fault in Nankoweap Creek. The obscure start of the Butte Fault route is located across the creek about 100 yards southwest. (See page 237 Nankoweap Trail.)

Nankoweap Creek/Nankoweap Saddle/Kwagunt Creek

Mile 0. Nankoweap Creek, Elevation 3,280 feet (1,000 meters), Muav Limestone: Elevation Gain to Nankoweap Saddle 1,400 vertical feet/Elevation Loss to Kwagunt Creek 1,320 vertical feet. From Nankoweap Creek, you have two choices of routes that closely parallel one another to reach Kwagunt Creek. Either follow the hogback of the Butte Fault on its east or west side up and over the 4,680-foot Nankoweap Saddle in the Muav Limestone/Carbon Canyon Formation between Point 4,810 and Point 5052 on your Nankoweap Mesa Quadrangle (7.5 minute) map. Or follow the north/south drainage system that contours the west side of 6,316-foot Nankoweap Mesa. From Nankoweap Saddle, the route descends into Kwagunt Creek.

Kwagunt Creek/Malgosa Divide/Malgosa Creek

Mile 3.85. Kwagunt Creek, Elevation 3,360 feet (1,024 meters), Muav Limestone, seasonal water: Elevation Gain to Malgosa Divide 1,300 vertical feet/Elevation Loss to Malgosa Creek 380 vertical feet. Once you reach Kwagunt Creek, you should have a good feel for the Butte Fault and be able to read the lay of the land ahead. From Kwagunt Creek the route climbs up to the 4,660-foot Malgosa Divide in the Tapeats Sandstone/Surprise Canyon Formation, contours the west side of 5,584-foot Malgosa Crest, then drops into Malgosa Creek. Major John Wesley Powell named Kwagunt Creek after a Unikarets Paiute man named *Kwaganti*, "quiet man," who lived in "Kwagunt Valley" because it offered refuge from the Yavapai-Apache who reportedly attacked his family. In his 1872 diary, Powell expedition photographer John K. Hillers recounted the chilling aftermath of Kwagunti witnessing his parents' and brother's murders: "Next morning about sun up some white men came close to our camp and began to shoot. Our men got their guns and started to shoot at the white men. My sister and myself ran and hid in the rocks. We hid all day and everything was very still. When we dared to come out we looked around and found all the Indians dead." A creek dwelling, corrugated pottery shards, shattered metates, abstract red pictographs, and spiral petroglyphs seen along Kwagunt Creek are mute testimony the area was inhabited long before Kwagunti lived there.

Malgosa Creek/No Name Divide/Awatubi Creek

Mile 5.5. Malgosa Creek, Elevation 4,280 feet (1,305 meters), Surprise Canyon/Redwall Limestone: Elevation Gain to No Name Divide 800 vertical feet/Elevation Loss to Awatubi Creek 890 vertical feet. From Malgosa Creek the route crosses the 5,050-foot No Name Divide in the Surprise Canyon/Redwall Limestone below the west side of 6,377-foot Kwagunt Butte on your Cape Solitude Quadrangle (7.5 minute) map. Malgosa Creek, Canyon, and Crest were named after Pablo de Melgosa (with an e), one of conquistador García López de Cárdenas's men who failed to reach the "large river" at the bottom of the Grand Canyon during their journey of discovery in September 1540.

What a practice to name and misspell canyon landmarks after someone who never made the rim-to-river trek, in Melgosa's case from the South Rim near Desert View to the Colorado River. Incredibly, Arizona rock climbers Larry Trieber, Bruce Grubbs, and party made it to the summit of the imposing Kwagunt Butte on March 24, 1979. The ascent was one of the last major ones in the Grand Canyon, and it required a brutal multiday trek into the canyon just to reach the foot of the climb. Trieber summarized climbing such a difficult to reach-summit-and-return canyon peak. "The problems of climbing temples in the Grand Canyon are as complex as those found in remote mountain ranges. Only the climbs are located in a vast canyon, and are on desert mountains."

Awatubi Creek/Awatubi Divide/Sixty-mile Creek

Mile 7.15. Awatubi Creek, Elevation 4,160 feet (1,268 meters), Wescogame, Manachaka, and Watahomigi Formations: Elevation Gain to Awatubi Divide 770 vertical feet/Elevation Loss to Sixty-mile Creek 772 vertical feet. From Malgosa Creek the route climbs over the 4,930-foot Awatubi Divide in the Tapeats Sandstone and Wesco-Mana-Wata Formations beneath 5,403-foot Awatubi Crest, and descends into Sixty-mile Creek on your Cape Solitude topo. The Creek and Crest take their name from Awatobi, a sixteenth-century Hopi pueblo whose name is derived from *awata*, "bow." The Bow Clan symbol can still be seen at *Tutuventiwngwu*, "Place of the Clan Rocks," at Willow Springs, Arizona. Many Hopi inscribed their clan symbols at Willow Springs during their difficult and dangerous ritual pilgrimages to collect salt at their sacred mine in the eastern Grand Canyon called *Öngtupqa*, "Salt Canyon."

Sixty-mile Creek/Chuar Saddle/East Fork-West Fork Carbon Creek Confluence

Mile 9.05. Sixty-mile Creek, Elevation 4,160 feet (1,268 meters), Temple Butte and Wesco-Mana-Wata Formations: Elevation Gain to Chuar Saddle 739 vertical feet/Elevation Loss to East-West Fork Confluence 1,547 vertical feet. From Sixtymile Creek the route climbs over 4,987-foot Chuar Saddle in the Surprise Valley/Redwall Limestone beneath 6,394-foot Chuar Butte on your Cape Solitude topo, descends into the East Fork, and follows the creek route as it contours the western ramparts of 6,300-foot Temple Butte to its confluence with the West Fork of Carbon Creek. This confluence is located due west of the 5,308-foot south summit of Temple Butte. Chuar Butte takes its name from Chuarrumpeak, a Kaibab Paiute chief who was one of Powell's principal ethnographic sources and translators. A skilled orator among the Paiute, Chuarrumpeak guided Powell to the Unikaret Plateau far to the west where the Major traveled overland to investigate the murders of three crew members who abandoned his maiden Colorado River expedition at Separation Rapids in 1869. (See page 313 Western Grand Canyon Trails.) Eighty-seven years later Chuar Butte was the tragic scene of a disastrous mid-air collision when a United Airlines DC-7 and a Trans World Airline Super Constellation collided on June 30, 1956, killing all 128 people. *Life* Magazine called it "Commercial Aviation's Worst Disaster" in the July 16, 1956, issue. Deadly gusts and sixty mile an hour winds reportedly prevented Army and Air Force helicopter pilots from landing. As a result, "American and Swiss mountain climbers were lowered on spots inaccessible to helicopters, seeking bodies and . . ." Many victims were buried in the Grand Canyon Pioneer Cemetery.

East Fork–West Fork Carbon Creek Confluence/Lava Canyon/ Colorado River

Mile 12.6. East Fork-West Fork Carbon Creek Confluence, Elevation 3,340 feet (1,018 meters), Carbon Canyon Member: Elevation Gain to Lava Canyon 0 vertical feet/Elevation Loss to Colorado River 600 vertical feet. From the East Fork-West Fork Carbon Creek Confluence on your Cape Solitude topo, you can trace Carbon Canyon south/southeast around the base of Temple Butte through the Tapeats Sandstone and Escalante Member to the Colorado River at Mile 14.5 (River Mile 64.4). I continued south where I eyeballed a route over the low unnamed saddle between BM 3471 and the northwest point of 3,945-foot Chuar Lava Hill, descended the Cardenas Basalt into Lava Canyon, turned left (southeast) and followed the beautiful creek bed through the "horse thief" portal in the Ochoa Formation between Chuar Lava Hill and 4,241-foot Lava Butte to the Colorado River. Before cowboy Jack Fuss could start riding north across the Butte Fault to join the 1924 "Great Kaibab Deer Drive," he and his outfit had to swim their herd of steeds across the Colorado River, leading them while paddling calfskin wooden kayaks to reach the mouth of Lava Canyon. In a 1975 Coconino County Public Library interview, Fuss recounted the epic crossing, in part: "And then, you see, the river was rough, 'cause there wasn't no dams in it, then . . . Oh, it was sure dangerous, and that river was really somethin' then. And we had to make that sandbar, else we'd have gone down the river. But we finally made it. And after we got that big mule across, well, then the other horses would see him . . . So we swam each horse, each one of them twenty-seven horses across, one at a time. And I had to row one [kayak], and then George [McCormick] would row one, because nobody else knew how to row. Well, we got there . . . It was moonlight." Imagine paddling twenty-seven backpacks one at a time across the wild Colorado River that Fuss said was 200 to 300 feet wide (two to three miles total) before your group starts its trek across the Butte Fault to reach the head of the Nankoweap Trail.

Colorado River/River Crossing

Mile 16.9. Colorado River, Lava Canyon Rapids, Mile 65.5, Elevation 2,740 feet (835 meters), Cardenas Basalt. At Lava Canyon Rapids, (not to be confused with Lava Falls at Mile 179.5 one hundred and fifteen miles downstream), you can follow the sandy river path 125 yards upstream from Lava Canyon to a narrow river crossing point and paddleraft 300 to 400 feet across the river to the opposite tamarisk tree-choked sandbar to reach the Bemer Trail at Palisades Creek. During an 8.5-day journey run below the North Rim following the North Trans Canyon Trails and Routes, I swam across the Colorado River—don't try it!—in a light CO_2-charged scuba diver vest, and followed the Beamer Trail west to reach my first resupply point at the foot of the Tanner Trail.

River Crossing: Depending on the weather and the river flow, this crossing is not as benign as the South Bass/North Bass river crossing appears to be. The river here is colder and wider. (See page 57, Hazards, River Crossings.)

Lava Canyon/Beamer Trail/Tanner Trail

From McCormick's Copper Blossom Mine site near Palisades Creek (River Mile 65.5) on the south side of the Colorado River, follow the Beamer Trail 3.5 miles west to the foot of the Tanner Trail at Mile 20.4. (See page 185 Beamer Trail.)

Additional Considerations

If you've reached the Colorado River, or any point in between the river and the Nankoweap Trailhead, you can retrace your route back up to the trailhead; or cross the river in the right conditions with the proper packraft and required PFD (Personal Flotation Device), hike 3.5 miles on the Beamer Trail, and nine miles up the Tanner Trail to the South Rim, or you can continue following the Trans Canyon Trails and Routes forty-five miles west to Bright Angel Campground and Phantom Ranch, where you can return to the North Rim via the 14.2-mile North Kaibab Trail or the South Rim via the 9.5-mile Bright Angel Trail.

Travel Notes

- Elevation: 3,280-feet Nankoweap Creek, 5,050-feet No Name Saddle, to 2,740-feet Colorado River.
- Biotic Communities: Piñon Juniper, Lower Sonoran Desert, and Desert Riparian.
- Total Elevation Loss: 5,509 vertical feet (with Nankoweap Trail 6,046 feet descent 11,555 vertical feet). Are your knees ready?!

- Total Elevation Gain: 5,509 vertical feet (with Nankoweap Trail 6,046 feet ascent 11,555 vertical feet).
- Mileage Point to Point: 16.9 miles (with Nankoweap Trail 30.9 miles).
- Mileage Roundtrip: 33.8 miles roundtrip (with Nankoweap Trail 61.8 miles).
- Water: Nankoweap Creek and Colorado River; Kwagunt Creek (seasonal).
- Seasons: Stay out during the summer. Fall through spring. Late winter and spring normally offer the best prospects for water.
- Maps: Nankoweap, Nankoweap Mesa, Cape Solitude, and Desert View Quadrangles (7.5 minute).
- Escape Routes: Nankoweap Trail to North Rim or Colorado River, Kwagunt Creek to Colorado River, East Fork of Carbon Creek and Lava Canyon to Colorado River.

Mile 0. Colorado River, Elevation 2,680 feet (817 meters), Dox Sandstone, Tanner Canyon/North Tonto Route East/Migration Route.

This untamed route traces what may be the mythic course of the Zuni migration route, *Chimik'yanakona penane*, their ancestors once followed from their sacred place of emergence, *Chimik'yana'kya*, "origin place," at Ribbon Falls on Bright Angel Creek and presumably traveled east across the North Tonto Route East, and along the river, to the confluence of the Colorado and Little Colorado Rivers, and beyond.

Colorado River/Tanner Canyon/Basalt Creek/Unkar Creek
Rapids, River Mile 68.5, Tanner Beach Camp Zone BB9. From the foot of the Tanner Trail, you can hike nine miles out to the South Rim, or continue following the Trans Canyon Trails and Routes and walk west across Tanner Creek Delta to a river crossing point above Basalt Creek Delta on the opposite (north) side of the Colorado River. From Basalt Creek at Mile 1 on your Desert View Quadrangle (7.5 minute), follow the right (north) riverbank downstream through heavy stands of Tamarisk trees along the Dox Sandstone approximately 3.25 miles to Unkar Creek. (See page 57 Hazards, River Crossings.)

North Tonto Route East/Unkar Creek/The Tabernacle
Mile 4.25. Colorado River, Elevation 2,623 feet (799 meters), Dox Sandstone, Unkar Rapids, River Mile 72.4. The fertile 125-acre delta was the seasonal home of Ancestral Puebloans who terraced-farmed the delta between 850 and 1200. Immediately west of Unkar Creek is a prominent ridgeline of Dox Sandstone. Climb two thousand vertical feet up this northwest-trending ridgeline to a break in the Tapeats Sandstone and follow a narrow strip of the Tonto Formation southwest beneath the rim from BM 5072 and 6,406-foot Rama Shrine to the unnamed 4,650-foot saddle on the northwest side of the

4,802-foot The Tabernacle. Distance 4.25 miles, Elevation Gain 2,027 feet, Water Colorado River; Seasonal Water Unkar Creek; Escape Routes via Tanner Trail or Colorado River, Map Cape Royal Quadrangle (7.5 minute), Camping at-large low impact. (See page 308, Unkar Creek, Colorado River Trails.)

North Tonto Route East/The Tabernacle/Clear Creek Trail

Mile 8.5. Tabernacle Saddle, Elevation 4,650 feet (1,417 meters), Bright Angel Shale/Tonto Formation. When Powell expedition photographer E. O. Beaman and his assistant reached the headwaters of the Deer Creek Falls in 1872, he wrote ". . . we found ourselves in the heart of the American Alps." One can only wonder how Beaman would have described the natural sky walk along the North Tonto beneath the snow-covered rim, wind-sculpted temples, and islands in the sky of 7,721-foot Wotans Throne, 7,533-foot Vishnu Temple, 6,761-foot Angels Gate, and 7,458-foot Point Sublime, among others. The breathtaking landmarks tower above as you journey west along this rugged skywalk through the inner canyon into the western horizon. Tabernacle Saddle is the starting point for the North Tonto Route, which is devoid of any trails until you reach the Clear Creek Trail. Once you leave Tabernacle Saddle, you'll need to decide whether your best course of travel is to follow the outer rim of the Tonto Formation along the Tapeats Sandstone or stay high and shadow the base of the Muav Limestone to try to shave some distance off the long and circuitous miles. From Tabernacle Saddle on your Cape Royal topo, follow the North Tonto around the south side of 4,990-foot Sheba Temple to the head of Asbestos Canyon. There's a break in the Tapeats Sandstone you'll have to scout in order to reach seasonal springs in the east and west fork of Asbestos Canyon. From the head of Asbestos Canyon follow the North Tonto around the southern points of BM 5659 until you reach the unnamed 4,450-foot saddle on the northeast side of 5,105-foot Newberry Butte.

There's a break through the Muav Limestone in Newberry Saddle, which will cut three to three-and-a-half miles off the West Tonto to reach the head of Vishnu Creek. If you trek this route during the spring, there's a fair chance of finding seasonal water in the head of Vishnu Creek, which also makes a spectacular camping spot. From the head of Vishnu Creek it's a long haul southwest before contouring in and around the tributary drainages of 5,525-foot Hall Butte, 5,200-foot Hawkins Butte, and 5,572-foot Howlands Butte to the Clear Creek descent on your Phantom Ranch Quadrangle (7.5 minute) map. There are no shortcuts in between. The standard descent into Clear Creek is down the drainage running west from the 5,370-foot Angels Gate/Wotans Throne Saddle. If you're a skilled climber and canyoneer, there's a steep and exposed shortcut straight down a terraced crevice through the Tapeats Sandstone into Clear Creek north of Howlands Butte. Eyeball the route to make sure you're in the right chimney before committing yourself.

From the bed of Clear Creek at the foot of the climbers' descent line, head downstream for about 200 yards before turning right (north) up the tributary fork of Clear Creek to reach the Clear Creek Trail, Elevation loss 1,410 feet; Water Clear Creek, Cheyava Falls, and Colorado River; Seasonal Water Unkar Creek and Vishnu Creek; Escape Routes Unkar Creek to Colorado River and Clear Creek Trail to Phantom Ranch; Maps Desert View, Cape Royal, and Phantom Ranch Quadrangles (7.5 minute); Camping dispersed in Clear Creek Zone AK9.

Warning: Be aware of flashflood dangers.

Clear Creek Trail
Clear Creek Trail/Phantom Ranch/Bright Angel Creek and Campground

Mile 36. (Bright Angel Campground nine miles), Clear Creek, Elevation 3,240 feet (988 meters), Tapeats Sandstone, perennial water, Clear Creek. The Clear Creek Trail is unquestionably the best section of trail this side of the Thunder River Trail on the entire Trans Canyon Trails and Routes. The Civilian Conservation Corp trail is straight forward and easy to follow from Clear Creek to Zoroaster Canyon and Sumner Wash all the way to the Phantom Ranch canteen. Distance nine miles, Elevation Gain 500 feet, Elevation Loss 1,260 feet; Water Clear Creek, Phantom Ranch; Seasonal Water Sumner Wash; Escape Route Phantom Ranch, Map Phantom Ranch Quadrangle (7.5 minute), Camping at-large low impact Sumner Wash Zone AK9 and designated Bright Angel Campground.

Lost Paradise

In December 1933, a Civilian Conservation Corp trail crew worker climbed into a cave and discovered ancient split twig figurines he put in his pocket so he could mail them home to his parents as mementos from his Grand Canyon adventure. Fortunately, the fragile effigies were recovered. Archaeologists who later excavated what they called Luka Cave reported that the figurines, similar to those excavated from *Tsé'áán Ketán,* "Prayer Stick Cave," across the canyon dated back to Archaic peoples 4,000 years ago.

Tread lightly. Clear Creek is a culturally sensitive area for Native Peoples. It abounds with dwellings that, unfortunately, have been dug up, picked over, rummaged through, and stolen by many visitors. This extraordinary settlement illuminates a lost paradise that thrived sight unseen until 1903.

Cheyava Falls

Mile 36. (BAC 12.9 miles), Cheyava Falls, Elevation 5,680 feet (1,731 meters), Redwall Limestone, perennial water. To reach spectacular Cheyava Falls from Clear Creek, hike,

A climber peers over the 7,646-foot-high summit of Shiva Temple soaring into the Trinity Canyon abyss. Isis Temple is in the background. Copyright © John Annerino Photography.

ford, scramble, and bushwhack past Obi Canyon 3.9 miles upstream to the foot of the tallest waterfall in the Grand Canyon. Cascading seven-hundred feet into Clear Creek, Cheyava Falls was the canyon's last cataract to be discovered and the most difficult to explore. First seen through binoculars from the South Rim in 1903 by tourist guide William Beeson who thought it was "a huge sheet of ice," Emery and Ellsworth Kolb surmised it was a seasonal waterfall. The Kolbs named it Cheyava Falls they mistakenly believed to be a Hopi word meaning "intermittent." It's actually a Southern Paiute name for the edible plant *Chee-ava,* which grows at *Chee-ava-pa*, Buckhorn Springs, in Zion National Park, Utah.

Many years passed before the Kolbs attempted to explore the misty white plume from the North Rim in 1930. It turned into a life and death epic. Using ropes, pulleys, and guile to descend sheer stair-step escarpments, the Kolbs got cliffed-out, lowered their heavy packs, lassoed a fir tree, traversed the rope hand over hand long before slacklining became popular, and slid a large fir tree three hundred feet down the talus to negotiate another death-defying span before using a 125-foot rope to reach the brink of Cheyava Falls. Caught by nightfall, the Kolbs bivouacked without food or water, cached their cameras at daybreak the following morning, and returned to the North Rim for rations and more rope. The next day, they lugged another 200 feet of rope to their bivouac site to use with the 400 feet threaded through their block and tackle suspended from a makeshift boom of timbers. Spent from their miserable bivouac the night before, and the grueling resupply trek, they were not ready for Cheyava Falls until 5 p.m. the following day. They went out of food and water again, and darkness crept in with head winds of an approaching storm. They pushed on. Wedging a log across a crevice, Emery lowered Ellsworth down an overhanging cliff of Redwall Limestone they called the "blue lime" when they were suddenly hammered by an electrical storm. "The lightning struck many times close by," Emery said, his hair standing on end. "So strong was the wind I had fear of being blown from the cliff. I withdrew from the edge, tying the rope to a small pinyon, leaving my brother dangling in the air."

Lashed by violent wind, hail, and rain, Ellsworth spun around helplessly in the overhang until the storm finally abated. When it did, Emery lowered Ellsworth a long pole so he could touch the wall and unwind himself in the dark. Incredibly, Emery hauled his 165-pound brother up hand-over-hand inch-by-inch 200 dead drop feet. Emery was so exhausted from his heroic efforts to save his brother, he couldn't even ride in the car when they finally reached it the North Rim the next day. He hired an airplane for sixty dollars to fly him back to the South Rim. After another valiant attempt to explore Cheyava Cave several years later, Emery offered their gear to anyone who wanted to explore the 600-foot-long stream cave behind the falls and wrote: ". . . there is still opportunity for the adventurous person to further explore the cave. Our boom yet hangs over the cliff, patiently waiting for the next explorer."

Clear Creek Trail/Sumner Wash/Bright Angel Creek

Mile 43. (BAC 2 Miles), Sumner Wash, Elevation 3,740 feet (1,140 meters), Tonto Formation, seasonal water. Named after one of Major Powell's 1869 boatman, John "Captain Jack" Sumner, Sumner Wash offers 4th Class passage through the Redwall Limestone for climbers planning to scale 7,551-foot Brahma Temple or nearby 7,123-foot Zoroaster Temple. Before Donald G. Davis and Clarence "Doc" Ellis made the first ascent of Brahma Temple, Davis described it as "one of the largest and most imposing Canyon summits yet remaining untested as to its accessibility without hardware." During their lightening first ascent of Brahma Temple on May 15, 1968, Davis and Ellis climbed 5,071 vertical feet up from Phantom Ranch, reached the un-trod temple summit, and returned to Phantom Ranch in fourteen hours. It was an incredible first that entailed twelve miles of rugged trekking and 10,042 vertical feet of elevation gain and loss that eclipsed others who were considered expert canyoneers. Arizona Republic photographer Christine Keith made the first known women's ascent of Brahma Temple on May 6, 1978.

Bright Angel Campground

Mile 45. Bright Angel Campground, Elevation 2480 feet (756 meters), Vishnu Schist. From Bright Angel Campground, you can hike 14.2 miles up the North Kaibab Trail to the North Rim, hike 9.5 miles up the Bright Angel Trail to the South Rim, or continue following the Trans Canyon Trails and Routes. (See page 227 North Kaibab Trail, or page 101 Bright Angel Trail.)

North Tonto Route West

Utah Flats/North Tonto Route West/Crystal Rapids

Mile 0. From Bright Angel Campground, (directly above Campsite 1), climb 2,004 vertical feet up the well-worn track that follows the hanging boulder-strewn drainage called "Piano Alley" through the Vishnu Schist to a notch in the sheltered overhangs of the Bass Formation. This is the passageway to the Hakatai Formation. The tendency is to climb high at this point, but this is not the route to Phantom Canyon or the Cheops/Isis Saddle. Stay in the Hakatai Formation as you contour southwest around the base of 5,401-foot Cheops Pyramid and Point 5206 on your Phantom Ranch Quadrangle (7.5 minute) map until you reach the northwest arm of Ninety-one Mile Creek beneath point 3860 on your Shiva Temple Quadrangle (7.5 minute) map. Climb up this arm to the North Tonto Formation. From Ninetyone Mile Creek, stay on the Tonto Route West as it contours around the south and southwest points of 7,006-foot Isis Temple to the northeast arm of Trinity Creek. This arm will take you into Trinity Creek, where seasonal water can sometimes be found. (The source I drank from was a foul-tasting "elixir," so look for the best source). Continue on the Tonto Route West and head toward BM 3970 on your Shiva Temple topo and contour around the south side of this point. Just about the time you think you're headed into no man's land—and you are, apart from the drone of scenic air tours—drop your pack and detour south to the edge of the Tonto Formation overlooking the Upper Granite Gorge.

Grand Canyon Cableway Survey

In 1919, the National Park Service temporarily approved an aerial tramway from the South Rim's 7,065-foot Hopi Point down to 5,031-foot Dana Butte where it would cross a half-mile above the Colorado River to the north Tonto Formation and link 6,012-foot Tower of Set, 6,613-foot Osiris Temple, and 7,646-foot Shiva Temple with the North Rim's 7,766-foot Tiyo Point. The brainchild of San Francisco engineer George K. Davol who'd installed wire rope mining cableways in California, the high wire aerial tram was envisioned to lure more tourists to the Grand Canyon much the way the controversial Grand Canyon Escalade proposes to do at the confluence of the Colorado and Little Colorado Rivers. The Santa Fe Railroad green lighted Davol's survey proposal, and between August and November 1919 Davol's six man survey crew traversed the route by foot, raft, and rope from the South Rim to the spectacular point on which you're standing. According to the National Archives, the cableway was shelved by millionaire-turned-National Park Service Director Stephen Tyng Mather when Grand Canyon National Park was established in 1920 because it was ". . . too costly, and damaging to the canyon's ecology."

Reverse your detour back to the Tonto Route West. From BM 3970, continue traipsing in and around the tentacles of 6,012-foot Tower of Set to the head of Ninety-four Mile Creek on your Grand Canyon Quadrangle (7.5 minute) map until you reach the westernmost arm coming down off 6,129-foot Tower of Ra at Point 6002 on your Shiva Temple topo. This arm points in the general direction of the descent to Crystal Creek along the ridge west of the drainage beneath BM 3639. Eyeball the route through the Tapeats Sandstone and Vishnu Schist down to Crystal Creek before committing yourself. This descent is longer, looser, and more difficult than the climber's descent into Clear Creek. Distance 26.25 miles, Elevation Gain 2,004 feet, Elevation Loss 1,110 feet, Water Phantom Ranch and Colorado River, Seasonal Water Trinity Creek, Escape Route Phantom Ranch, Maps Phantom Ranch, Grand Canyon, and Shiva Temple Quadrangles (7.5 minute), Camping at-large low impact on Utah Flats and Tonto Route West.

Colorado River/Crystal Creek/Tuna Creek

Mile 26.25. Colorado River, Elevation 2,330 feet (710 meters), Vishnu Schist, Crystal Rapids, River Mile 98. This two-mile riverside stretch through the Vishnu Schist and quartz along the right (north) side of the Colorado River to regain the Tonto Route West above Tuna Creek is as short, difficult, and time-consuming as any two miles on the Trans Canyon Trails and Routes. From Crystal Creek to the mouth of Tuna Creek, you need to pick, choose, boulder hop, and clamber your way along the path of least resistance. Difficult to imagine historic fourteen-inch rains hammered the North Rim in December 1966 created catastrophic flash floods that roared down Crystal Creek at 29,000 CFS (cubic feet per second) that swept mud, debris, boulders, and timbers into the Colorado River creating Crystal Rapids, one of the most feared rapids in North America. The avalanche of stony debris stands between you and Tuna Creek. Distance two miles to Tonto Route West, Elevation Gain 1,170 feet, Water Crystal Creek and Colorado River, Escape Route river runner's overlook Crystal Rapids (summer), Map Havasupai Point Quadrangle (7.5 minute), Camping at-large low impact Crystal Creek delta and Tuna Creek.

Midnight Freefall into the Abyss

During a training flight from Tonopah, Nevada, to Tucson, Arizona, on June 21, 1944, three airmen were ordered to bail out of a B-24 when all four engines died. Jumping through the bomb bay at 24,000 feet, the trio hurtled through black skies at two in the morning into one of the worst drop zones on Earth and deployed their T-4 parachutes just as the B-24's engines restarted. Their olive drab, 22-foot-diameter canopies flowered open and violently jerked their backs and wrenched their canvas harnesses. They were Lieutenant Charles Goldblum, Flight Officer Maurice J. Cruickshank, and Corporal Roy W. Embanks. Cruickshank slammed down on the North Tonto above Tuna Creek and broke his right foot. Embanks managed to survive a landing four hundred feet below the Tonto Formation, but it was too dark to see where he crash landed. Goldblum snagged his chute on the edge of a Tapeats Sandstone cliff a thousand feet above the Colorado River. Hanging in his harness, Goldblum climbed hand over hand up the slippery shroud lines and groped for his companions on the pitch black Tonto Formation. When the HALO jumpers (High Altitude Low Opening, the first American airmen to do so), found one another the next morning they limped and stumbled down to the Colorado River to quench their ravage thirst, then climbed back up Tuna Creek where they hunkered down in a cave. They weren't sure when or if the cavalry was coming. Ed Laws delivered mail on horseback from Kanab, Utah, to Lee's Ferry, Arizona, not far from the 1776 Domínguez and Escalante route. Dr. A. A. MacRae, on the other hand, was a Princeton graduate and a professor of Old Testament history. In Laws and MacRae you couldn't find two more unlikely partners to form a search and rescue team. In a remarkable feat of canyoneering, Laws and MacRae descended 4,463 vertical feet, and pieced together on-site a rugged ten-mile cross-country route that lead from 7,763-foot Point Sublime to the stranded airmen in 19.5 hours. When Laws and MacRae finally reached the bearded, sunburned aviators who'd been marooned for nine days, they were living high on K-rations dropped by parachutes they'd said tasted like turkey. Still feeling western, Laws quipped, "You boys sure are suffering in comfort." When the trio finally emerged from the Grand Canyon, NBC and the local press were waiting to hear their tale. Cruickshank gave them what they wanted: "I wanted to go back to that [wildcat] den on our fourth day. We were so hungry, and I hoped that cat had come back so we could eat it. I would have tackled it with my bare hands for food."

Tonto Route West/Tuna Creek/North Bass Trail

Mile 27.75. Colorado River, Elevation 2,310 feet (704 meters), Vishnu Schist, Tuna Creek Rapids, River Mile 99. From the mouth of Tuna Creek, climb up what appears to be granodiorite 1,170 vertical feet through the Vishnu Schist and Tapeats Sandstone to regain the Tonto Route West on your Havasupai Point Quadrangle (7.5 minute) map. Once you've regained the route, contour west of BM 3919 in and around the twin pincers of 5,832-foot Scorpion Ridge, around the head of Emerald Canyon all the way to the head of Monadnock Amphitheater. Turn (left) southwest and follow the Tonto Trail Route West toward the southern point of BM 4621, contour northwest until you reach BM 3962 on the western arm of 6,379-foot Evans Butte toward the head of Hotauta Canyon, (named for the eldest son of Captain Navajo, *Gtata*, "Porcupine," 1889). There are several faults leading from Hotauta Amphitheater down to the Colorado River at Bass Rapids. Study your line of descent to the river before committing yourself. North of Point 3962 I glissaded, jumped, and ran down the loose scree, ledges, terraces, and breaks through the Hakatai Shale, sills, and dikes to the foot of the North Bass Trail along river's edge. Distance 18.48 miles, Elevation Gain 1,430, Elevation Loss 1,542; Water Colorado River; Seasonal Water Drainage 3239 north of the west pincer of Scorpion Ridge, Emerald Canyon maybe, both arms of Monadnock Amphitheater belw Tapeats Sandstone; Escape Routes South Bass Trail, North Bass Trail, Colorado River (summer); Maps Havasupai Point and Shiva Temple Quadrangles (7.5 minute), Camping at-large low impact North Tonto and Bass Beach BQ9.

North Bass Trail
Colorado River/North Bass Trail/Muav Saddle

Mile 46.25. Colorado River, Elevation 2,198 feet (670 meters), Vishnu Schist, Bass Rapids, River Mile 107.5. From the Colorado River hike 12.5 miles up the North Bass Trail to Muav Saddle at route Mile 58.75. (See page 251 North Bass Trail.)

Muav Saddle/Saddle Canyon/Tapeats Creek/Thunder River

Mile 0. Muav Saddle, Elevation 6,711 feet (2,046 meters), Coconino Sandstone, water Muav Saddle Spring (seasonal). There is no trail down Saddle Canyon, but I found the riparian course the prettiest stretch on the entire Trans Canyon Trails and Routes. There aren't any real route finding difficulties—follow the drainage—but several of the upper formations of the Esplanade and Supai may require doubling back and scouting to find the easiest and safest line of descent if you get cliffed-out. From Muav Saddle head northwest off the saddle below the 1925 "Muav Saddle Snowshoe Cabin," (Teddy's Cabin), down Saddle Canyon through Gambel oak and dense Manzanita, Ponderosa pine trees, snags, and blow-down-covered Esplanade Sandstone and Hermit Shale 1.15 miles to Grassy Canyon on your King Arthur Castle Quadrangle (7.5 minute) map. The *cañoncito*, "little canyon," enters from right (east). Powell Spring is located 300 yards upstream. From the mouth of Grassy Canyon continue bushwhacking, boulder hopping, and slaloming down through the trees and ledges three miles through the Supai Formation to Stina Canyon. I contoured around the pour offs I encountered en route on the right (east). Others reported contouring left (west). Above the confluence of Stina Canyon there's a Redwall Limestone pour off I avoided on the right (east), a narrow water-polished Redwall Limestone chute and plunge pools I slid down and waded through, and an eight-foot jump-down plunge pool I made after I tossed my gear down ahead of me. Stina Canyon is in the Supai/Wescogome Formations and enters from the right (east). From Stina Canyon continue down canyon 0.75 miles through the Muav Limestone to the confluence of Crazy Jug Canyon (Timp Canyon tributary), which enters from the north on your Tapeats Amphitheater Quadrangle (7.5 minute) map. From here down to Thunder River heavy runoff and flash floods pose life-threatening hazards to avoid at all costs. But the narrows need to be crossed—there's no practical way I found to skirt the narrows on the right (north) side all the way to Thunder River. Turn left (west/northwest) at the Crazy Jug confluence where Tapeats Creek begins and head downstream through the Muav Limestone, Bright Angel Shale, and Tapeats Sandstone 2.9 miles to the confluence of Tapeats Spring Creek, which enters from the right (north). From the Tapeats Creek confluence continue 1.75 miles downstream to Thunder River. You'll need to ford Tapeats Creek above this confluence. I found a stout-looking century plant stalk and tried pole-vaulting the deep rapid white water creek. Don't do this! The stalk snapped—it worked for me the day before while crossing flood swollen Shimumo Creek—and I got swept helplessly downstream until I managed to hook my arm around the root of a cottonwood tree. Distance 9.55 Miles, Elevation Loss 4,266 feet; Water Muav Saddle Spring, Saddle Canyon, Tapeats Creek, and Thunder River; Escape Routes Swamp Point, Colorado River, and Thunder River Trailheads; Maps King Arthur Castle and Tapeats Amphitheater Quadrangle, (7.5 minute), and North Kaibab National Forest

Road Map; Camping at-large low impact Muav Saddle, Saddle Canyon, and designated Upper Tapeats Camp Zone AW7.

Note: I wore a light CO_2-charged scuba diver vest for safety while tracing Shinumo Creek, Saddle Canyon, and Tapeats Creek during mid-May spring runoff. From my canyon journey running experience, no other time of the year offered me the environmental margin of safety for sleeping bagless bivouacs and drinking water sources to run trans canyon from the Nankoweap Trailhead.

Thunder River Trail
Thunder River Trail/Indian Hollow/End
Mile 9.55. Thunder River/Tapeats Creek Confluence, Elevation 2,445 feet (745 meters), Muav Limestone-Tapeats Sandstone. From the confluence hike 11.35 miles up the Thunder River Trail to the Indian Hollow Trailhead. (See page 265 Thunder River Trail.)

- Managing Agency: Grand Canyon National Park.
- Backcountry Information Center: for information call (928) 638–7875.
- Critical Backcountry Updates visit www.nps.gov/grca/planyourvisit/trail-closures.htm
- NPS Grand Canyon Hiker 24 Hour Emergency Phone Number and Email
  - Phone (928) 638–7805
  - Email: grca_bic@nps.gov (Use this if the phone line is busy)

A boatwoman hiker wades North Canyon's deep plunge pool.

25

Colorado River Trails: Riverside Hikes, Trails, and Routes

"I searched about for a few minutes for a more easy way; what was my surprise at finding a stairway, evidently cut in stone by human hands! . . . I stood where a lost people had lived centuries ago, and looked over the same strange land. I gazed off to great mountains to the north-west, slowly covered by night until they were lost, and then turned toward camp. It was no easy task to find my way down the wall in the darkness, and I clambered about until nearly midnight, before I arrived there."

—Major John Wesley Powell, 1869
The Cañons of the Colorado

INTRODUCTION

Many rewarding hikes lead from the banks of the Colorado River into the corridors of stone, water, and light that drain into the timeless river. Short riverside strolls, day hikes, ambitious treks, and canyoneering adventures offer exciting passageways to see and explore the Colorado River and its tributary creeks, canyons, and gorges.

River Miles

The U.S. Geological Survey implemented a system whereby all Colorado River miles are counted downstream. In this chapter they begin with River Mile 0 at Lee's Ferry, the "put-in" for all Grand Canyon River trips, and end at River Mile 225.9 at Diamond

Creek, the "take out" for most river trips. Included with each river hiking milepost entry is the name of the destination, followed by RR or RL, (facing downstream RR is river right, and RL is river left), elevation, geology at river level, and the elevation drop of each corresponding river rapid.

Escape Routes

Before satellite communications, tracking, and messaging, "escape routes" were an essential consideration for river runners and hikers. In the event of an emergency, knowledgeable river runners and hikers would know which tributary canyons offered the best options for self-rescues and river-to-rim escape routes. Listed at the end of each river hike entry are escape routes, when known, in the event you have an emergency and a satellite or ground-to-air communications failure.

Maps

At the end of each river hike milepost the names of the U.S Geological Survey Quadrangles (7.5 minute) maps are included. Each of these topographical maps features the river hike entry and the Colorado River corridor downstream to the next named map.

LANDFORM

From 10,175-foot La Poudre Pass in Colorado's Never Summer Mountains, the Colorado River, together with the Green River, drains 254,000 square miles of the Colorado Plateau and descends over ten thousand vertical feet to the Colorado River Delta at the head of Mexico's Sea of Cortés 1,450 miles downstream. The most celebrated, culturally rich, and adventure-filled stretch of the Colorado River is the 225 miles of white water and pool-drop rapids that tumble through the Grand Canyon between Lees Ferry at River Mile 0 and Diamond Creek at River Mile 225.9.

HISTORICAL OVERVIEW

Hikers, river runners, and readers have long associated riverside walking, hiking, and exploration with the historic Colorado River journeys that began with Major John Wesley Powell's 1869 Geographical Expedition through the "great unknown." You needn't hike far from your raft to see masonry cliff dwellings, storage granaries, pot shards, lithic scatters, agave roasting pits, pictographs and petroglyphs, and mining camps. These cultural artifacts, sometimes sacred objects, and historical relics offer mute testimony that beginning 4,000 years ago, perhaps earlier, Archaic peoples, and later ancestral Puebloans, *Hisat.sinom,* Anaasázi, Cohonina, Mukwic, Hopi, Navajo, Southern Paiute, and Pai, as well as explorers, prospectors, miners and a rogue's gallery of early river runners who probed, hiked, explored, and climbed nearly every nook, cranny, cliff, canyon and mesa throughout the Grand Canyon. It would be something if you weren't following an early traveler's ghost trail of yucca fiber sandals, deerskin moccasins, or leather boots. Savor the incredible access and opportunity the Colorado River offers versus arduous rim-to-river hiking and exploration.

Río Colorado

The name *Río Colorado,* "Red River," was used by many explorers and prospectors to describe their journeys down, and their trails that lead to, the Colorado River. *Colorado Chiquito* was also used to describe the Little Colorado River. Both names and variations are derived from Spanish Jesuit missionary explorer and cartographer Padre Eusebio Francisco Kino's 1701–02 map engraving, *Paso por Tierra a la California,* "Passage by Land to California," where Padre Kino's river name, *Río Colorado del Norte,* "Red River of the North," first appeared.

Mile 0 Marble Canyon to Mile 60

Mile 0. Lees Ferry RR, Elevation 3,116 feet (950 meters), Moenkopi Formation. (The Kaibab Limestone appears downstream at River Mile 1.) Before the area was settled, Lee's Ferry was traditionally used by the Hopi for many generations to collect cottonwood at *Neneqpi Wunasivu* to carve sacred ceremonial prayer sticks called *paahos.* Lee's Ferry was named for pioneer Mormon cattleman and settler John D. Lee who established the first reliable ford across the Colorado River in 1871. It was the only ford for hundreds of miles in either direction between Hites Crossing (Dandy Crossing), Utah (1880), and Pierce Ferry, Arizona (1876), near the head of steamboat navigation. Navajo cowboys who also used Lee's Ferry called it *Tó Ha'naant'eetiin,* "Where They Crossed Against the Current," and the Kaibab Paiute called it *Paru,* "intersection of rivers." Lees Ferry is located on the Colorado River near the mouth of Paria Canyon. Paria Canyon is the first of four major tributary canyons that drain into the Colorado River in Arizona, including Little Colorado River Gorge, Kanab Creek Canyon, and Cataract-Havasu Canyons.

THE HIKES

Paria Canyon

If you have time, explore the vicinity above the mouth of Paria Canyon before putting on the river. From the wooden footbridge crossing the Paria River near the trailhead, you can take pleasant strolls around the Lee's Ferry homestead Lee's wife, Emma, called "Lonely Dell," the historic pioneer cemetery, and the southern end of the Paria Canyon-Vermilion Cliffs National Monument. The mile-long trail hugs the left (west) side of the Paria River, the traditional travel corridor and hunting grounds the Kaibab Paiute called *Pareya-pa*, "elk water," where you can hike or run up and down Paria Canyon as far as you like.

End-to-End

The forty-two mile trek through the narrows, plunge pools, and "quicksand" through the mesmerizing incised meanders of Buckskin Gulch and the slick rock corridor of Paria Canyon to Lees Ferry takes three to four days. It's one of my favorites.

Map: Lees Ferry Quadrangle (7.5 minute)

Mile 3. Cathedral Wash RR (Three Mile Wash), Elevation 3,110 feet+/- (948 meters), Toroweap Formation. It's an enjoyable and straightforward 1.25-mile hike and 324 vertical foot climb up this dry wash to the Lee's Ferry Road. No water. The route is sometimes used by trout fishermen who hike downstream to fish the Colorado River. *Escape Route*: Lees Ferry Road to Highway 89A.

Mile 4.3. Navajo Bridge, Elevation 3,100 feet +/- (945 meters), Coconino Sandstone. (The Hermit Shale appears downstream at Mile 5.2). Navajo high scalers and iron workers who built the 467-feet tall and 834-feet span bridge in 1929 called it *Na'ní'á Hatsoh,* "Big Bridge." When Western novelist Zane Grey described the horse ford at the head of Marble Canyon in his novel, *The Last of the Plainsmen* (1907), he wrote: "I saw the constricted rapids, where the Colorado took its plunge into the box-like head of the Grand Canyon of Arizona; and the deep, reverberating boom of the river, at flood height, was a fearful thing to hear."

Mile 7.5. Badger Canyon RR, Elevation 3,060 feet +/- (933 meters), Hermit Shale, Badger Creek Rapid (fifteen-foot drop). You can take a mile hike up the boulder-strewn narrows of Badger Canyon until it dead-ends in an overhanging cul de sac of Kaibab Limestone. No water. Or you can canyoneer five miles top-to-bottom with good sense, two ropes, and climber's webbing.

Jackass Creek RL. The rugged 2.6-mile hike and 847-vertical-foot climb through the Coconino Sandstone offers an exciting short technical section that requires use of a fixed forty-foot hand line to climb up a ledgy pour off. No water. The Navajo sometimes hike the canyon to fish the Colorado River.

Stay Safe: Bring your own short climbing rope or dependable nylon bowline.

Escape Route: US Highway 89A.

Mile 11.2. Soap Creek RR, Elevation 3,048 feet (929 meters), Hermit Shale, Soap Creek Rapids (seventeen foot drop). Returning from a "communitarian expedition" to the Hopi Mesas during the winter of 1858, Mormon missionary explorer Jacob Vernon Hamblin and his party faced thirst and starvation. In his 2015 report, *Slickrock Missions,* historian Todd Compton wrote: "Jacob Hamblin shot a badger, and when they camped at the next creek, Soap Creek, he cooked it. His bad cooking skills are memorialized for all time by this last name, for the badger, when cooked, turned into soap." During explorer Clyde L. Eddy's second Colorado River expedition in 1927, one of his crew members found a trove of letters sent from Teardale, Utah, dated January 12, 1894. Addressed to her two sons, W. E. and E. R. Mendenhall, the distraught unnamed mother reportedly wrote, ". . . how is it possible for you to get supplies enough to keep from famishing from hunger?" No one knows what happened to mama's boys. There is no record of a successful 1894 Grand Canyon Colorado River expedition. They either drowned or sealed their fate canyoneering up Soap Creek Canyon.

The Hike: The four-mile trek and 1,030-vertical foot climb out to US Highway 89A is a rugged and exposed canyoneering adventure along ledges and pour offs. Seasoned backcountry trout fisherman sometimes negotiate Soap Creek Canyon to fish the trout rich river confluence, which regularly yields some anglers their six-fish-a-day limit. No water.

Map: Bitter Springs Quadrangle (7.5 minute)

Mile 12. Salt Water Wash RL, Elevation 3,031 feet +/- (924 meters), Esplanade Sandstone, Brown's Riffle. A rock inscription here reads: "F. M. Brown Pres. D.CC. & P.RR Co was drowned July 10, 1889, opposite this point." Frank M. Brown was president of the Denver, Colorado, and Pacific Railway, and he accompanied Chief Engineer Robert Brewster Stanton during his first expedition to survey a proposed railroad line through the Grand Canyon. Strange but true, Peter Hansbrough who inscribed Brown's memorial, and the ill fated expedition cook Harry Richards, drowned three days later in Twenty-five Mile Rapids. Expedition members were not wearing cork life preservers because Brown was watching the railroad's pennies and rejected the idea.

The Hike: It's a four-mile trek and 1,472-vertical foot climb up Salt Water Wash to Highway 89A. Cairns mark the way up the steep, boulder-clogged lower half of this route until the wash opens up and walking becomes enjoyable. No water.

Escape Route: This is the last not-very-practical route to reach Highway 89A.

Mile 17. Rider Canyon/House Rock Wash RR, Elevation 2,995 feet (913 meters), Supai Sandstone, House Rock Rapid (ten-foot drop). During Stantons's second Denver, Colorado, and Pacific Railway Survey Expedition in 1890, photographer Franklin A. Nims was seriously injured in a twenty foot fall while trying to take a picture of the crew. How the unconscious, broken-boned expedition Nims was lifted and carried up this treacherous canyon before Stanton resumed his journey is a mystery.

The Hike: If you lunch or camp at House Rock Rapid, you can take a charming half-mile hike through the Supai narrows to a chockstone (a boulder wedged in a chimney or narrow canyon) that can be climbed on the left. From the river, you can also tackle the beautiful 3.4-mile long trek and 1,651-foot climb and canyoneering adventure through narrows, pour offs, plunge pools, and squeeze tunnels to reach the canyon rim.

Escape Route: This is not a practical escape route. Once out of Rider Canyon you need satellite communication to call for a rescue helicopter or a high clearance vehicle to meet you at the old trailhead sign. Or walk the maze of dirt roads criss-crossing House Rock Valley to reach Highway 89A.

Mile 20.5. North Canyon RR, Elevation 2,980 feet +/- (908 meters), Supai Sandstone, North Canyon Rapid (twelve-foot drop). This is a regular mile-long jaunt up the bed of North Canyon for river runners captivated by a path that leads through terra cotta narrows and scalloped slabs of Supai Sandstone to a reflective plunge pool beneath water polished stone at trail's end. No potable water.

Map: Emmett Wash Quadrangle (7.5 minute)

Mile 22.2. Twenty-two Mile Wash RL, Elevation 2,963 feet +/- (903 meters), Supai Sandstone. Widely spaced cairns mark the steep, sometimes exposed route through the Supai Sandstone to a good viewpoint of the Colorado River approximately one mile from camp. No water.

Escape Route: A route has been linked from the Supai through the Coconino Sandstone to reach the rim and Highway 89A. However, the exposed, waterless route should be avoided by inexperienced canyoneers.

Mile 29. Shinumo Wash RL, Silver Grotto, Elevation 2,920 feet +/- (890 meters), Redwall Limestone, Twenty-nine Mile Rapid (7 foot drop). Shinumo Wash, or *Tó hajisho'*, "Dragging Up Water" trail, was first used by Navajo to haul Colorado River water up to the rim in goat skin bags. It's a sacred cultural landscape of the Diné. Ancestral Hopi reportedly stopped nearby at 6,523-foot Shinamu Altar, *Pongyatuyqa*, on their ancient clan migrations and it remains a sacred cultural landscape of the Hopi.

The Hike: A riverside hike up this water-polished chute leads to the incredible setting of Silver Grotto. Several boulder moves on slick limestone may require spotting one another before wading or swimming through the cool plunge pools to Silver Grotto.

Map: North Canyon Point Quadrangle (7.5 minute)

Mile 31.5. South Canyon RR, Elevation 2,877 feet (877 meters), Redwall Limestone, Poison ivy. After their disastrous 1889 expedition, Stanton and his surviving crew members cached their gear and oars in what became known as Stanton Cave a quarter-mile downstream, and climbed out of South Canyon. It's not an easy canyoneering trek under the best conditions. Years later, during the Frazier-Hatch brothers' 1934 "Dusty Dozen" river expedition, pioneer boatman Alton Hatch was poking around a two-tiered Redwall Limestone cave and discovered remains he hadn't expected. On July 22, he wrote he found ". . . the skeleton of a man. He had dark hair, wore buckskin clothes. Had both legs broken . . ." Judging from the buckskin clothing, he may have been Kaibab Paiute who were well known for their prowess hunting mule deer on nearby

Buckskin Mountain (Kaibab Plateau), and for tanning and trading the soft buckskins to the Navajo, Hopi, and Havasupai. Or he may well have been a Navajo medicine man, *ha'athali,* "singer," who forded the Colorado River at Lees Ferry, *Tó Ha'naant'eetiin,* or crossed Marble Canyon from the 5,810-foot east rim of Tatahatso Point and used the declivitous Navajo route, *Adahíiná,* "Trail Where People Moved Down," to ford the river and climb up to the sacred cave. Seen near his buckskin-covered body was a rifle scabbard and split twig figurines that archaeologists, who've unearthed them elsewhere in Grand Canyon cave shrines, believe were offered as effigies for a successful hunt, in this case deer and bighorn sheep. Conceivably he was a medicine man who fell while making a dangerous ritual rim-to-river-to-rim pilgrimage to make a sacred offering in a "Prayer Stick"-type cave shrine near the rainbow-hued Redwall Limestone falls of Vaseys Paradise. (Twenty-six years later a Navajo medicine man died during a pilgrimage to *Tooh Ahidiilíní,* the sacred Confluence of the Colorado and Little Colorado Rivers. (See page 166 Medicine Man Trail.) Unfortunately, commercial river runners used to guide passengers to view South Canyon's "Mystery Skeleton." By the 1980s, the elder's desecrated remains had been picked apart and scavenged by ravens and visitors.

    The Hikes: From camp you can take a short walk through South Canyon's Redwall narrows. You can embark on a serious 6.5-mile trek and 2,539-vertical foot climb up South Canyon that leads beyond Bedrock Canyon through the boulder-strewn streambed, loose scree, narrows, chutes, and "if-you-fall-you-die" dropoffs to the rim of Marble Canyon's longest tributary canyon. Or you can follow the short, well-beaten river routes downstream to Stanton Cave; or hike below Stanton Cave to marvel at the riverside garden and twin gushets of 120-foot tall Vaseys Paradise (Poison ivy).

    Tread Gently: Vaseys Paradise, *Yam'taqa,* is a sacred cultural landscape of the Hopi who once journeyed here for its hallowed waters.

Stanton Cave

During the Hatch brothers' same low water "Dusty Dozen" river journey Alton's younger brother, Bus, discovered a trove of split twig figurines in Stanton Cave's large solution chamber. Archaeologists later excavated the cave floor and split twig figurine caches and removed 165 "magico-religious ritual" effigies similar to those unearthed at *Tsé'áán Ketán,* "Prayer Stick Cave," dating back to Archaic peoples 4,000 years ago. (See page 111 South Kaibab Trail.) At Prayer Stick Cave a hank of dark human hair was also seen dangling and excavated from the cave ceiling with what appeared to be two prayer sticks, *k'eet'áán* (Navajo) or *paahos* (Hopi). The fact that the cordage-wrapped hair from Prayer Stick Cave, and the "Mystery Skeleton" from the South Canyon cave, were found in association with the ritual effigies is an enlightening connection that suggests to me Native Peoples have continued to pay sacred homage throughout the epochs in once-secret cave shrines in historic times and perhaps up to the present day in what they've nearly always professed to non-Indians is hallowed ground. Furthermore, 1954-era archaeologists (*Bilagáana,* "White Man") admittedly created and used Navajo (*Diné*) names to obfuscate their work and the locations of two cave shrines they were excavating, *Tsé'áán bidá,* "Rock Cave," and *Tsé'áán Ketán,* "Prayer Stick Cave." Stanton Cave was sealed with a porous 2,000-pound steel grated door in 1997 to prevent looting yet allow colonies of Townsend's big-eared bats *(Corynorhinus townsendii)* access to fly in and out from their ceiling roosts.

Mile 33. Redwall Cavern RL Elevation 2,876 feet (877 meters), Redwall Limestone. This is a great place to stretch your legs and marvel at the corrasion, or lateral cutting power, of the Colorado River over eons. In his river journal entry for August 8, 1869, Major Powell wrote that the ". . . vast half-circular chamber, which, if utilized for a theater, would give sitting to 50,000 people." Twenty thousand people is estimated to be closer to the mark. On occasion orchestras journey down the Colorado River to take advantage of the Redwall chamber's natural acoustics.

Mile 34.8. Nautiloid Canyon RL, Elevation 2,870 feet (873 meters), Redwall Limestone. The indelible imprints of 400-million-year-old fossilized nautiloids (*Rayonnoceras spp.*) are found in this remarkable canyon. Some are two feet long. The short side trip up Nautiloid Canyon involves several boulder moves on polished limestone to reach its

Exploring Marble Canyon Dam Site, site of the the Sierra Club's/*New York Times*'s "battle ads" to "Save Grand Canyon From Being Flooded." Copyright © John Annerino Photography.

terminus at the base of an overhanging section of Redwall Limestone. Depending on the river level, a raft may be required to ferry hikers to the start of this enchanting route.

Map: Tatahatso Point Quadrangle (7.5 minute)

Mile 39.5. Marble Canyon Dam Site RL, Elevation 2,860 feet +/- (872 meters), Redwall Limestone. Marble Canyon (Redwall Canyon) Dam site and drift tunnel. Between 1949 and 1951 the U.S. Bureau of Reclamation constructed a 3,400-foot long aerial tram from the 5,702-foot rim of Tatahatso Point nicknamed "Henry Lane's Elevator" to ferry men and equipment down to the Colorado River to drill, blast, test, and explore the feasibility of building what was also called the Redwall Canyon Dam. As the conservation movement grew across the nation, so did opposition to the proposed dam. Spearheaded by environmentalist David R. Brower, the Sierra Club took out full-page "battle ads" in the *New York Times* on June 9, 1966, to ". . . Save Grand Canyon From Being Flooded . . . For Profit." Congress listened, so did President Lyndon B. Johnson who established Marble Canyon National Monument in 1969. National Monument status stopped future construction of Bureau of Reclamation Chief Floyd Dominy's dream of building the inner canyon hydroelectric generating "cash register" facility.

The Hike: River runners sometimes stop to stroll though the dark, fifty foot deep (seven foot tall, five foot wide) drift tunnel.

Map: Marble Canyon National Monument (historical) topo map

Mile 41. Buck Farm Canyon RR, Elevation 2,851 feet +/- (869 meters), Muav Limestone. You can take a wonderful two-mile round trip hike up Buckfarm Canyon that involves boulder-hopping, clambering up exposed stair steps, and cat walking across Muav ledges. Or you can hike 0.4 miles downstream to look for Albert "Bert" Loper's boat. The pioneer river runner's boat washed up here after the seventy-nine-year-old "Grand Old Man of the Colorado" reportedly died of a heart attack when his boat capsized upstream in 24.5-Mile Rapid on July 8, 1949.

Map: Buffalo Ranch Quadrangle (7.5 minute)

Mile 43. *Anaasází* Footbridge RR, Bridge Elevation 3,270 feet +/- (997 meters), Muav Limestone. Long before Navajo high scalers built Navajo Bridge across the Colorado River in 1929—and iron-worker Lane McDaniel died falling 470 feet into the river—the *Anaasází*, "Enemy Ancestors," constructed a driftwood log footbridge across a deadly gap in the crumbling Muav Limestone ledge circa 1100. Supported by Grand Canyon archaeologists Robert C. Euler and A. Trinkle Jones who were conducting a helicopter survey in the area, Colorado River dory boatman Kenton Grua and boatwoman Ellen Tibbits free climbed from the river 1,000 vertical feet up the ancient route to 4,484-foot Point Hansbrough. The river-to-rim route was one leg of a cross-canyon trail that may have linked the Anaasází's Eminence Fault route less than a mile downstream. Rock climbers who later climbed up to the footbridge rated the climb exposed 5.7 difficulty. They found it frightening and tipped their hats to the Anaasází who managed to haul heavy wooden logs up the cliffs with yucca fiber ropes to cross the span.

Mile 43.8. Eminence Break RL, 2,826 feet +/- (861 meters), Muav Limestone. From camp at the foot of President Harding Rapids (four foot drop), a steep rugged prehistoric route follows the northwest-trending canyon and climbs 2,984 vertical feet up through the Redwall, Supai, Coconino, and Kaibab formations—some call the "ledges of death" route—to the 5,810-foot east rim of Tatahatso Point (*Bidáá Hatsoh*, "Big Rim") on Navajo lands. This precipitous and exposed route was later named *Adahííná*, "Trail Where People Moved Down," and used by Navajo on the run from Colonel Christopher "Kit" Carson's and the Army's merciless campaign against them in 1863–64. The Diné came together and forged a daring rim-to-river trail by carving and chiseling stone steps, placing stone riprap, and stacked trail markers down to the Colorado River where they found sanctuary in the narrow chasm of Marble Canyon, farmed corn, and grazed their stock. If I'd doubted their ancestors, the *Anaasází*, first used this precipitous route it was dispelled during a trek about midway when I picked up—and returned—a sharp narrow two-inch long white arrowhead that may have dated between 1450 and 1600. This area remains part of the Diné.s sacred cultural landscape.

Escape Route: I wouldn't.

Map: Tatahatso Point Quadrangle (7.5 minute)

Mile 47. Saddle Canyon RR, Elevation 2,821 feet +/- (860 meters), Redwall Limestone. The 1.1-mile romp up Saddle Canyon climbs 339 vertical feet through the holly and redbuds to a small beautiful cascade at trail's end.

Mile 52. Nankoweap Canyon RR, Elevation 2,787 feet (849 meters) Bright Angel Shale, Nankoweap Rapids (twenty-seven-foot drop). The most popular hike at Nankoweap is the steep hike up to the Ancestral Puebloan granaries. (See page 248 Nankoweap Trail.) On occasion some river runners trek the ten-mile Nankoweap/Butte Fault/Kwagunt Creek loop. Most river-runners day hiking this rugged loop often prefer to be picked up at the river camp immediately below Kwagunt Rapids at Mile 56 rather than contend with the boulders and tamarisk trees between the two creeks. The river runner trails in the Nankoweap Delta area are heavily braided. Volunteers have realigned them to prevent erosion. Stay on the marked trails.

Map: Nankoweap Mesa Quadrangle (7.5 minute)

Mile 56. Kwagunt Creek RR, Elevation 2,763 feet (842 meters), Bright Angel Shale, Kwagunt Rapids (seven foot drop). The two-mile trek climbs 597 vertical feet up Kwagunt Creek and leads to the Butte Fault's storied "Horse Thief Trail." (See page 275 Butte Fault.)

Mile 61.5. Little Colorado River/Colorado River Confluence RL, Elevation 2,722 feet (830 meters), Tapeats Sandstone. This is the sacred Confluence of eleven culturally affiliated tribes, including the Hopi (*Hopitu Shinumu*), Navajo (*Diné*), Kaibab Paiute (*Kaipa'pici*), Havasupai (*Havsuw' Baaja*), Zuni (*A:shiwi*), and other Native Peoples who oppose construction of the proposed Grand Canyon Escalade project. (See page 188 Colorado and Little Colorado Rivers.)

The Hikes
Beamers Cabin

The most popular day hike at the mouth of the Little Colorado River Gorge is the short ramble to Beamers Cabin on the south side of the Little Colorado River. Rebuilt by prospector and pioneer Ben Beamer from a 4,000-year old Archaic cliff dwelling, "Beamer's Cabin" was first seen and described by Major John Wesley Powell during his maiden voyage down the Colorado River in 1869. On August 10, Major Powell wrote: "I return to camp about three o'clock and find that some of the men have discovered ruins and many fragments of pottery; also etchings and hieroglyphics on the rocks."

John Wesley Powell Route

More time-consuming, strenuous, and dangerous is the river-to-rim route some can-yoneers have mistakenly called the "Walter Clement Powell route" and named after Major Powell's cousin, Clem. Following a rough occasionally cairned line up steep talus, boulder-strewn slopes, precipitous interconnecting shelves, ledges, and cliffs, the rugged route climbs 2,690 vertical foot from the mouth of the Little Colorado River and tops out of the gorge on the 6,061-foot west rim of the Painted Desert Façade on Navajo Nation lands. According to Major Powell's diary entries for August 10 and 11, the one-armed explorer who the Kaibab Paiute called *Kapurats*, "Arm-Off," pioneered the daunting route solo without ropes that the controversial Grand Canyon Escalade gondola tramway would ferry 10,000 visitors a day down the John Wesley Powell Route into the remote Little Colorado River Gorge. On August 11, 1869, Powell wrote:

> We find to-night, on comparing the readings of the barometers, that the walls are about 3,000 feet high—more than half a mile—an altitude difficult to appreciate from a mere statement of feet. The slope by which the ascent is made is not such a slope as is usually found in climbing a mountain, but one much more abrupt—often vertical for many hundreds of feet,—so that the impression is given that we are at great depths, and we look up to see but a little patch of sky.

That description and assessment would have stopped most, but not Powell who still reeled from pain seven years after much of his right arm was shot off by a muzzle-loaded .50- or .58-caliber Minié ball during the Civil War Battle of Shiloh in 1862. On August 12, 1869, Powell described his difficult ascent, in part, from the expedition's camp on the east side of the *Colorado Chiquito* (Little Colorado): "This morning I spend two or three hours in climbing among these shelves, and then I pass above them and go up a long slope to the foot of the cliff and try to discover some way by which I can reach the top of the wall; but I find my progress cut off by an amphitheater. Then I wander away around to the left, up a little gulch and along benches, climbing from time to time, until I reach an altitude of nearly 2,000 feet and can get no higher. From this point I can look off to the west, up side canyons of the Colorado, and see the edge of a great plateau . . ."

End-to-End

The difficult yet sublime fifty-seven-mile trek through the flash flood swept mud, boulders, narrows, soaring walls, and turquoise travertine pools of the Little Colorado River Gorge takes 3.5 days to reach the confluence of the Colorado and Little Colorado Rivers from Cameron, Arizona, on US Highway 89. Once at the confluence you need to hike 8.5 miles across the Beamer Trail and nine miles up the Tanner Trail to the 7,380-foot trailhead at trek mile 74.5. The mid-May 5.5-day trek through the extraordinary seldom-traveled gorge and sere headwinds across the Beamer Trail remains my favorite solo chasm journey. (See page 159 Tanner Trail.)

Map: Cape Solitude Quadrangle (7.5 minute)

Mile 61.5. Beamer Trail RL, Little Colorado River Gorge to Mile 68.5 Tanner Canyon Rapids. It's an 8.5 mile trek from the Little Colorado River Gorge to the foot of the Tanner Trail. Use your raft as a downstream shuttle or hike out-and-back in either direction from a river camp near Mile 65.5 Palisades Creek RL. (See page 278 Beamer Trail.)

Mile 64.5. Carbon Creek RR to Mile 65.4 Lava Canyon RR. From Carbon Canyon Rapids you can take a rugged and beautiful three-mile loop trek up Carbon Creek, across the saddle on the west side of 3,945-foot Chuar Lava Hill, and hike down the bed of Lava Canyon to Lava Canyon Rapids (four foot drop). Use your raft as a downstream shuttle or hike out-and-back from either river camp at Carbon or Lava Creeks. (See page 277 Butte Fault.)

Mile 68.5. Tanner Canyon RL, Elevation 2,680 feet (817 meters), Dox Sandstone, Tanner Rapids (twenty foot drop).

Tanner Canyon Trail Crossroads

The nine-mile rim-to-river Tanner Trail can be used as a river access trail, or as an *Escape Route:* Desert View Watch Tower visitors would probably notice, weather permitting, line-of-sight mirror flashes from Tanner Beach. There's an NPS Ranger Station at Desert View.

The ten-mile Escalante Route RL from Tanner Canyon leads past Cardenas Creek to River Mile 76.5 at Red Canyon at the foot of the New Hance Trail RL. (See page 195 Escalante Route/"Blessingway Trail".)

Map: Desert View Quadrangle (7.5 minute)

Mile 71. Cardenas Creek RL, Elevation 2,640 feet +/- (805 meters), Dox Formation. The well marked mile-long river runner's trail climbs 400 vertical feet to the Ancestral Puebloan Hilltop Ruin and Unkar Rapids overlook. *Note:* You can walk here from Tanner Canyon, but crossing "Furnace Flats" during the summer isn't a hike most enjoy. (See page 195 Cardenas Creek.)

Mile 72.4. Unkar Creek RR, Elevation 2,623 feet (799 meters), Dox Sandstone, Unkar Rapids (25-foot drop). A pine pitch-covered Havasupai water basket, Hopi ollas, and a wooden hut noted during Major John Wesley Powell's Second Colorado River Expedition in 1872 indicates the delta was also used in the historic era by other Native Peoples, including the Southern Paiute and the Zuni whose migration route crossed Unkar Delta. When Powell Expedition member Frederick S. Dellebaugh was hunting bighorn sheep in the area on August 27, 1872, he noted the wooden structure that was believed to be the work of Southern Paiute: "Near this point there was a small abandoned hut of mesquite logs."

The Hike: The park has developed the 0.8 Unkar Delta Trail that loops through the fertile 125-acre delta that was an important seasonal home for Ancestral Puebloans. From 850 to 1200, they terrace-farmed the rich soil for corn, beans, and squash, and crafted and fired hand-painted ollas for storage.

Mile 75.2. Seventy-five Mile Creek RL, Elevation 2,580 feet +/- (786 meters), Shinumo Quartzite, Nevills Rapid (sixteen foot drop). An easy quarter-mile hike leads through the enchanting narrows of ancient stone.

Map: Cape Royal Quadrangle (7.5 minute)

Mile 76.5. Red Canyon RL, Elevation 2,578 feet (786 meters), Hakatai Shale, Hance Rapids (thirty-foot drop).

Red Canyon Trail Crossroads

The 6.5-mile rim-to-river New Hance Trail can be used as a river access trail, or as a difficult *Escape Route*. (See page 198 New Hance Trail.) The Escalante Route ends here.

The 121.4-mile Tonto Trail starts here and ends at River Mile 114.5 Garnet Canyon RL. (See page 206 Tonto Trail.)

Mile 77 Upper Granite Gorge to Mile 118

Mile 81.5. Grapevine Creek RL, Elevation 2,510 feet +/- (765 meters), Vishnu Schist, Grapevine Rapids (eighteen-foot drop). From the camp above Grapevine Rapids you can scramble along the Vishnu Schist to gain the mouth of Grapevine Creek and explore the rugged tributary narrows in the Vishnu Schist.

    Map: Phantom Ranch Quadrangle (7.5 minute)

    Mile 84. Clear Creek RR, Elevation 2,475 feet +/- (754 meters), Tapeats Sandstone-Vishnu Schist. From the small camp above Clear Creek, you can skirt around the dark granite and drop into the streambed of Clear Creek to visit a beguiling maidenhair fern-draped waterfall a half-mile upstream. If you want to explore beyond, you can bypass the falls on the left (west) in order to continue up Clear Creek for as far as time permits. Over the years river runners have hiked up Clear Creek to the east end of the Clear Creek Trail, then followed the nine-mile Civilian Conservation Corps trail west to Phantom Ranch where they were picked up by a downstream shuttle raft the same day. (See page 281 Clear Creek Trail.)

Mile 87.5 Kaibab (Black) Suspension Bridge

Mile 87.5. Bright Angel Creek RR, Elevation 2459 feet (747 meters), Vishnu Schist.

Bright Angel Creek Trail Crossroads

- For Bright Angel Trail, Bright Angel (Silver) Suspension Bridge, Colorado River Trail, Kaibab (Black) Suspension Bridge, Bright Angel Campground, Phantom Ranch, and Bright Angel Creek area walks (see page 108).
- South Kaibab Trail (see page 110 South Kaibab Trail).
- North Kaibab Trail and Ribbon Falls Trail (see page 224 North Kaibab Trail).
- Clear Creek Trail (see page 281 North Trans Canyon Trails and Routes).
- Emergency Help: There's a National Park Ranger Station at the mouth of Bright Angel Creek. There's also a pay phone, food, and refreshments at Phantom Ranch.

Mile 88.3 Bright Angel (Silver) Suspension Bridge

Mile 89. Pipe Creek RL, Elevation 2,410 feet +/- (735 meters), Vishnu Schist, Pipe Springs Rapid (seven-foot drop). Pipe Creek Rest House marks the junction of the eight-mile Bright Angel Trail to the South Rim. From the Rest House the two-mile Colorado River Trail leads 1.3 miles east to the Bright Angel Creek (Silver) Suspension Bridge to Bright Angel Campground and 0.7 miles further to the Kaibab (Black) Suspension Bridge at the foot of the six-mile South Kaibab Trail to the South Rim.

Mile 95. Hermit Creek RL, Elevation 2,390 feet +/- (728 meters), Vishnu Schist, Hermit Rapids (fifteen-foot drop). Most folks are so excited about rafting Hermit Rapids' rollicking wave train they miss the opportunity to hike the area. If you camp overnight above Hermit Rapids, you can hike 1.2 miles up Hermit Creek to explore its spring-fed stream, or you can hike 2.7 miles to visit the remains of Historic Hermit Camp and the aerial tramway that once resupplied the Santa Fe Railroad's "luxurious tourist accommodations." The 9.7-mile rim-to-river Hermit Trail can be used as a long river access trail, or as an Escape Route (see page 120 Hermit Trail). To hike the Tonto Trail from Hermit Creek to Boucher Creek (see page 203 Tonto Trail West).

Map: Grand Canyon Quadrangle (7.5 minute)

Mile 96.5. Boucher Creek RL, Elevation 2,375 feet +/- (724 meters), Vishnu Schist, Boucher Rapid (thirteen foot drop). If you stop or camp overnight above Boucher Rapids you can take a pleasing 1.5-mile hike up the streambed to see the winter camp of Louis de Bouchere. The romantic white bearded "hermit" rode a white mule and told only white lies. The 10.8-mile rim-to-river Boucher Trail can be used as a long river access trail, or as a long and arduous *Escape Route* (see page 125 Boucher Trail).

Mile 98. Crystal Creek RR, Elevation 2,320 feet +/- (707 meeters), Vishnu Schist, Crystal Rapids (seventeen-foot drop). The most popular short hike at Crystal Creek is the river runners overlook where the merits of running the most feared rapids in North America are debated. A thirty-three-foot tour bus sized motor raft flipped on the high water days of June 1983, when 97,300 CFS roared through the Grand Canyon from the cavitating spillways of Glen Canyon Dam 113.2 miles upstream. One-hundred fourteen years earlier, Major Powell discribed high masonry dwellings high above the deadly rapid that hadn't existed until historic floodwaters roaring down from the North Rim created it in 1967. On August 17, 1869, Powell wrote: "Walk up creek 3 miles. Grand scenery. Old Indian Camps." (See page 285 North Trans canyon Trails and Routes.)

Map: Shiva Temple Quadrangle (7.5 minute)

Mile 107.5. Bass Canyon RL, Elevation 2,203 feet +/- (671 meters), Bass Formation, Bass Rapid (five foot drop). The 7.8-mile rim-to-river South Bass Trail is sometimes used as a river access trail by backpackers and pack rafters hiking rim-to-river-to-rim via the South Bass and North Bass Trails. Unless you have a vehicle parked or waiting at the South Bass Trailhead it would be a long and remote Escape Route. (See page 135 South Bass Trail.)

Map: Havasupai Point Quadrangle (7.5 Minute)

Mile 108.5. Shinumo Creek RR, Elevation 2,198 feet (670 meters), Vishnu Schist, Shinumo Rapid (eight foot drop). You can hike 1.5 miles to the shade and charm of Bass's historic Shinumo Camp and Garden. The 13.5-mile rim-to-river North Bass Trail is sometimes used as a river access trail by backpackers and pack rafters hiking rim-to-river-to-rim via the North Bass and South Bass Trails. Unless you have a vehicle parked

A river hiker's reflection, Fern Glen Canyon, Colorado River. Copyright © John Annerino Photography.

or waiting at the North Bass Trailhead it would be a long and remote Escape Route (see page 248 North Bass Trail).

Mile 116.5. Royal Arch Creek RL, Elevation 2,115 feet +/- (645 meters), Tapeats Sandstone. From the river, it's a "must see" quarter-mile hike and scramble to Elves Chasm. Viewed alone, the spring-fed waterfall grotto is a captivating oasis of running water, polished stone, and bouquets of maidenhair ferns, red monkey flowers, and yellow columbines.

Map: Explorers Monument Quadrangle (7.5 minute)

Mile 120 Conquistador Aisle to Mile 123

Mile 120. Blacktail Canyon RR, Elevation 2,096 feet (639 meters), Tapeats Sandstone, Great Unconformity. From the mouth of what's also called One Hundred and Twenty Mile Creek, this delightful saunter through stream cobbles leads through acoustical narrows beneath towering ledges of Tapeats Sandstone to what most visitors consider a cul de sac.

It's a great place for contemplation or exploration. There is an exposed route through the Tapeats Sandstone near the head of Blacktail Canyon on its east side to the Tonto Formation. You can run or hike east across the Tonto upstream to River Mile 119 where you'll need to scout the descent off the Tonto Formation through the Tapeats Sandstone down the least intimidating line back to the river. From Mile 119, you can loop west cross-country back downstream along the river to the mouth of Blacktail Canyon. No water on the Tonto Route.

Warning: The Blacktail Ascent and Tonto Route is for experienced canyoneers only.

Mile 127 Middle Granite Gorge to Mile 131

Mile 131.8. Stone Creek RR, Elevation 1,988 feet (606 meters), Diabase, Hakatai Shale, Bass Formation, Dubendorff Rapid (fifteen foot drop). From your camp at Dubendorff Rapids below the mouth of Stone Creek, you can hike two miles up the course of Stone Creek to one of the prettiest secluded waterfalls in the canyon. Or you can find the break in the Bass Formation and follow a faint desert bighorn trail two miles downstream west along the rim of Hakatai Shale in and around One Hundred and Thirty three Mile Creek to the east rim overlooking the mouth of Tapeats Creek. From the Tapeats Creek overlook, you can use a trail that follows the east side of Tapeats Creek down to the river. Return the way you came or use your raft as a downstream shuttle pickup. No water.

Warning: The route is not for inexperienced canyoneers.

Map: Powell Plateau Quadrangle (7.5 minute)

Mile 133.5. Tapeats Creek RR, Elevation 2,003 feet (611 meters), Diabase-Bright Angel Shale, Tapeats Rapid (15 foot drop). This is another must stop and layover for river runners, hikers, and trout fishermen. Tapeats Creek offers access to fishing and three enticing hikes: the 2.8-mile trail to Thunder River Falls; the 4.2-mile trail and streamside bushwhack to Tapeats Falls; and the 6.2-mile hike past Thunder River over Surprise Valley to Deer Creek Falls and your downstream shuttle raft at River Mile 136. (See page 265 Thunder River Trail.)

Mile 135 Granite Narrows to Mile 136

Mile 136. Deer Creek RR, Elevation 1,936 feet (590 meters), Granite-Tapeats Sandstone, Deer Creek Falls (190 feet tall), Colorado River in Granite Narrows (seventy-six feet wide). The most popular hike from the foot of Deer Creek Falls is the mile-long clamber past poison ivy up to Deer Creek Narrows. This is the heart of Kaibab Paiute holy land they revere as *Puaxant Tuvip*, "power land."

Tread Lightly: This is the heart of the Kaibab Paiute holy land. From Deer Creek Falls you can also trek 7.5 rugged cross-country river miles downstream to Kanab Creek in the footsteps of Powell Expedition photographer E. O. Beaman who made the journey in 1872. (See page 267 Deer Creek Trail.)

Map: Fishtail Mesa Quadrangle (7.5 minute)

Cogswell Butte

A rewarding river to summit hike is the short, steep trek from Surprise Valley up to the 4,545-foot summit of Cogswell Butte (see page 267).

Be Careful: A thirty-four-year-old Colorado River guide was reported missing from Panchos Kitchen river camp on September 12, 2016. His body was discovered near Mile 139 on September 20, 2016.

R.I.P. Joshua Tourjee.

Mile 143.5. Kanab Creek Canyon RR, Elevation 1,887 feet (575 meters), Muav Limestone, Kanab Rapid (twelve-foot drop). Navigating high water in battered wooden boats and facing what he felt was imminent disaster, Major Powell ended his second Colorado River Expedition at Kanab Creek on September 8, 1872. The following day expedition topographer and geologist Almon Harris Thompson wrote: "It is nonsense to think of trying the "lower land" with this water. . . .The major told the boys of our decision this morning. All were pleased. The fact is, each one is impressed with the impossibility of continuing down the river." That put the expedition between a rock and a hard place. Met by a pack string from Kanab, Utah, expedition members still faced a grueling trek and ride through immense boulders that choked the 3,000-foot deep canyon narrows in their return to civilization. Pow-

Panning gold, Colorado River gold miner, 1898, George Wharton James photo.

ell's cousin and expedition member Walter Clement Powell described the route: "The trail is simply "Jackassable and hardly passable." In other words, the terrain was too narrow and rugged for heavily laden mules—one of the reasons William Wallace Bass favored burros.

The Hikes
Whispering Falls Canyon
From the confluence of the Colorado River, you can hike around the deep sandal- and shoe-sucking mud and thread huge boulders 3.5 miles upstream to the junction of Whispering Falls Canyon. Turn right (east) and dance across the Muav Limestone ledges 0.2 miles to a crystal clear deep pool of water. Spawned by a captivating garden of maidenhair ferns and it offers a refreshing sight and welcome spray.

End-to-End
From Nagles Crossing south of Fredonia, Arizona, you can trek fifty-seven miles through sand, stream cobble, flash flood swept boulders and huge broken timbers across precipitous ledges beneath springs that seep from towering walls through Kanab Creek Canyon to the Colorado River. Then what?! Retrace the rugged course of the Powell expedition and the footsteps of destitute gold rush prospectors back to Fredonia; trek the river upstream and climb out Deer Creek and Thunder River Trail; or, if the NPS still permits, hitchhike to Havasu Canyon and hike eighteen miles up Havasu and Hualapai Canyons to Hualapai Hilltop. If you have the patience to wait. It took me thirty-six hours in the August heat until a boatwoman I'd worked with spotted me trekking west along the Colorado River RL from the mouth of Kanab Creek.

Map: Kanab Point Quadrangle (7.5 minute)

Mile 148. Matakatamiba Canyon RL, Elevation 1,839 feet (561 meters), Muav Limestone, Matakatamiba Rapid (three-foot drop). From the river, hike, wade, and body-bridge the striated creek-polished Muav Limestone ledges 0.4 miles into Matakatamiba amphitheater. On a quiet day, the hallowed chamber offers beauty, solace, and soft rock to nap on. In deference to Havasupai spiritual beliefs I personally don't visit the traditional use area above the amphitheater.

Mile 156.5. Havasu Canyon RL, Elevation 1,790 feet +/- (546 meters), Muav Limestone, Havasu Rapids (three-foot drop). From the river runners "parking lot" at the mouth of Havasu Canyon, it's a four mile stream-crossing wade, hike, and 363-ver- tical-foot climb to Beaver Falls near the confluence of Havasu and Beaver Canyons. Hikers and river runners spend time at the forty-foot high falls cliff jumping into the travertine pool, swimming the subterranean "green room," relaxing, and predicting the odds of flash floods. That's never a good bet in Havasu Canyon during July–August monsoons.

End-to-End

From Moqui Tank on the rim of the Coconino Plateau you can trek forty-two miles in the footsteps of the Hopi and Navajo down the beautiful but austere Moqui Trail Canyon through the dry and desolate "Kuhni Desert" to the life saving confluence of Cataract and Havasu Canyons past Supai all the way to the Colorado River. Coming at the end of a 210-mile journey run across the Hopi-Havasupai trade route from Oraibi to Supai, the blistering Moqui Trail Canyon/Cataract Canyon stretch was a tough nut to crack. Special permit required. (See page 179, Moqui (*Móka*) Trail.)

Map: S B Point Quadrangle (7.5 minute)

Mile 164.5. Tuckup Canyon RR, Elevation 1,760 feet +/- (536 meters), Muav Limestone, 164 Mile Rapid (four foot drop). From the river you can hike one mile up the streambed, skirt flint napped sharp shattered boulders that have fallen from cliffs overhead, chimney the ten foot tall channel-blocking chockstone on the left, and follow the stream-polished ledges through the deep narrows that glow with refracted morning and afternoon light. Some distance upstream, below the confluence of Tuckup and Cottonwood Canyons, is the twenty-six foot span, fourteen foot tall Conglomerate Arch.

Mile 166.5. National Canyon RL, Elevation 1,744 feet (532 meters), Muav Limestone. National Canyon, *Chikoráma*, is a sacred cultural landscape of the Havasupai. Compared to Matakatamiba and Tuckup Canyon narrows, the one-mile hike through the wide gravel mouth of National Canyon is boulder-strewn and often exposed to the sun until you reach the Muav Patio streams and slot canyon. An early morning or late afternoon hike displays the distinct character of the western Grand Canyon's Mojave Desert tributary canyons.

Map: Fern Glen Canyon Quadrangle (7.5 minute)

Mile 168. Fern Glen Canyon RR, Elevation 1,736 feet +/- (529 meters), Muav Limestone, Fern Glen Rapid (three foot drop). From the small arch near the mouth of Fern Glen Canyon, the charming one-mile hike beneath the "Weeping Walls" of spring-fed maidenhair ferns is one of my favorite short canyon romps. It requires scrambling and chimneying up a boulder slide on the left that some commercial river runners safeguard with a belay rope. In the narrows beyond, you can stair step up easy but exposed Muav ledges on the right side of a thirty-foot boulder wedged into the canyon narrows to reach the overhanging pouroff and rest stop at trail's end.

Mile 179.5. Lava Falls RR, Elevation 1,680 feet +/- (512 meters), Gray Ledge Basalt-Uinkaret Lava Flow, Lava Falls Rapids (thirteen-foot drop). From the pullout above Lava Falls there are two hikes. The most popular is the short, normally sun-scorched hike through the black lava to the heart-thumping river runners overlook of

Lava Falls. Still contested to this day, the Big Drop rapids may have been navigated by horse thief and prospector James White who lashed himself to a crude log raft two years before Major John Wesley Powell's first successful descent in 1869. The most dangerous hike is the proven-to-be-deadly, mercilessly steep 1.5-mile Lava Falls Route (see page 234 Western Grand Canyon Trails).

   Map: Vulcans Throne Quadrangle (7.5 minute)

   Mile 188. Whitmore Wash RR, Elevation 1,603 feet +/- (489 meters), Cenozoic Basalt, Whitmore Rapid (three foot drop). *Escape Route:* Upstream from Whitmore Wash at River Mile 187.5, the Bar 10 Ranch operates a seasonal helipad and helicopter service for river runners. They also operate the 4,500 feet long, thirty-three feet wide Bar 10 Airstrip (Indicator 1Z1) at the ranch they call "Whitmore International Airport." Contact the Bar 10 Ranch before your river journey to see what emergency services they offer in the event of a hiking or river running mishap in the area. Phone: (435) 628–4010, (800) 582–4139; Fax: (435) 628–5124. Visit www.bar10.com/

   Map: Whitmore Rapids Quadrangle (7.5 minute)

Mile 216 Lower Granite Gorge to Mile 264

Mile 225.9. Diamond Creek RL, Elevation 1,362 feet (415 meters), Diamond Creek Rapid (twenty-five foot drop), Colorado River takeout. *Escape Route*: Peach Springs on US Route 66 is located twenty-two miles up the Diamond Creek Road.

   Map: Diamond Peak Quadrangle (7.5 minute)

- Managing Agency: Grand Canyon National Park.
- Backcountry Information Center: for information call (928) 638–7875.
- Critical Backcountry. Updates visit www.nps.gov/grca/planyourvisit/trail-closures.htm
- NPS Grand Canyon Hiker 24 Hour Emergency Phone Number and Email
  - Phone (928) 638–7805
  - Email: grca_bic@nps.gov (Use this if the phone line is busy)

"Mohave men Panambona and Mitiwara," Colorado River at Diamond Creek, 1871, Timothy H. O'Sullivan stereograph, Library of Congress.

26

Western Grand Canyon Trails

"We believe in Jacob [Hamblin], and look upon you as a father. When you are hungry, you may have our game. You may gather our sweet fruits. We will give you food when you come to our land. We will show you the springs and you may drink; the water is good. We will be friends and when you come we will be glad. We will tell the Indians who live on the other side of the great river that we have seen *Ka'purats*, 'arm off,' [Powell] and that he is the Indians' friend. We will tell them he is Jacob's friend."

—Shiv'wits Paiute chief, September 19, 1870
Yevingkarere, "Mount Trumbull"

LANDFORM

Once the ancestral lands of the Southern Paiute, the untamed 11,000-square-mile Arizona Strip forms one of the loneliest and most desolate and rugged tracts of land in the American West. Comprised of four major plateaus named after Southern Paiute bands—Kaibab, Kanab, Uinkaret, and Shivits—this vast, sparsely populated region of Great Basin Desert reels southward from the Vermilion Cliffs sixty desolate miles to the edge of the western Grand Canyon. Today, it includes Pipe Spring National Monument, Grand Canyon-Parashant National Monument, and western Grand Canyon National Park.

Toroweap Point looking west. Pioneer photographer John K. "Jack" Hillers's Camera Station 61, April 1, 1872. Copyright © John Annerino Photography.

Mutungw, "Yellow Rock Water," Pipe Spring

For thousands of years the ancient spring of *Mutungw,* "Yellow Rock Water," known today as Pipe Springs, has been the most dependable water source for travelers journeying across the vast, seemingly bleak homelands of the Southern Paiute. The Kaibab and Shivwits Paiute had long used Mutungw as they journeyed from one distant water hole to the next, hunting, gathering, growing small plots of maize, beans, and squash, and trading with the Havasupai and Hualapai on the far side of the "great river" they reached by using one of twenty-three traditional cross-canyon trails. Mormon pioneer missionary families depended on its life-saving waters during their struggles across the Honeymoon Trail from St. George, Utah, to the Little Colorado and Gila River Valleys, Arizona; as did lumberman who fell, chained, bucked, and hauled one million board feet of timber from 8,029-foot Mount Trumbull across the Temple Trail to build the St. George Utah Temple in 1877. Hordes of gold seekers also stopped at the oasis to fill their canteens and wooden barrels before heading down Kanab Creek Canyon hell-bent on finding the mother lode at the Colorado River. The Kaibab and Shivwits Paiute's cottonwood tree–shaded artesian spring was renamed after pioneer waggoner, polygamist, and silver miner William Haynes "Gunlock Bill" Hamblin, who reportedly shot a hole through Indian missionary Dudley Leavitt's meerschaum pipe from fifty paces at the spring in 1852. There was no arguing with Gunlock Bill, brother of Jacob Hamblin, about the new name. Leavitt was the great grandfather of Mountain Meadows Massacre historian and author Juanita Brooks. In 1870, Mormon leader Brigham Young organized forty church members to build a native stone masonry fort they called Winsor Castle around the area's four springs, Fort Spring, Spring Room Spring, Tunnel Spring, and West Cabin Spring that once flowed freely from the Sevier Fault in the Navajo Sandstone and Kayenta Formation. Young, who founded Salt Lake City and was the governor of Utah, was known as "American Moses" among his followers and the men, women, and children who toiled in the high desert to build "Brigham's Bastion," according to Juanita Brooks, "to protect the church's all-important tithing [cattle] herd from Native American raiders."

- Directions: From Fredonia, Arizona, drive fifteen miles west on Highway 389 to Pipe Spring National Monument, Arizona.
- The Hikes: Ranger Guided Day Hikes and Tours
- Camping: Kaibab Paiute Tribe Campground
- Contact: Pipe Spring National Monument
  - Visit: www.nps.gov/pisp/index.htm
  - HC 65 Box 5,406 Pipe Springs Road Fredonia, AZ 86022
  - Phone: (928) 643–7105

The Arizona Strip

Major John Wesley Powell was the first non-Native to explore what he called "that difficult region" south of Pipe Spring in 1870. On September 13 he wrote: "We followed this Indian trail toward the east all day, and at night camped at a great spring, known to the Indians as "Yellow Rock Water." What made Powell's overland journeys distinct from the lifeless "Indian ruins" he visited during his first 1869 Colorado River expedition the year before were the living Native Peoples he traveled amongst and depended upon, lead by Kaibab Paiute leader, guide and translator, Chuar'rumpeak. Powell had two pressing reasons to visit the unknown region south of Pipe Springs. He wanted to investigate the fate of William Dunn and Seneca and O. G. Howland, three men who'd abandoned his 1869 Geographic Expedition down the Colorado River at Separation Canyon. And he wanted to explore the possibility of establishing resupply caches for his Second Powell Expedition in 1871–72. To do so, Powell also enlisted Mormon missionary, explorer, and diplomat Jacob Vernon Hamblin to work with Chuar'rumpeak as liaisons with the Shivwits Paiute he'd smoke a peace pipe with while traveling overland through the Paiute homeland of *Nungwuh Tuhveep*.

Major John Wesley Powell and Tau-Gu, Great Chief of the Pai-Utes, 1874, John K. Hillers's stereoview photo.

Venturing southward from the prehistoric way station of Pipe Spring, Powell embarked on one of the most unusual murder investigations and reconnaissances in the annals of American West. Unbeknownst to Powell, he would be journeying along the ceremonial pilgrimage route of the Kaibab Paiute between Mount Trumbull and Toroweep Point. And he was about to be told face-to-face who killed the Dunn-Howland trio. In the remote forests of *Uinkaret Kaiv*, "Place of Pines," beneath the lonely heights of *Yevingkarere*, "Mount Trumbull," you can still hear the wind howling through the trees and feel the power of what the Shiv'wits Paiute chief told Powell late one night in the company of Hamblin and Chuar'rumpeak. As the roaring fire blazed and sent burning embers spiraling into the dark starlit heavens, the unidentified Shiv'wits chief spoke: "Last year we killed three white men. Bad men said they were our enemies. They told great lies. We thought them true. We were mad; it made us big fools. We are very sorry. Do not think of them; it is done; let us be friends . . ." Powell concluded his murder investigation and traveled among the Shivwits and Kaibab Paiute. He climbed their highest mountain, drank from their sacred water holes, and nearly perished of thirst with his men and horses struggling down the frightening ledges of Whitmore Canyon to reach the Colorado River in the depths of the western Grand Canyon. Powell would have perished without his Paiute guides: "I have prided myself on being able to grasp and retain in my mind the topography of a country; but these Indians [Paiute] put me to shame . . . They know every rock and every ledge, every gulch and canyon, and just where to wind among these to find a pass; and their knowledge is unerring." Nearly a century and a half later it's still possible to follow in the footsteps of Powell, Hamblin, Chuar'rumpeak, and the Southern Paiute through this alluring seldom-traveled region.

Directions

For all hikes and treks use the 58.9-mile unimproved Sunshine Road, (County Road #109 and Road #115). The well-marked turnoff is located on Highway 389, six miles west of Fredonia, Arizona, and five miles east of Pipe Spring National Monument.

Travel Advisory

The condition of the graded all-weather dirt Sunshine Road varies from normal tire-shredding gravel and stones during hot wind-blown dust storms to axle-burying ponds of standing water and mud during torrential monsoon summer rains and flash-floods. Then, there's winter snow. There are no facilities. Tow-out costs rival the price of a catered glamping getaway. Come prepared with adequate provisions of water, food, gas, tools, two spare tires, tire plugs, portable air compressor, and a shovel. Bring a copy of the AAA Guide to Indian Country map, and print out a copy of the Grand

Canyon-Parashant National Monument road map, which covers the entire Arizona Strip.

Visit: www.nps.gov/hfc/carto/PDF/PARAmap1.pdf

GRAND CANYON-PARASHANT NATIONAL MONUMENT

Established by President William J. Clinton on January 11, 2000, the 1.1 million acre Grand Canyon-Parashant National Monument sits in the heart of the Arizona Strip. Wild, remote, and rugged, it is a modern no-man's land that lures hikers, backpackers, adventurers, and spirited individuals who've grown weary of crowds, traffic congestion, and smog—what environmental essayist Edward Abbey who lived in nearby Wolf Hole called "industrial tourism"—that characterize some of the region's national parks and monuments.

Enepi Pikavo, "Witch Water Pocket," Day Hike

One of the first things Powell wrote about when he headed south from Pipe Spring on the morning of September 14, 1870, was the region's paucity of water sources: "Not more than a half-dozen are known in a district of country large enough to make many good-sized counties in Illinois. There are no running streams, and these springs and water pcokets—that is, holes in rocks that hold water from shower to shower—were our only dependence." Powell relied on Chuar'rumpeak's knowledge to lead his party along the ancient footpaths from one aboriginal water hole to the next. At twilight on Day Two, Powell finally reached Witches Water Pocket, forty-odd miles south of Pipe Spring. It was one of the Kaibab Paiute's most storied water holes. On September 15, Powell wrote: "During the rainy season the water rolls down the mountain-sides, plunging over precipices, and excavating a deep basin in solid rock below. This basin, hid from the sun, holds water the year-round . . . The Indians call it *U-nu-pin Pika-vu,* that is, '"Elfin Water-Pocket.'" Fortunately, this lava pool has not been developed, as early Mormon settlers and cattlemen had done for most water holes that sustained their families and livestock on the Arizona Strip. Today, Witches Water Pocket retains the same allure it had when cartographer Clarence E. Dutton retraced Powell's route to survey the western Grand Canyon during the summer of 1880. Dutton wrote: "In every desert the watering places are memorable, and this one is no exception. It is a weird spot. Around it are the desolate Phlegraean fields, where jagged masses of black lava still protrude through rusty, decaying cinders . . . The pool itself might well be deemed the abode of witches." That's what Chuar'rumpeak told Frederick S. Dellenbaugh, one of Powell's expedition members, when he visited the eerie waterhole: "They said the locality was a favorite haunt of witches."

The Hike: From the roadside pull off, the 3.65 mile secondary road walk and cross country hike begins off the Sunshine Road. (See Directions below). Get your bearings on your Vulcans Throne Quadrangle (7.5 minute) map, and hike 1.5 miles south to BM 5192. Turn right (west) and hike 1.4 miles to BM 2240 and stop. Key off of 5921 hill and hike north/northwest a halfmile or so through black lava, piñon juniper, beavertail cacti, and staghorn cholla to the wash that contours the base of the hill. Powell climbed and described the unnamed landmark hill as "a huge pile of volcanic scoria, loose and light as cinders from a forge, which gave way under my feet as I climbed with great labor." Turn left (west) at the base of the hill and follow the rugged ravine a quarter-mile or more to what the Paiute also called, *Enepi Pikavo,* "Witch Water Pocket."

Directions

Drive approximately forty-two miles south on the Sunshine Road (County Road # 109) to BM 5265 located in the small pass between the Towoweap Cliffs on your left (east) and 5921 hill on your right (west). Refer to your Vulcans Throne Quadrangle (7.5 minute) map. Pull off on the secondary road on the eastern border of the 7,880 acre Mount Trumbull Wilderness to start the hike.

Travel Notes

- Primary Access: Sunshine Road from Highway 389.
- Elevation: 5,265-feet Sunshine Road to 5,330-feet Witches Water Pocket.
- Biotic Community: Piñon juniper woodland, Great Basin Desert.
- Elevation Gain and Loss: 211 vertical feet each way.
- Mileage: 7.3 miles (3.65 miles one way).
- Water Sources: Witches Pool (seasonal, purify before drinking, and strain the "wigglers" Powell nonchalantly drank in front of his men and said: "I haven't seen any wigglers.")
- Escape Route: Back the way you came.
- Seasons: All year.
- Map: Vulcans Throne Quadrangle (7.5 minute), Grand Canyon-Parashant NM road map.
- Camping: Tuweep Campground, no camping within 0.5 miles of Witches Water Pocket.
- Managing Agency: Grand Canyon-Parashant National Monument.
- Public Lands Information Center (NPS, BLM, U.S. Forest Service). 345 East Riverside Drive, St. George, UT 84790
  - Phone (435) 688–3200, Fax (435) 688–3388
  - Visit: www.nps.gov/para/index.htm

Shaman petroglyph, Nampaweap trail shrine. Copyright © John Annerino Photography.

Nampaweap, "Foot Canyon," Trail Day Hike

Mile 0. Nampaweap Trailhead, Elevation 6,366 feet (1,940 meters), Volcanic Basalt, no water. The leisurely 0.75-mile hike to Nampaweap Canyon reveals a captivating landscape spiritually linked to the Kaibab Paiute's Toroweap ceremonial lands of *Mukunta'uipi*. Of all places to view stone murals of petroglyphs pecked into black lava cliffs, boulders, and columns, the craggy and wooded canyon beneath Mount Trumbull seems an unlikely location. Here, along the timeless corridor, thousands of petroglyphs have been pecked, chiseled, and incised by ancient foot travelers into fine-grained igneous basalt that represent the Bighorn Sheep Song, ceremonies, hunts, maps, springs, fields of corn, and creation stories that still speak to Kaibab Paiute who come to pay homage at the sacred rocks that tell stories whispered by their ancestors. It is a place of *puha*, "power," prayer, and ceremony where sacred spring water is offered by pilgrims who "look and listen" but do not touch the rocks. Powell and Dutton made no mention of this once secret canyon en route to the Colorado River. But one of Powell's expedition photographers, John K. "Jack" Hillers, visited the stony ravine on April 1, 1872, where he took the first recorded photograph of the Southern Paiute's trail shrines. In his diary entry for the day, Hillers wrote: "Andy [Hattan] and myself started toward the Colorado [River]—took a picture of some Moqui hieroglyphics which were situated in a gulch near the foot of Mt. Trumbull."

The Hike: From the Nampaweap Trailhead, hike downhill 0.75 miles east on the abandoned two-lane dirt road through piñon, juniper, and ponderosa pine and descend 200 vertical feet to the head of what Mormon settlers called Billy Goat Canyon for the profusion of Mountain Sheep (*Ovis Canadensis*) petroglyphs.

Tread Lightly: Several Paiute elders expressed concern that the area should be fenced off from outsiders.

Map: Mount Logan Quadrangle (7.5 minute)

Directions

Drive 45.7 miles south on the Sunshine Road (County Road #109) to the junction of County Roads 5 and 115. Turn right (west) on County Road 5 and drive 3.2 miles west to the Nampaweap turnoff. Turn left (south) on Road 1028 and drive past the Arkansas Ranch (private) 1.1 miles to the Nampaweap Trailhead.

WESTERN GRAND CANYON NATIONAL PARK

Bordered on the east by the deep, rugged course of Kanab Creek Canyon, on the north by a sea of Great Basin Desert, on the west by the stark plateaus and canyons of Grand Canyon-Parashant National Monument, and on the south by sheer cliffs that plummet over 3,000 feet to the Colorado River, the western Grand Canyon remains the wild

Twilight, Son of Lava Falls, Colorado River, Western Grand Canyon. Copyright © John Annerino Photography.

canyon country that first lured explorers, prospectors, surveyors, pioneers, and cattlemen into the heart of what was once popularly known as "the strip." It's just the kind
of country that still tugs at the souls of desert rats, canyoneers, adventurers, artists, and
Native Peoples.

Whitmore Canyon River Route

Few people realize the Shivwits and Kaibab Paiute first used the route to ford the
Big Water to hunt and gather, for vision quests, and to trade, war, and Ghost Dance
with the Havasupai and Hualapai. One of the twenty-three traditional cross-canyon
trails the Shivwits and Kaibab Paiute used was their trail down Whitmore Canyon.
When Powell asked if there was a way down to the Colorado River near *Mukunta'uipi*
(Toroweap), he wrote the Shivwits Paiute told him ". . . years ago, a way was discovered by which parties could go down, but that no one had attempted it for a long
time; that it was a very difficult and dangerous undertaking to reach *pianukwintu*
"big water"." Instead, the Shivwits guided Major Powell and expedition cartographer
Captain Francis M. Bishop overland across what was marked on their map as "Wonsits
Tiravi" [*Wonsits Tiravu*, "Antelope Plain"], between the volcanic cinder cones in the
pass between Mt. Trumbull and 7,866-foot Mt. Logan (*Yevimpur Wekavika*), via Big
Springs (*Aqáp'u*) and Hells Hollow, and over the Hurricane Ledges (*Tsingkawihav*)
where Powell, Captain Bishop, and their horses nearly met their fate descending into,
and climbing out of, Whitmore Canyon: "In a few minutes he [the Shivwits guide]
returned and told us there was a little water in the pocket below. But it was vile and
nauseating, and our ponies refused to drink it . . . We started, leading our ponies, a
wall upon our left, unknown depths on our right. At places our way was along shelves
so narrow or so sloping that I ached with fear lest a pony should make a misstep and
knock a man over the cliff with him," Powell wrote during his reconnaissance to use
Whitmore Canyon as his resupply route for the Second Powell Expedition down the
Colorado River in August 1872. Further study of Powell's journal and it appears his
torch lit midnight descent through the precipitous cliffs of Whitmore Canyon was the
explorer's most dangerous rim-to-river canyon trek he'd made during his entire 1869
voyage along the 930-mile stretch of the Green and Colorado Rivers from Green River,
Wyoming, to the confluence of the Virgin River, Nevada.

Powell wrote: "We feared that we should have to stay there clinging to the rocks
until daylight . . . Soon every man of our party had a torch of his own, and the light by
the river, and the lights in the opposite gulch, and our own torches, made more manifest
the awful darkness which filled the tremendous gorge. We were hungry and thirsty and
almost starved, and we lay down on the rocks to drink. Then we made a cup of coffee, and,
spreading our blankets on a sand beach, we were lulled to sleep by the roaring Colorado."

The Old Ones (*Enugwuhype*) Trail

Based on ethnographic accounts of ancestral Southern Paiute constructing trails and more than 100 round stone shelters on the neighboring *Unav-Nuquaint*, "Little Springs Lava Flow," it's safe to assume their ancestors, the *Enugwuhype*, first used tumpline burden baskets to move volcanic cinders and stones for travel down what remains of their aboriginal trail along the Lava Falls Route to the Colorado River for hunting, gathering, trade, and ceremony between 1075 and 1100.

Lava Falls Route

As far as can be discerned, two of Powell's 1872 Colorado River expedition crew members, Frederick S. Dellenbaugh and Captain Pardyn Dodds, made the first recorded historic descent of the Lava Falls Route. During an overland survey before the Second Powell Expedition down the Colorado River launched from Lees Ferry on August 17, Dellenbaugh wrote: "On the 20th [April] Dodds and I climbed down the cliffs about three thousand feet to the water at a rapid called Lava Falls. Across the river we could see a very large spring [Warm Springs], but of course we could not reach it." That's as succinct and as accurate a description of the Lava Falls Route as there is. If you're primed, acclimated, and canyon fit for the adventure, you can follow the historic route of Dellenbaugh and Dodds to one of the most storied rapids in North America. How better to emulate these early canyoneers than to follow in their footsteps.

Directions

Drive 45.7 miles south on the Sunshine Road (County Road #109) to the junction of County Roads 5 and 115. Continue straight on County Road 115 and drive 13.1 miles south to the Tuweep Campground. From the Tuweep Campground early the next morning, drive 1.9 miles north back up the Sunshine Road to the Lava Falls Route turnoff on the left (west) side of the road. From this secondary road junction at BM 4575, drive across Toroweap Lake *Tu-roump-pi-ca-vu*, 2.4 miles along the northwest/west slope of Vulcans Throne to the trailhead.

Volcans Throne

Grand Canyon geologist Clarence E. Dutton named 5,102-foot Vulcans Throne when he retraced Powell's route from Pipe Spring during the summer of 1880. In his scientific, precisely phrased tome, *The Tertiary History of the Grand Cañon District, with Atlas* (1882), Dutton wrote "there stands a basaltic cinder cone immediately upon the brink of the inner gorge. Its altitude above the surrounding plane is 580 feet. The summit is readily gained, and it is an admirable stand-point from which the entire panorama may be viewed. We named it Vulcan's Throne." Vulcans Throne is spiritually linked with the Kaibab Paiute's Toroweap ceremonial landscape of *Mukunta'uipi*.

Warning

The primitive 1.5-mile Lava Falls Route is the Grand Canyon's shortest, toughest, and driest rim-to-river route. Make no mistakes this route demands self-rescue skills—there's no one else out here—excellent physical conditioning to trek half-a-Grand Canyon (5,000 vertical feet) out-and-back in three miles, honed route finding skills, endurance, and good judgment. Step-for-step midsummer the Lava Falls Route is more treacherous than Arizona's/Sonora, México's *El Camino del Diablo*, "The Road of the Devil," which has claimed thousands of lives throughout its recorded history.

Lava Falls Route

It's important for you to consider your motives for embarking on what recently proved to be a deadly route for three fit hikers who died within "earshot" of the remote Lava Falls Route parking area—there's no phone, emergency water, or facilities. It's a shade less, south-facing route exposed to the sun. Summertime this is one of the last places on earth you should consider hiking. Go explore the Kaibab Plateau's increasingly rare old growth forests of Ponderosa pines (*Pinus ponderosa*). (See page 221 North Rim Trails.) Black scoria lava and basalt ground temperatures soar between too-hot-to-touch or fall-down-on 140 to 160 degrees Fahrenheit. A simple misstep, twisted ankle, or wrenched knee quickly levels the playing field for the most seasoned and fit canyoneers, athletes, and "tough guys." Whether you follow this rugged route to emulate the Paiute, Powell's men, or because you just want to reach the Big Water, the Toroweap Route is anything but an aesthetically pleasing "hike," as most people define the term. It plummets 2,500 vertical feet in 1.5 miles, a greater elevation loss than Black Canyon of the Gunnison National Park's established rim-to-river routes. Here, the 600 square mile, 600,000 year old Uinkaret Volcanic Field is tilted at a 45-degree angle and can throw you to your knees during the descent—and wring the last drop of moisture out of your body and cracked lips during the debilitating stumble, scramble, and shuffle out. There is little more to say about the sketchy route snaking its way through glass-black lava too hot for Grand Canyon pink rattlesnakes (*Crotalus oreganus abyssus*) most times of the year, other than follow the rock cairns during the decent and, once you turn around, trace the ghost white crosses shining the way back out of the fearsome rubble of lava. It's not popularly known who white-washed the crosses in place on the fingertip- and palm-burning black lava, but they bare a faint resemblance to the mysterious two-foot tall white cross pecked into the Phlegraean basalt of Witches Water Pocket above the initials "PE" [Powell

Expedition?] that may have been carved by one of Powell's men during their visit to the haunted pool on September 15, 1870. Whatever reasons you have for using the Lava Falls Route, you need to cache water during the descent: one quart *minimum* for every 500 to 700 vertical feet you descend.

Backstory: I first trekked the Lava Falls Route one scorching mid-summer afternoon during a solar eclipse to photograph river runners plunging through Lava Falls. It's the shortest route anywhere on which I'd ever cached water. I prehydrated drinking one gallon of water at the trailhead, cached one gallon during the descent, and carried and drank from one more gallon to and from the river. Before I began my late afternoon ascent, I soaked in the cool river water fully clothed except for shoes and socks to lower my core temperature. On the way out the cold wet clothes insulated me from the elevated air and ground temperatures until I reached my water cache midway up the route. Once the clothes dried, and my core temperature returned to normal, the trail blazes and cairns started to look like a procession of crosses and stone memorials in the shimmering heat waves as I picked my way up to the lava rim in the solar breeze that blew across the black dome of Vulcans Throne.

Mile 0. Lava Falls Route Trailhead, Elevation 4,180 feet +/- (1,274 meters), Gray Ledge Basalt-Uinkaret Lava Flow, no water, Rim View South/SE: Colorado River at Prospect Canyon and Colorado River at Lava Falls. "West of Vulcan's Throne there is a place where it is practicable to descend from the esplanade to the river," Dutton wrote, then he warned, "The way is difficult and at times well calculated to daunt the most active climber." From the trailhead follow the faint impression of a trail until it disappears in the look-alike cinder, lava stones, and boulders, and follow the cairns, your instinct, and route finding skills down to the Colorado River.

In the hazy, sweaty, squinty-eyed heat of summer, a series of topographical features stand out. In the clear crisp hiking days of fall through spring you may view them quite differently. So use your best judgment.

Vulture Valley

So I named it for the turkey vultures I watched circling overhead in the hot summer thermals, the shadows of their long wings scything over the route like a pair of black guillotines. Vulture Valley is a steep slope leading from the trailhead down to the brink of the topographical formation called Lava Falls. (Allow twenty minutes or more for your ascent.)

Lava Falls

Two boulder moves must be negotiated in descending the Lava Falls feature from Vulture Valley to Finger Rock Ridge. (Allow twenty minutes or more for your ascent.)

The Chute
From Finger Rock Ridge, you face the grungiest section on the Lava Falls Route—a knee-wrenchingly steep chute filled with ankle-knocking, feet-pulverizing rock. Two boulder moves must also be negotiated on this leg to reach the river's edge. (Allow thirty minutes or more for your ascent.)

River's Edge
Now that you're this far, the scramble across the boulder slide through the mesquite, barrel cactus, and creosote to Lava Falls Rapid will seem like a walk, 'er stumble, in the park. (Allow fifteen to twenty minutes for your return.)

Mile 1.5. Colorado River, Elevation 1,680 feet +/- (512 meters), Gray Ledge Basalt-Uinkaret Lava Flow, Lava Falls Rapids (thirteen foot drop). River View South: Lava Falls and Warm Springs across the Colorado River. Lava Falls is a ritual landmark spiritually linked to the Kaibab Paiute's Toroweap ceremonial landscape. You can lunch in the shade beneath Scout Rock, the river runners' overlook, and wonder how in the world you're going to hike out? (Soak in the still upstream waters to cool off. Take your time climbing out. Go safely and steadily). And you can study the legendary rapids some believe was first run in 1867 by a sunburned and emaciated horse thief and prospector named James White. In their book, *The Big Drops: Ten Legendary Rapids* (1989), Roderick Nash and Robert Collins wrote,

> Think of a weakened, dazed man, looking up from his logs at the line across the river, listening to the boom of Lava, and thinking, in desperate condition, that he might as well hang on and hope for the best. Then the sickening first drop and brown water tearing at his body and smashing it against the wood and, finally, the calm below and wondering how much more he could take before death. He took enough to get out barely alive and tell a tale nobody would, at first, believe. We do.

So do I. Return the way you came, and be grateful you don't have to try running Lava Falls on a driftwood log raft.

Travel Notes
- Warning: Do not hike the Lava Falls Route in the summer.
- Primary Access: Sunshine Road, Tuweep Campground.
- Elevation: 4,180-feet Lava Falls Route rim to 1,680-feet Colorado River.
- Biotic Communities: Piñon juniper woodland, Great Basin Desert scrub, and Mojave Desert scrub.

- Elevation Loss and Gain: 5,000 feet (2,500 vertical feet each way).
- Mileage: Three miles (1.5 miles one way to the Colorado River).
- Water Sources: Colorado River. No water en route.
- Cache Points: Vulture Valley, Lava Falls, Finger Rock Ridge, and wherever you can find a sliver of shade.
- Tuweep Ranger Station: From Highway 389, the NPS Ranger Station is located 53.5 miles south on the Sunshine Road. Stop and get your permits there.
- Emergencies: From Tuweep Campground, the Ranger Station is located 5.4 miles north on the Sunshine Road. From the Lava Falls Route parking, the Ranger Station is located 7.8 miles north.
- Escape Route: Rim or river? Whichever option offers you the best chance for survival. During a summer emergency you can wait overnight until daybreak and hike out well-hydrated from treated river water, full water jugs, and cool morning temperatures in two hours or less at 0.75 miles per hour walking and scrambling speed. (Nighttime without a good flashlight or full moonlight could turn into a real nightmare with cold blooded rattlesnakes who often bask on warm stones and pavement). You can approach a river outfitter, but remember they're focused on getting their crew and passengers through Lava Falls right-side-up! Bring your own satellite communications. If air tour operators are flying the western Grand Canyon you can try mirror signaling them and using satellite or ground-to-air communications.
- Seasons: Mid-fall to mid-spring.
- Maps: Vulcans Throne Quadrangle (7.5 minute), and optional Reconnaissance Map, Arizona Mt. Trumbull Sheet (March 1892).
- Camping: Tuweep Campground. Nine small campsites, one to six people each, picnic tables, grills, and a deluxe slick rock composting privy with an elevated front porch view. No water.
- Nearest Supply Points: Fredonia, Arizona, and Kanab, Utah.
- Backcountry Information Center: for information call (928) 638–7875.
- Critical Backcountry Updates visit www.nps.gov/grca/planyourvisit/trail-closures.htm
- NPS Grand Canyon Hiker 24 Hour Emergency Phone Number and Email
  - Phone (928) 638–7805
  - Email: grca_bic@nps.gov (Use this if the phone line is busy)

Toroweap Point Overlook

Road Mile 58.9. Toroweap Point, The Edge of the World, Elevation 5,055 feet +/- (1,541 meters), Esplanade Sandstone, Kaibab Paiute name *Mukunta'uipi* (Toroweap), Rim View South: Colorado River and Aubrey Cliffs. Toroweap Point is a sacred ceremonial landscape of the Kaibab Paiute. Major Powell never set foot on Toroweap Point, but his cartographic point man Clarence E. Dutton did in the summer of 1880. And when Dutton stood on the edge of that sheer cliff that drops like a stone 3,350-vertical feet into the gaping chasm formed by the Colorado River, he extolled its incomparable virtues: "It would be difficult to find anywhere else in the world . . . such dramatic and inspiring surroundings." Dutton was right about that. So was Frederick S. Dellenbaugh when he called it "the Edge of the World." It is. But to reach the edge of the planet requires a journey. It always does. If you're anywhere in Arizona but the Arizona Strip, you darn near have to drive through Utah or Nevada to reach it, the most remote, iconic and spectacular vista in America that sometimes appears on soda vending machines throughout the Southwest's celebrated Grand Circle of national parks.

Still, people come, not many, maybe hundreds. The curious. Free spirits. Foreign tourists piloting America's outback in rented sedans. Folks who prefer to travel off the tourist grid. Desert rats. Photographers, especially, covet the daunting view. Some get testy and possessive, and sometimes during the wee early morning hours before sunrise I've been surprised no one's been elbowed off the same trapdoor wide point-and-shoot-by-numbers spot, or simply fell screaming into the abyss still taking a "selfie" after jousting and hurdling through the aluminum thicket of tripod legs. Few think and turn around and see there's another picture there, or over there, or maybe a hundred wee yards in that direction. Hillers did walkabout the rim and take other rim-to-river views upstream and downstream. Rumor had it a while back one landscape photographer wanted to have a brass nameplate mounted on the edge of Toroweap Point. He was convinced other photographers were "stealing my picture." He didn't know, or didn't think anyone else would discover, that John K. "Jack" Hillers beat everyone to the punch. Hillers was one of Powell's 1872 expedition photographers, and on April 1, he took the first known-image from Toroweap Point. So a brass plate emblazoned with Hiller's name could be embedded in sandstone here. Were it not sacred to the Kaibab and Shivwits Paiute, there is room for one more brass benchmark in the Arizona Strip, especially for Hillers who, with Powell, went on to document the lifeways of the Southern Paiute and Hopi, among other Native Peoples who revere the Grand Canyon. "What a sight met my eyes!" Hillers wrote in his journal the same day Dellenbaugh and Dodds were trudging and staggering up the Lava Falls Route. "Looking down on the river from the top it appears to be nothing but a narrow gutter from top to bottom—I should judge about 4,000 feet and about 400 feet wide. It looked gloomy and forbidden. I counted eight rapids whose roar came up like a distant roll of thunder." Whether you ever take a picture from Toroweap Point, or bore your friends to tears with a twenty-eight-minute pirated-music Youtube video, you must go. If you do nothing else, just sit there. Take your time. Let the Canyon whisper its secrets to you.

Vision Quest, Seeking *Puha*

Where most come for the extraordinary view, solace, and beauty, the Southern Pai-ute sought spiritual renewal and visions during the long journey on foot across their ancestral landscape that followed the sacred trail south from *Mutungw,* "Yellow Rock Springs," through the waterless high desert past what Clarence Dutton named Wild Band Pockets for the wild horses he observed beneath *Yevingkarere,* "Mount Trumbull," to *Enepi Pikavo,* "Witch Water Pocket," across *Unav-Nuquaint,* "Little Springs Lava Flow," to secret springs and Nampaweap where they made offerings before arriving here at *Mukunta'uipi,* (Toroweap Canyon).

Peering over the edge, the Kaibab Paiute *Puha'gants,* "shamans," and pilgrims could see *Piapaxa 'Uipi,* "Big River Canyon," and Vulcan's Anvil, *Wi-Geth-Yea'a,* "Medicine Rock," seemingly floating in the middle of *Piapaxa,* "Big River." From the rim they could also see and hear the roar of Lava Falls that marked the location of their ceremo-nial rock shelter, yellow ochre streaked walls, and Water Baby Paintings where some shamans journeyed off the Toroweap Point rim on a pilgrimage to swim the Big River's pooled-up waters to scale Vulcan's Anvil. On the altar of volcanic stone that spewed from the molten core of Vulcans Throne and landed in the very depths of the earth during the time of their ancestors, the *Puha'gant* performed a ceremony for his patient or pilgrim, or he waited alone on the sacred mantel fasting and praying two to three days for the vision he sought. Then he climbed down into the Big River, swam to the south bank of the river, and made his way downstream to bathe in the holy waters of Warm Springs. Cleansed and enlightened, he swam back across the river and returned to his village then came along the paths of the Old Ones, *Enugwuhype.* Some shamans and pilgrims stayed right there at Toroweap Point where they looked, listened, and prayed until thirst, hunger, and privation, perhaps the sound of ravens, the shadow of an ant cast against the red sand, or the sight of a coyote walking up to him when the vision came, gave him the *puha,* and showed him the way most cannot imagine. Such places as *Mukunta'uipi* offered the "Elements of the Universe" elders told ethnographers they sought: "Paiutes believed that power (*puha*) could reside in any natural object, including animals, plants, stones, water, and geographic features, and that it habitually resided in natural phenomena such as the sun and moon, thunder, clouds, and wind."

The Way Home, Down the River, *Piapaxa,* "Big River"

Someone, somewhere, among the Paiute, or Pai, a shaman or a young man, who were intimately familiar with swimming the Colorado River, or fording it on a driftwood log raft, at low water during the warm "Indian Summer" days of fall, when the river temperature was 78 to 80 degrees Fahrenheit, had a different epiphany during their vision quest. If they'd journeyed east on foot along the river from their traditional trail down Whitmore Wash upstream to Vulcans, Anvil, *Wi-Geth-Yea'a*, "Medicine Rock," they were faced with a grueling 8.5 mile walk and stumble through river cobble, boulders, brush, 1,000-year-old driftwood piles that sometimes caught fire, and large timbers that had been swept downstream during spring floods just to reach their ceremonial site. Coming at the end of their vision quest, while enlightening, took a physical toll, and they knew that from the confluence of Whitmore Wash and the Colorado River they still needed to make the daunting sixty mile canyon and cross-country journey to get back home, a frightening journey that had pushed Major Powell, a veteran canyon explorer, and his men to their limits. Fatigued, the *Puha'gant*, or his apprentice, were still mentally prepared, physically fit, and knew the river better than most early river runners, including Major John Wesley Powell and James White. Why not push a driftwood timber into the river, hang on, and ride it down the Big River to their Whitmore Wash Trail?

In firsthand reports recounted by elders in his *Havasupai Ethnography*, (1928) ethnographer Leslie Spier documented the prowess of the Havasupai and Hualapai swimming and fording the Colorado River in the western Grand Canyon on logs and log rafts. Spanish explorer Captain Melchior Díaz had first reported witnessing Mojave men, women, and children navigating the lower Colorado River (*Río del Tizón*, "Firebrand River") on reed balsas and rafts north of Yuma in 1540. South of Yuma, Arizona, the Cocopah or *Cucapá* (*Xawill kwñchawaay*, "Those Who Live on the River") of Northern Baja, Mexico also used reed balsas to navigate strong river currents and deadly tidal bores where the Colorado River empries into Mexico's Sea of Cortés. Even further south the Seri (*Comcáac,* the "People") navigated the treacherous shark-infested currents and boils of the Little Channel of Hell paddling standing up paddle-board style—the first to do so—on reed balsas (*hascám*) between mainland Sonora, Mexico, and Tiburon Island in the Sea of Cortés where Norwegian ethnographer and explorer Thor Heyerdahl had traveled to study the Seri's use of reed balsas for his sea faring Atlantic Ocean crossing Ra Expeditions. One of the earliest accounts of Native People navigating the Colorado River through the Grand Canyon is the "myth" of *Ti-Yo.* In every story there's a grain of truth. Sometime before 1894, *Wi-Ki*, a Hopi Rattlesnake Chief from Wàlpi reportedly told ethnographer J. Walter Fewkes about Ti-Yo. The "youth," as he was also called, hollowed out a cottonwood log canoe with a stone axe, cured it with burning charcoal and embers, sealed it with pine pitch, and embarked on a legendary river journey from *Tokòonavi Wuhkokiekeu* (Navajo Mountain village) down *Pisisvayu* (Colorado River) to *Paatuwaqatsi*, "the ocean," (Gulf of California) and beyond to *Yupqöyve*, "the place beyond the horizon" during a Hopi migration. In his ethnographic report, "The Snake Ceremonials at Walpi," Fewkes recounted the story, in part, that Ti-yo ". . . floated over smooth waters and swift-rushing torrents, plunged down cataracts, and for many days spun through wild whirlpools where black rocks protruded their heads like angry bears."

The long-standing controversial debate about the "first man through" has always centered around Major Powell's 1869 Geographic Expedition and James White 1867 river escape—what about the Hopi? *Bahanna* (non-Hopi) archaeologists nearly always prefer physical proof they can carbon date, catalog, and store on a museum shelf or display in a museum diorama. It's the rare enthoarchaeologist or historian who will rely on oral history alone. The 65th Congress, 1st Session, Senate Resolution No. 79, June 4, 1917, Document No. 42 concurred White as "First Traversing the Grand Canyon of the Colorado." Think of a shaman or young Paiute, "looking up from his logs at the line across the river," running the *Piapaxa*, "Big River" from Lava Pinnacle (Vulcans Anvil) through Lava Falls down the Slot Run tracing the "bubble line" between the Ledge Hole and V-Wave, the right run around Meteor Rock and the boat crunching Black Rock on river right, or what some river guides call the "cheat run" between Pyramid Rock and behind Domer Rock on river left near Warm Springs. I don't think it's question of if the Paiute or Pai ran the same falls Major Powell's 1869 expedition portaged their wooden boats around. It's a question of river flow. At what water level and CFS (cubic feet per second) were the Colorado River's first indigenous river runners able to successfully navigate Lava Falls on a driftwood timber or yucca fiber cordage-bound log raft 10.2 miles downstream to Whitmore Wash, or beyond? In 1924 the record low flow for the Colorado River was 700 cfs. The 1955 DeSaussure Western Speleological Institute Expedition, "Terminated [their river] trip at Bright Angel [Creek] on July 28 due to low water . . ." Between 1866 and 1933 the Colorado River at Lees Ferry reportedly froze-over nine times. During one two-week period after January 15, 1878, the river ice was so thick, "Mormon missionaries crossed on the ice pulling wagons across [four horse-drawn 1,500 pound wagons]." Think about the possibilities. And imagine the petroglyph or pictograph that the Paiute or Pai driftwood whitewater river runner might have carved or painted after his own incredible Colorado River journey. Or recounted like the Hopi.

Backstory: Sometime back, I applied for and received permission from the National Park Service to launch what I proposed as "The James White Expedition." I was convinced I could survive running the Colorado River on a rudimentary log raft, given the right environmental conditions. In the end, I bowed out, not for the inherent risks—I faced worse on my trans canyon North Rim journey run—but for the style. Park rules necessitated a support crew of rafts and kayakers, precluded the use of natural wood fires for warmth, and river temperatures released from Glen Canyon Dam averaged a hypothermic 45–50 degrees Farhenheit in contast to low river flows and balmy 78 degree temperatures early fall predam days, requiring the use of a dry suit for prolonged cold water immersion. It was certainly not the style of James White I wanted to emulate, nor the indigenous Colorado River runners who undoubtedly preceded White's voyage wherever his true point of embarkation was.

Saddle Horse Springs Day Hike

For those who want to dance along the Edge of the World, you can trace the Saddle Horse Spring Trail. No doubt it had its beginnings with sheepherder and prospector Henry Covington. According to a documentary film script by Elinor Lin Mrachek, Covington "prospected along the rim and the inner gorge around 1917." That's not all Covington did. Somewhere over the "Edge of the World," the polygamist reportedly "kept one of his wives in an old Indian cave near his mine." But Covington wasn't the only one furbishing "honeymoon suites" hidden from the outside world, prying eyes, and federal agents who in 2016 were still rounding up and trying to end plural marriages Arizona Strip communities were infamously known for, including Pipe Spring. According to historian Kathy McCoy, Pipe Spring ". . . also served as an important refuge for Mormon polygamists, who fiercely resisted federal government efforts to stamp out a practice believed by them to be divinely ordained [Mormon *Doctrine and Covenants, Section 132*]. During the period of heaviest prosecution of polygamists, the fort [Winsor Castle] sequestered a considerable number of plural wives and their children." Mrachek wrote that cattleman Al Craig refurbished two caves near the bottom of the canyon and called it "Son-of-a-Bitch Hotel" because it was so difficult and dangerous to reach "few have ever spent the night or would have the courage to ever return."

The Hike: About 0.5 miles north of Toroweap Point on the Tuweep Campground road, you can pick up the 1.15 mile Saddle Horse Trail on the right (east) side of the road. It loops counterclockwise east 0.3 miles to the rim overlooking the Colorado River, and contours 0.45 miles north across the Esplanade to Saddle Horse Springs. The Supai Sandstone micro oasis of clear, knee-deep water, wild grapes, and cane also offers stunning views of Saddle Horse Canyon and the Colorado River. Head southwest 0.4 miles to return to Tuweep Campground near Campsite 5.

Tuckup (*Tekape*) Trail Day and Overnight Hikes and Treks

Mystifying pictographs, hidden cliff dwellings, and secret springs dating back 3,000 years indicate the Tuckup Trail was used by Archaic peoples, Mukwic (ancestral Paiute), and Kaibab Paiute many generations before explorers, prospectors, surveyors, and cattleman first used the faint serpentine sixty-mile path to cross the Esplanade Formation between Toroweap Point and Tuckup Canyon. It's the kind of spirit land the Shiv'wits Paiute chief had spoken to Powell about: "The pines sing and we are glad. Our children play in the warm sand; we hear them sing and are glad. The seeds ripen and we have food to eat and we are glad. We do not want their good lands; we want our rocks and the great mountains where our fathers lived." The musty July evening I bounded through this captivating redrock desert, peacefully running so effortlessly beneath towering cliffs that I was drawn farther and farther toward the horizon through piñon and juniper and gnarly stands of yucca wafting against the blue skies until I realized I was becoming dehydrated and needed to retrace the powdery red path before it showed its teeth. Given the time and water, I wanted to keep following the enchanting track to journey's end. Among the Southern Paiute, it's been recorded, "Running can be both a way of traveling for a man seeking power or a vision."

The Hike: From Tuweep Campground, hike north toward 5,855-foot Toroweap Point cliffs, skirt the head of Saddle Horse Canyon, and follow the serpentine path that unwinds before you, twisting and turning across the rust-red rim of the Esplanade around the head of Burro Canyon, Cove Canyon, and Big Point Canyon as far as your dreams, energy, and water permit.

Directions

You can access the Tuweep Trail off the Sunshine Road 0.7 miles north of the Tuweep Campground turnoff, or from Campsite 10 in Tuweep Campground.

Additional Considerations

To hike the Tuckup Trail sixty miles point-to-point you need a shuttle vehicle parked or waiting at the Tuckup Trailhead. Permanent water is only found at Willow Spring, Cottonwood Spring, and Schmutz Spring. Fall through spring seasonal water can usually be found along the route in the Esplanade Sandstone's ephemeral water pockets during and after summer monsoons and seasonal rain throughout the year. Check with the BIC and Tuweep Ranger Station.

Directions

From Highway 389, drive thirty-two miles south on the Sunshine Road (County Road #109) and turn left (south) off the Sunshine Road and drive south past June Tank BM 5303 to reach the remote 5,847-foot Tuckup Trailhead.

Maps: Refer to the Heaton Knolls, Hancock Knolls, and Fern Glen Canyon Quadrangles (7.5 minute).

Trace the following bench marks on your topographical maps across the secondary nonmaintained, high clearance roads leading to the Tuckup Trailhead: BM 5303 June Tank, BM 5614 bare left, BM 5813 continue straight, BM 5905 continue straight, BM 5918 turn left (south), BM 5902 turn left (east/southeast), Tuckup Trailhead.

Travel Notes

- Primary Access: Tuweep Campground.
- Elevation: 4,590-feet Tuweep Campground to 4,584-feet Cove Canyon.

- Biotic Community: Piñon juniper woodlands, Great Basin Desert scrub.
- Elevation Loss and Gain: 800 feet (400 vertical feet each way).
- Mileage: Nine miles (4.5 miles one way to Cove Canyon).
- Water: Saddle Horse Spring, Tuweep Ranger Station; Esplanade water pockets (seasonal).
- Cache Points: Saddle Horse Canyon, Burro Canyon.
- Escape Route: Tuweep Campground.
- Seasons: All year.
- Maps: Vulcans Throne Quadrangle (7.5 minute), Reconnaissance Map, optional Arizona Mt. Trumbull Sheet (March 1892).
- Camping: Tuweep Campground, and at-large, low-impact camping. Don't bust the crust.
- Nearest Supply Points: Fredonia, Arizona, and Kanab, Utah.
- Backcountry Information Center: for information call (928) 638–7875.
- Critical Backcountry Updates visit www.nps.gov/grca/planyourvisit/trail-closures.htm
- NPS Grand Canyon Hiker 24 Hour Emergency Phone Number and Email
  - Phone (928) 638–7805
  - Email: grca_bic@nps.gov (Use this if the phone line is busy)

Major John Wesley Powell's watch, GCNP Museum Collection.

Afterword

"Keep the Grand Canyon of Arizona as it is. We have gotten past the stage, my fellow
citizens, when we are to be pardoned if we simply treat any part of our country as
something to be skinned for two or three years for the use of the present generation.
Whether it is the forest, the water, the scenery, whatever it is, handle it so that your
children's children will get the benefit of it. . . Keep the forests in the same way. Preserve
them for that use, but use them so that they will not be squandered; will not be wasted."

—President Theodore Roosevelt, May 6, 1903
South Rim, Grand Canyon Game Preserve

ONE CAN ONLY IMAGINE WHAT ROOSEVELT WOULD MAKE OF
Grand Canyon National Park in the twenty-first century, which now faces many of the
same critical issues that threaten our nation's urban cities, suburban areas, and farm,
ranchlands, and wildlands. It's important to touch upon them so you're aware of the
volatile tug-of-war between locals whose livelihood depends on area jobs and environ-
mentalists who often live in distant cities far removed from the stormy skies that hover
beyond the sunset-hued scenic vistas and the at once peaceful and sublime inner Canyon sanctuaries of stone, water, and light.

Poor Air Quality
From Four Corners's coal-fired power generating plants, regional pollution carried into the
park from distant metropolitan cities, local traffic smog, forest fires, and controlled burns.

Contaminated and Depleted Groundwater
From uranium mining, development, traffic, acid rain and runoff, and *fecal coli* from trespass cattle and human waste poisons depleted wells and aquifers, and once-clear, clean, and
sweet rivers, streams, springs, and seeps that threaten pristine, increasingly rare biological
communities that plants, mammals, birds, fish, invertebrates, and people depend upon.

Old-Growth Forest Destruction
From overlogging, wild land fires, fire suppression, controlled burns, and fire and log-
ging roads on the 1,152 square mile Kaibab Plateau, which contains the Southwest's last
stands of rare old-growth forests of Ponderosa pines (*Pinus ponderosa*).

Noise

From overcrowding, park traffic congestion, tour buses, shuttles, trucks, cars, scenic air and helicopter tours, and motorized rafts.

Inner Canyon Development

As this goes to press, the Navajo National Tribal Council in Window Rock, Arizona, is considering proposed legislation to build the controversial Grand Canyon Escalade Project at the confluence of the Colorado and Little Colorado Rivers that has generated mixed support and public outcry. (See page 189 Beamer Trail.)

Water, Critical Needs, and the Trans Canyon Pipeline

The aging, deteriorating, frequently patched-and-repaired fifty-one-year-old pipeline has withstood snow and monsoon storms, flashfloods, and rock fall, yet still carries 500,000 gallons of water a day from Roaring Springs from the North Rim to the South Rim. It sustains the critical needs of park operations, visitor services, commercial concessions, housing, employees, and five million visitors a year. Now in urgent need of repair, the prohibitive estimated cost for the park's budget is between $100 million to $150 million. One flashflood too many, it ruptures, and everyone goes back to where he or she came from. How the park came to depend on a single source of water in a region that's been reeling from a 100-year drought cycle remains puzzling.

Selected
Bibliography

Abbey, Edward. *Black Sun, A Novel*. New York: Simon and Schuster, 1971.

———. *Desert Solitaire: A Season in the Wilderness*. New York: Ballantine, 1968.

———. *Slickrock: Endangered Canyons of the Southwest*, (photographs by Philip Hyde). Layton, UT: Peregrine Smith Books, 1987.

Adams, Eilean. *Hell or High Water: James White's Disputed Passage through Grand Canyon, 1867*. Logan: Utah State University Press, 2001.

Annerino, John. *Colorado Plateau: Wild and Beautiful,* (photographs by the author). Helena, MT: Farcountry Press, 2014.

———. *Indian Country: Sacred Ground, Native Peoples,* (photographs, essays, and Native American glossary by the author). New York: W. W. Norton, 2007.

———. "Rowing Home: An Adventure Photographer Follows in the Wake of a Grand Canyon Explored," (photographs by the author). *Arizona Highways Magazine*, Vol. 82, No. 8 (August 2006): 10–17.

———. *Hiking the Grand Canyon, A Sierra Club Totebook*. San Francisco: Sierra Club Books, 2006.

———. "The Grand Canyon Explored, A Fact-filled Pullout Mega-map," (cartography and historic photos edited by the author). *National Geographic Adventure*, Vol. 6, No. 2 (March 2004): 66–68.

———. *Canyons of the Southwest: A Tour of the Great Canyon Country from Colorado to Northern Mexico,* (photographs by the author). San Francisco: Sierra Club Books, 2000.

———. Apache: *The Sacred Path to Womanhood,* (photographs by the author). New York: Marlowe and Company, 1999.

———. *People of Legend: Native Americans of the Southwest,* (photographs by the author). San Francisco: Sierra Club Books, 1996.

Arizona, the Grand Canyon State; A State Guide, Compiled by workers of the Writers Program of the Work Projects Administration in the State of Arizona. New York: Hastings House, 1941.

Arizona Graphic, Vol. I, No. 4 (October 7, 1899): 2.

Armstrong, Margaret. "Canyon and Glacier." San Francisco. *Overland Monthly*, Vol. 59, No. 2 (February 1912): 95–99.

Avery, Ben. "Huge Unsupported Cable Starts Dam Project. Marble Canyon Dam Site Line is World's Longest." *Arizona Republic,* Sunday (June 25, 1950): 6.

Ayer, Emma Augustus Burbank. *A Motor Flight through Algeria and Tunisia.* Chicago: A.C. McClurg & Co., 1911.

Baars, Donald L. *The Colorado Plateau: A Geologic History.* Albuquerque: University of New Mexico Press, 1983.

Barnes, William C. *Arizona Place Names.* Tucson: University of Arizona Press, 1988.

Bartlett, Katharine. "How Don Pedro de Tovar Discovered the Hopi and García López de Cárdenas Saw the Grand Canyon, with Notes upon Their Probable Route." *Plateau*, Vol. 12, No. 3 (January 1940): 37–45.

Bass, William Wallace. *Bass Camp: The Grand Canyon of Arizona.* Under the Direct Supervision of W. W. Bass, Grand Canyon, Arizona, June 1904. No imprint.

Belknap, Buzz, and Loie Belknap-Evans. *Grand Canyon River Guide.* Evergreen, CO: Westwater Books, 2001.

Bierce, Ambrose. *The Letters of Ambrose Bierce,* (edited by Bertha Clark Pope, memoir by George Sterling). San Francisco: Book Club of California, 1922.

Bill, Donald J., et al. "Historical and 2009 Water Chemistry of Wells, Perennial and Intermittent Streams, and Springs in Northern Arizona." U.S.G.S Scientific Investigations Report 2010–5025. Reston, VA: U.S. Geological Survey, 2010.

Billingsley, George H., et al, and Ryan Clark. *Geologic Map of the Grand Canyon and Vicinity.* Flagstaff, AZ: U.S. Geological Survey, 2014, Mapbox Interactive: online, rclark.github.io/grand-canyon-geology/.

Billingsley, M. W. *M. W. Billingsley's 51 years with the Hopi people Behind the Scenes in Hopi Land,* self-published, 1971, no imprint.

Bolton, Herbert E. *Pageant in the Wilderness: The Story of the Escalante Expedition to the Interior Basin, 1776. Including the Diary and Itinerary of Father Escalante.* Translated and Annotated. Salt Lake City: Utah Historical Society, 1950.

Bourke, John G. *On the Border with Crook,* illustrated. New York: Charles Scribner's Sons, 1891.

Bowden, Charles. "Grand Canyon Trek: A Personal Journey Through a Vertical World." *Arizona Highways Magazine,* Vol. 60, No. 9 (September 1984): 16–31.

Brew, J. O. "Hopi Prehistory and History to 1850," in *Handbook of North American Indians, Southwest,* Vol. 9: 514–23. Washington, DC: Smithsonian Institution, 1979.

Brewer, Rev. William A. "Into the Heart of Cataract Cañon, Grand Cañon of Arizona. *Sierra Club Bulletin.* San Francisco, Vol. 4, No. 2 (June 1902): 77–77.

Brooks, Juanita, and Robert Glass Cleland, eds. *A Mormon Chronicle: The Diaries of John D. Lee, 1848–1876,* Vol. 2. Salt Lake City: University of Utah Press, 1983.

Brower, David Ross. *The Place No One Knew: Glen Canyon on the Colorado*, (photographs by Eliot Porter). Layton, UT: Peregrine Smith Books, 1988.

Brown, Bryan. T., and M. Susan Moran. "An Inventory and Classification of Surface Water Resources in Grand Canyon National Park, AZ." A Final Report to the Division of Resource Management, Grand Canyon National Park. Part I (Water Resources Inventory) of the 208 Water Quality Project, October 1979.

Brown, David E., and Carlos A. López González. *Borderland Jaguars / Tigres de la Frontera*. Salt Lake City: University of Utah Press, 2001.

Brown, David E., ed. *The Wolf in the Southwest: The Making of An Endangered Species*. Tucson: University of Arizona Press, 1983.

Brugge, David M. "Navajo Prehistory and History to 1850," in *Handbook of North American Indians, Southwest*, Vol. 10: 489–501. Washington, DC: Smithsonian Institution, 1983.

"Cameron to Retain Bright Angel Trail: Land Office Fails to Prove Any of the Allegations." *Arizona Journal-Miner*, Prescott, Arizona, (September 29, 1905): 5.

Carmony, Neil B., and David E. Brown, eds. *The Wilderness of the Southwest: Charles Sheldon's Quest for Desert Bighorn Sheep with the Havasupai and Seri Indians*. Salt Lake City: University of Utah Press, 1993.

Carmony, Neil B., ed. "The Grand Canyon Deer Drive of 1924: The Accounts of Will C. Barnes and Mark E. Musgrave." *Journal of Arizona History*, Vol. 43, No. 1 (Spring 2002): 41–64.

Casanova, Frank E. "Trails to Supai in Cataract Canyon." *Plateau*, Vol. 39, No. 3 (Winter 1967): 124–30.

Chimoni, Harry, Zuni/A:shiwi, and E., Richard Hart. "Zuni Emergence Myth." Institute of the North American West, and Zuni Cultural Advisory Team, presented October 22, 1994, Western History Association, Albuquerque, New Mexico.

"Chronology of Grand Canyon Trails." Grand Canyon National Park, AZ, unpublished manuscript, n.d.

Claflin, William H., Jr. "Three Months with the Champion Cougar Hunter." *Recreation: The "Been There" Sportsman Magazine*, Vol. 54, No. 1, New Series (January 1916): 211–212.

Collins, Robert O., and Roderick Nash. *The Big Drops: Ten Legendary Rapids*. San Francisco: Sierra Club Books, 1978.

Colton, Harold S. "Principal Hopi Trails." *Plateau*, Vol. 36, No. 3 (Winter 1964): 91–94.

———. *Black Sand: Prehistory in Northern Arizona*. Albuquerque: University of New Mexico Press, 1960.

———. "Prehistoric Trade in the Southwest." *Scientific Monthly*, Vol. 52 (April 1941): 308–19.

Compton, Todd. *Slickrock Missions: Jacob Hamblin's Communitarian Expeditions Across the Colorado.* St. George, Utah: Dixie State University, 2015.

Cordell, Linda S. "Prehistory: Eastern Anasazi," in *Handbook of North American Indians, Southwest,* Vol. 9: 131–51. Washington, DC: Smithsonian Institution, 1979.

Coping, Cindy, ed. "Discrepancies and Inconsistencies Discovered as of August 12, 2012 in Peer-Reviewed Literature and Other Reports of Historic Records of Jaguar sightings in New Mexico and Arizona." Green Valley, AZ: SACPA, 2012, online.

Corle, Edwin. "Trail Wise and Trail Weary," in *Listen, Bright Angel.* New York: Duell, Sloan and Pearce, 1946.

Coues, Elliot, ed. *On the Trail of a Spanish Pioneer: The Diary and Itinerary of Francisco Garcés (Missionary Priest) in His Travels Through Sonora, Arizona, and California, 1775–1776.* Translated from an Official Contemporaneous Copy of the Original Manuscript, and Edited, with Copious Critical Notes by Elliot Coues. 2 Vols. New York: Francis P. Harper, 1900.

Crampton, C. Gregory. *Land of Living Rock: The Grand Canyon and the High Plateaus: Arizona, Utah, Nevada.* New York: Alfred A. Knopf, 1972.

Curtis, Edward S. *The Hopi, Vol. 12, The North American Indian* (1907–1930). Cambridge, MA: University Press, 1922, Plate No. 420.

Cushing, Frank Hamilton. "The Nation of Willows." *Atlantic Monthly,* (September, October 1882): 362–74, 541–49.

Davis, Dan. "A Traverse of the Colorado River from Lees Ferry to Lake Mead." Grand Canyon National Park, AZ, unpublished manuscript, November 19, 1957: 19 pages.

———. "Voyages Down the Colorado: 1825–1956." Grand Canyon National Park, AZ, unpublished manuscript, chronology and notations (November 19, 1957, December 12, 1956): 29 pages.

———. "River to Rim Routes." Grand Canyon National Park, AZ, unpublished manuscript, n.d. 16 pages.

Dawson, Thomas F. *The Grand Canyon, An Article: Giving the Credit of First Traversing the Grand Canyon of the Colorado to James White, A Colorado Gold Prospector, Who It Is Claimed Made the Voyage Two Years Previous to the Expedition Under the Direction of Major J. W. Powell in 1869.* 65th Congress, 1st Session, Senate Resolution No. 79, June 4, 1917, Document No. 42. Washington, DC: U.S. Government Printing Office, 1917.

Debo, Angie. *Geronimo: The Man, His Time, His Place.* Norman: University of Oklahoma Press, 1976.

Dellenbaugh, Frederick S. *A Canyon Voyage: The Narrative of the Second Powell Expedition Down the Green-Colorado River from Wyoming, and the Explorations on Land, in the Years 1871 and 1872.* New Haven, CT: Yale University Press, 1926.

————. *The Romance of The Colorado River: The Story of its Discovery in 1540, with an Account of the Later Explorations, and with Special Reference to the Voyages of Powell Through the Line of the Great Canyons.* New York and London: G. P. Putnam's Sons and Knickerbocker Press, 1902.

Doheny, Edward L., Charles W. Gilmore, and Samuel Hubbard. *The Doheny Scientific Expedition to the Hava Supai Canyon, Northern Arizona, October and November, 1924.* San Francisco: Sunset Press, 1925.

Dobyns, Henry F., and Robert C. Euler. "The Dunn-Howland Killings: Additional Insights." *Journal of Arizona History* Vol. 21, No. 1 (Spring 1980): 87–95.

Dudley, Gail. *Grand Canyon's Scariest Trail,* cover feature: "Nankoweap: The Most Difficult Trail in the Grand Canyon," (photographs by Richard L. Danley). *Arizona Highways Magazine* Vol. 72, No. 10 (October 1996): 7–11.

Dutton, Clarence Edward. *Tertiary History of the Grand Canyon District, with Atlas.* Department of Interior Monographs of the United States Geological Survey, Vol. 2. Washington, DC: U.S. Government Printing Office, 1882.

Eddy, Clyde L. *Down the World's Most Dangerous River.* New York: Frederick A. Stokes, 1929.

Eddy, Clyde L., and Peter D. Miller, ed. *A Mad Crazy River: Running the Grand Canyon in 1927.* Albuquerque, NM: University of New Mexico Press, 2012.

Eiseman, Fred. B. "The Hopi Salt Trail." *Plateau,* Vol. 32, No. 2 (October 1959): 25–32.

Euler, Robert C. "The Canyon Dwellers." *American West,* Vol. 4, No. 2 (May 1967): 22–27, 67–71.

Euler, Robert C., ed. *The Archaeology, Geology, and Paleobiology of Stanton Cave, Grand Canyon National Park, Arizona.* Monograph No. 6. Grand Canyon, AZ: Grand Canyon Natural History Association, 1984.

Euler, Robert C., Don. D. Fowler, and Catherine S. Fowler. "The Archaeology of the Canyon Country," in *John Wesley Powell and the Anthropology of the Canyon Country,* Geological Professional Paper 670. Washington, D.C.: U.S. Government Printing Office, 1969.

Euler, Robert C., M. E. Cooley, and B. N. Aldridge. "Effects of the Catastrophic Flood of December 1966, North Rim Area, Eastern Grand Canyon, Arizona." Geological Survey Professional Paper. Washington, DC: U.S. Government Printing Office, 1977.

Euler, Robert C., and A. Trinkle Jones. *A Sketch of Grand Canyon Prehistory.* Grand Canyon, AZ: Grand Canyon Natural History Association, 1979.

Farmer, Malcolm F., and Raymond DeSaussure. "Split-Twig Animal Figurines." *Plateau,* Vol. 27, No. 4 (April 1955): 13–23.

Felger, Richard Stephen, and Mary Beck Moser. *People of the Desert and the Sea: The Ethnobotany of the Seri Indians.* Tucson: University of Arizona Press, 1985.

Fenton, Frank, (screenplay), and Louis Lantz, (story). *The River of No Return.* Los Angeles, CA: 20th Century-Fox, 1954.

Ferguson, T. J., G. Lennis Berlin, and Leigh J. Kuwanwisiwma. "*Kukhepya*: Searching for Hopi Trails." *Landscapes of Movement: Trails and Paths in Anthropological Perspective,* November 18, 2004, 103rd Annual Meeting of the American Anthropological Association, San Francisco, California.

Ferrall, L. L. Sydney, personal correspondence to Mr. Glen E. Sturdevant, Park Naturalist, Grand Canyon, Ariz., L. L. Ferrall, Phoenix, Ariz., Dec. 10, 1927. Grand Canyon Pioneer Society, Flagstaff, Arizona.

Fewkes, J. Walter. "The Snake Ceremonials at Walpi." *A Journal of American Ethnology and Archaeology,* Vol. 4. Boston: Houghton, Mifflin and Co., 1894.

Fletcher, Colin. *The Man Who Walked Through Time: The Story of the First Trip Afoot Through the Grand Canyon.* New York: Alfred A. Knopf, 1967.

Foster, Dennis. "The Walcott Journal: Deciphering the Grand Canyon Expedition of 1882–1883" presentation, Grand Canyon Historical Society Symposium, January 28, 2012, Shrine of Ages, Grand Canyon National Park, Arizona.

Freeman, Lewis R. "Surveying the Grand Canyon of the Colorado: An Account of the 1923 Boating Expedition of the United States Geological Survey." *National Geographic Magazine,* Vol. 45, No. 5 (May 1924): 472–548.

Fuss, John W. "Jack," interviewer Susan L. Rogers, with Marie Fuss. "Oral History Interview with John W. "Jack" Fuss," November 25, 1975. Flagstaff City-Coconino County Public Library Oral History Project, Arizona.

Fuss, Jack, interviewer Marie "Mimi" Fuss. "Jack Fuss and the Great Kaibab Deer Drive." *Boatman's Quarter Review: The Journal of Grand Canyon River Guides,* Vol. 17, No. 2 (Summer 2004): 16–23.

Galloway, Donald G., Joel C. Janetski, and Omar C. Stewart. "Ute," in *Handbook of North American Indians, Great Basin,* Vol. 11: 336–67. Washington, DC: Smithsonian Institution, 1986.

Garrett, H. Dean. "Traveling the Honeymoon Trail: An Act of Faith and Love," in *Regional Studies in Latter-day Saints Church History, Arizona,* (eds. H. Dean Garrett and Clark V. Johnson). Department of Church History and Doctrine, Brigham Young University, Provo, Utah, 1989.

Gaylord, A., "Into the Grand Canyon, and Out Again, by Airplane," in *Literary Digest,* (October 7, 1922): 63–64, 66.

Geiger, Tom. "Trans Canyon Waterline," and "Grand Canyon Geology and the History of Park Water Systems." *Courier, News Magazine of the National Park Service,* Vol. 37, No. 4. (April 1992): 19–20, 21.

Ghiglieri, Michael P., and Thomas M. Myers. *Over the Edge; Death in Grand Canyon*. Flagstaff, AZ: Puma Press, 2001.

Granger, Byrd H. *Grand Canyon Place Names*. Tucson: University of Arizona Press, 1960.

———. *William C. Barnes' Arizona Place Names*, (illustrations Anne Merriam Peck). Tucson: University of Arizona Press, 1979.

Gregory, David A., and David R. Wilcox. *Zuni Origins: Toward a New Synthesis of Southwestern Archaeology*. Tucson: University of Arizona Press, 2007.

Gregory, Herbert Ernest, and Robert C. Moore. *The Kaiparowits Region: A Geographic and Geologic Reconnaissance of Parts of Utah and Arizona*. Washington, DC: U.S. Government Printing Office, 1931.

Grey, Zane. *The Last of the Plainsmen*. New York: Outing Publishing Company, 1908.

———. *Roping Lions in the Grand Canyon*. New York Grosset & Dunlap, 1924.

Hamblin, W. Kenneth, and Joseph R. Murphy. *Grand Canyon Perspectives: A Guide to the Canyon Scenery by Means of Interpretive Panoramas*. Geology Studies, Special Publications No. 1. Provo, UT: Brigham Young University, 1969.

Hayden, F. V. *Annual Report of the United States Geological and Geographical Survey of the Territories Embracing Colorado and Parts of Adjacent Territories: Being a Report of Progress of the Exploration for the Year 1874*, (photographer William Henry Jackson, guest artist Thomas Moran). Washington, DC: U.S. Government Printing Office, 1876.

Heald, Weldon F. "How Deep Are Those Mexican Barrancas," (photographs by the author). *Pacific Discovery*, Vol. 11, No. 5 (Sept.-Oct. 1958): 22–27.

Heyerdahl, Thor. *The Ra Expeditions*. New York: Doubleday, 1971.

Hirst, Stephen. *I Am the Grand Canyon: The Story of the Havasupai People*. Grand Canyon, AZ: Grand Canyon Association, 2006.

Holmes, E. Burton. *Burton Holmes Travelogues, With Illustrations from Photographs by the Author. Vol. 12. The Yellowstone National Park; The Grand Cañon of Arizona; Moki Land*. Chicago and New York: Travelogue Bureau, 1919.

———. *Travelogues, With Illustrations from Photographs by the Author, Vol. 6*. New York: McClure Co., 1901.

Horan, James David. *Desperate Men: The James Gang and the Wild Bunch*. Lincoln: University of Nebraska Press, 1949.

Hose, Louise D. "Secrecy: An Alternative and Successful Model for Cave Exploration." National Speleological Society, *NSS Bulletin*, Vol. 54, No. 1 (June 1992): 17–24.

Hovey, H. G. "On the Rim and in the Depths of the Grand Canyon." *Scientific American,* Vol. 67 (August 6, 1892): 87–89.

Huntoon, Peter Wesley. *The Hydro-mechanics of the Ground Water System in the Southern Portion of the Kaibab Plateau, Arizona, PhD Dissertation.* Tucson: University of Arizona, 1970.

Hyde, Bessie Haley. *Wandering Leaves: Created 1901–1928,* unpublished collection of poems, 51 pages, Glen Hyde Collection, NAU Cline Library Collections and Archives.

Ives, Joseph Christmas. *Report Upon the Colorado River of the West: Explored in 1857 and 1858.* Washington, DC: U.S. Government Printing Office, 1861.

James, George Wharton. *In and Around the Grand Canyon: The Grand Canyon of the Colorado River in Arizona* (With Numerous Illustrations). Boston: Little, Brown and Company: 1900.

———. *The Indians of the Painted Desert Region: Hopis, Navahos, Wallapais, Havasupais* (With Numerous Illustrations from Photographs). Boston: Little, Brown and Company, 1904.

———. *The Grand Canyon of Arizona: How to See It* (With Numerous Illustrations of Points of Interest and Maps). Boston: Little, Brown and Company, 1910.

Kelly, Isabel T., and Catherine S. Fowler. "Southern Paiute," in *Handbook of North American Indians: Great Basin,* Vol. 11: 368–97. Washington, DC: Smithsonian Institution, 1986.

Kenney, Ray. "A 16th-century Spanish Inscription in Grand Canyon? A Hypothesis." *Park Science,* Vol. 27, No. 2 (Fall 2010): 58–63.

Khera, Sigrid, and Patricia S. Mariella. "Yavapai," in *Handbook of North American Indians, Southwest,* Vol. 10: 38–54. Washington, DC: Smithsonian Institution, 1983.

Kino, Fray Eusebio Francisco, *Passo por Tierra a la California, Río Colorado del Norte,* map engraving, from 1701, in *Passage by land to California. Discover'd by Father Eusebius Francis Kino, a Jesuit; Between the Years 1698 & 1701: Containing Likewise the New Missions of the Jesuits.* E. Bowen Sc., London, England, 1701.

Kolb, Ellsworth, and Emery Kolb. "Experiences in the Grand Canyon," (photographs by the authors *National Geographic Magazine,* Vol. 26, No. 2 (August 1914): 125, 127.

Kolb, Emery C. "Cheyava Falls," in History and Exploration of the Grand Canyon Region. *Nature Notes, Natural History Bulletin,* No. 2 (November 1935): online.

———. *Through the Grand Canyon from Wyoming to Mexico,* (photographs by Emery and Ellsworth Kolb). New York: Macmillan Co., 1920.

Kluckhorn, Clyde Kay Maben. *Navaho Witchcraft.* Papers of the Peabody Museum of American Archaeology and Ethnology, Vol. 22, No. 2, 1944, Harvard University.

Lange, Arthur L. "An Earthquake Underground." *Cave Notes: Publication of Cave Research Associates,* Vol. 3, No. 2 (March/April 1961): 10.

Lange, Arthur L., Raymond de Saussure, ed. "Activities." *Cave Notes: Publication of Cave Research Associates*, Vol. 1, No. 6 (November/December 1959): 27.

Linford, Laurance D. *Tony Hillerman's Navajoland: Hideouts, Haunts, and Havens in the Joe Leaphorn and Jim Chee Mysteries*. Salt Lake City: University of Utah Press, 2011.

———. *Navajo Places: History, Legend, Landscape*. Salt Lake City: University of Utah Press, 2000.

Lummis, Charles Fletcher. *A Tramp Across the Continent*. New York: Charles Scribner's Sons, 1892.

Matthes, François Émile. "Breaking a Trail Through Bright Angel Canyon." *Grand Canyon Nature Notes*, Vol. 2, No. 6 (November 1927):1–4.

Matthes, François Émile, topography, and Edward Morehouse Douglas, geographer in charge. "The Grand Canyon of the Colorado River," Bright Angel Quadrangle, USGS 1:48000-scale. Reston, VA: U. S. Geological Survey, 1903.

Matthews, Washington. *The Mountain Chant: A Navajo Ceremony*. U.S. Bureau of American Ethnology, Fifth Annual Report, 1883–84. Washington, DC: Smithsonian Institution, 1887.

McClintock, J. H. *Mormon Settlement in Arizona: A Record of Peaceful Conquest in the Desert*. Phoenix: Manufacturing Stationers, Inc., 1921.

McKoy, Kathy, Historian, National Park Service, Intermountain Region, Denver, CO. "Pipe Spring National Monument Historic District," Fredonia, Mohave County, AZ. National Register of Historic Places Registration Form, NPS 10–9003, (July 5, 2000): 25.

W. J. McGee, "The Supai Group of Arizona." U.S.G.S. Professional Paper 1173. Washington: U.S. Government Printing Office, 1982.

———. "Kanab Canyon: The Trail of Scientists." *Plateau*, Vol. 18, No. 3 (January 1946): 33–42.

———. "On Canyon Trails." *Grand Canyon Nature Notes,* Vol. 8, No. 6 (September 1933): 173–77, 191–94.

McGuire, Randal H., and Ruth Van Dyke. "Dismembering the Trope: Imagining Cannibalism in the Ancient Pueblo World," in *Social Violence in Prehispanic American Southwest*, eds. Deborah L. Nichols and Patricia L. Crown. Tucson: University of Arizona Press, 2008.

McGuire, Thomas R. "Walapai," in *Handbook of North American Indians, Southwest*, Volume 10: 25–37. Washington, DC: Smithsonian Institution, 1983.

Mead, Jim I. "Harrington's Extinct Mountain Goat (*Oreamnos harringtoni)* and its Environment in the Grand Canyon, Arizona." Tucson: University of Arizona, PhD Dissertation, 1983.

Melis, Theodore S., William M. Phillips, Robert H. Webb, and Donald J. Bills. "When the Blue Green Waters Turn Red, Historical Flooding in Havasu Creek, Arizona."

U.S. Geological Survey Water-Resources Investigations Report 96—4059, Bureau of Reclamation. Tucson, AZ: U.S. Department of Interior, 1996.

Merakis, Lisa. "4,000-year-old UFO Found in Grand Canyon! U.S. Military Rushes Alien Starship to Secret Base: Inside: Amazing Proof of Alien Colony in America—3,500 years before Columbus." "*Nothing but the Truth*"-*Weekly World News* (September 27, 1994): cover story.

Merbs, Charles F., and Robert C. Euler. "Atlanto-occipital fusion and spondylolisthesis in an Anasazi skeleton from Bright Angel Ruin," Grand Canyon National Park, AZ. *American Journal of Physical Anthropology*, Vol. 67, Issue 4 (August 1985): 381–391.

Merriam, C. Hart. "Results of a Biological Survey of the San Francisco Mountain Region and Desert of the Little Colorado, Arizona." *North American Fauna*, Vol. 3 (September 11, 1980). U.S. Division of Agriculture, Division of Ornithology and Mammalogy. Washington, DC: U.S. Government Printing Office, 1890.

Metzger, D. G. *Geology in Relation to Availability of Water Along the South Rim Grand Canyon National Park, Arizona. Hydrology of the Public Domain.* Geological Survey Water Supply Paper, 1478-C. Washington, DC: U.S. Government Printing Office, 1961.

Mooney, James. *The Ghost-dance Religion and the Sioux Outbreak of 1890,* in Fourteenth Annual Report of the Bureau of American Ethnology to the Secretary of the Smithsonian Institutions, 1892–93. Washington: U.S. Government Printing Office, 1896.

Monroe, Harriet. "Its Ineffable Beauty," in W. J. Black, *The Grand Canyon of Arizona: Being a Book of Words from Many Pens, About the Grand Canyon of the Colorado River in Arizona.* Published by the Passenger Department of Santa Fe, 1906.

Mowat, George. "Silent River Cave" photo. *Cave Notes, Publication of Cave Research Associates,* Vol. 2, No. 3 (May/June 1960): Cover. [". . . photo was touched up with a cumulous cloud to obscure distinctive buttes in the background." Hose, 1992. [7,801-foot Kibbey Butte.]

Muir, John. "The Grand Cañon of the Colorado," in *Steep Trails: California, Utah, Nevada, Washington, Oregon, The Grand Canyon,* (William Frederic Bade, ed). Boston and New York: Houghton Mifflin Company, 1918.

———. "The Grand Cañon of the Colorado." *Century Magazine,* Vol. 55 (November 1902): 107–116.

———. *Our National Parks: Sketches from the Atlantic Monthly.* Boston, New York: Houghton Mifflin and Co., 1901.

Obregón, Baltasar de. *Obregón's History of 16th Century Explorations in Western America, Entitled Chronicle, Commentary, or Relation of the Ancient and Modern Discoveries in New Spain and New Mexico, Mexico, 1584,* (Translated, Edited, and Annotated by

George P. Hammond and Agapito Rey). Los Angeles: Wetzel Publishing Company, Inc., 1928.

"Old Navajo Medicine Man, Third Tanner Trail Victim, *Arizona Daily Sun* (June 27, 1960): 1.

Palmer, William R. "Indian Names in Utah Geography." *Utah Historical Quarterly*, Vol. 1, No. 1 (January 1928): 22 pages.

Parker, O. K. "Through the Grand Canyon, To the Colorado River in a 1914 Metz 22 Speedster." *California Outlook,* Vol 17. No. 26, (December 26, 1914): 22, online.

Pattie, James Ohio, and Timothy Flint, ed. *The Personal Narrative of James Ohio Pattie, of Kentucky: During an Expedition from St. Louis, through the Vast Regions between that place and the Pacific Ocean, and thence back through the city of Mexico to Vera Cruz. During Journeyings of Six Years, in which He and His Father, Who Accompanied Him, Suffered Unheard of Hardships and Dangers . . .* Cincinnati, OH: John H. Wood, 1831.

Peattie, Roderick, ed. *The Inverted Mountains: Canyons of the West*, (contributors Weldon F. Heald, Edwin D. McKee, Harold S. Colton). New York: Vanguard Press, 1948.

"Perilous Searching Operation, After Commercial Aviation's World Disaster." *Life Magazine*, Vol. 41, No. 3 (July 16, 1956): 19–21.

Plog, Fred. "Prehistory: Western Anasazi," in *Handbook of North American Indians, Southwest,* Volume 9: 108–130. Washington, DC: Smithsonian Institution, 1979.

Powell, J. W. *Explorations of the Colorado River of the West and Its Tributaries: Explored in 1869, 1870, 1871, and 1872.* Washington: U.S. Government Printing Office, 1875.

Powell, J. W., Director, Modeled by Edwin E. Howell, *Grand Cañon of the Colorado River of the West and the Cliffs of Southern Utah* map, Washington: U.S. Geological Survey, Library of Congress, 1910.

Powell, Major J. W. *An Overland Trip to the Grand Cañon,* (and "Map of the Grand Cañon of the Colorado Showing Route Traveled by Major Powell"). Palmer Lake, CO: Filter Press, 1974.

Powell, J. W., and A. H. Thomson. *Photographic Documentation of the U.S. Topographical and Geological Survey of the Colorado River of the West*, (photographer John K. Hillers). Washington: J. F. Jarvis, 1874.

Powell, Walter Clement. "Journal of W. C. Powell, April 21, 1871-December 7, 1872," (Charles Kelly, ed.). *Utah Historical Quarterly*, Vols. 16–17 (1949): 257–478.

Reisner, Marc. *Cadillac Desert: The American West and Its Disappearing Water.* New York: Penguin Books, 1986.

Renshawe, Jon R., assistant. *Map of Grand Canyon National Park.* U. S. National Park Service. Washington: U.S. Government Printing Office, 1926.

Resser, Charles E. "The Search for Ancient Life Forms in the Rocks of the Western United States," in *Explorations and Field-Work of the Smithsonian Institution in 1930*. Washington: Smithsonian Institution, 1931.

Rice, Steven E. "Surveying Leandras Cave, Longest in Arizona," Reports From the Field. *Inside Earth*, Vol. 15, No. 1 (Spring 2012): 4–5. [Cover photo Abyss River Cave].

Roessel, Robert A., Jr. "Navajo History, 1850–1923," in *Handbook of North American Indians, Southwest*, Vol. 10: 506–23. Washington, DC: Smithsonian Institution, 1983.

"Rogers Clubb, Jr. son of a Vancouver, British Columbia, professor, has been missing since Friday . . ." *Arizona Republic*, Sunday, (August 4, 1963): 1.

Roosevelt, Theodore. *A Book-Lover's Holidays in the Open*. New York: Charles Scribner's Sons, 1916.

————. *The Works of Theodore Roosevelt. Presidential Addresses and State Papers*, Part One. New York: P. F. Collier and Son, 1905.

————. "At Grand Canyon, Arizona, May 6, 1903." Presidential Speech to "Mr. Governor, and you, my Fellow-Citizens . . ."

Rusho, W. L. and C. Gregory Crampton. *Desert River Crossing: Historic Lee's Ferry on the Colorado River*. Salt Lake City, UT: Peregrine Smith, 1975.

Schwartz, Douglas W. "Havasupai," in *Handbook of North American Indians, Southwest*, Vol. 10: 13–24. Washington, DC: Smithsonian Institution, 1983.

————. "An Archaeological Survey of Nankoweap Canyon, Grand Canyon National Park." *American Antiquity*, Vol. 28, No. 3 (January 1963): 289–302.

Schwartz, Douglas W., Arthur L. Lange, and Raymond DeSaussure. "Split-Twig Figurines in the Grand Canyon." *American Antiquity*, Vol. 23, No. 3 (January 1958): 264–274.

Seargeant, Helen Humphreys. "Mooney Falls," *Arizona Highways Magazine*, Vol. 35, No. 8 (August 1959): 23–24.

Sekaquaptewa, Emory, Cultural Editor, et al. *Hopi Dictionary: Hopìikwa Lavàytutuveni: A Hopi–English Dictionary of the Third Mesa Dialect With an English-Hopi Finder List and a Sketch of Hopi Grammar*. Tucson: University of Arizona Press, 1998.

Smith, Robert L. *Venomous Animals of Arizona,* (illustrations by Joel Floyd). Tucson: University of Arizona, College of Agriculture, 1982.

Spier, Leslie. *Havasupai Ethnography*. American Museum of Natural History, Anthropological Papers, Part 3, Vol. 29 (1928): 381–392.

Stanton, Robert Brewster, and James McGowan Chalfant. *Colorado River Controversies*. New York: Dodd, Mead & Co., 1932.

Stewart, Kenneth M. "Mohave," in *Handbook of North American Indians, Southwest*, Vol. 10: 55–70. Washington, DC: Smithsonian Institution, 1983.

Steere, Peter. "National Forest Fire Lookouts in the Southwestern Region, USDA Forest Service." National Register of Historic Places Nomination Form, U.S. Department of the Interior, National Park Service (December 14, 1987): 1–115.

Stoffle, Richard W., et al. "Ghost Dancing the Grand Canyon: Southern Paiute Rock Art, Ceremony, and Cultural Landscapes." *Current Anthropology* Vol. 41, No. 1 (February 2000): 11–38.

Stone, Julius F. *Canyon Country: The Romance of a Drop of Water and a Grain of Sand,* (photography by Raymond A. Cogswell). New York & London: G. P. Putnam's Sons, 1932.

Strong, L. *Silent River Cave Trip Report for 23–24 July 1976 with Observations on Previously Unrecorded Geological and Biological Features in the Cave*; an unpublished report submitted on 19 September 1976 to the files of Grand Canyon National Park, 3 p.

"Summary of Location and Discharge for Springs, Seeps, and Springs." Bureau of Land Management, Northern Arizona Proposed Withdrawal Draft Environmental Impact Statement, Appendix D February 2011 D-1. Table D-1.

Talayesva, Don C. *Sun Chief: The Autobiography of a Hopi Indian*, (Leo W. Simmons, ed.). New Haven, CT: Yale University Press, 1948.

Titiev, Mischa. "A Hopi Salt Expedition." *American Anthropologist*, Vol. 39, No. 2 (April–June 1937): 244–258.

Tower, Donald B. "The Use of Marine Mollusca and Their Value in Reconstructing Prehistoric Trade Routes in the American Southwest." *Papers of the Excavator's Club*, Vol. 2, No. 3 (1945): 1–55.

Tom, Gary, and Ronald Holt, "The Paiute Tribe of Utah," in *History of Utah's Indians*, (Forrest S. Cuch, ed.). Salt Lake City: Utah Division of Indian Affairs/Utah State Division of History, 2000.

Upchurch, Jonathan. "The "Monte Video" Inscription at Grand Canyon National Park: Why It's Likely from the Bass Tourist Era." *Park Science*, Vol. 30, No. 2 (Fall 2013): 6–11.

Van Valkenburgh, Richard F., Lucy Wilcox Adams, and John C. McPhee. *Diné Bikéyah (The Navajo's Country)*. Window Rock, AZ: United States Department of Interior, Office of Indian Affairs, Navajo Service, 1941.

Walcott, Charles D. "Report of Mr. Charles D. Walcott," *Fourth Annual Report of the United States Geological Survey 1882–1883*. Washington: U.S. Government Printing Office, 1884.

Wall, Leon, and William Morgan, translator. *Navajo-English Dictionary*. U.S. Department of Interior, Bureau of Indian Affairs. Window Rock, AZ: Navajo Agency, Division of Education, 1958.

Warner, Charles Dudley, "On the Brink of the Canyon," in W. J. Black, *The Grand Canyon of Arizona: Being a Book of Words from Many Pens, About the Grand Canyon of the Colorado River in Arizona.* Published by the Passenger Department of Santa Fe, 1906.

Webb, Robert H., Theodore S. Melis, and Richard A. Valdez. "Observations of Environmental Change in Grand Canyon, Arizona." U.S. Geological Survey, Water-Resources Investigations Report 02–4080, prepared in Cooperation with Grand Canyon Monitoring and Research Center, Tucson, AZ, 2002.

Wieland, Laurence. *The Grand Canyon Panorama Project.* Austin, Texas, 2016, online.

Wills, John. "On Burro'd Time: Feral Burros, the Brighty Legend, and the Pursuit of Wilderness in the Grand Canyon." *Journal of Arizona History,* Vol. 44, No. 1 (Spring 2003): 1–24.

Wheeler, Captain George M. *Report Upon the United States Geographical Surveys West of the One Hundredth Meridian,* Vol. 1, Geographical Report, (photographers Timothy H. O'Sullivan and William Bell). Washington: U.S. Government Printing Office, 1875.

Woods, G. K., collected and compiled by. *Personal Impressions of the Grand Cañon of the Colorado River near Flagstaff, Arizona: As Seen Through nearly Two Thousand Eyes, and Written in the Private Visitors' Book of the World-Famous Guide, Capt. John Hance, Guide, Story-teller, and Path-finder.* Published for G. K. Woods, Flagstaff, Arizona Territory. San Francisco: Whitaker & Ray Company, 1899.

Work, Hubert, Secretary, U.S. Department of the Interior, and Stephen T. Mather, Director, National Park Service. *Grand Canyon National Park, Arizona: Rules and Regulations.* Washington: U.S. Government Printing Office, 1923.

Wyland, Leland C. "Navajo Ceremonial System," in *Handbook of North American Indians, Southwest,* Vol. 10: 536–557. Washington, DC: Smithsonian Institution, 1983.

Photography & Illustration Credits

Page 10. Above the Rim. "Through the Grand Canyon to the Colorado River in a Metz 22 Speedster, 1914, photo by O. K. Parker, Reporter. Source: online.

Page 62. "A Hopi Man," Edward S. Curtis photogravure, plate no. 420. Library of Congress, No known restrictions on publication. www.loc.gov/rr/print/res/369_curt.html

Page 65. "Pachilawa—Walapai chief," Pachilawa—Walapai chief, 1907, Edward S. Curtis, Library of Congress Curtis no. 2429–07. No known restrictions on publication.

Page 75. *Life Zones of the Grand Canyon* graph, 1890, artist not attributed. Source: C. Hart Merriam, (see bibliography).

Page 81. *Geology of the Grand Canyon* graph, artist not attributed. Source USGS, McKee, W. J., McGee, W. J. 1982, (see bibliography).

Page 98. "Big Jim, Havasupai chief," 1915, Emery Kolb photo, South Rim Kolb Studio. Source: Grand Canyon National Park Museum Collection. http://creativecommons.org/licenses/by/4.0/

Page 109. An ancient spilt-twig figurine excavated from a remote cave. Source: GCNP Museum Collection, NPS photo. http://creativecommons.org/licenses/by/4.0/

Page 116. Mary Jane Colter's Hermits Rest featured in souvenir postcard," 1932, painted by Gunnar Mauritz Widforss. Source: Fred Harvey, GCNP Museum Collection. http://creativecommons.org/licenses/by/4.0/

Page 118. Architect Mary Elizabeth Jane Colter, 1892, photographer not attributed, online.

Page 128. Prospector Louis D. Boucher atop his white mule, "Calamity Jane," 1910, E. W. Murphy photo. Source: GCNP Museum Collection. http://creativecommons.org/licenses/by/4.0/

Page 134. "Captain Burro," ca. 1900, Fredrick Hamer Maude hand-colored lantern slide. Source: GCNP Museum Collection. http://creativecommons.org/licenses/by/4.0/

Page 143. Ancestral Puebloan Tusayan black on red bowl, 1050-1150 AD, GCNP Museum Collection. http://creativecommons.org/licenses/by/4.0/

Page 166. "A Navaho shaman," 1879, John K. Hillers albumen silver print Source: Library of Congress Hillers no 99472516. No known restrictions on publication.

Page 174. Havasupai horseman, *Hamteq*, "Nighthawk," 1899 Henry G. Peabody photo. Source: GCNP Museum Collection http://creativecommons.org/licenses/by/4.0/

Page 177. "Havasupai sweat bath," Cataract Canyon, 1924, Robert L. Carson/Doheny Scientific Expedition photo. Source GCNP Museum Collection. http://creative-commons.org/licenses/by/4.0/

Page 194. "Navajo brave and his mother," 1873, Timothy H. O'Sullivan stereoview, 1873. Source: Library of Congress O'Sullivan no. 72. No known restrictions on publication.

Page 230. "Zuni girl," 1903, Edward S. Curtis photogravure. Source: Library of Congress Curtis no. 825.

Page 261. Wovoka, Ghost Dance shaman, circa 1890, photographer not attributed, possibly Lorenzo D. Creel. Source: online.

Page 270. Maj. J. W. Powell Expedition Journal, April 21, 1871, kept by Walter Clement Powell. Source: GCNP Museum Collection. http://creativecommons.org/licenses/by/4.0/

Page 309. Panning gold, Colorado River gold miner, 1898, George Wharton James photo. Source: James, 1900, (see bibliography).

Page 313. "Mohave men Panambona and Mitiwara," Colorado River near Diamond Creek, 1871, Timothy H. O'Sullivan stereograph. Source: Library of Congress.

Page 317. Major John Wesley Powell and Tau-Gu, Great Chief of the Pai-Utes, 1873, John K. Hillers photo. Source: Powell, J. W., and A. H. Thomson., 1874 (see bibliography).

Page 336. Major John Wesley Powell's watch. Source: GCNP Museum Collection. http://creativecommons.org/licenses/by/4.0/

About the Author

Author self-portrait, Coyote Wash, Utah, at the end of a month-long journey run from Mexico.

John Annerino is an award-winning photographer, author, and journalist of distinguished photography books, illustrated nonfiction books, magazine and news features, and color maps and calendars of the American West and Old Mexico.

John's assignment, consultant, and published work includes ABC News *Primetime, America 24/7: Extraordinary Images of One American Week, Arizona Highways* ("Rowing Home: An Adventure Photographer Follows in the Wake of a Grand Canyon Explorer" and "Adventure: Documenting the Quest"), *BrownTrout*, Heard American Indian Museum (Native Speaker on the Tarahumara), *Life Magazine* (Pima), *National Geographic Adventure* ("The Grand Canyon Explored"), *National Law Journal* (Environmental Law), Native Peoples (Mountain Pima), *Newsweek* (Hopi), *New York Times Travel* (Tarahumara) and *Magazine, Outdoor Photography UK* ("Colorado Plateau Wild and Beautiful"), *People* (Navajo Code Talkers), *Scientific American, Time, Travel & Leisure* (Grand Canyon cover shoot), Sierra Club Books, W. W. Norton, and as a contract photographer for TimePix and Liaison International photo agencies. John received a Book Builder's West Outstanding Photography award for his Sierra Club Book, *Canyons of the Southwest,* Southwest Book of the Year Best Reading awards for *Vanishing Border-*

lands, and *The Virgin of Guadalupe*, and a Society of Publication Designers Award for photography in the *National Geographic Adventure* border feature, "Along the Devil's Highway."

Explorations:

John spent most of his life exploring the *terra incognita* of the American West and Mexico—as an adventurer, conservationist, and scholar of Southwestern history. In his quest to explore its mythic landscapes and secret places, John climbed its hallowed mountains, rowed its wild and scenic rivers, and traced ancient Indian paths on foot through canyons and painted deserts. Among his explorations by foot, raft, rope, camera, and pen, John worked as an outdoor educator, climbing guide, and survival instructor in Arizona and Mexico; heliac wildlands fire crew leader in Alaska's Kenai Peninsula, Washington's North Cascades National Park, and Montana's Pasayten Wilderness; and a white-water boatman-photographer on the Forks of the Kern River, Golden Trout Wilderness, California; Green and Yampa Rivers, Dinosaur National Monument, Utah; Colorado River, Grand Canyon National Park, and Upper Salt River Canyon Wilderness, Arizona; and Rio Grande, Big Bend National Park, Texas/Río Bravo del Norte, Maderas del Carmen UNESCO Biosphere Reserve, Mexico.

John cut his teeth exploring the Grand Canyon, safely guiding students down the Canyon's trails, and as a veteran Colorado River boatman and paddle captain. Rediscovering routes of Native Peoples and explorers, John canyoneered the length of the Canyon's longest tributary chasms: Little Colorado River Gorge, Buckskin Gulch/ Paria Canyon, Cataract/Havasu Canyons, and Kanab Creek Canyon; hiked each of the Canyon's rim-to-river miner trails; and made the Canyon's first journey runs: six-day inner-Canyon below the South Rim; seven-day, 210-mile spirit run on the old Hopi/Havasupai trade route from Oraibi to Havasupai; and an an eight-and-a-half day adventure run off-the-grid below the North Rim. Tracing Indian paths and historic trails John ran 750 miles of Arizona wilderness from Mexico to Utah, and led the first modern, unsupported crossing of the *El Camino del Diablo*, "The Road of the Devil," on foot, midsummer. To date, John has explored more than 59,773 recorded miles on-foot of Native American routes and trails in the canyons, deserts, and mountains of the Great Southwest.